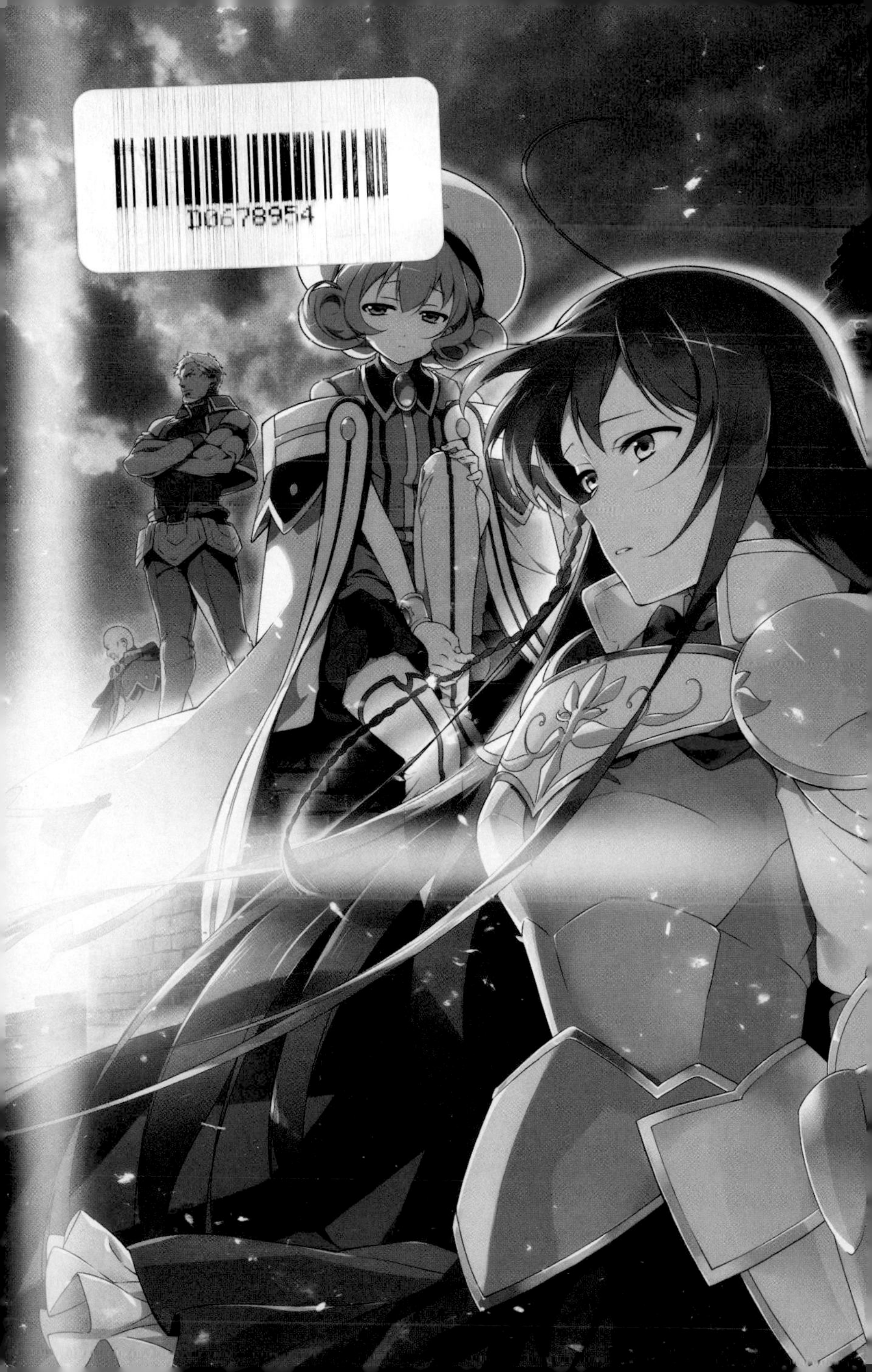

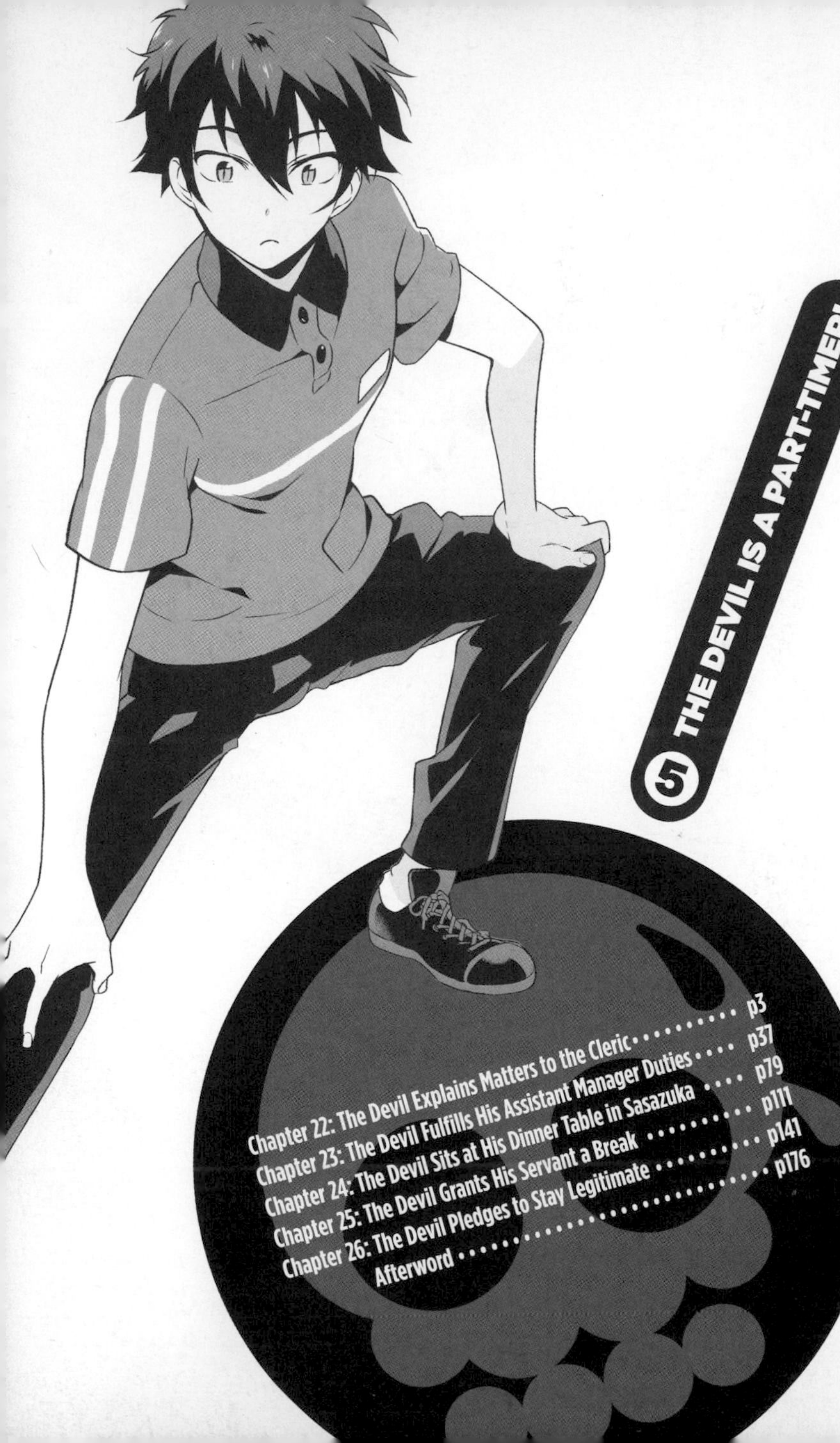

⑤ THE DEVIL IS A PART-TIMER!

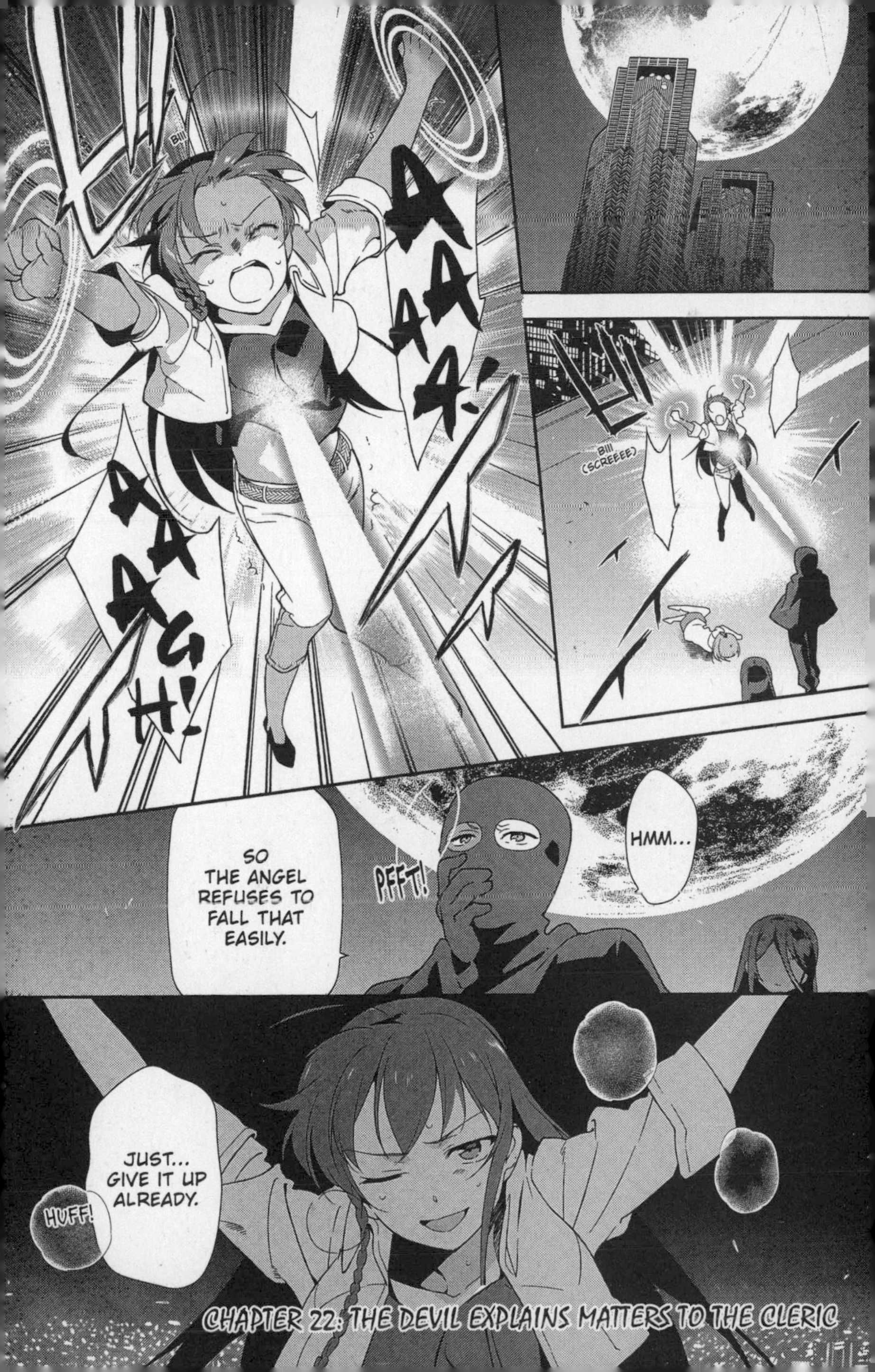
BIII
(SCREEEE)
BIII
AAAA!
AAAAGH!
HMM...
PFFT!
SO THE ANGEL REFUSES TO FALL THAT EASILY.
JUST... GIVE IT UP ALREADY.
HUFF!
CHAPTER 22: THE DEVIL EXPLAINS MATTERS TO THE CLERIC

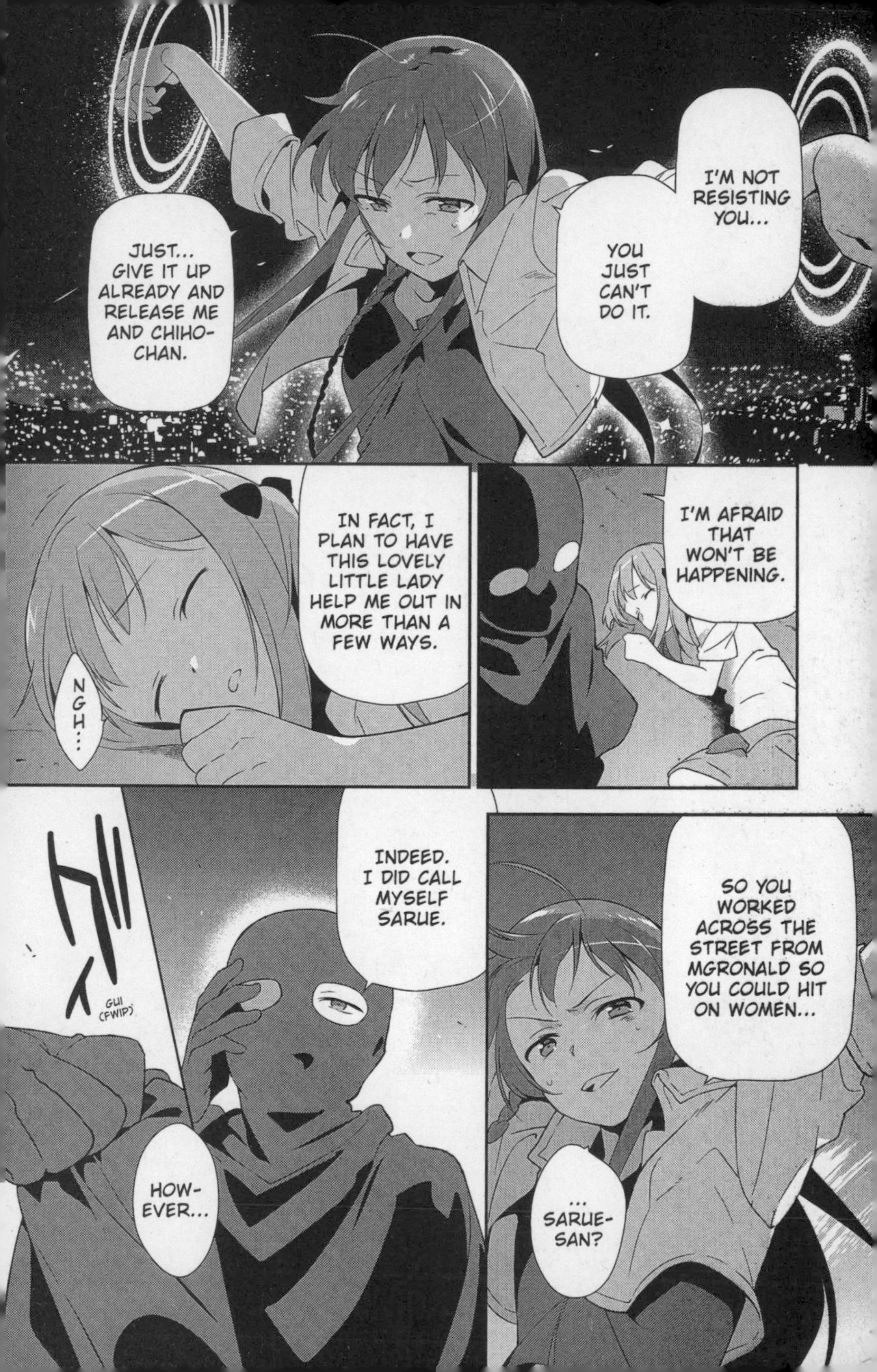
I'M NOT RESISTING YOU...
YOU JUST CAN'T DO IT.
JUST... GIVE IT UP ALREADY AND RELEASE ME AND CHIHO-CHAN.
I'M AFRAID THAT WON'T BE HAPPENING.
IN FACT, I PLAN TO HAVE THIS LOVELY LITTLE LADY HELP ME OUT IN MORE THAN A FEW WAYS.
NGH...
SO YOU WORKED ACROSS THE STREET FROM MGRONALD SO YOU COULD HIT ON WOMEN...
...SARUE-SAN?
INDEED. I DID CALL MYSELF SARUE.
GUI (FWIP)
HOW-EVER...

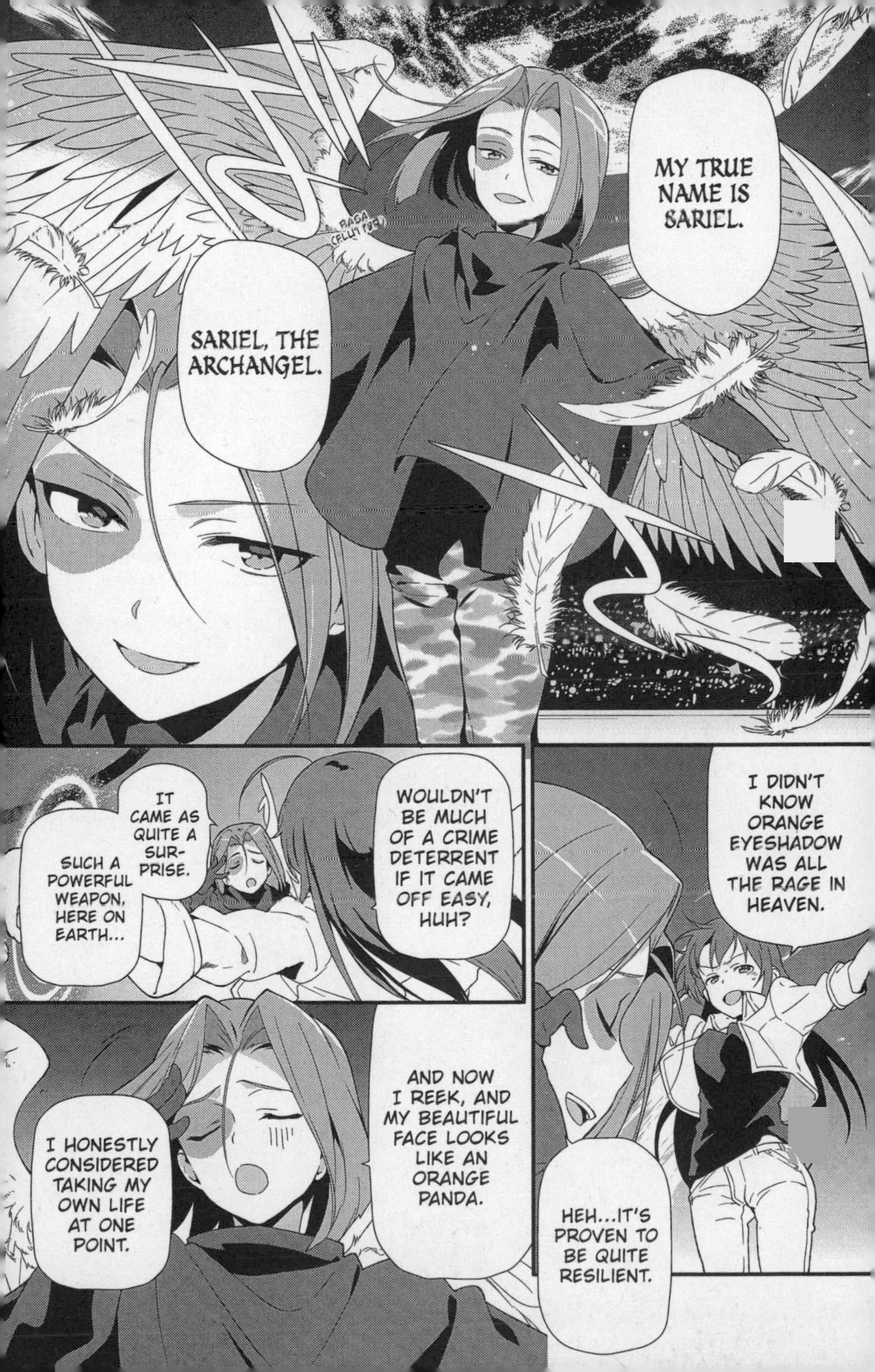
MY TRUE NAME IS SARIEL.
BASA
SARIEL, THE ARCHANGEL.
I DIDN'T KNOW ORANGE EYESHADOW WAS ALL THE RAGE IN HEAVEN.
HEH...IT'S PROVEN TO BE QUITE RESILIENT.
WOULDN'T BE MUCH OF A CRIME DETERRENT IF IT CAME OFF EASY, HUH?
IT CAME AS QUITE A SUR-PRISE.
SUCH A POWERFUL WEAPON, HERE ON EARTH...
AND NOW I REEK, AND MY BEAUTIFUL FACE LOOKS LIKE AN ORANGE PANDA.
I HONESTLY CONSIDERED TAKING MY OWN LIFE AT ONE POINT.

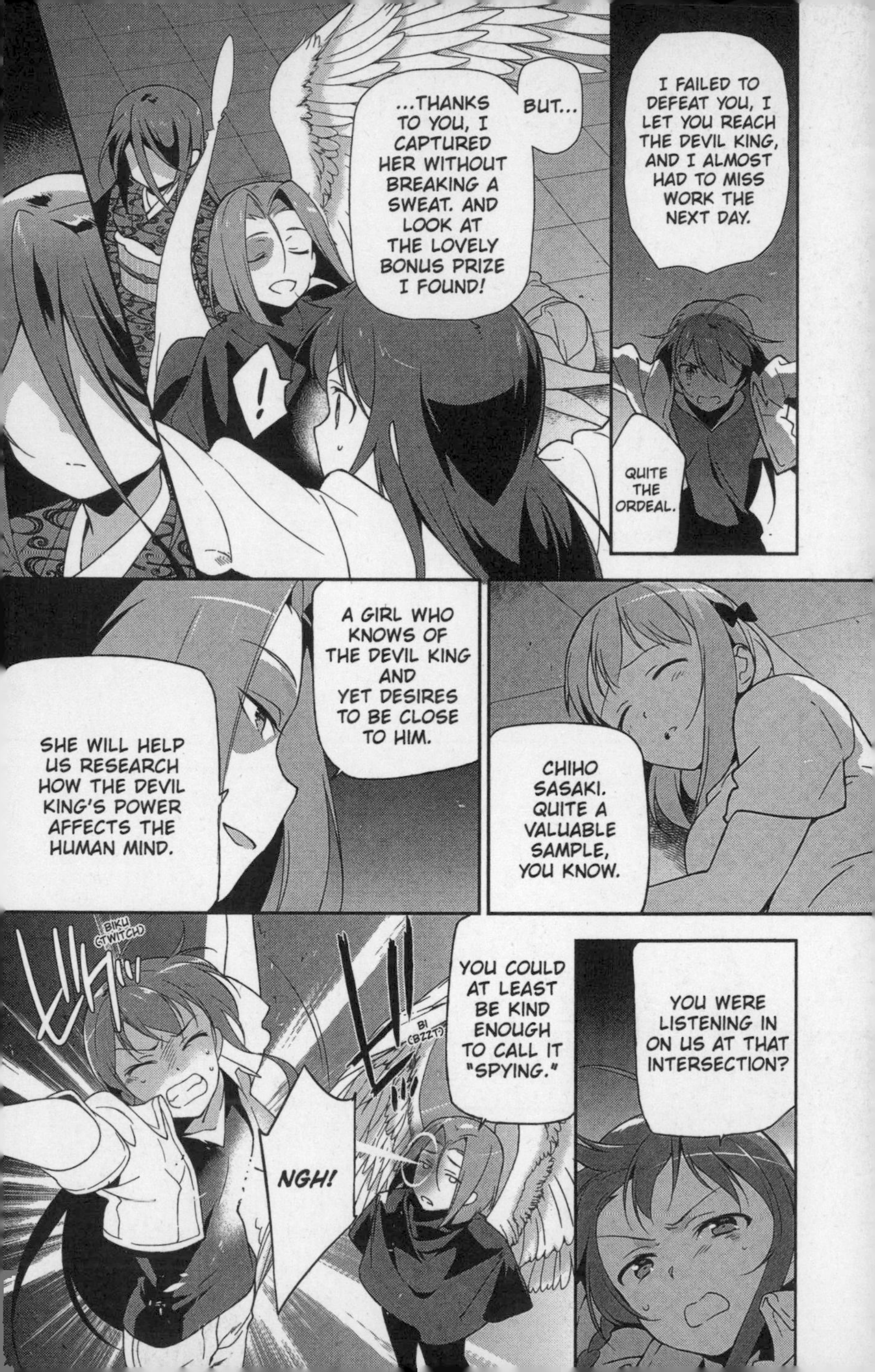

I FAILED TO DEFEAT YOU, I LET YOU REACH THE DEVIL KING, AND I ALMOST HAD TO MISS WORK THE NEXT DAY.
QUITE THE ORDEAL.
BUT...
...THANKS TO YOU, I CAPTURED HER WITHOUT BREAKING A SWEAT. AND LOOK AT THE LOVELY BONUS PRIZE I FOUND!
!
CHIHO SASAKI. QUITE A VALUABLE SAMPLE, YOU KNOW.
A GIRL WHO KNOWS OF THE DEVIL KING AND YET DESIRES TO BE CLOSE TO HIM.
SHE WILL HELP US RESEARCH HOW THE DEVIL KING'S POWER AFFECTS THE HUMAN MIND.
YOU WERE LISTENING IN ON US AT THAT INTERSECTION?
YOU COULD AT LEAST BE KIND ENOUGH TO CALL IT "SPYING."
BI (BZZT)
NGH!
BIKU (TWITCH)

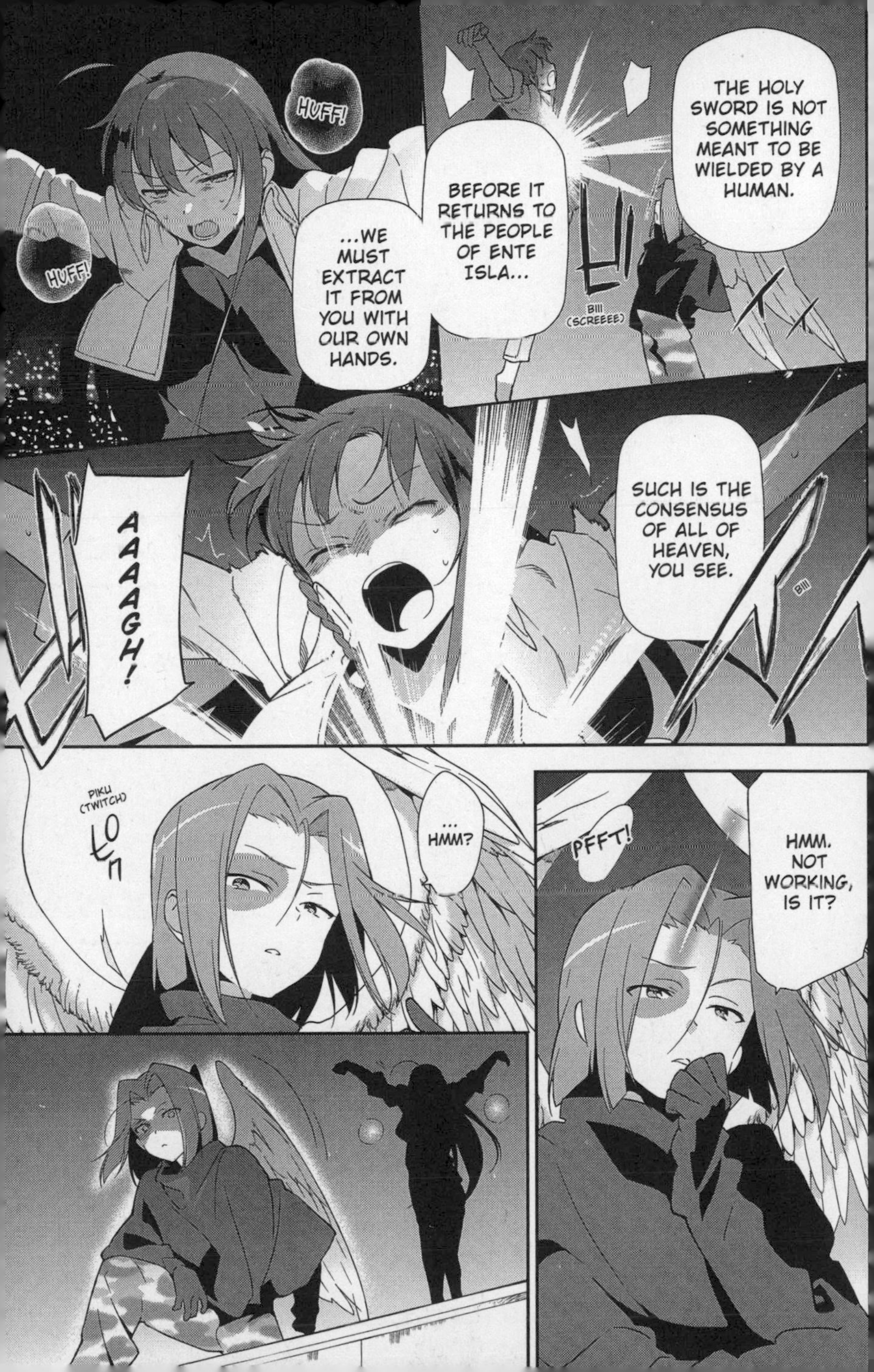
THE HOLY SWORD IS NOT SOMETHING MEANT TO BE WIELDED BY A HUMAN.
BIII (SCREEEE)
BEFORE IT RETURNS TO THE PEOPLE OF ENTE ISLA...
...WE MUST EXTRACT IT FROM YOU WITH OUR OWN HANDS.
HUFF!
HUFF!
SUCH IS THE CONSENSUS OF ALL OF HEAVEN, YOU SEE.
BIII
AAAAGH!
HMM. NOT WORKING, IS IT?
PFFT!
... HMM?
PIKU (TWITCH)

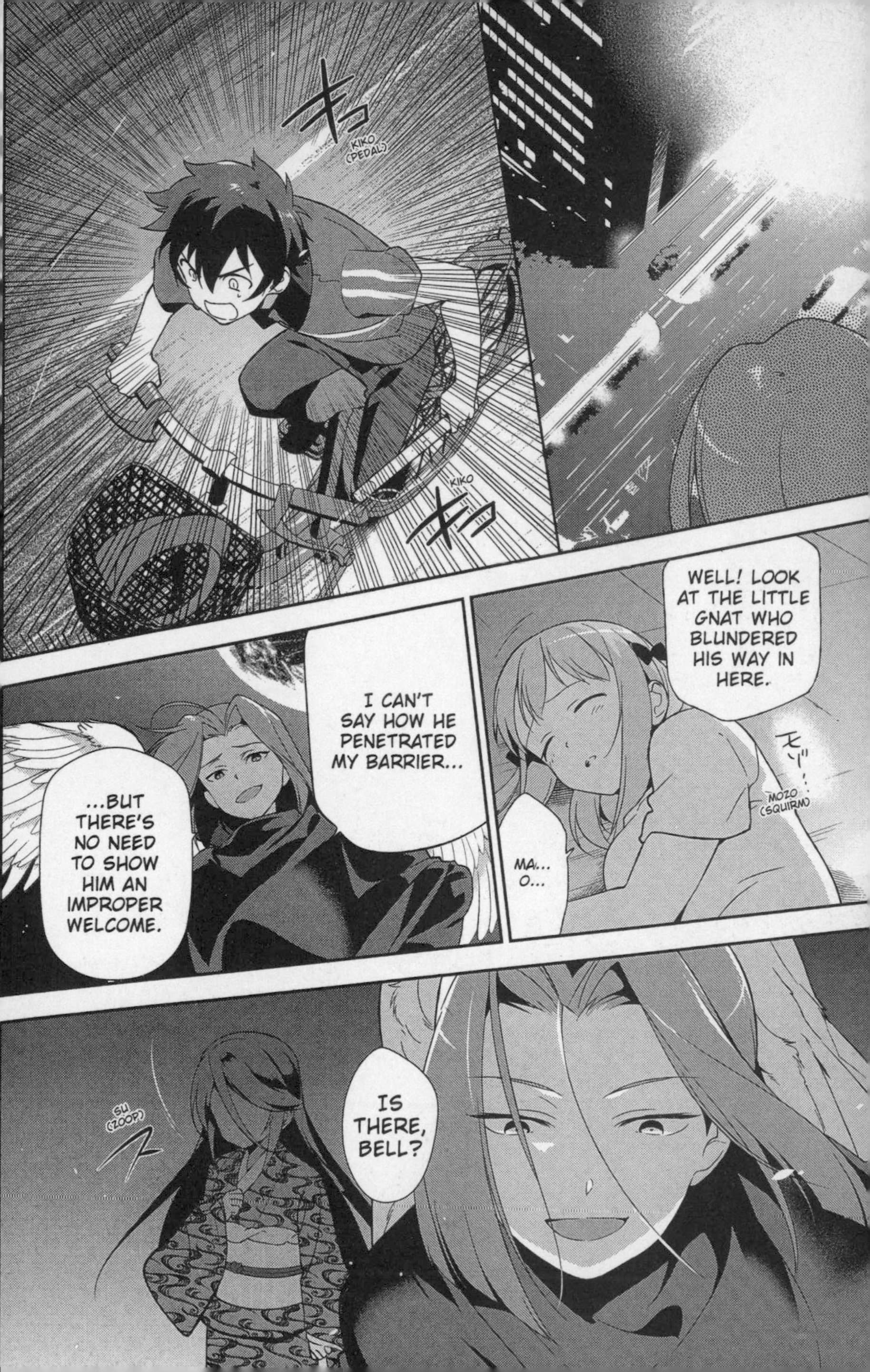

キコ
KIKO (PEDAL)
KIKO
キコ
WELL! LOOK AT THE LITTLE GNAT WHO BLUNDERED HIS WAY IN HERE.
モゾ
MOZO (SQUIRM)
MA... O...
I CAN'T SAY HOW HE PENETRATED MY BARRIER...
...BUT THERE'S NO NEED TO SHOW HIM AN IMPROPER WELCOME.
IS THERE, BELL?
SU (ZOOP)
ス

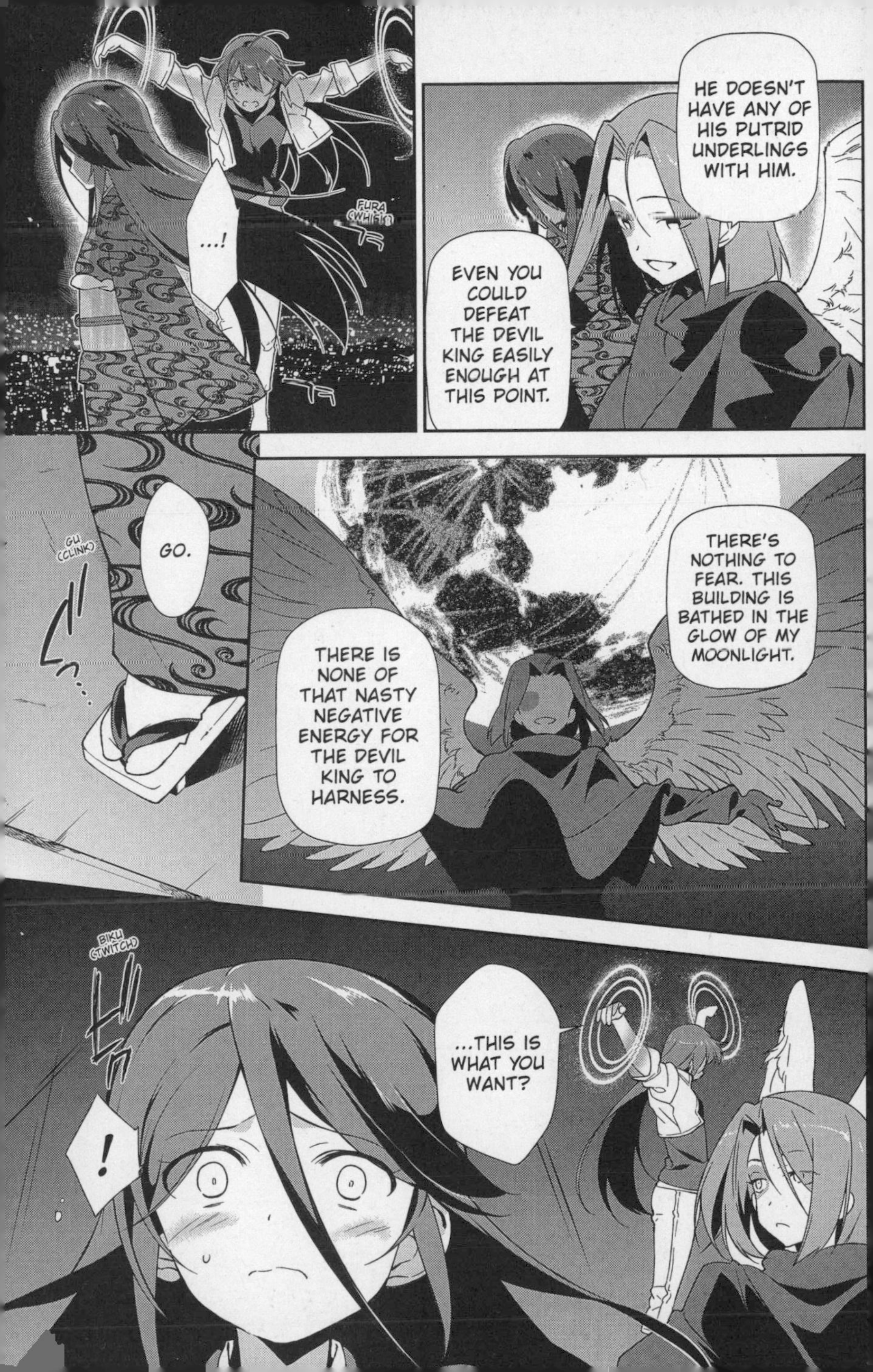
HE DOESN'T HAVE ANY OF HIS PUTRID UNDERLINGS WITH HIM.
EVEN YOU COULD DEFEAT THE DEVIL KING EASILY ENOUGH AT THIS POINT.
FURA (WHIFF)
...!
THERE'S NOTHING TO FEAR. THIS BUILDING IS BATHED IN THE GLOW OF MY MOONLIGHT.
THERE IS NONE OF THAT NASTY NEGATIVE ENERGY FOR THE DEVIL KING TO HARNESS.
GO.
GU (CLINK)
...THIS IS WHAT YOU WANT?
BIKU (TWITCH)
!

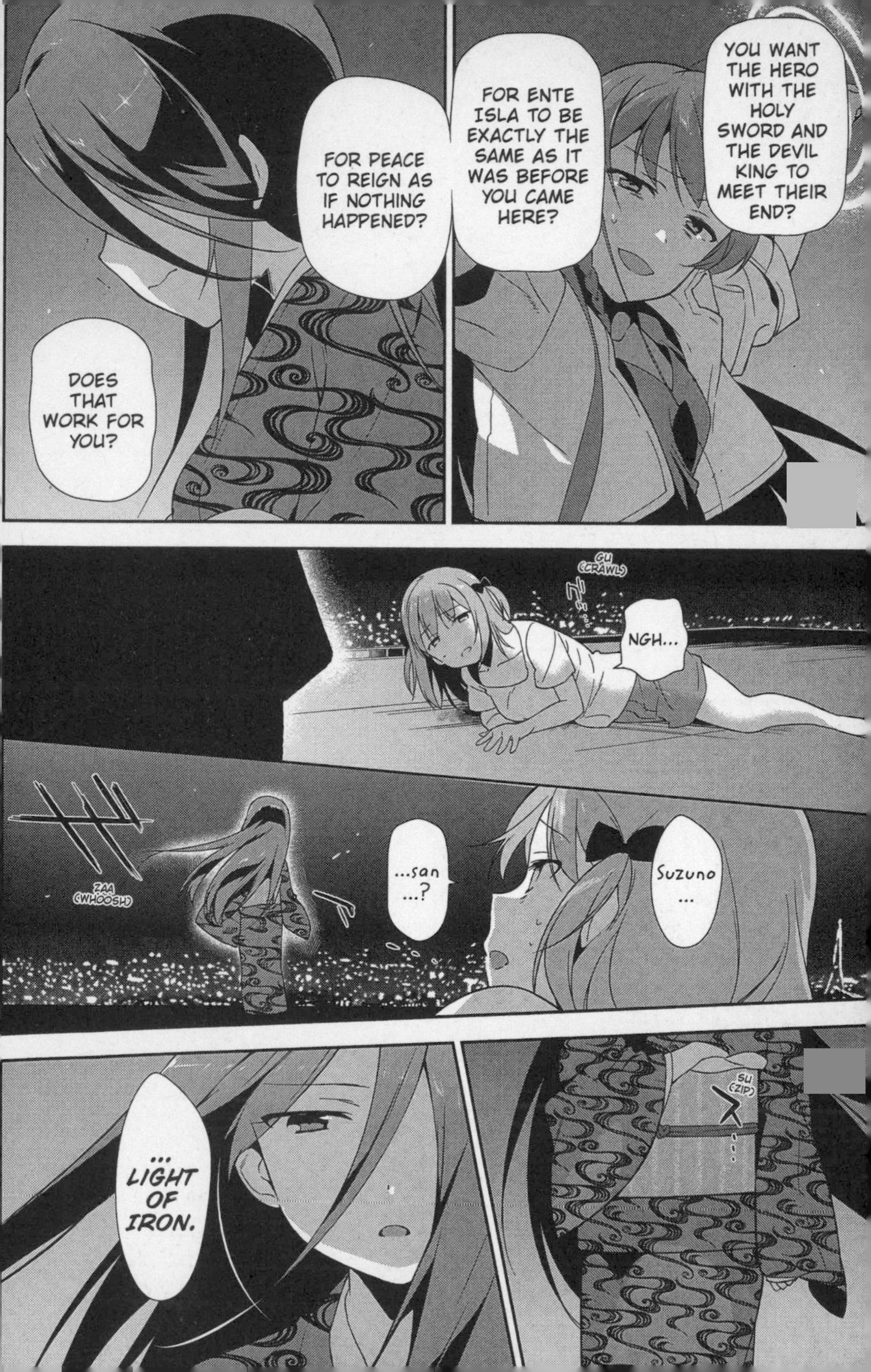
YOU WANT THE HERO WITH THE HOLY SWORD AND THE DEVIL KING TO MEET THEIR END?
FOR ENTE ISLA TO BE EXACTLY THE SAME AS IT WAS BEFORE YOU CAME HERE?
FOR PEACE TO REIGN AS IF NOTHING HAPPENED?
DOES THAT WORK FOR YOU?
GU (CRAWL)
NGH...
Suzuno ...
...san ...?
ZAA (WHOOSH)
SU (ZIP)
... LIGHT OF IRON.

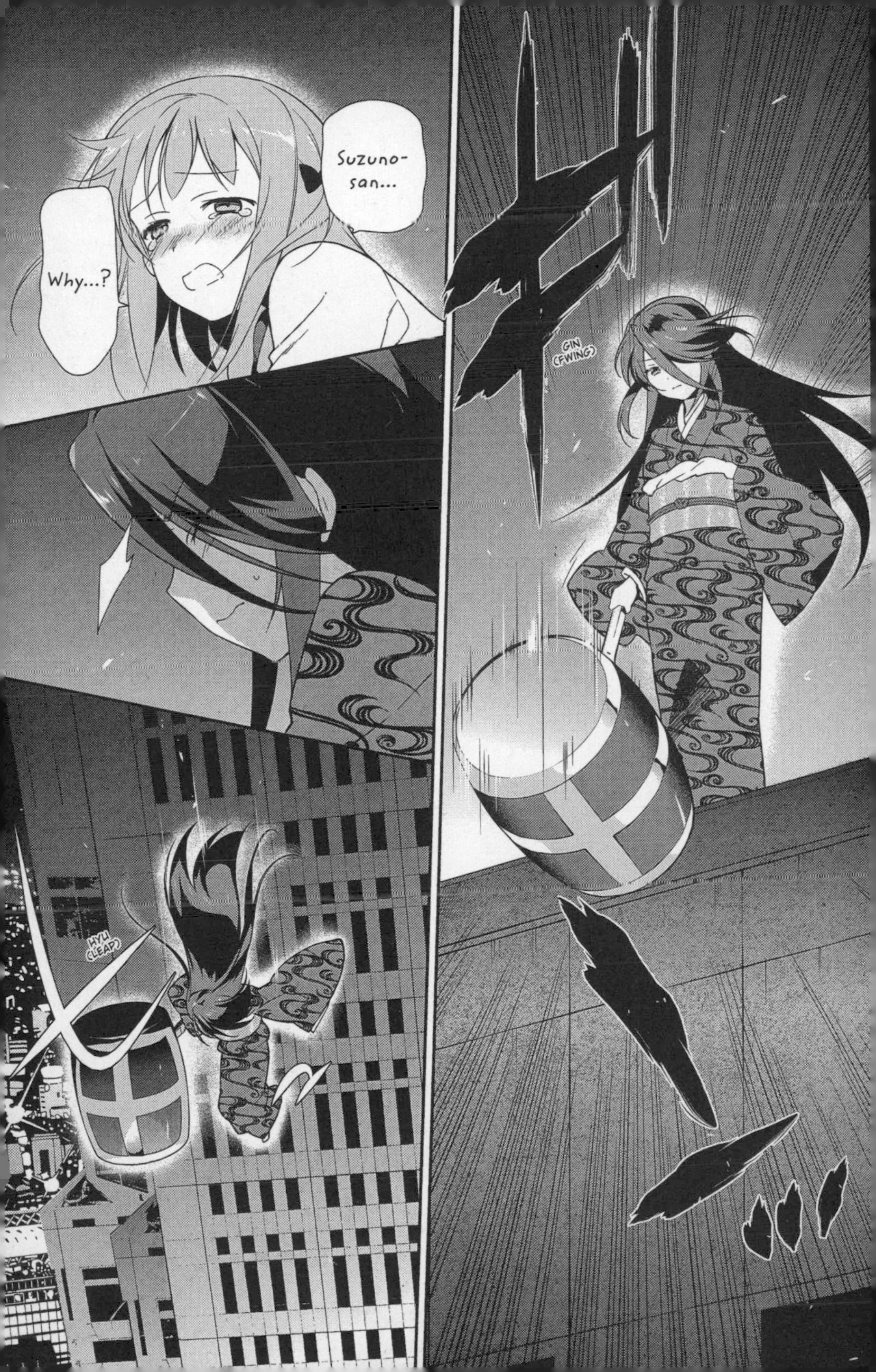
GIN (FWING)
Suzuno-san...
Why...?
HYU (LEAP)

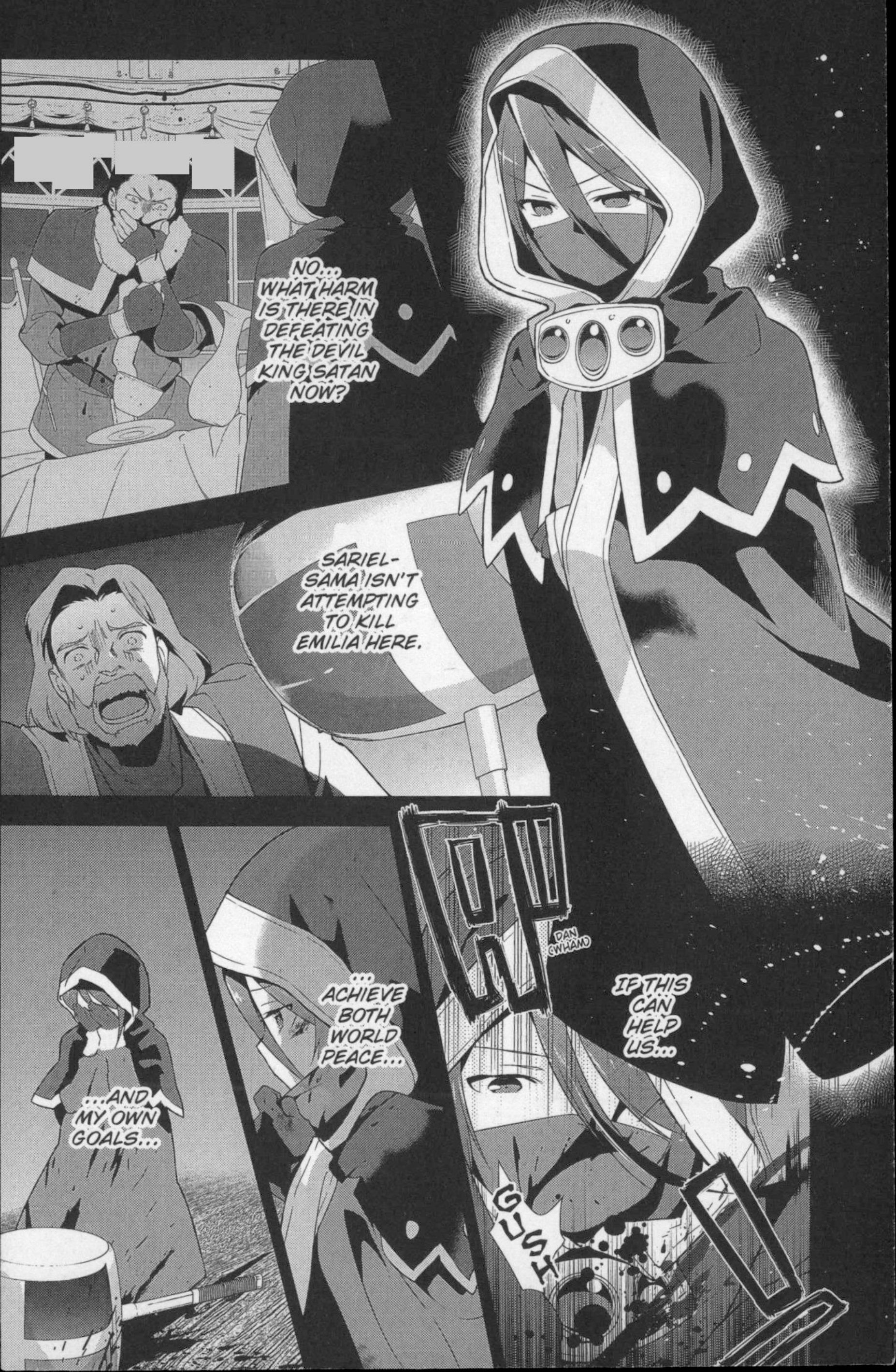
NO... WHAT HARM IS THERE IN DEFEATING THE DEVIL KING SATAN NOW?
SARIEL-SAMA ISN'T ATTEMPTING TO KILL EMILIA HERE.
IF THIS CAN HELP US...
DAN (WHAM)
GUSH
...ACHIEVE BOTH WORLD PEACE...
...AND MY OWN GOALS...

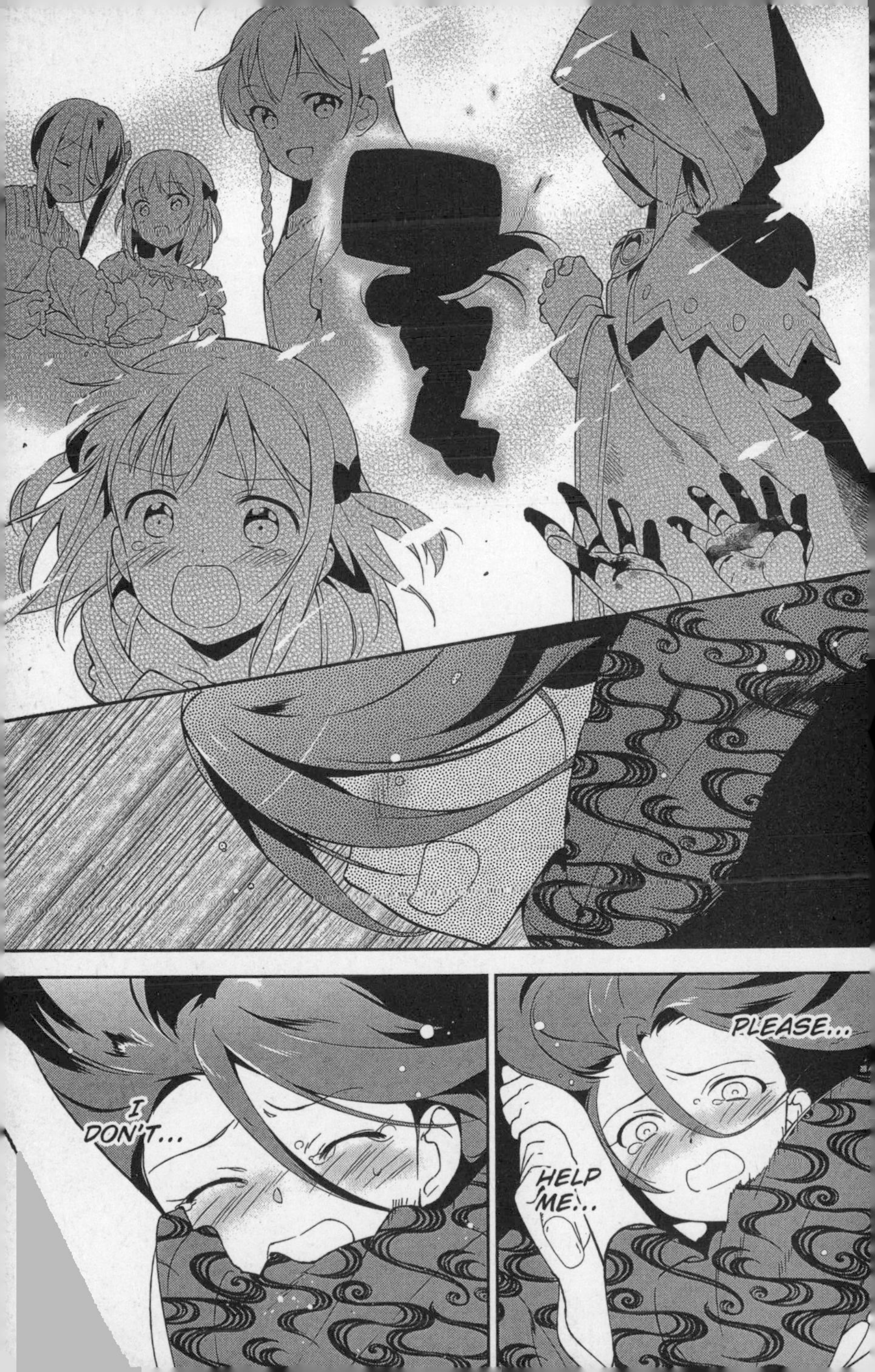
PLEASE...
HELP ME...
I DON'T...

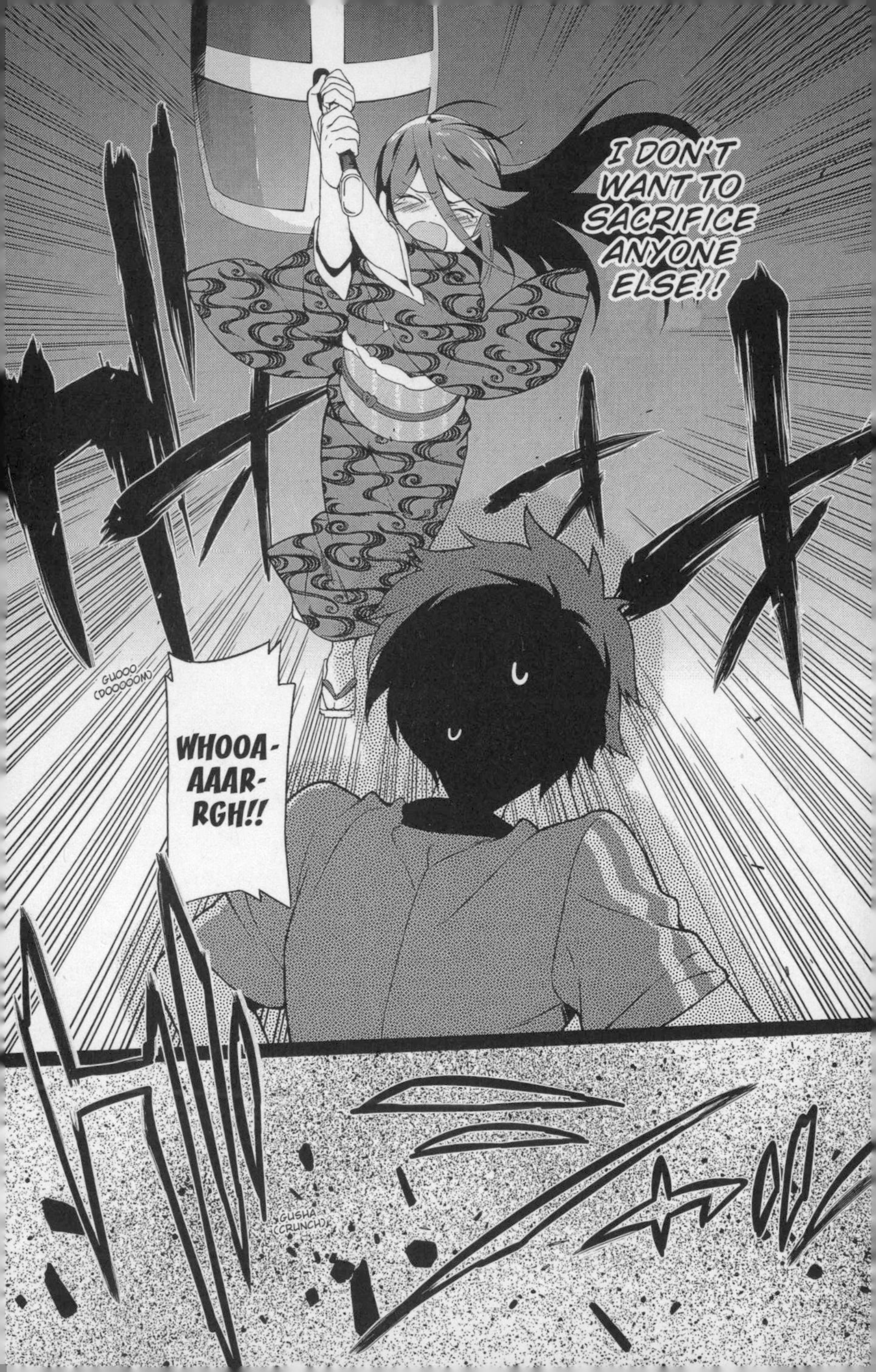
I DON'T WANT TO SACRIFICE ANYONE ELSE!!
GUOOO (DOOOOOM)
WHOOA-AAAR-RGH!!
GUSHA (CRUNCH)

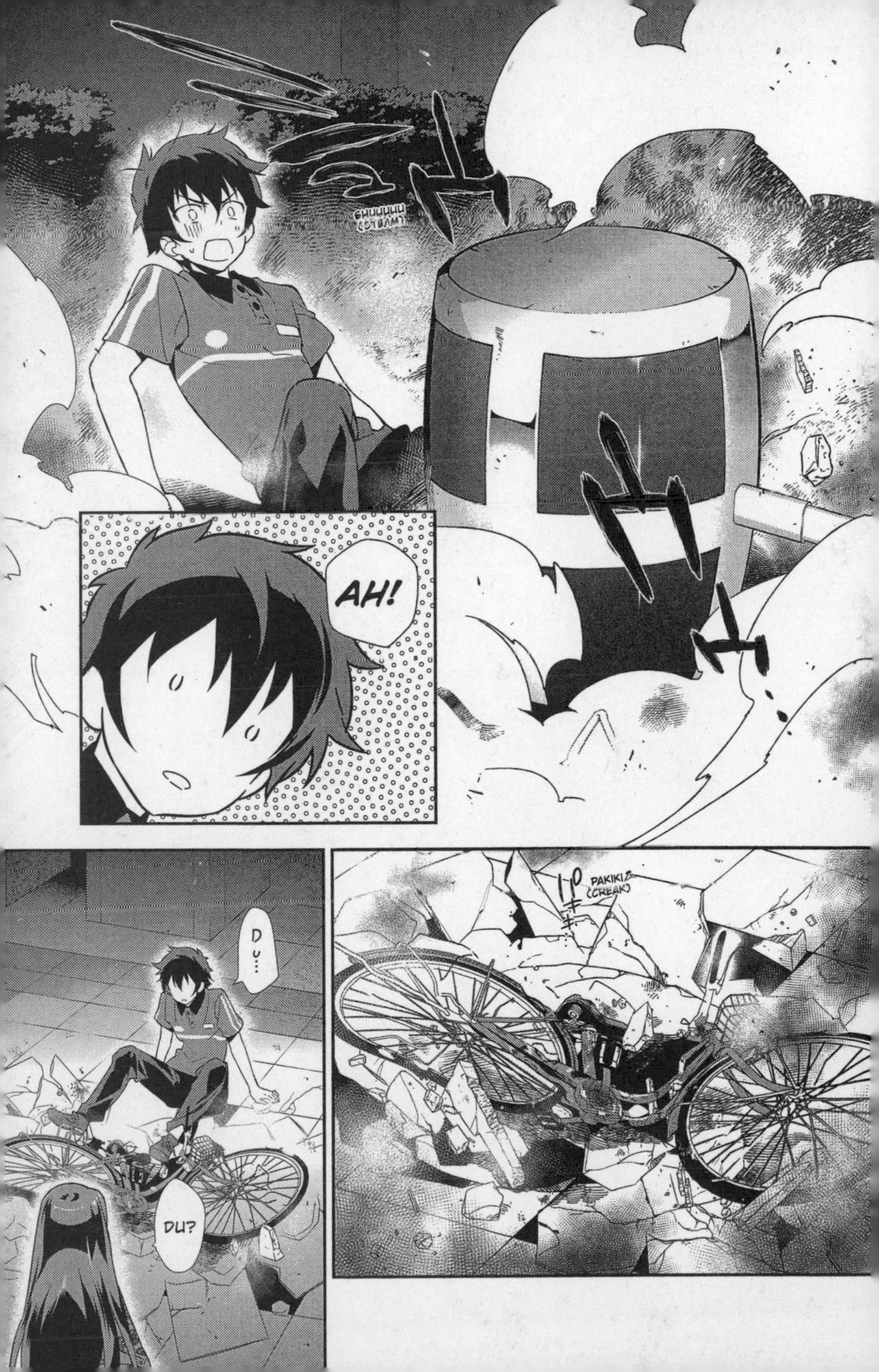
AH!
PAKIKI (CREAK)
DU...
DU?

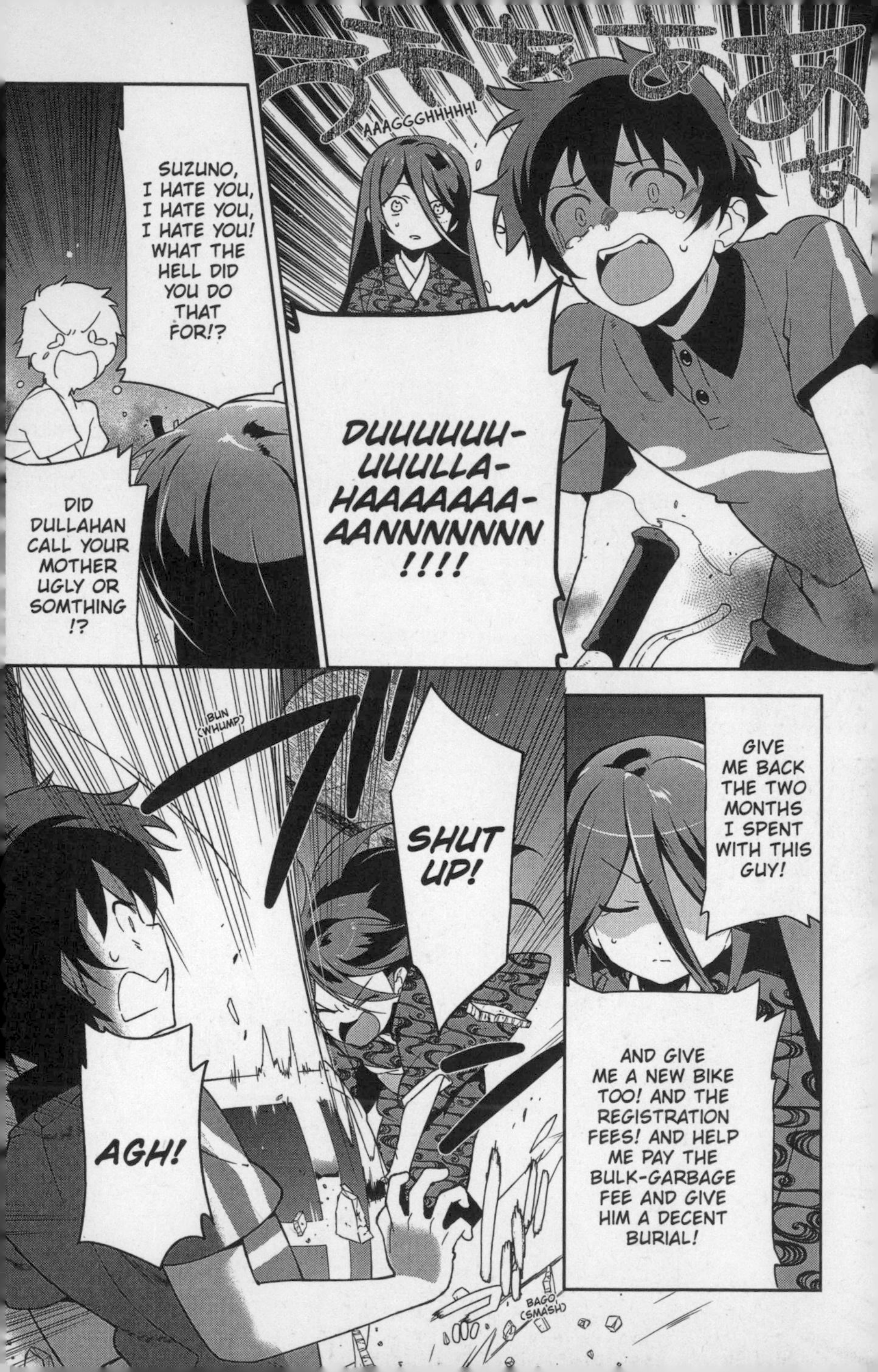
AAAGGGHHHHH!
DUUUUUUU-UUULLA-HAAAAAAA-AANNNNNNN!!!!
SUZUNO, I HATE YOU, I HATE YOU, I HATE YOU! WHAT THE HELL DID YOU DO THAT FOR!?
DID DULLAHAN CALL YOUR MOTHER UGLY OR SOMTHING!?
GIVE ME BACK THE TWO MONTHS I SPENT WITH THIS GUY!
AND GIVE ME A NEW BIKE TOO! AND THE REGISTRATION FEES! AND HELP ME PAY THE BULK-GARBAGE FEE AND GIVE HIM A DECENT BURIAL!
BUN (WHUMP)
SHUT UP!
AGH!
BAGO (SMASH)

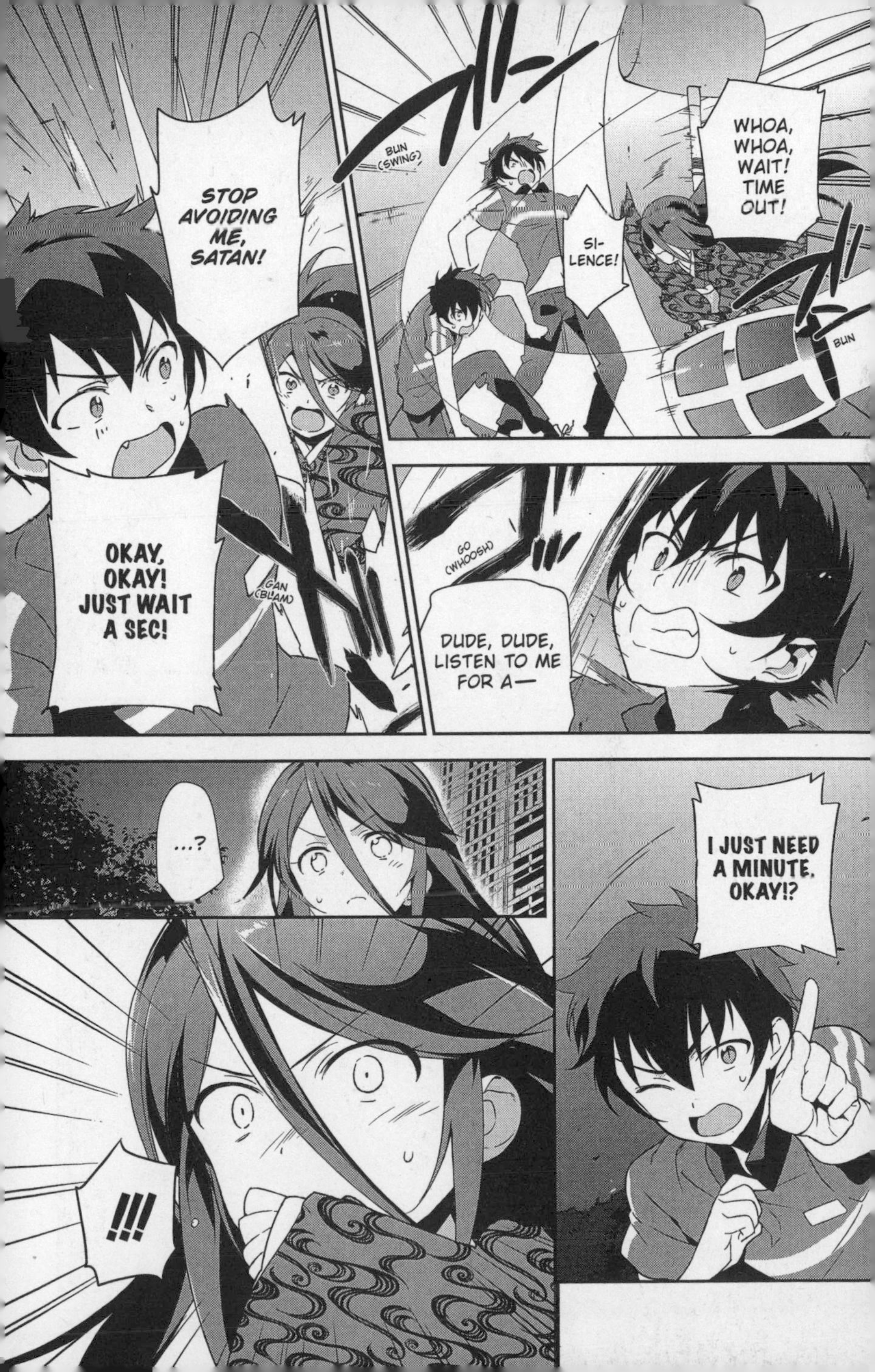
WHOA, WHOA, WAIT! TIME OUT!
BUN (SWING)
SI-LENCE!
BUN
GO (WHOOSH)
DUDE, DUDE, LISTEN TO ME FOR A—
STOP AVOIDING ME, SATAN!
OKAY, OKAY! JUST WAIT A SEC!
GAN (BLAM)
I JUST NEED A MINUTE, OKAY!?
...?
!!!

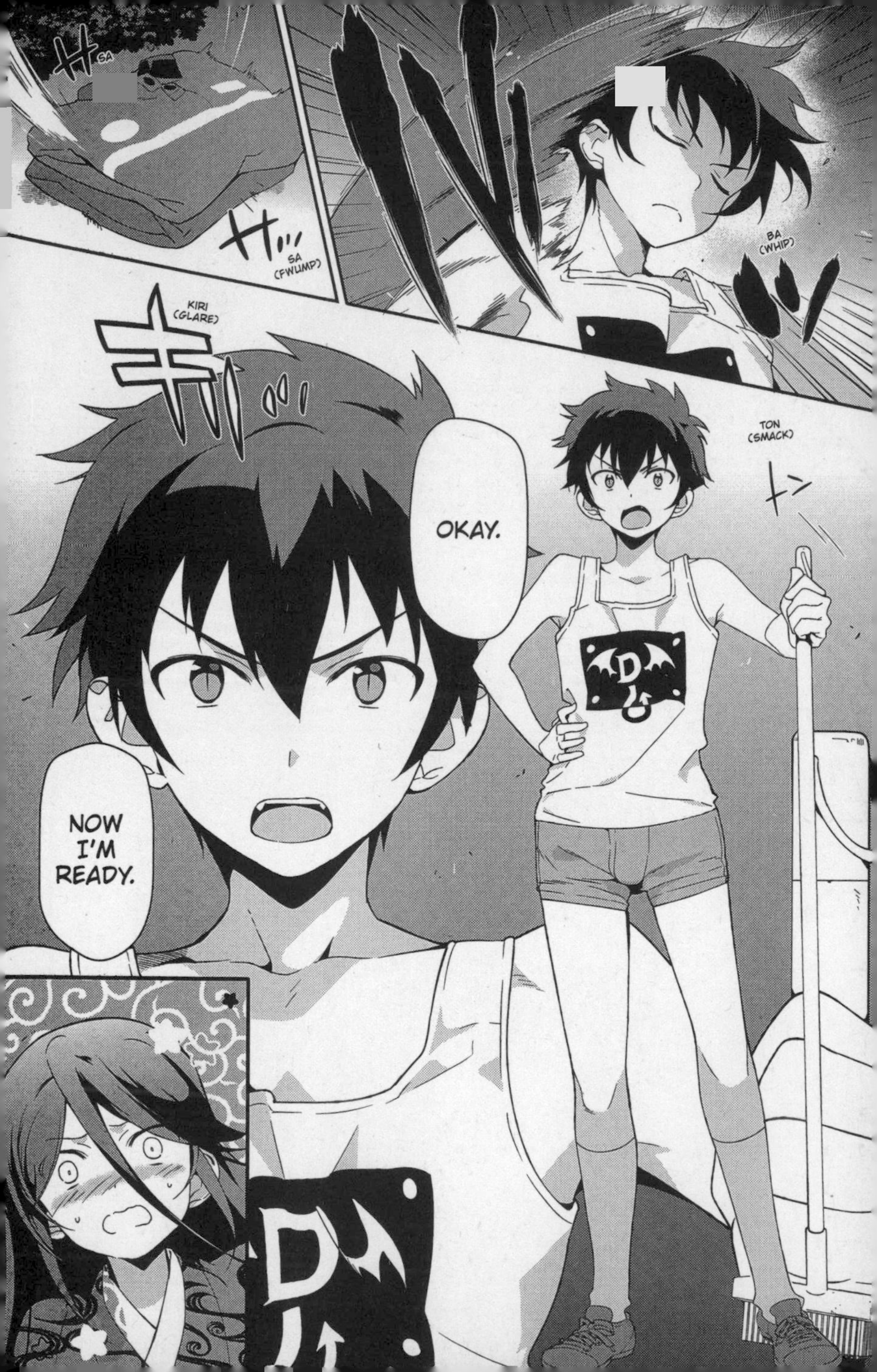
BA
(WHIP)
SA
SA
(FWUMP)
TON
(SMACK)
OKAY.
KIRI
(GLARE)
NOW
I'M
READY.

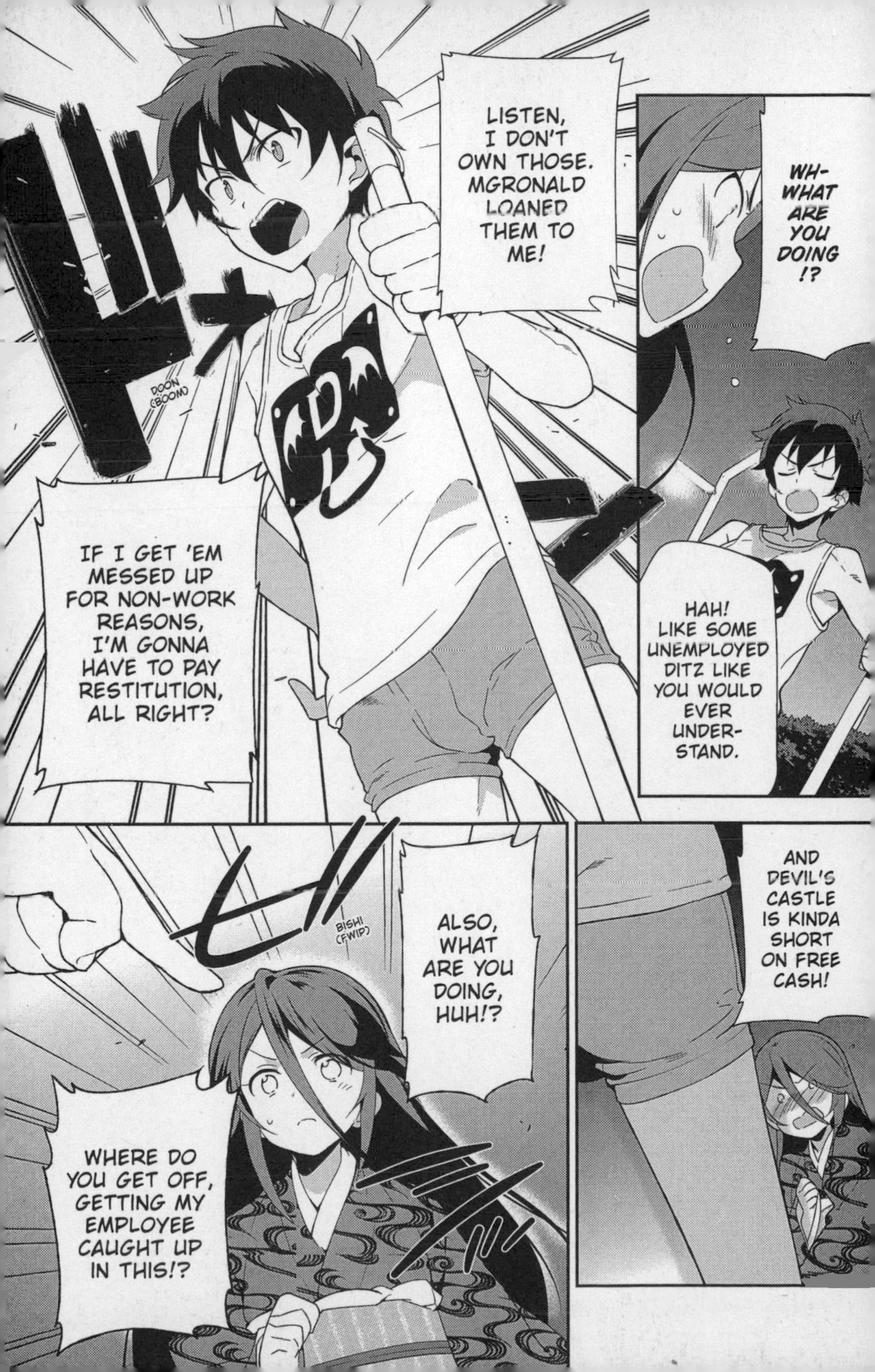
WH-WHAT ARE YOU DOING!?
HAH! LIKE SOME UNEMPLOYED DITZ LIKE YOU WOULD EVER UNDER-STAND.
LISTEN, I DON'T OWN THOSE. MGRONALD LOANED THEM TO ME!
DOON (BOOM)
IF I GET 'EM MESSED UP FOR NON-WORK REASONS, I'M GONNA HAVE TO PAY RESTITUTION, ALL RIGHT?
AND DEVIL'S CASTLE IS KINDA SHORT ON FREE CASH!
ALSO, WHAT ARE YOU DOING, HUH!?
BISHI (FWIP)
WHERE DO YOU GET OFF, GETTING MY EMPLOYEE CAUGHT UP IN THIS!?

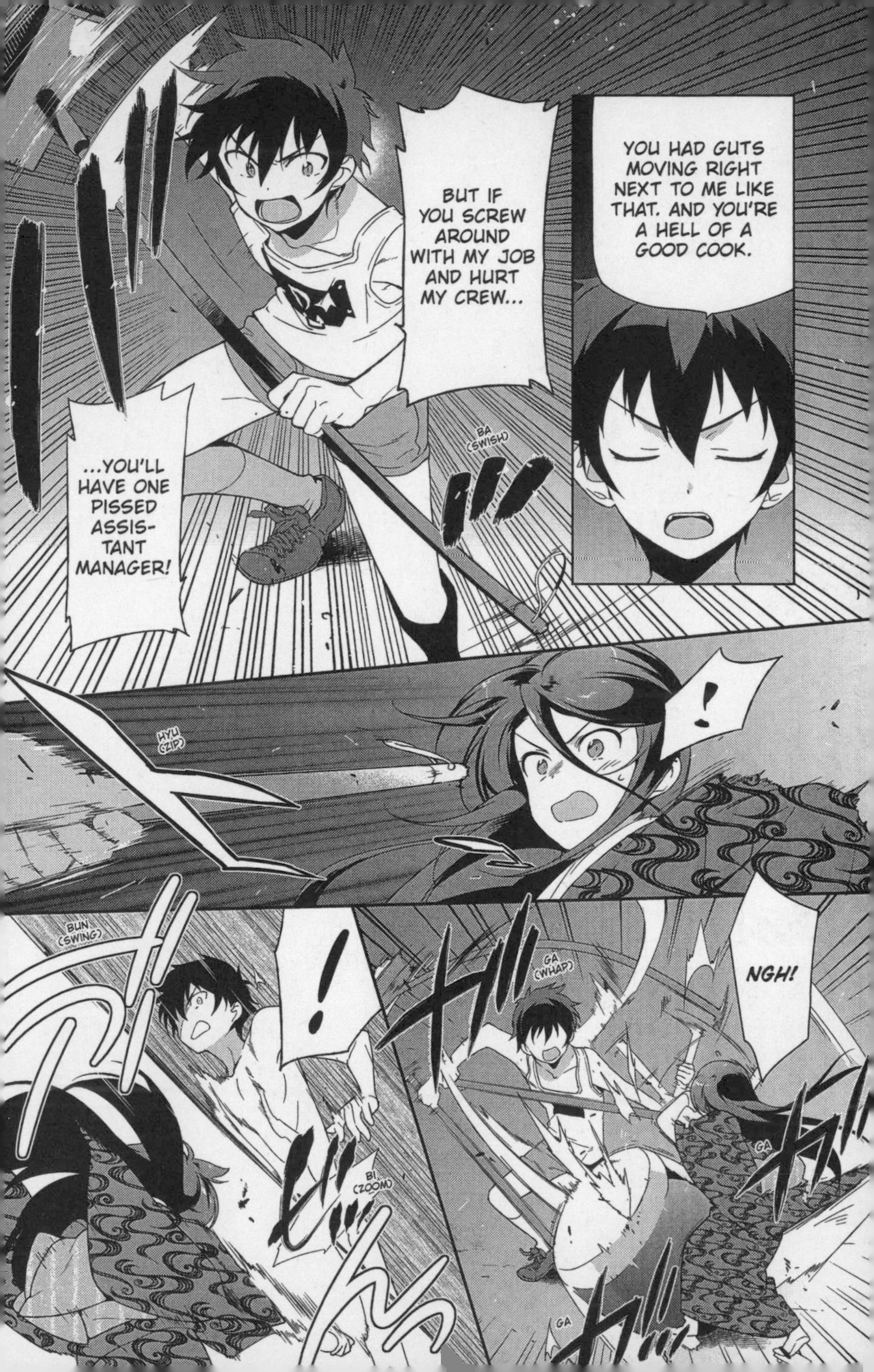
YOU HAD GUTS MOVING RIGHT NEXT TO ME LIKE THAT. AND YOU'RE A HELL OF A GOOD COOK.
BUT IF YOU SCREW AROUND WITH MY JOB AND HURT MY CREW...
BA (SWISH)
...YOU'LL HAVE ONE PISSED ASSIS-TANT MANAGER!
!
HYU (ZIP)
NGH!
GA (WHAP)
GA
GA
!
BUN (SWING)
BI (ZOOM)

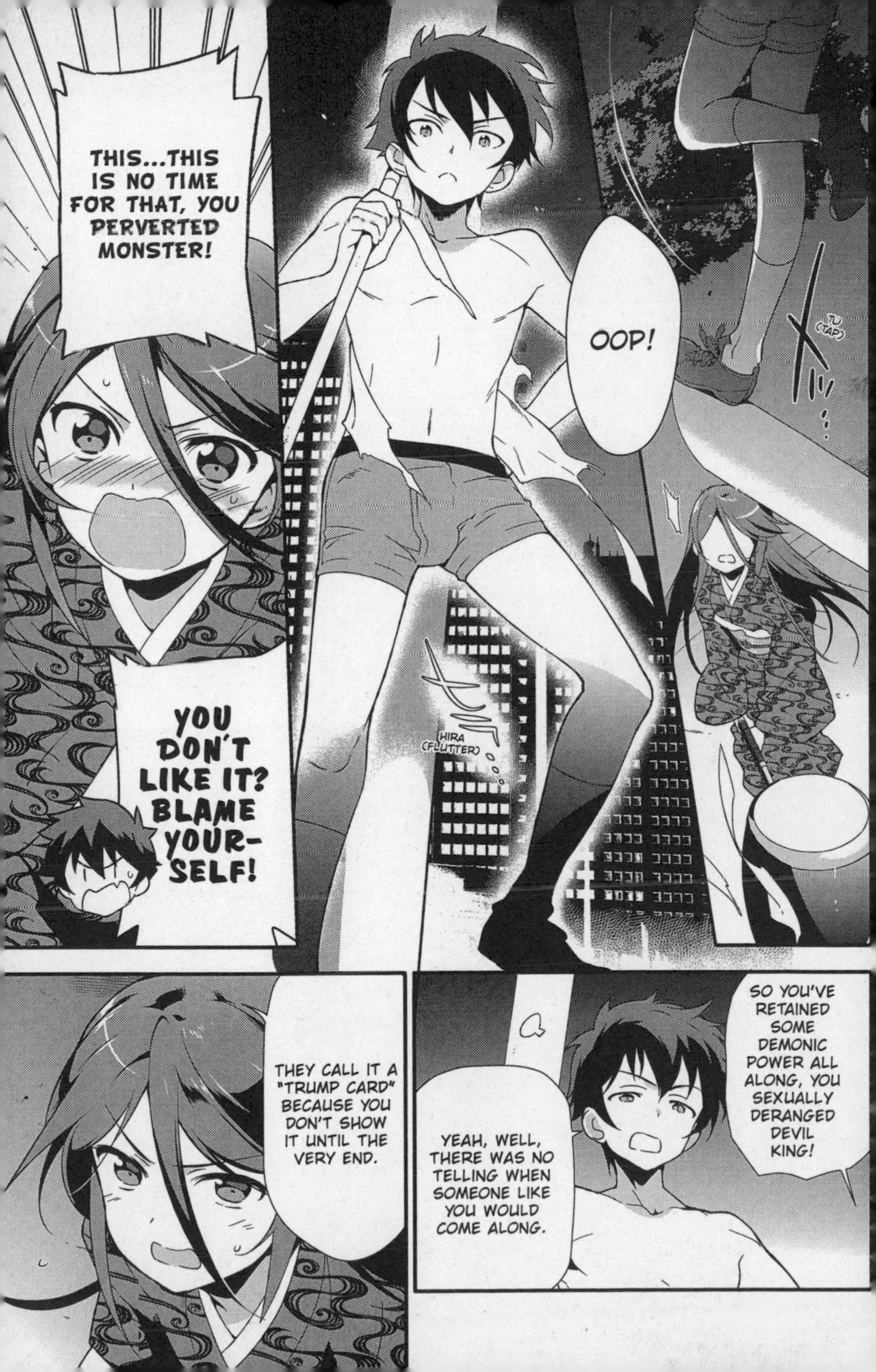
TU (TAP)
OOP!
HIRA (FLUTTER)
THIS...THIS IS NO TIME FOR THAT, YOU PERVERTED MONSTER!
YOU DON'T LIKE IT? BLAME YOURSELF!
SO YOU'VE RETAINED SOME DEMONIC POWER ALL ALONG, YOU SEXUALLY DERANGED DEVIL KING!
YEAH, WELL, THERE WAS NO TELLING WHEN SOMEONE LIKE YOU WOULD COME ALONG.
THEY CALL IT A "TRUMP CARD" BECAUSE YOU DON'T SHOW IT UNTIL THE VERY END.

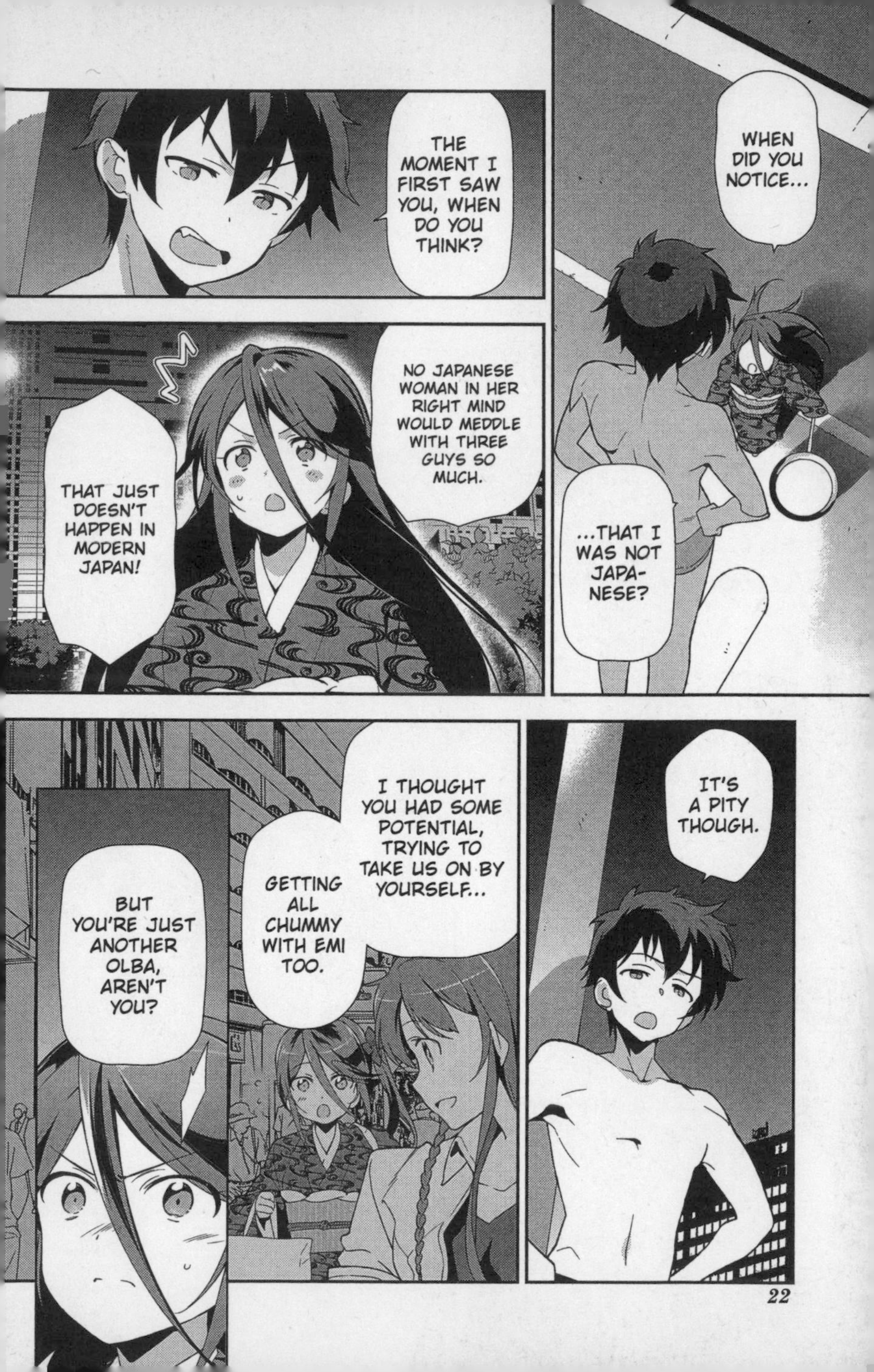
WHEN DID YOU NOTICE...
...THAT I WAS NOT JAPANESE?
THE MOMENT I FIRST SAW YOU, WHEN DO YOU THINK?
NO JAPANESE WOMAN IN HER RIGHT MIND WOULD MEDDLE WITH THREE GUYS SO MUCH.
THAT JUST DOESN'T HAPPEN IN MODERN JAPAN!
IT'S A PITY THOUGH.
I THOUGHT YOU HAD SOME POTENTIAL, TRYING TO TAKE US ON BY YOURSELF...
GETTING ALL CHUMMY WITH EMI TOO.
BUT YOU'RE JUST ANOTHER OLBA, AREN'T YOU?

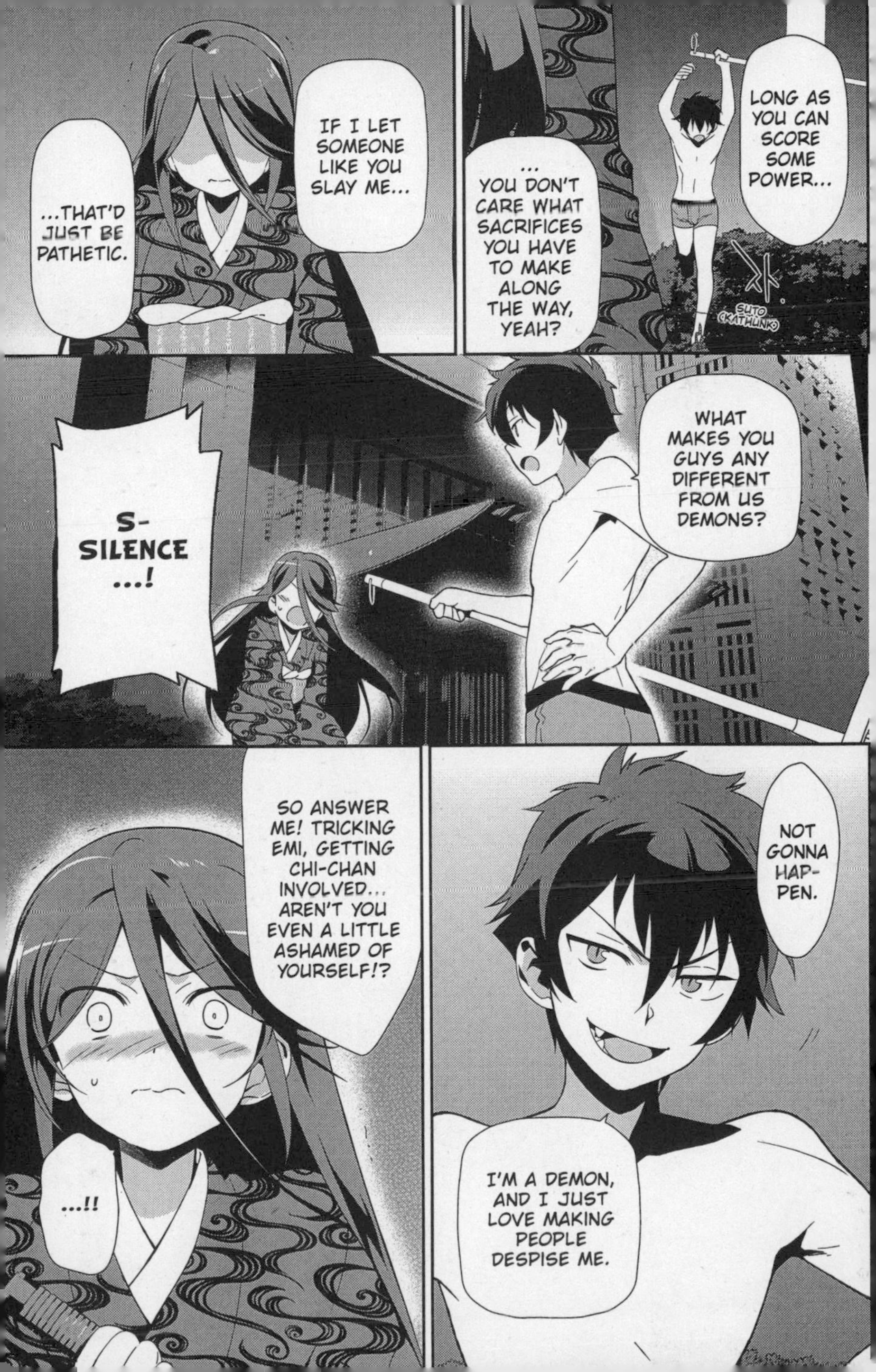
LONG AS YOU CAN SCORE SOME POWER...
... YOU DON'T CARE WHAT SACRIFICES YOU HAVE TO MAKE ALONG THE WAY, YEAH?
SUTO (KATHUNK)
IF I LET SOMEONE LIKE YOU SLAY ME...
...THAT'D JUST BE PATHETIC.
WHAT MAKES YOU GUYS ANY DIFFERENT FROM US DEMONS?
S-SILENCE ...!
NOT GONNA HAP-PEN.
I'M A DEMON, AND I JUST LOVE MAKING PEOPLE DESPISE ME.
SO ANSWER ME! TRICKING EMI, GETTING CHI-CHAN INVOLVED... AREN'T YOU EVEN A LITTLE ASHAMED OF YOURSELF!?
...!!

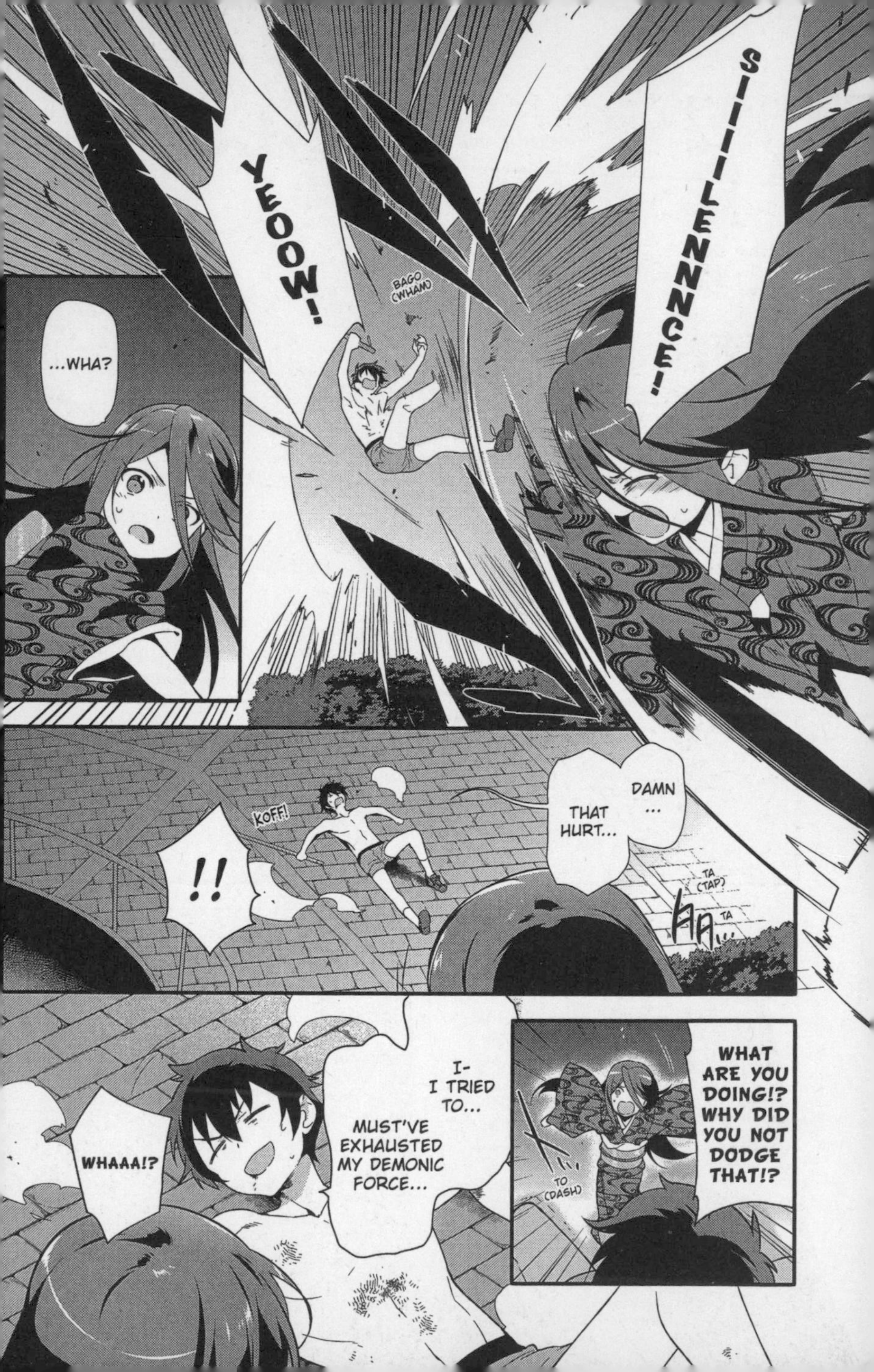
SIIIILENNNCE!
YEOOW!
BAGO (WHAM)
...WHA?
DAMN... THAT HURT...
TA (TAP) TA
KOFF!
!!
WHAT ARE YOU DOING!? WHY DID YOU NOT DODGE THAT!?
TO (DASH)
I- I TRIED TO...
MUST'VE EXHAUSTED MY DEMONIC FORCE...
WHAAA!?

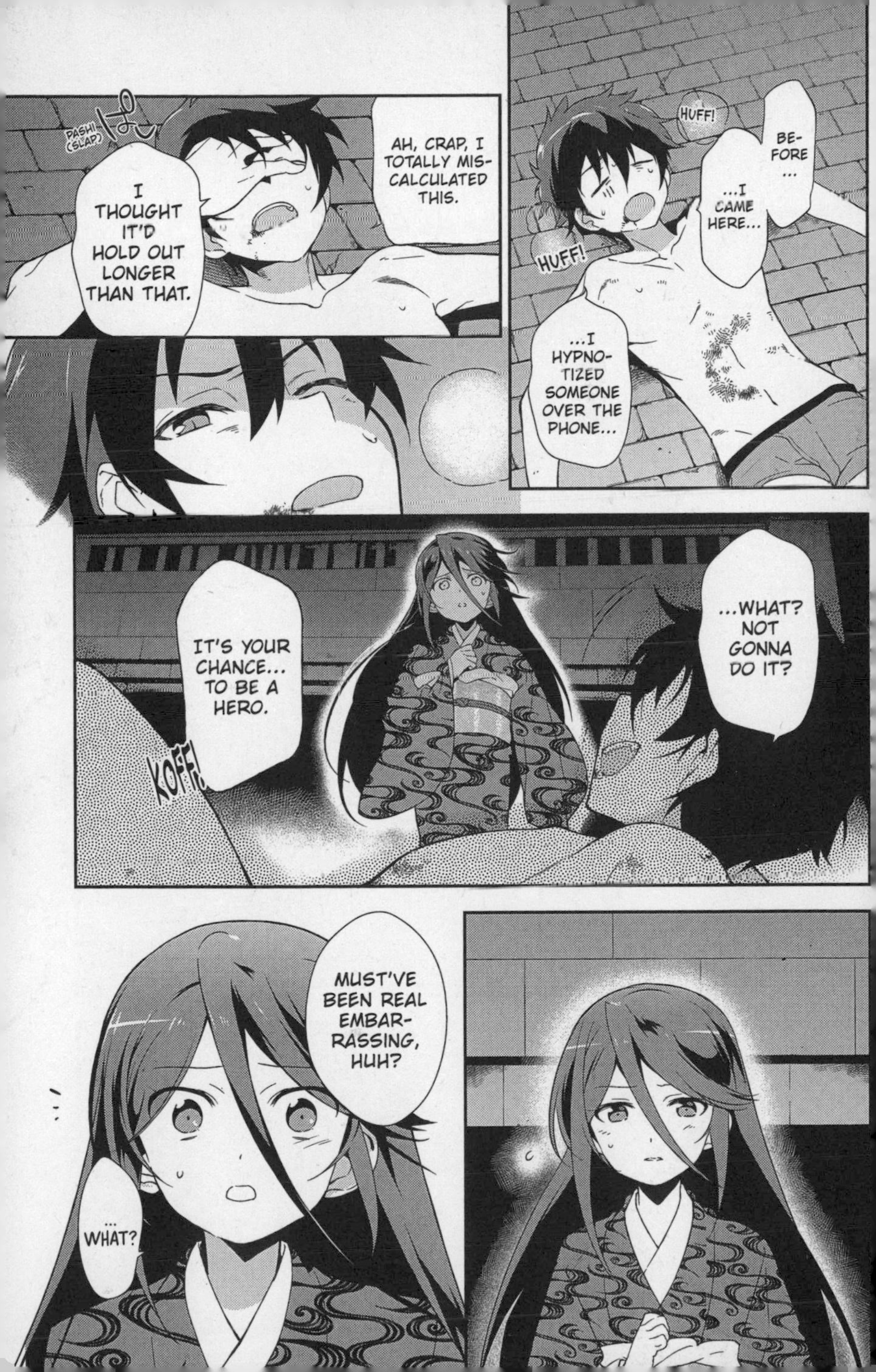
HUFF!
BE-FORE...
...I CAME HERE...
HUFF!
...I HYPNO-TIZED SOMEONE OVER THE PHONE...
PASHI (SLAP)
AH, CRAP, I TOTALLY MIS-CALCULATED THIS.
I THOUGHT IT'D HOLD OUT LONGER THAN THAT.
...WHAT? NOT GONNA DO IT?
IT'S YOUR CHANCE... TO BE A HERO.
KOFF!
MUST'VE BEEN REAL EMBAR-RASSING, HUH?
...WHAT?

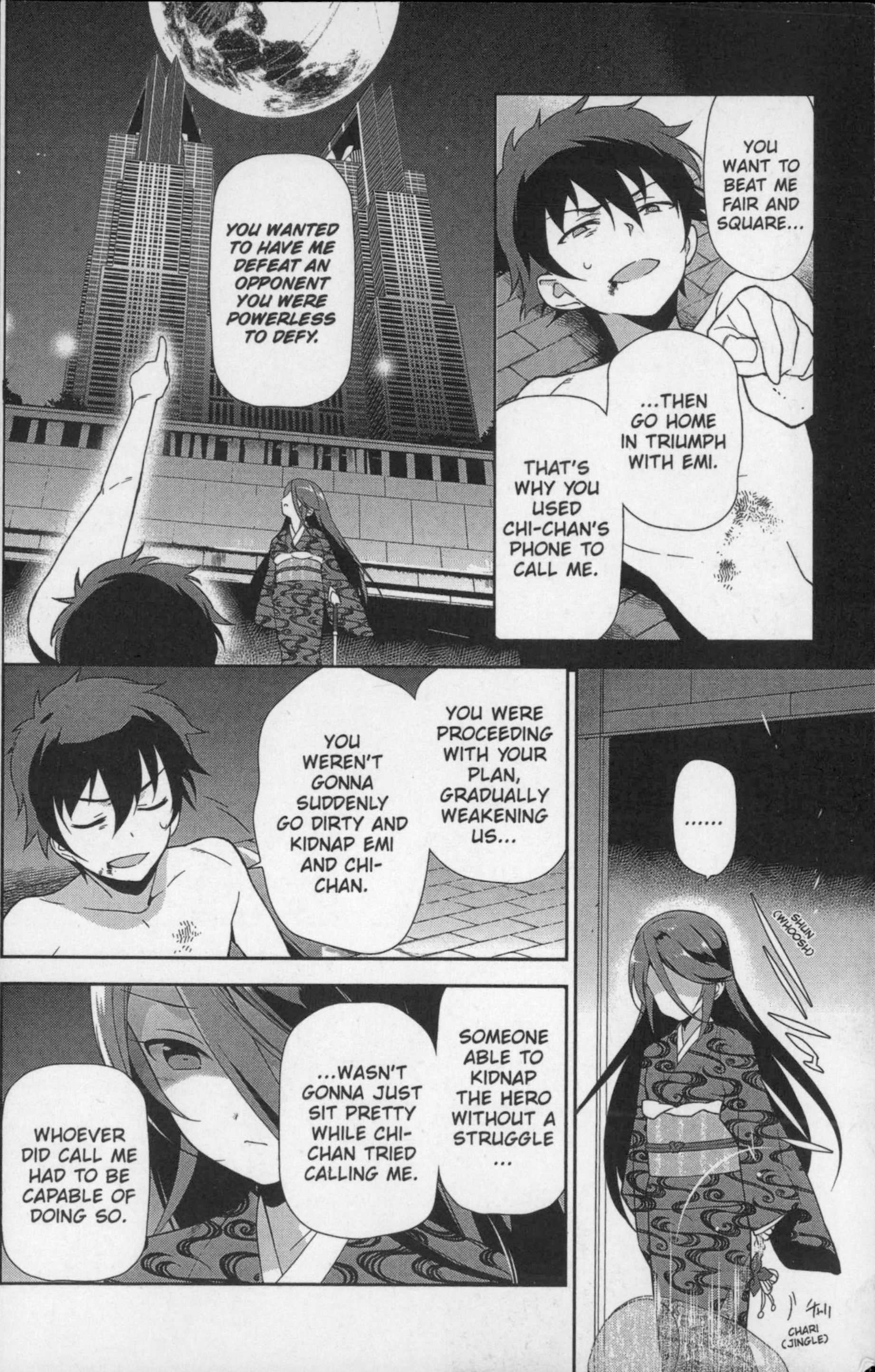
YOU WANT TO BEAT ME FAIR AND SQUARE...
...THEN GO HOME IN TRIUMPH WITH EMI.
THAT'S WHY YOU USED CHI-CHAN'S PHONE TO CALL ME.
YOU WANTED TO HAVE ME DEFEAT AN OPPONENT YOU WERE POWERLESS TO DEFY.
......
SHUN (WHOOSH)
CHARI (JINGLE)
YOU WERE PROCEEDING WITH YOUR PLAN, GRADUALLY WEAKENING US...
YOU WEREN'T GONNA SUDDENLY GO DIRTY AND KIDNAP EMI AND CHI-CHAN.
SOMEONE ABLE TO KIDNAP THE HERO WITHOUT A STRUGGLE...
...WASN'T GONNA JUST SIT PRETTY WHILE CHI-CHAN TRIED CALLING ME.
WHOEVER DID CALL ME HAD TO BE CAPABLE OF DOING SO.

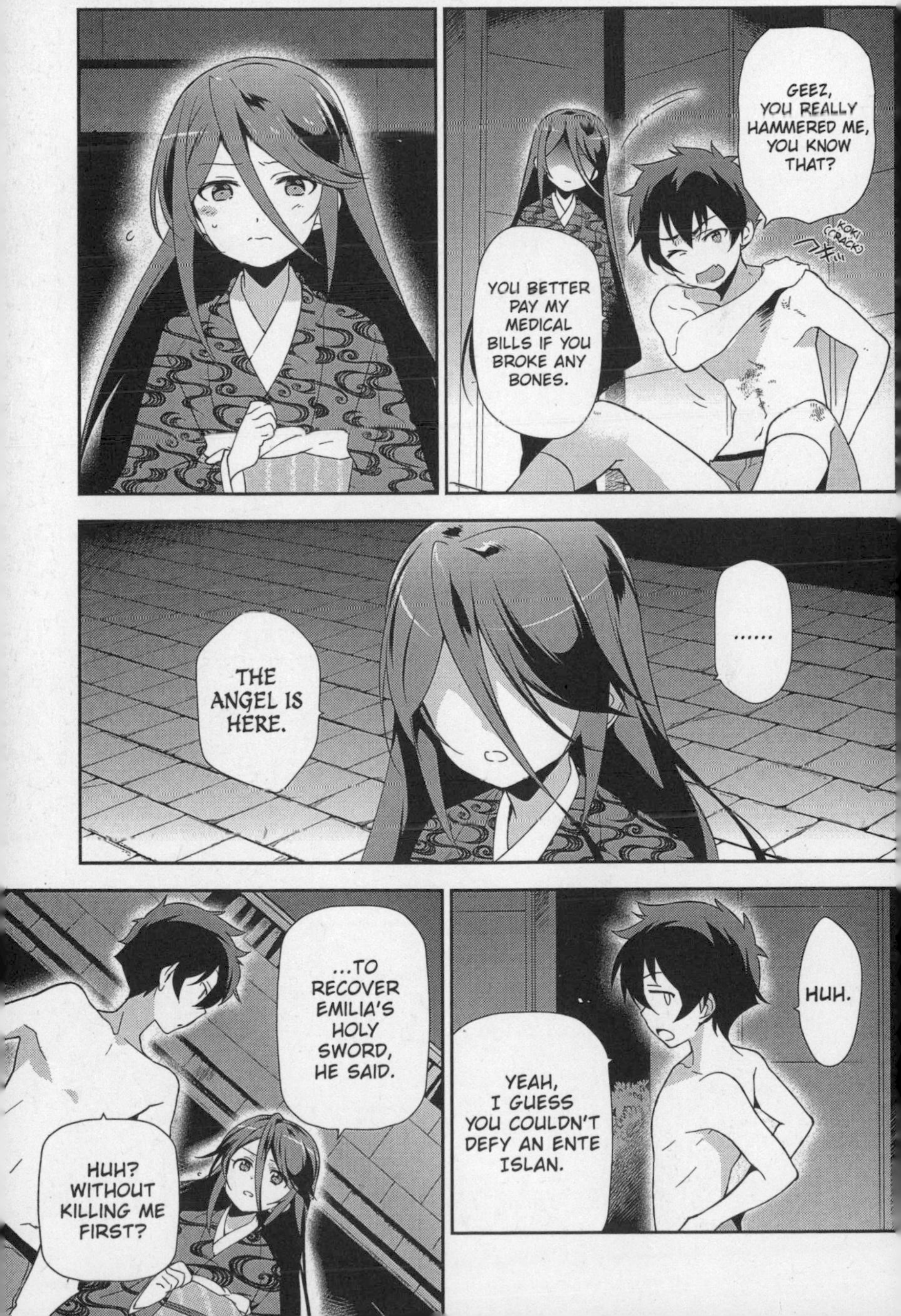
GEEZ, YOU REALLY HAMMERED ME, YOU KNOW THAT?
KOKI (CRACK)
YOU BETTER PAY MY MEDICAL BILLS IF YOU BROKE ANY BONES.
......
THE ANGEL IS HERE.
HUH.
YEAH, I GUESS YOU COULDN'T DEFY AN ENTE ISLAN.
...TO RECOVER EMILIA'S HOLY SWORD, HE SAID.
HUH? WITHOUT KILLING ME FIRST?

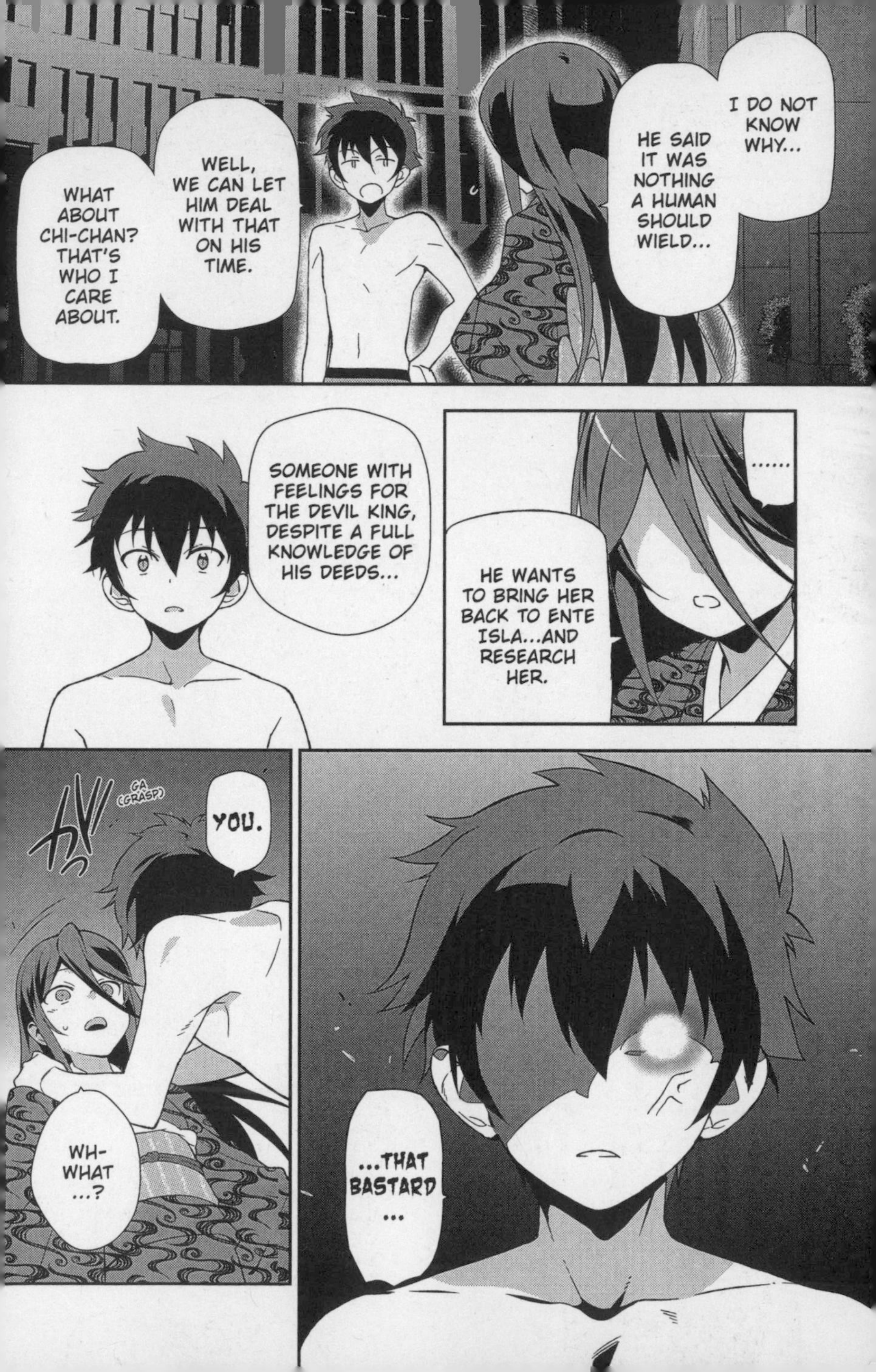
I DO NOT KNOW WHY...
HE SAID IT WAS NOTHING A HUMAN SHOULD WIELD...
WELL, WE CAN LET HIM DEAL WITH THAT ON HIS TIME.
WHAT ABOUT CHI-CHAN? THAT'S WHO I CARE ABOUT.
......
HE WANTS TO BRING HER BACK TO ENTE ISLA...AND RESEARCH HER.
SOMEONE WITH FEELINGS FOR THE DEVIL KING, DESPITE A FULL KNOWLEDGE OF HIS DEEDS...
...THAT BASTARD ...
GA (GRASP)
YOU.
WH-WHAT ...?

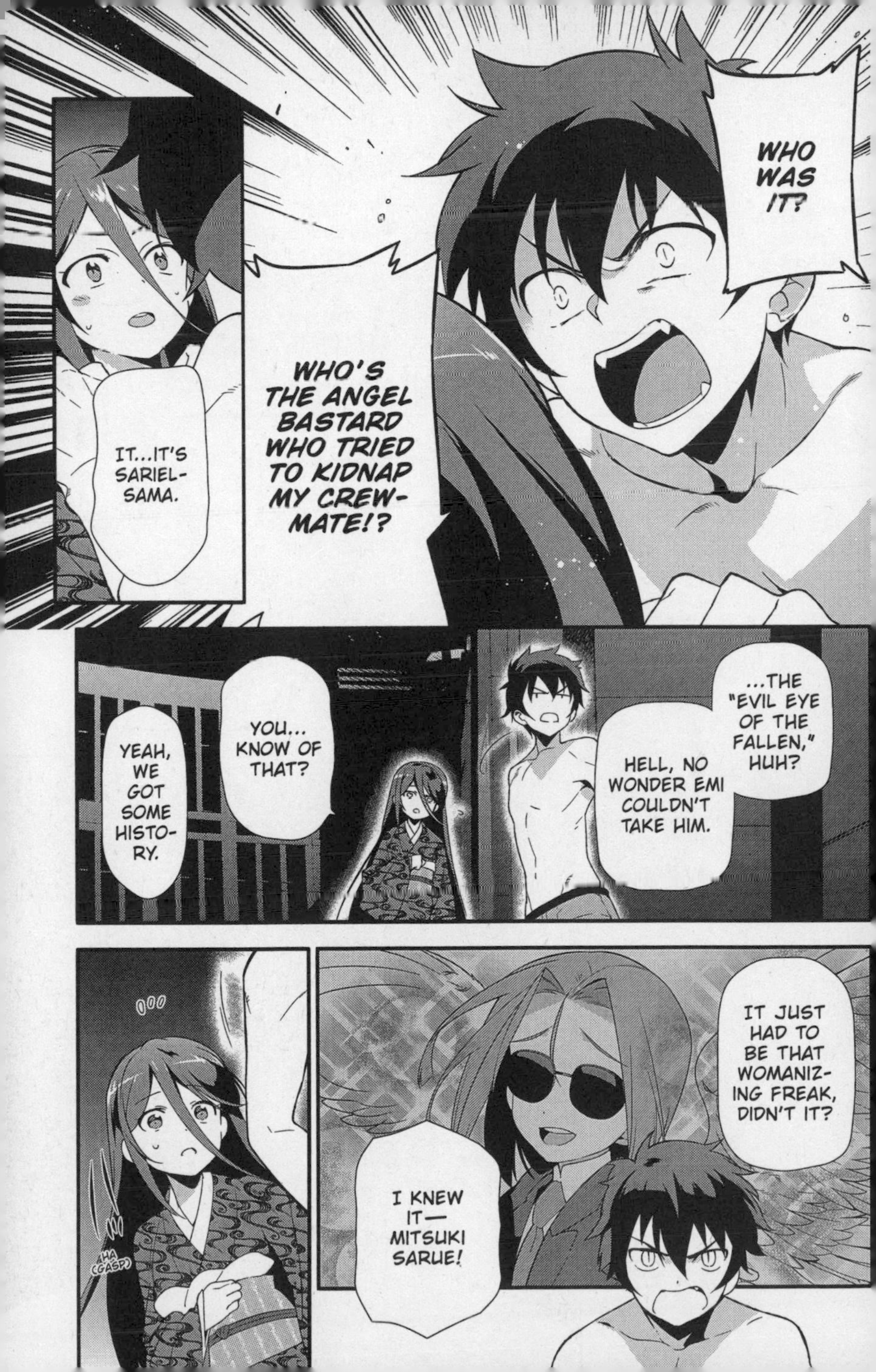
WHO WAS IT?
WHO'S THE ANGEL BASTARD WHO TRIED TO KIDNAP MY CREW-MATE!?
IT...IT'S SARIEL-SAMA.
...THE "EVIL EYE OF THE FALLEN," HUH?
HELL, NO WONDER EMI COULDN'T TAKE HIM.
YOU... KNOW OF THAT?
YEAH, WE GOT SOME HISTORY.
IT JUST HAD TO BE THAT WOMANIZING FREAK, DIDN'T IT?
I KNEW IT—MITSUKI SARUE!
HA (GASP)

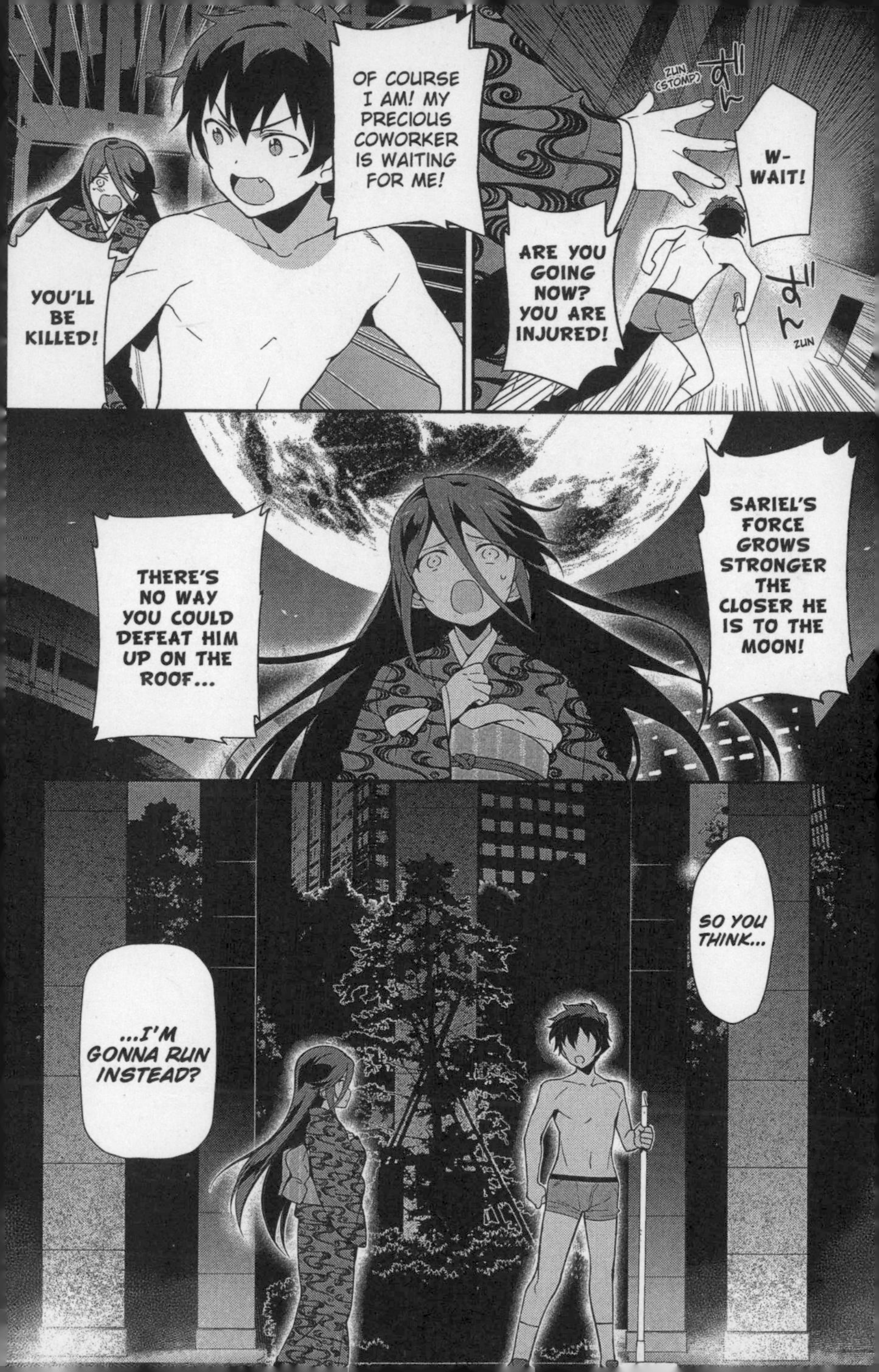
ZUN (STOMP)
W-WAIT!
ZUN
ARE YOU GOING NOW? YOU ARE INJURED!
OF COURSE I AM! MY PRECIOUS COWORKER IS WAITING FOR ME!
YOU'LL BE KILLED!
SARIEL'S FORCE GROWS STRONGER THE CLOSER HE IS TO THE MOON!
THERE'S NO WAY YOU COULD DEFEAT HIM UP ON THE ROOF...
SO YOU THINK...
...I'M GONNA RUN INSTEAD?

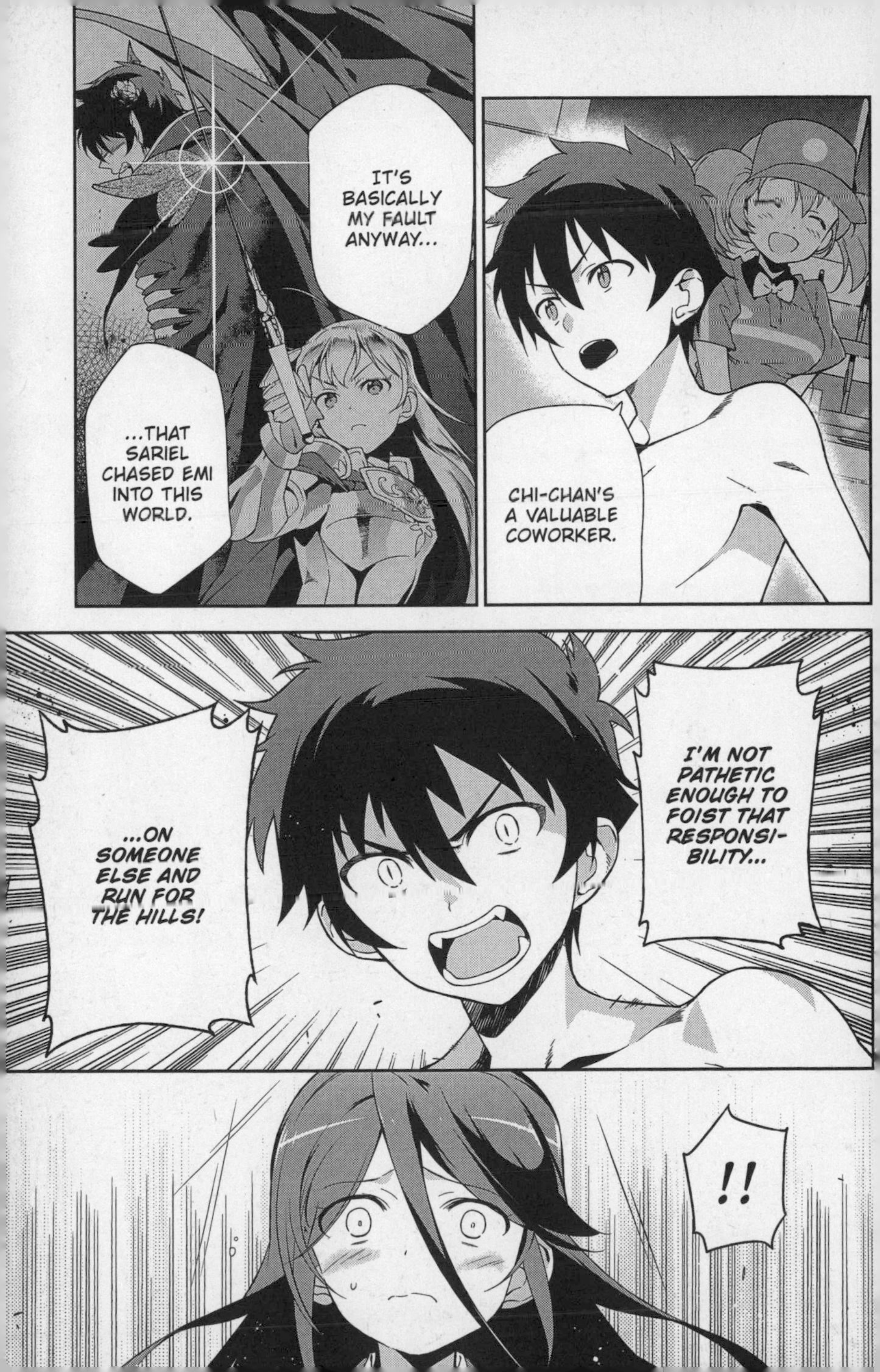
CHI-CHAN'S A VALUABLE COWORKER.
IT'S BASICALLY MY FAULT ANYWAY...
...THAT SARIEL CHASED EMI INTO THIS WORLD.
I'M NOT PATHETIC ENOUGH TO FOIST THAT RESPONSI-BILITY...
...ON SOMEONE ELSE AND RUN FOR THE HILLS!
!!

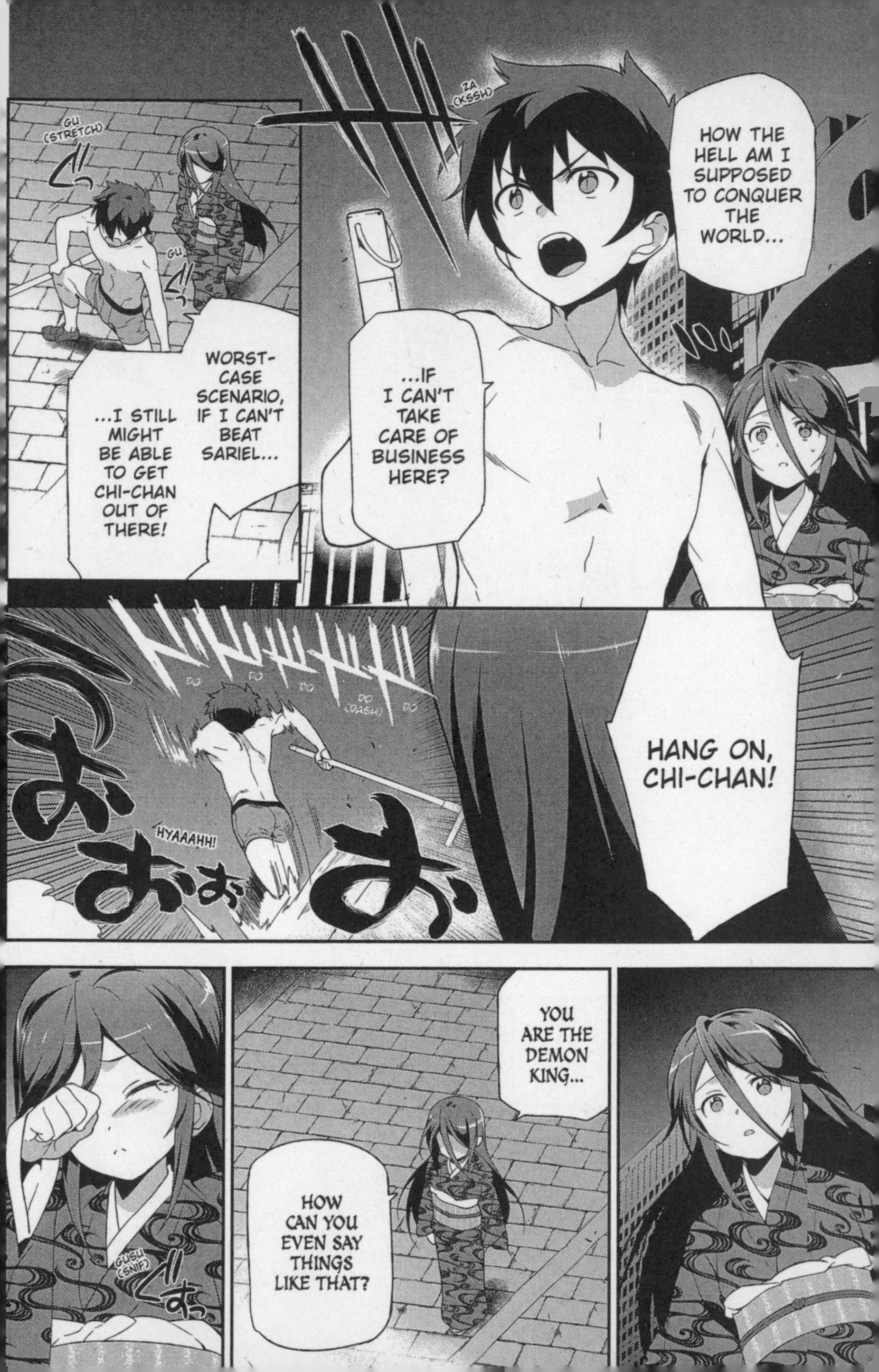
ZA (KSSH)
HOW THE HELL AM I SUPPOSED TO CONQUER THE WORLD...
...IF I CAN'T TAKE CARE OF BUSINESS HERE?
GU (STRETCH)
GU
WORST-CASE SCENARIO, IF I CAN'T BEAT SARIEL...
...I STILL MIGHT BE ABLE TO GET CHI-CHAN OUT OF THERE!
HANG ON, CHI-CHAN!
DO DO DO DO (DASH) DO
HYAAAHH!
YOU ARE THE DEMON KING...
HOW CAN YOU EVEN SAY THINGS LIKE THAT?
GUSU (SNIF)

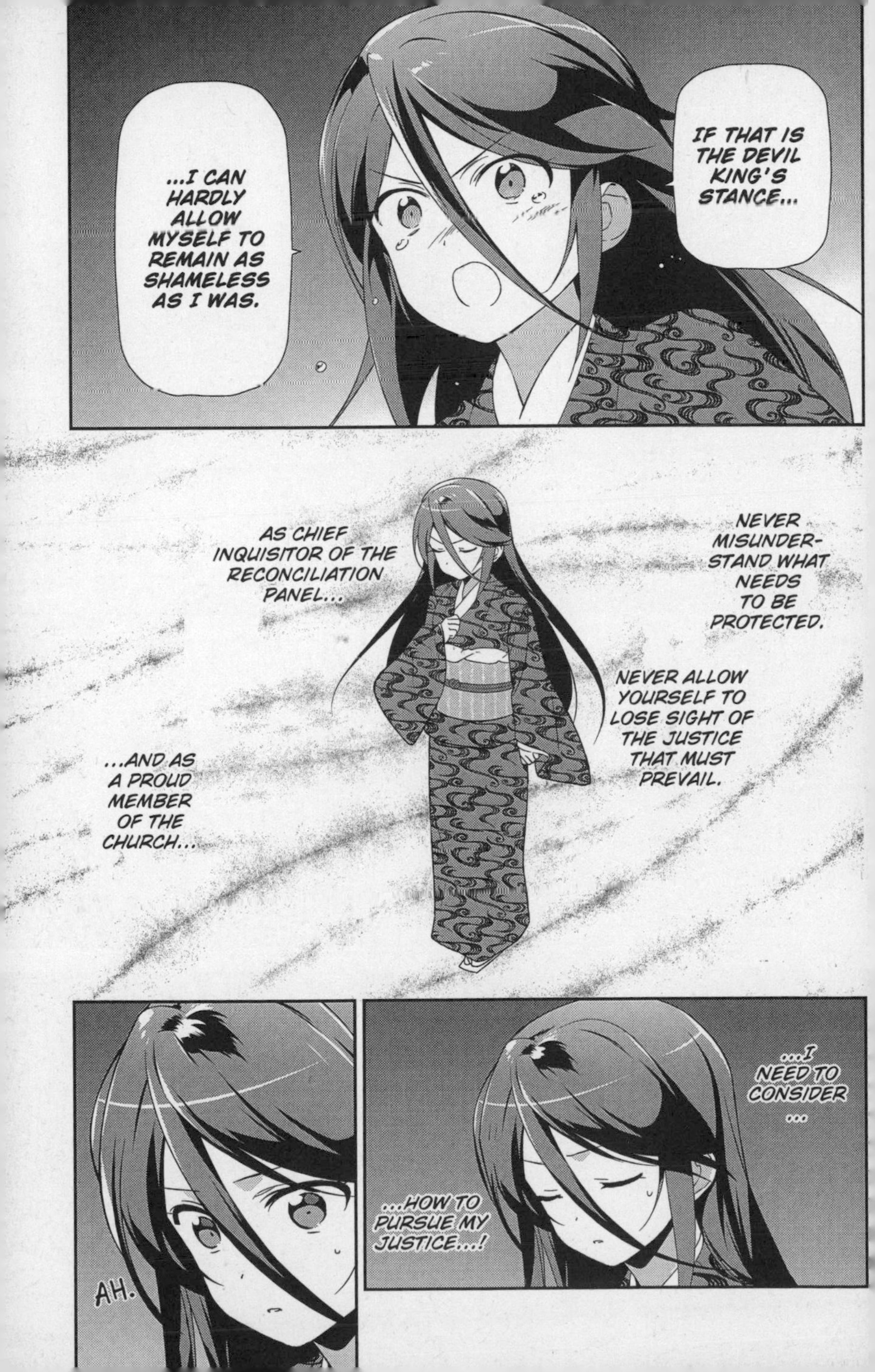
IF THAT IS THE DEVIL KING'S STANCE...
...I CAN HARDLY ALLOW MYSELF TO REMAIN AS SHAMELESS AS I WAS.
NEVER MISUNDERSTAND WHAT NEEDS TO BE PROTECTED.
AS CHIEF INQUISITOR OF THE RECONCILIATION PANEL...
NEVER ALLOW YOURSELF TO LOSE SIGHT OF THE JUSTICE THAT MUST PREVAIL.
...AND AS A PROUD MEMBER OF THE CHURCH...
...I NEED TO CONSIDER ...
...HOW TO PURSUE MY JUSTICE...!
AH.

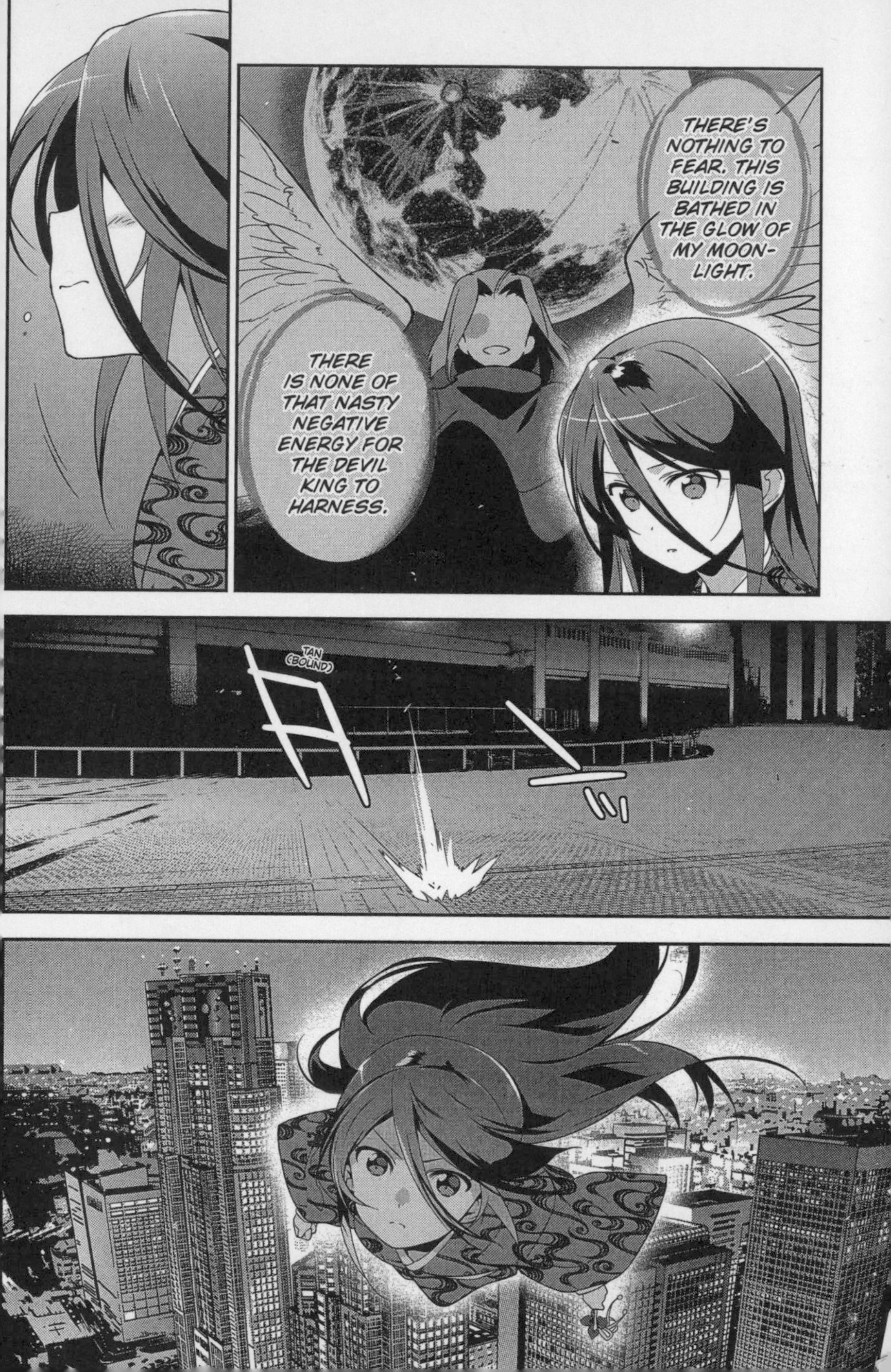
THERE'S NOTHING TO FEAR. THIS BUILDING IS BATHED IN THE GLOW OF MY MOON-LIGHT.
THERE IS NONE OF THAT NASTY NEGATIVE ENERGY FOR THE DEVIL KING TO HARNESS.
TAN (BOUND)

Sariel

THE DEVIL IS A PART-TIMER!

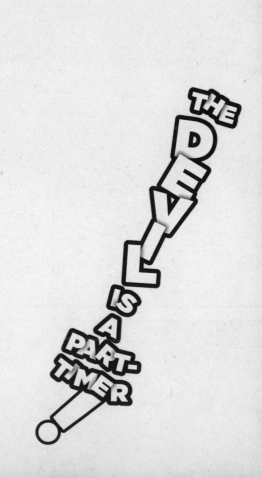

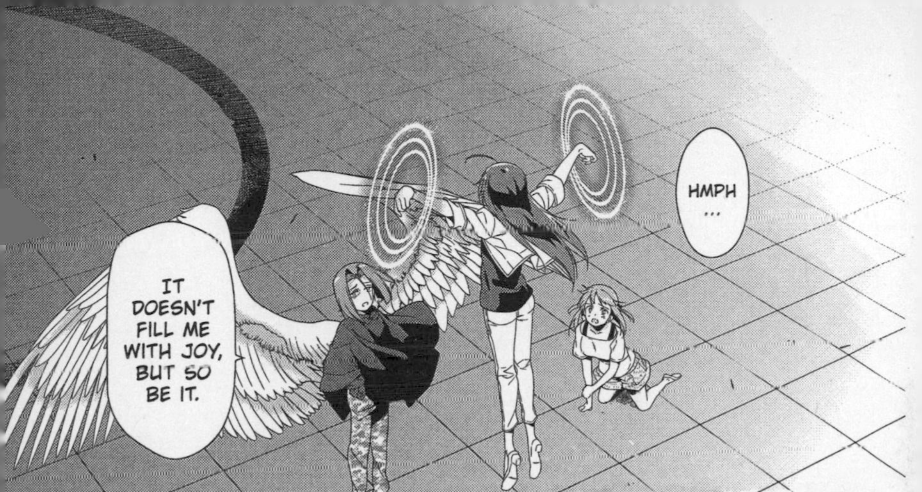
HMPH ...
IT DOESN'T FILL ME WITH JOY, BUT SO BE IT.

CHAPTER 23: THE DEVIL FULFILLS HIS ASSISTANT MANAGER DUTIES

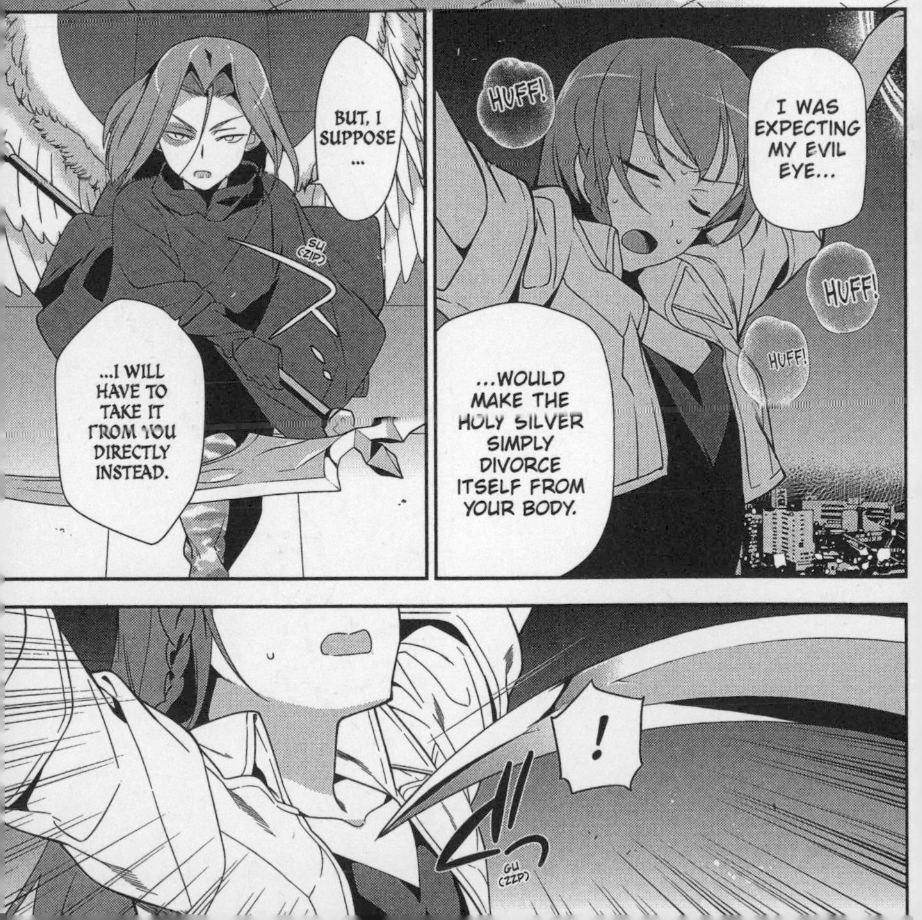
HUFF!
I WAS EXPECTING MY EVIL EYE...
HUFF!
HUFF!
...WOULD MAKE THE HOLY SILVER SIMPLY DIVORCE ITSELF FROM YOUR BODY.
BUT, I SUPPOSE ...
SU (ZIP)
...I WILL HAVE TO TAKE IT FROM YOU DIRECTLY INSTEAD.
!
GU (ZZP)

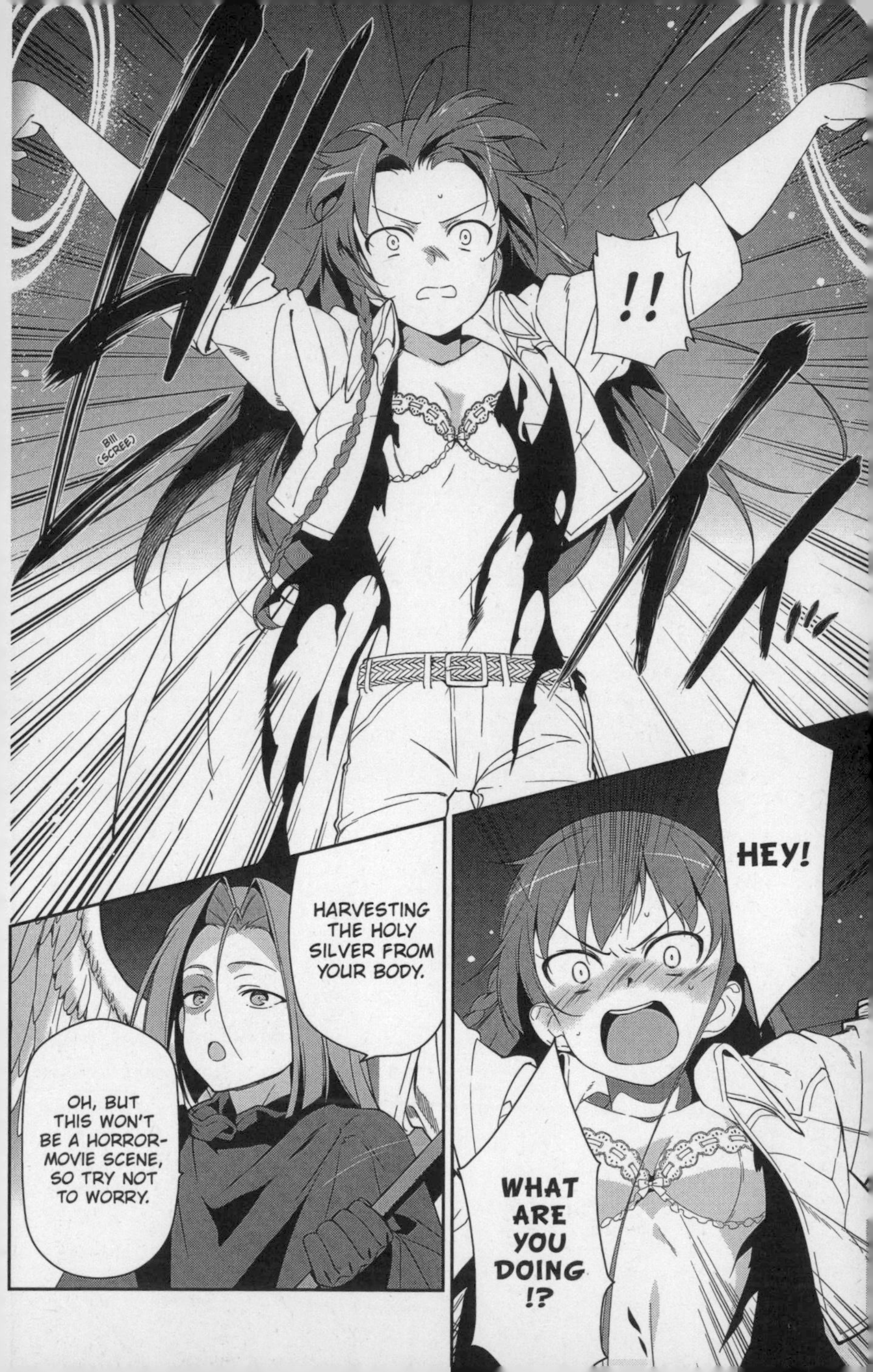
!!
BIII (SCREE)
HEY!
WHAT ARE YOU DOING!?
HARVESTING THE HOLY SILVER FROM YOUR BODY.
OH, BUT THIS WON'T BE A HORROR-MOVIE SCENE, SO TRY NOT TO WORRY.

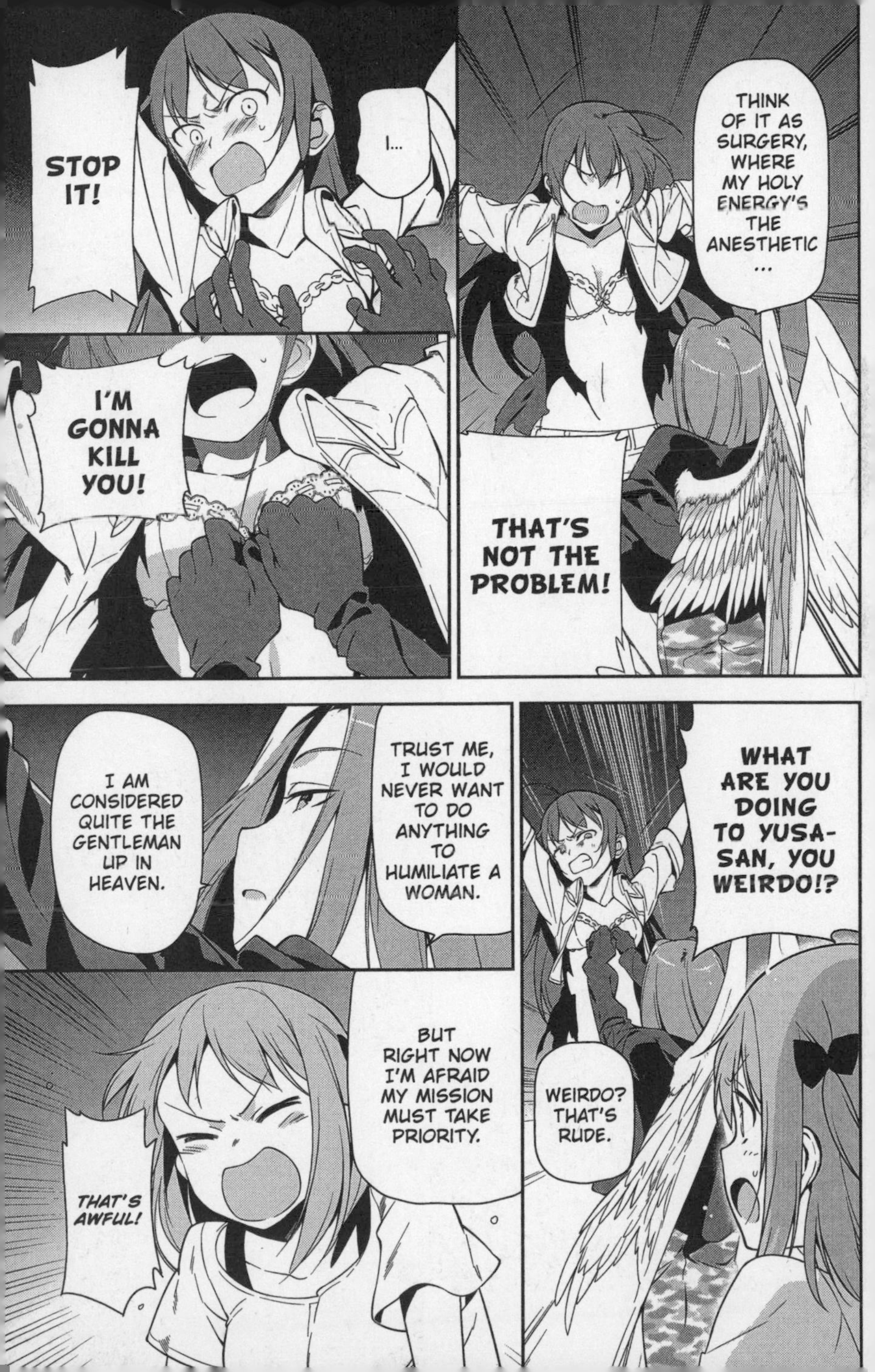
THINK OF IT AS SURGERY, WHERE MY HOLY ENERGY'S THE ANESTHETIC ...
THAT'S NOT THE PROBLEM!
I...
STOP IT!
I'M GONNA KILL YOU!
WHAT ARE YOU DOING TO YUSA-SAN, YOU WEIRDO!?
WEIRDO? THAT'S RUDE.
TRUST ME, I WOULD NEVER WANT TO DO ANYTHING TO HUMILIATE A WOMAN.
I AM CONSIDERED QUITE THE GENTLEMAN UP IN HEAVEN.
BUT RIGHT NOW I'M AFRAID MY MISSION MUST TAKE PRIORITY.
THAT'S AWFUL!

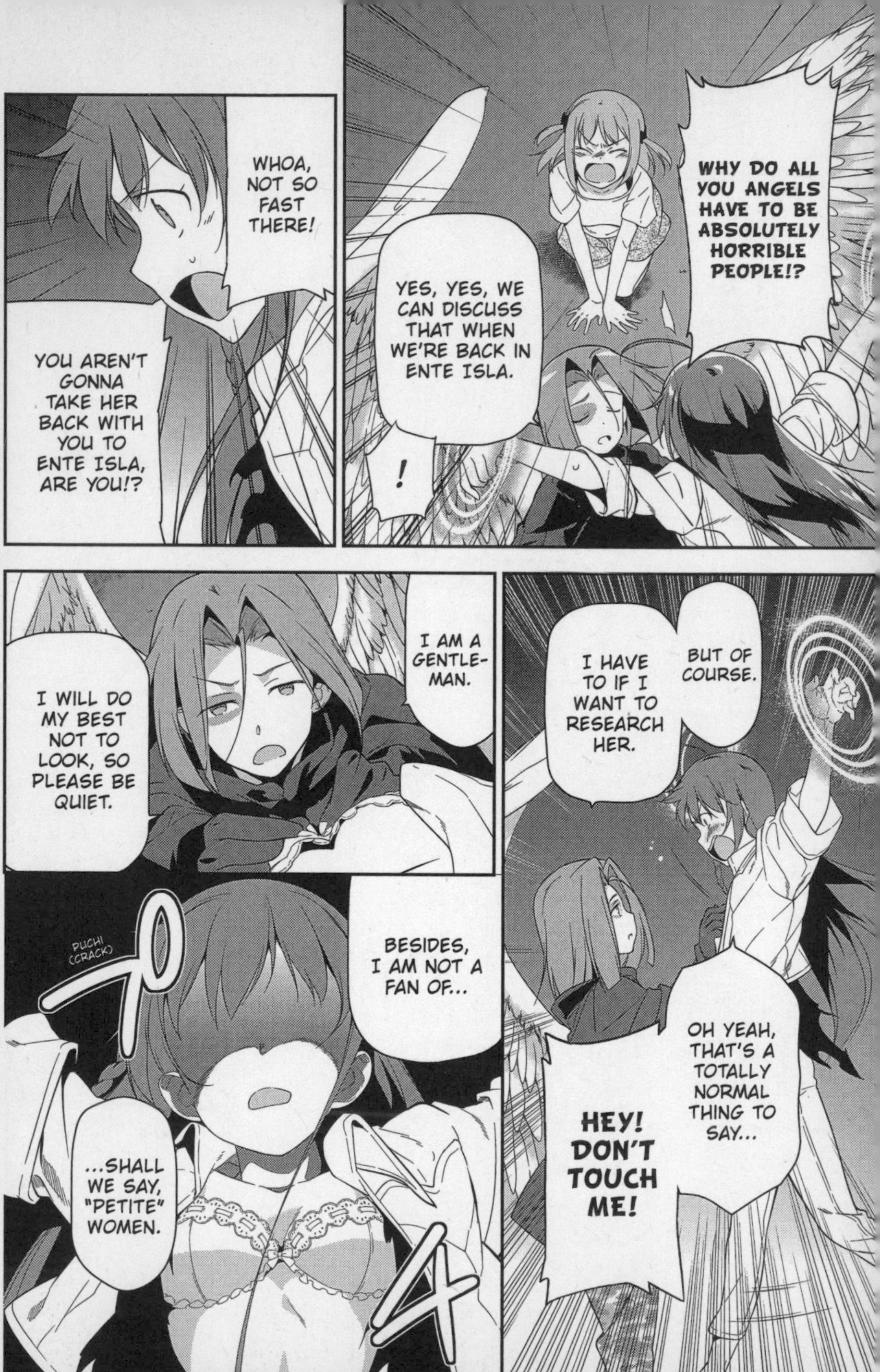
WHY DO ALL YOU ANGELS HAVE TO BE ABSOLUTELY HORRIBLE PEOPLE!?
YES, YES, WE CAN DISCUSS THAT WHEN WE'RE BACK IN ENTE ISLA.
!
WHOA, NOT SO FAST THERE!
YOU AREN'T GONNA TAKE HER BACK WITH YOU TO ENTE ISLA, ARE YOU!?
BUT OF COURSE.
I HAVE TO IF I WANT TO RESEARCH HER.
OH YEAH, THAT'S A TOTALLY NORMAL THING TO SAY...
HEY! DON'T TOUCH ME!
I AM A GENTLE-MAN.
I WILL DO MY BEST NOT TO LOOK, SO PLEASE BE QUIET.
PUCHI (CRACK)
BESIDES, I AM NOT A FAN OF...
...SHALL WE SAY, "PETITE" WOMEN.

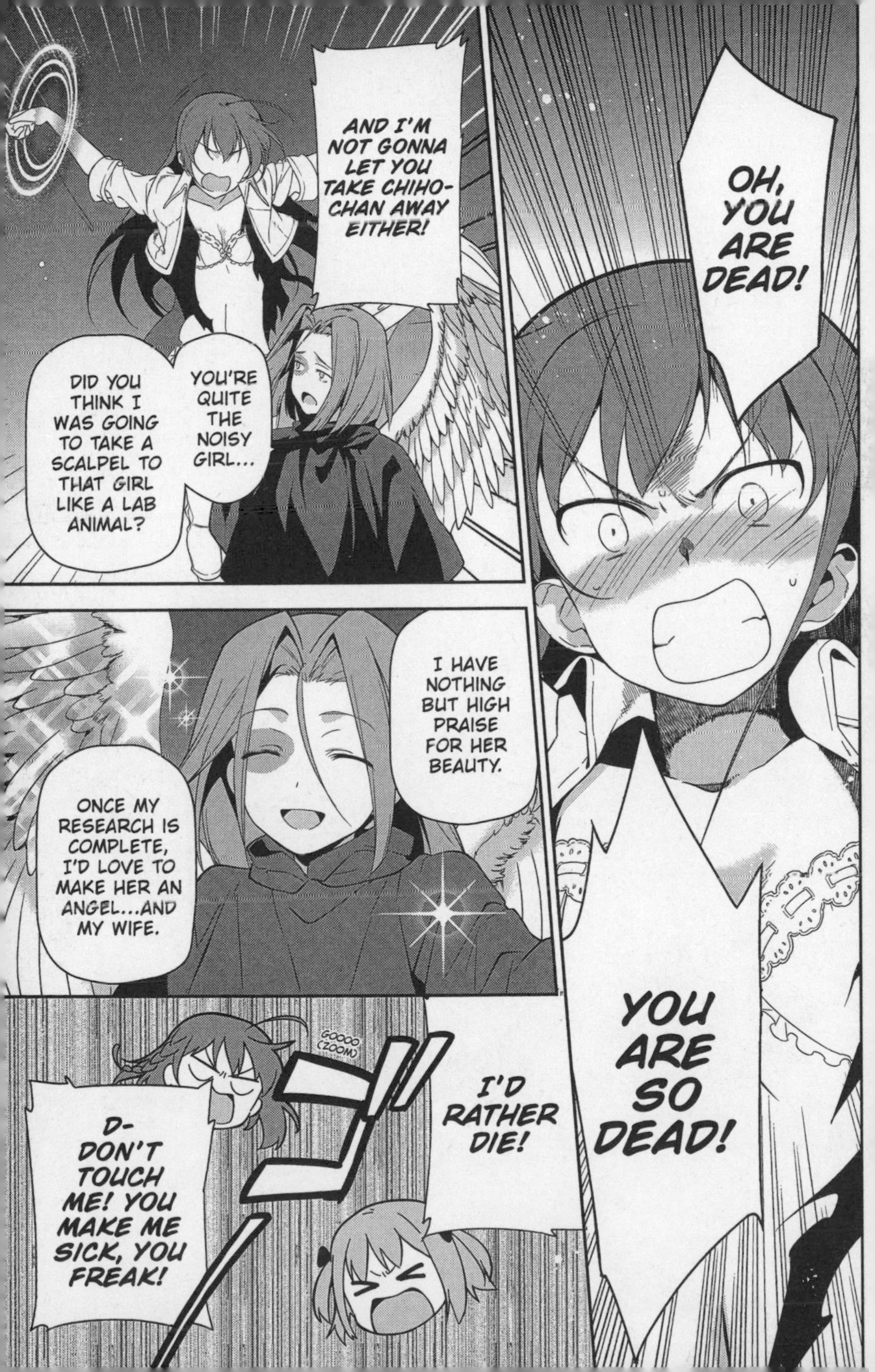
OH, YOU ARE DEAD!
YOU ARE SO DEAD!
AND I'M NOT GONNA LET YOU TAKE CHIHO-CHAN AWAY EITHER!
YOU'RE QUITE THE NOISY GIRL...
DID YOU THINK I WAS GOING TO TAKE A SCALPEL TO THAT GIRL LIKE A LAB ANIMAL?
I HAVE NOTHING BUT HIGH PRAISE FOR HER BEAUTY.
ONCE MY RESEARCH IS COMPLETE, I'D LOVE TO MAKE HER AN ANGEL...AND MY WIFE.
GOOOO (ZOOM)
I'D RATHER DIE!
D-DON'T TOUCH ME! YOU MAKE ME SICK, YOU FREAK!

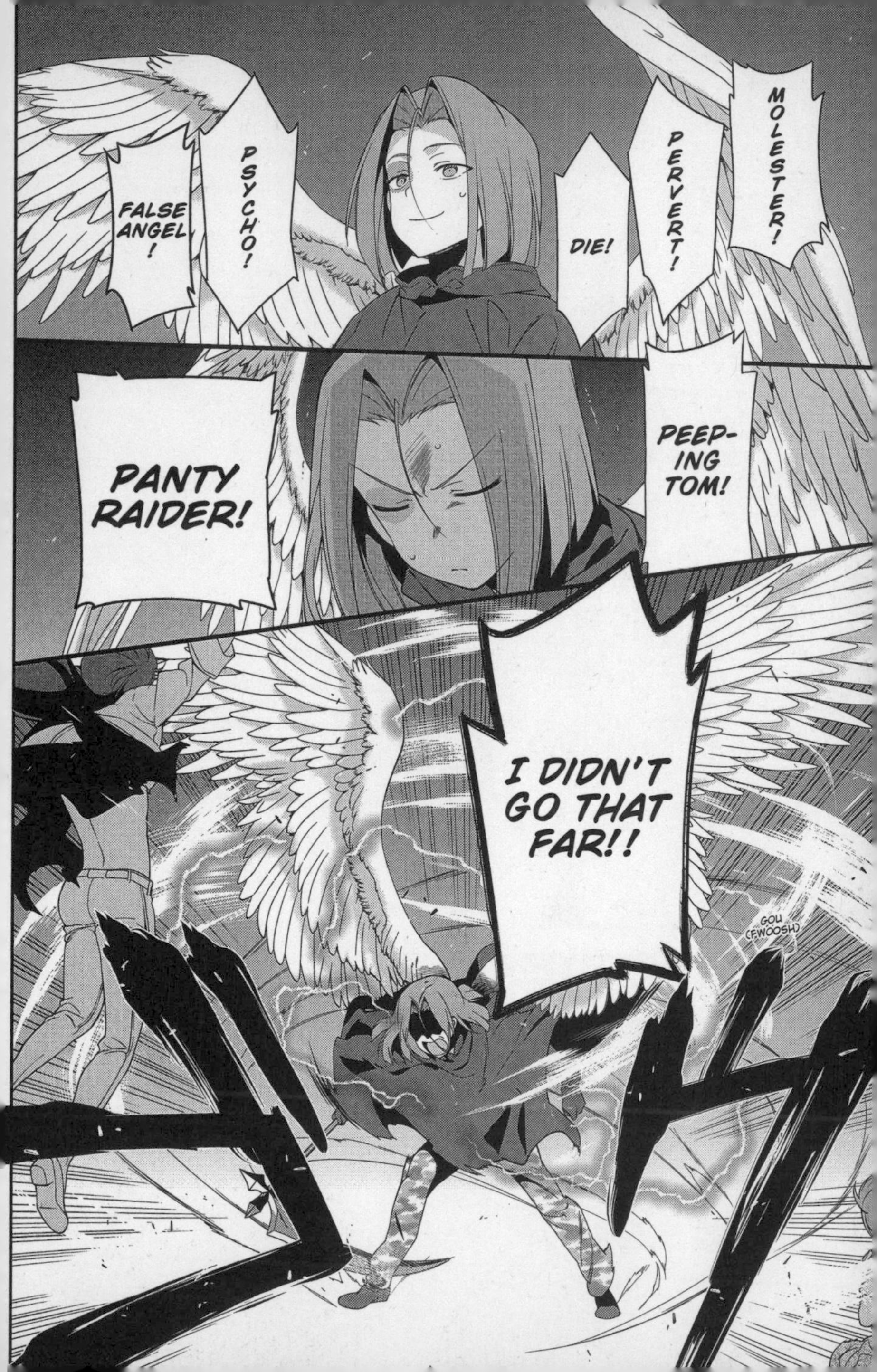
MOLESTER!
PERVERT!
DIE!
PSYCHO!
FALSE ANGEL!
PEEP-ING TOM!
PANTY RAIDER!
I DIDN'T GO THAT FAR!!
GOU (FWOOSH)

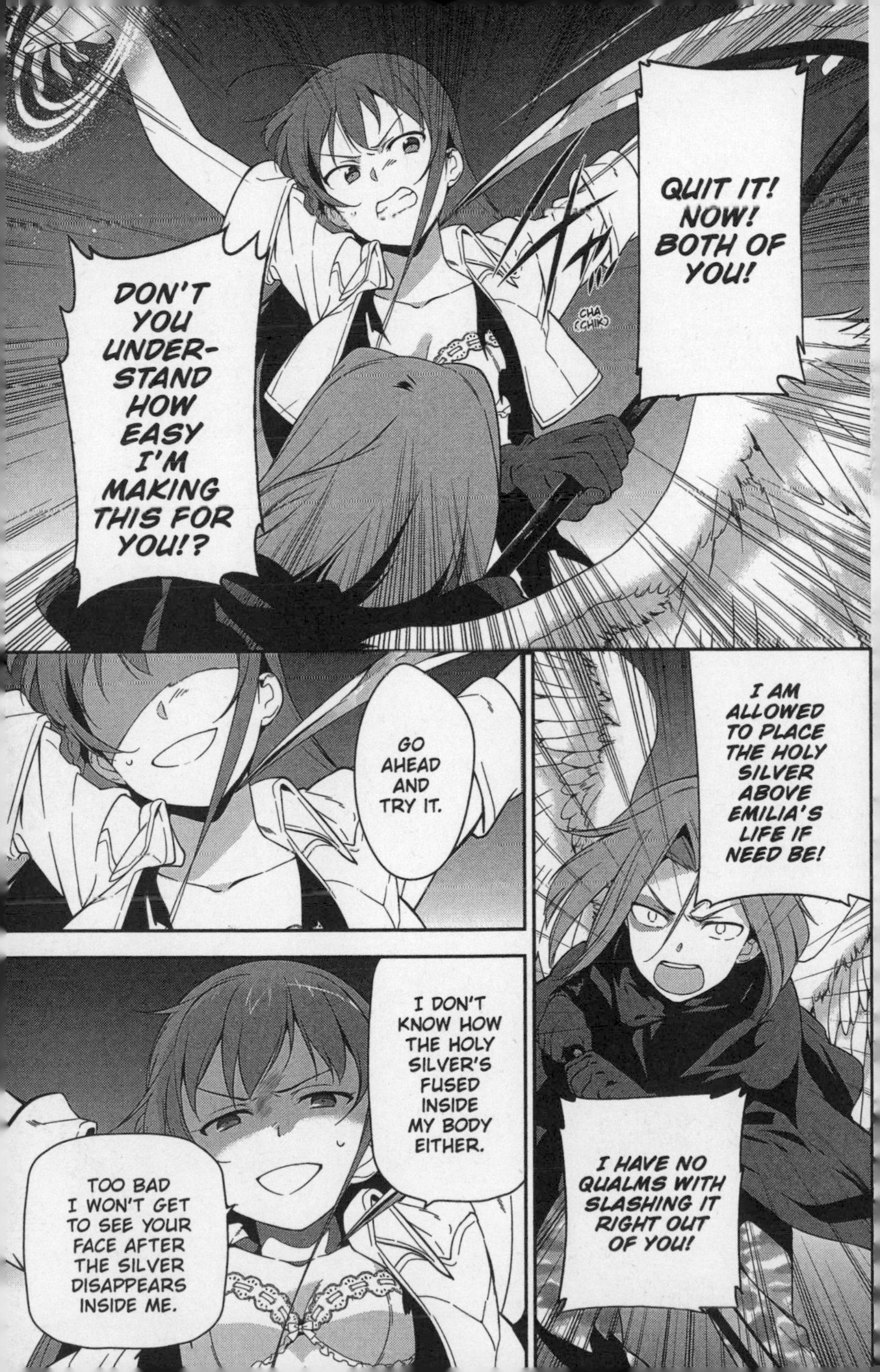
QUIT IT! NOW! BOTH OF YOU!
CHA CHIK
DON'T YOU UNDERSTAND HOW EASY I'M MAKING THIS FOR YOU!?
I AM ALLOWED TO PLACE THE HOLY SILVER ABOVE EMILIA'S LIFE IF NEED BE!
I HAVE NO QUALMS WITH SLASHING IT RIGHT OUT OF YOU!
GO AHEAD AND TRY IT.
I DON'T KNOW HOW THE HOLY SILVER'S FUSED INSIDE MY BODY EITHER.
TOO BAD I WON'T GET TO SEE YOUR FACE AFTER THE SILVER DISAPPEARS INSIDE ME.

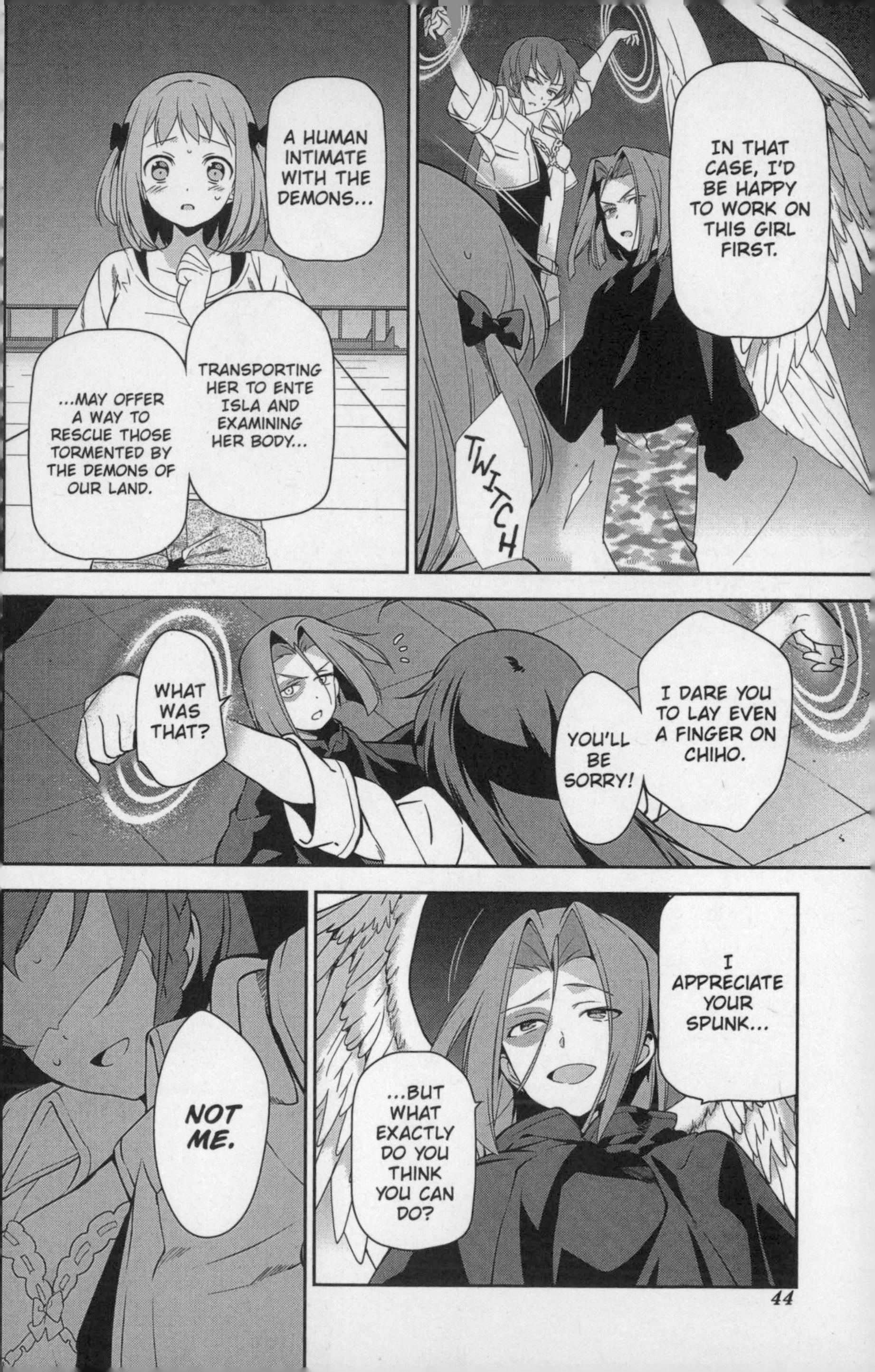
IN THAT CASE, I'D BE HAPPY TO WORK ON THIS GIRL FIRST.
TWITCH
A HUMAN INTIMATE WITH THE DEMONS...
TRANSPORTING HER TO ENTE ISLA AND EXAMINING HER BODY...
...MAY OFFER A WAY TO RESCUE THOSE TORMENTED BY THE DEMONS OF OUR LAND.
I DARE YOU TO LAY EVEN A FINGER ON CHIHO.
YOU'LL BE SORRY!
WHAT WAS THAT?
I APPRECIATE YOUR SPUNK...
...BUT WHAT EXACTLY DO YOU THINK YOU CAN DO?
NOT ME.

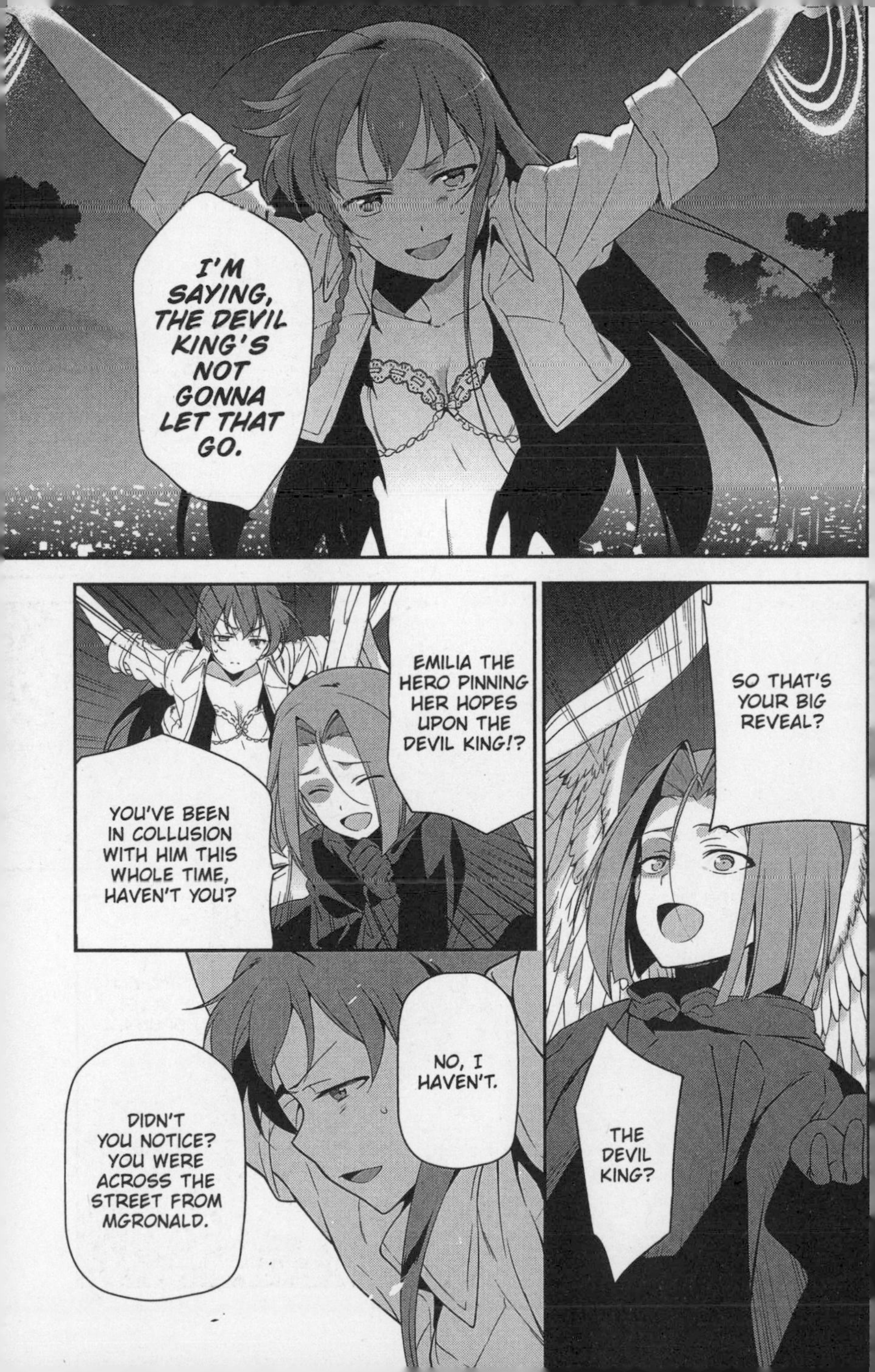
I'M SAYING, THE DEVIL KING'S NOT GONNA LET THAT GO.
SO THAT'S YOUR BIG REVEAL?
THE DEVIL KING?
EMILIA THE HERO PINNING HER HOPES UPON THE DEVIL KING!?
YOU'VE BEEN IN COLLUSION WITH HIM THIS WHOLE TIME, HAVEN'T YOU?
NO, I HAVEN'T.
DIDN'T YOU NOTICE? YOU WERE ACROSS THE STREET FROM MGRONALD.

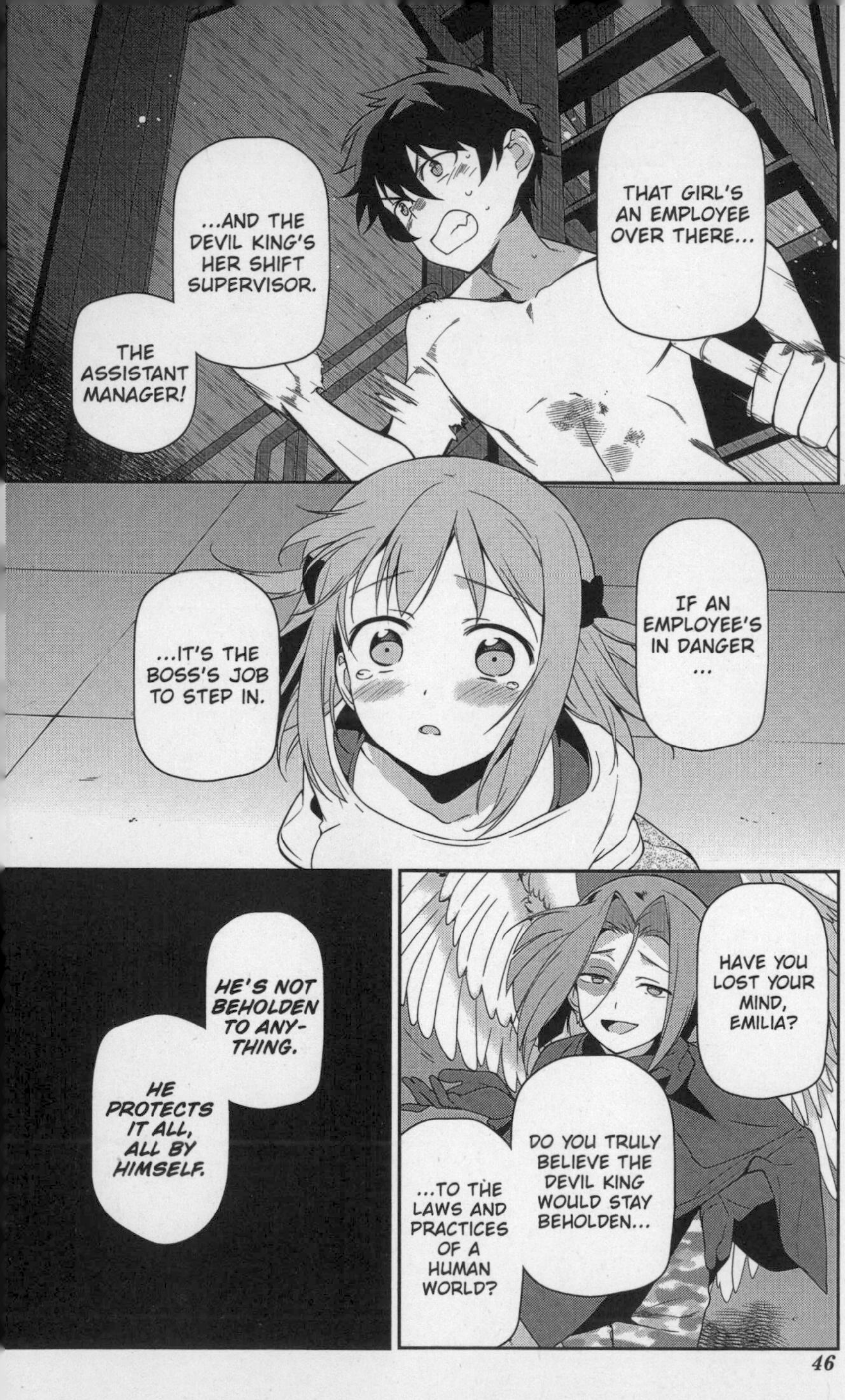
THAT GIRL'S AN EMPLOYEE OVER THERE...
...AND THE DEVIL KING'S HER SHIFT SUPERVISOR.
THE ASSISTANT MANAGER!
IF AN EMPLOYEE'S IN DANGER ...
...IT'S THE BOSS'S JOB TO STEP IN.
HAVE YOU LOST YOUR MIND, EMILIA?
DO YOU TRULY BELIEVE THE DEVIL KING WOULD STAY BEHOLDEN...
...TO THE LAWS AND PRACTICES OF A HUMAN WORLD?
HE'S NOT BEHOLDEN TO ANY-THING.
HE PROTECTS IT ALL, ALL BY HIMSELF.

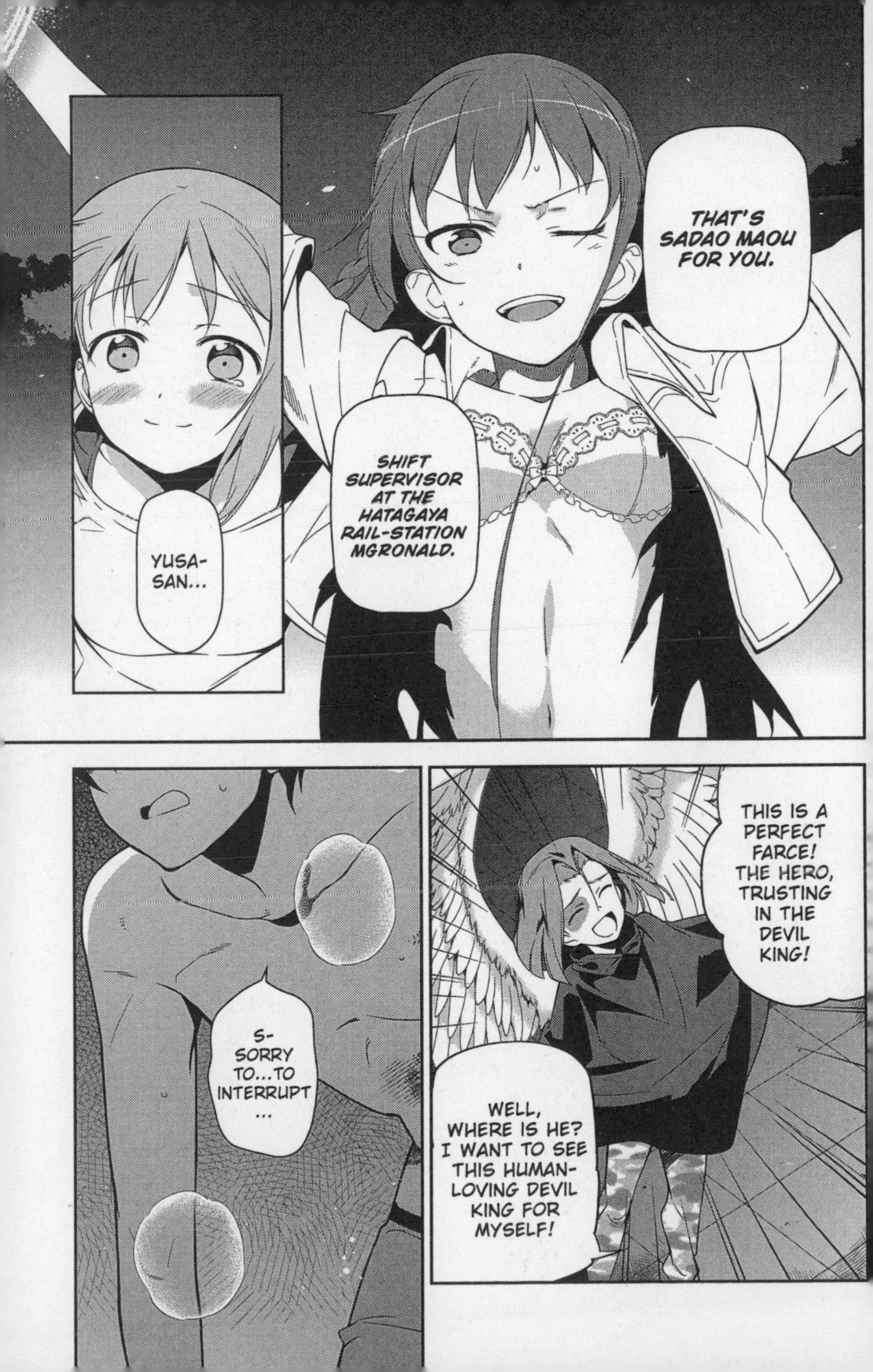
THAT'S SADAO MAOU FOR YOU.
SHIFT SUPERVISOR AT THE HATAGAYA RAIL-STATION MGRONALD.
YUSA-SAN...
THIS IS A PERFECT FARCE! THE HERO, TRUSTING IN THE DEVIL KING!
WELL, WHERE IS HE? I WANT TO SEE THIS HUMAN-LOVING DEVIL KING FOR MYSELF!
S-SORRY TO...TO INTERRUPT...

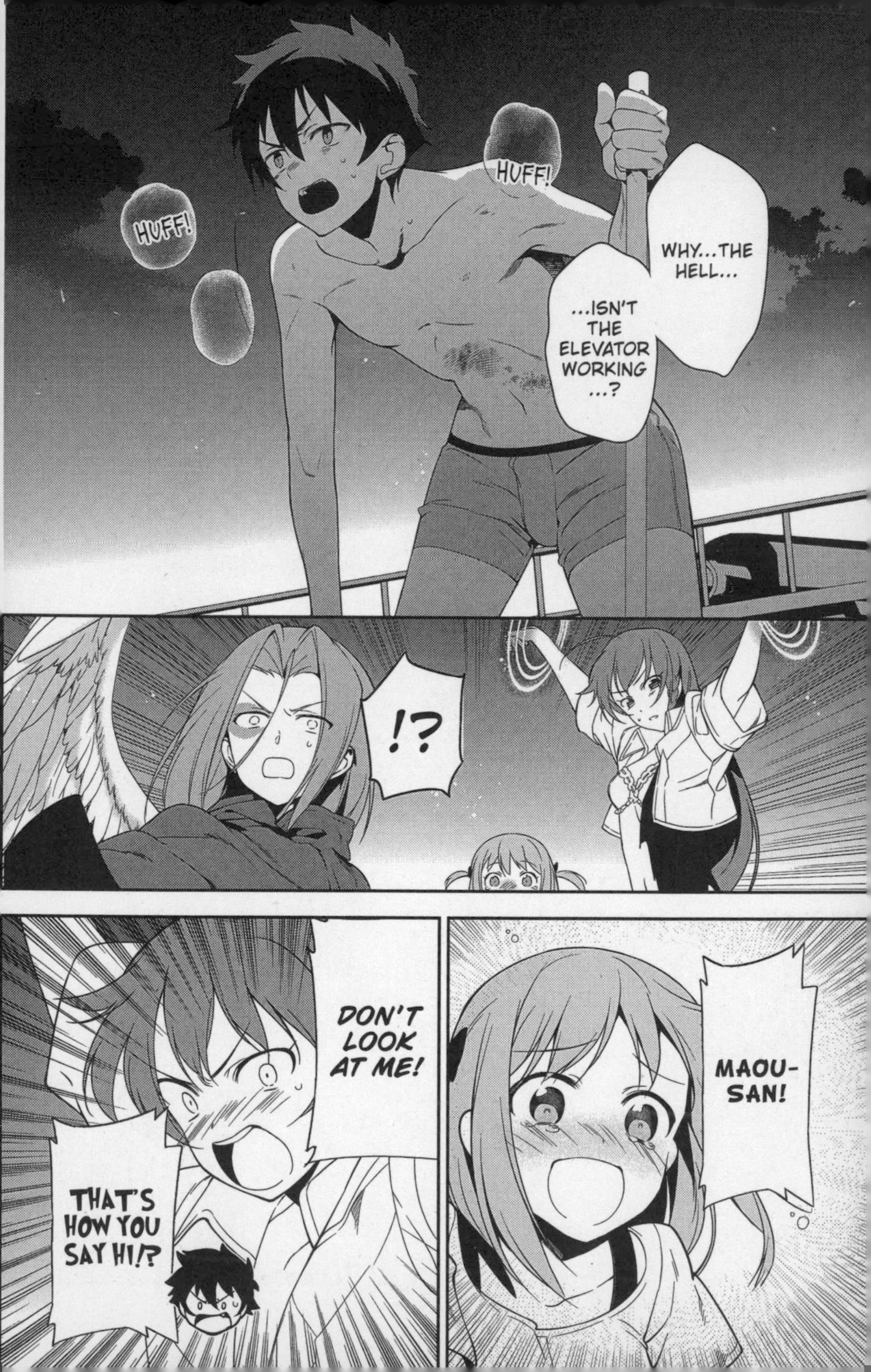
HUFF!
HUFF!
WHY...THE HELL...
...ISN'T THE ELEVATOR WORKING...?
!?
MAOU-SAN!
DON'T LOOK AT ME!
THAT'S HOW YOU SAY HI!?

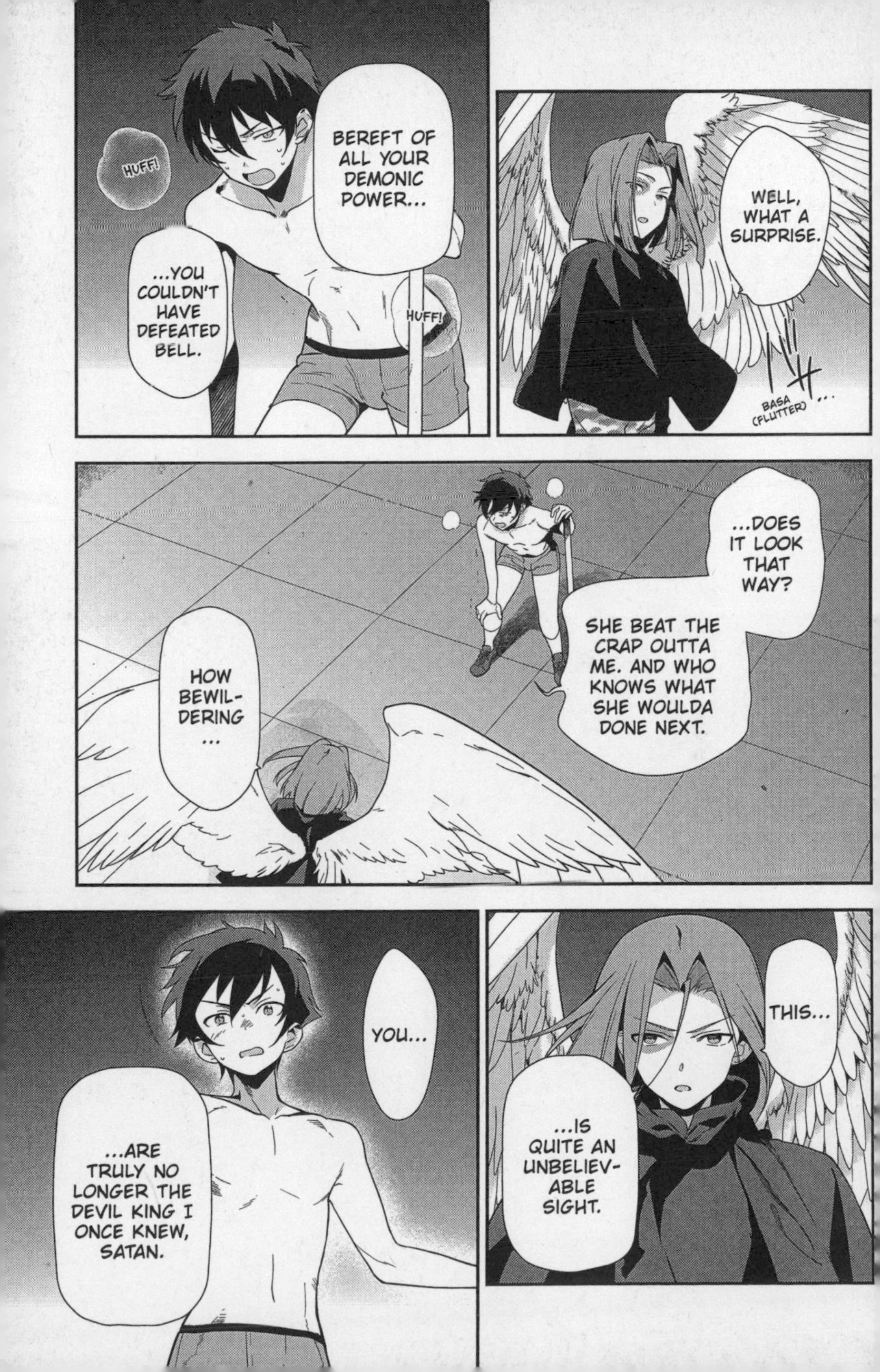
WELL, WHAT A SURPRISE.
BASA (FLUTTER)...
BEREFT OF ALL YOUR DEMONIC POWER...
HUFF!
...YOU COULDN'T HAVE DEFEATED BELL.
HUFF!
...DOES IT LOOK THAT WAY?
SHE BEAT THE CRAP OUTTA ME. AND WHO KNOWS WHAT SHE WOULDA DONE NEXT.
HOW BEWIL-DERING...
THIS...
...IS QUITE AN UNBELIEV-ABLE SIGHT.
YOU...
...ARE TRULY NO LONGER THE DEVIL KING I ONCE KNEW, SATAN.

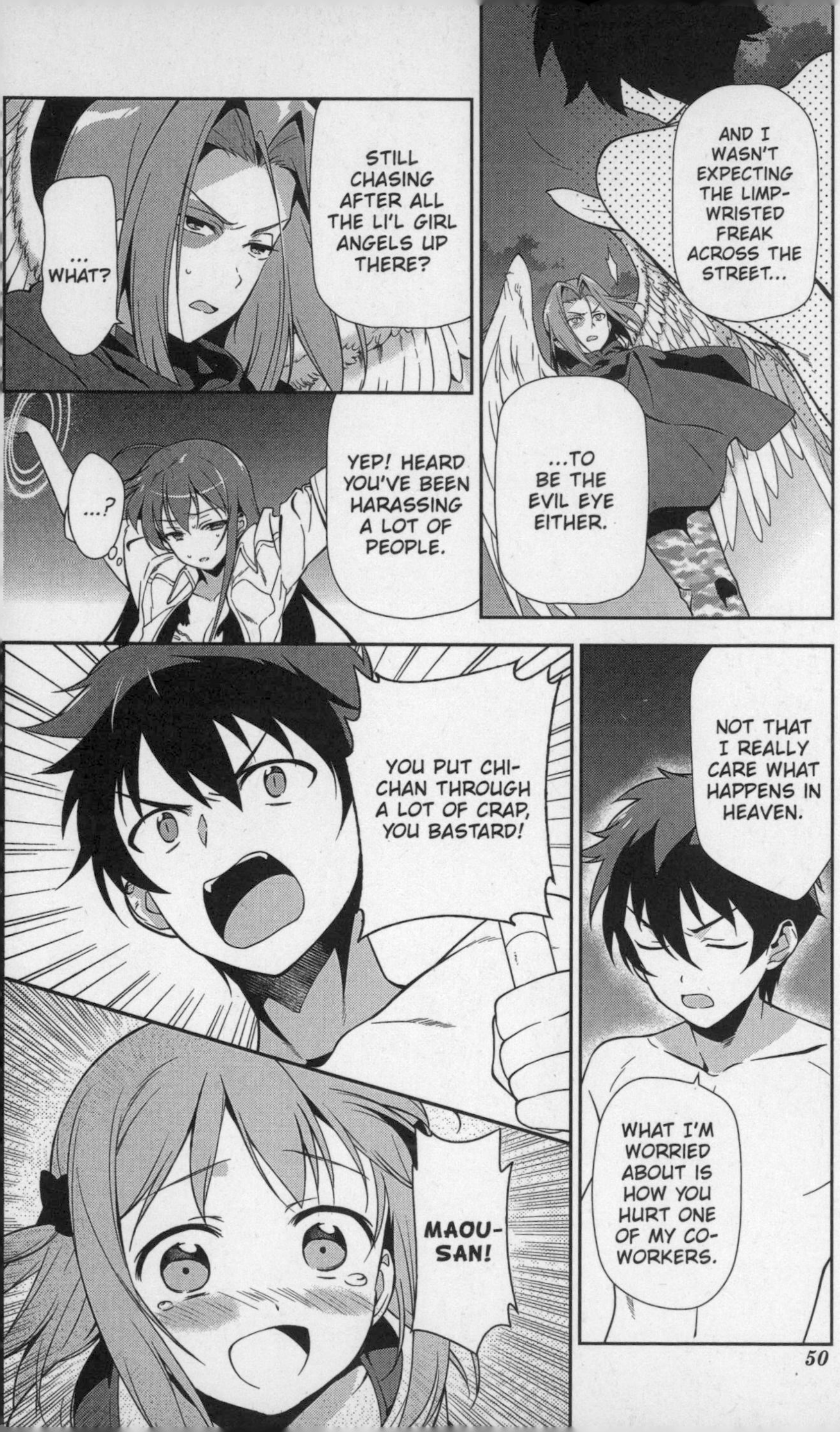
AND I WASN'T EXPECTING THE LIMP-WRISTED FREAK ACROSS THE STREET...
...TO BE THE EVIL EYE EITHER.
STILL CHASING AFTER ALL THE LI'L GIRL ANGELS UP THERE?
... WHAT?
YEP! HEARD YOU'VE BEEN HARASSING A LOT OF PEOPLE.
...?
NOT THAT I REALLY CARE WHAT HAPPENS IN HEAVEN.
WHAT I'M WORRIED ABOUT IS HOW YOU HURT ONE OF MY CO-WORKERS.
YOU PUT CHI-CHAN THROUGH A LOT OF CRAP, YOU BASTARD!
MAOU-SAN!

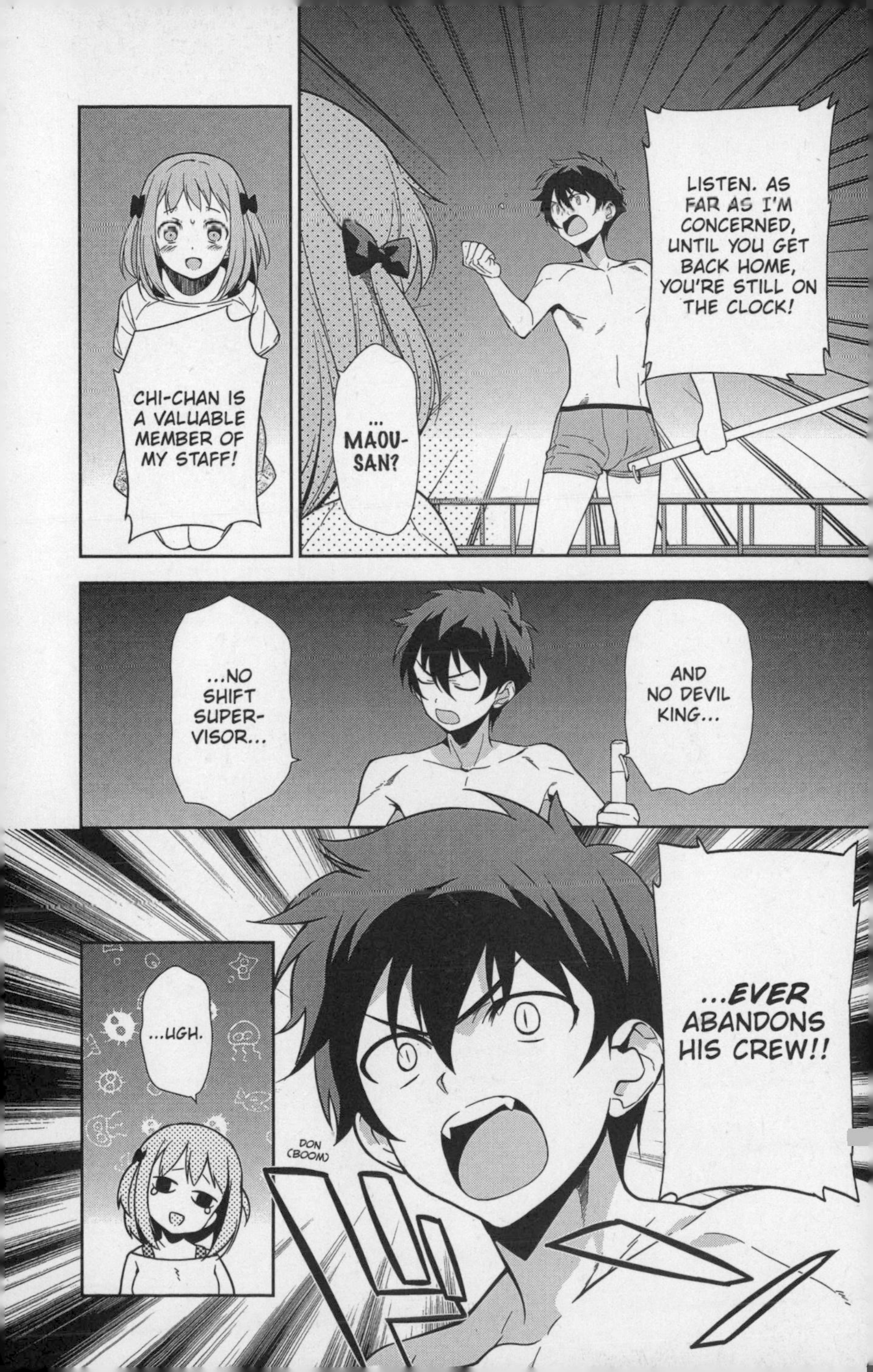
LISTEN. AS FAR AS I'M CONCERNED, UNTIL YOU GET BACK HOME, YOU'RE STILL ON THE CLOCK!
... MAOU-SAN?
CHI-CHAN IS A VALUABLE MEMBER OF MY STAFF!
AND NO DEVIL KING...
...NO SHIFT SUPER-VISOR...
...*EVER* ABANDONS HIS CREW!!
DON (BOOM)
...UGH.

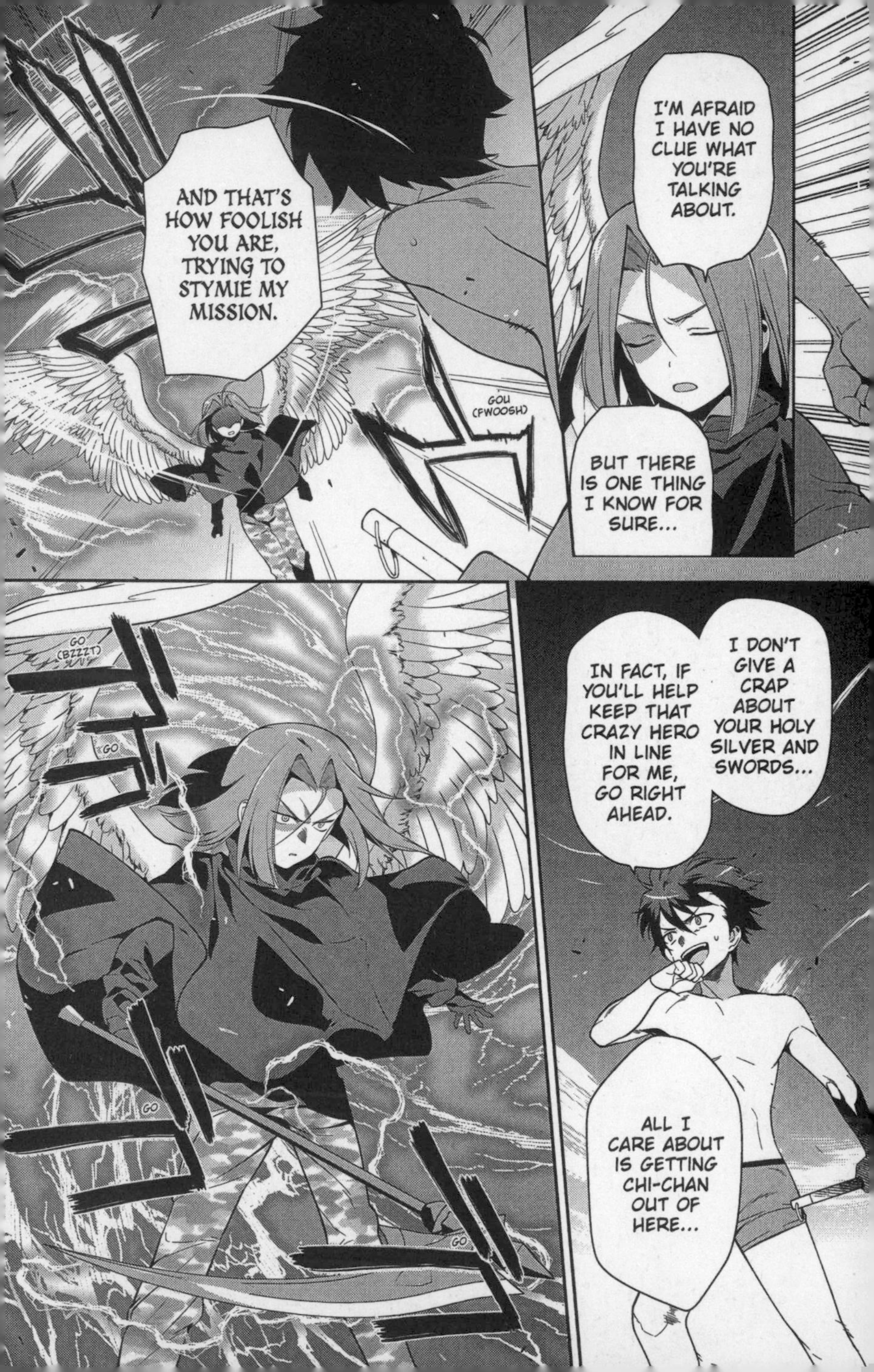
I'M AFRAID I HAVE NO CLUE WHAT YOU'RE TALKING ABOUT.
BUT THERE IS ONE THING I KNOW FOR SURE...
AND THAT'S HOW FOOLISH YOU ARE, TRYING TO STYMIE MY MISSION.
GOU (FWOOSH)
I DON'T GIVE A CRAP ABOUT YOUR HOLY SILVER AND SWORDS...
IN FACT, IF YOU'LL HELP KEEP THAT CRAZY HERO IN LINE FOR ME, GO RIGHT AHEAD.
ALL I CARE ABOUT IS GETTING CHI-CHAN OUT OF HERE...
GO (BZZZT)
GO
GO
GO

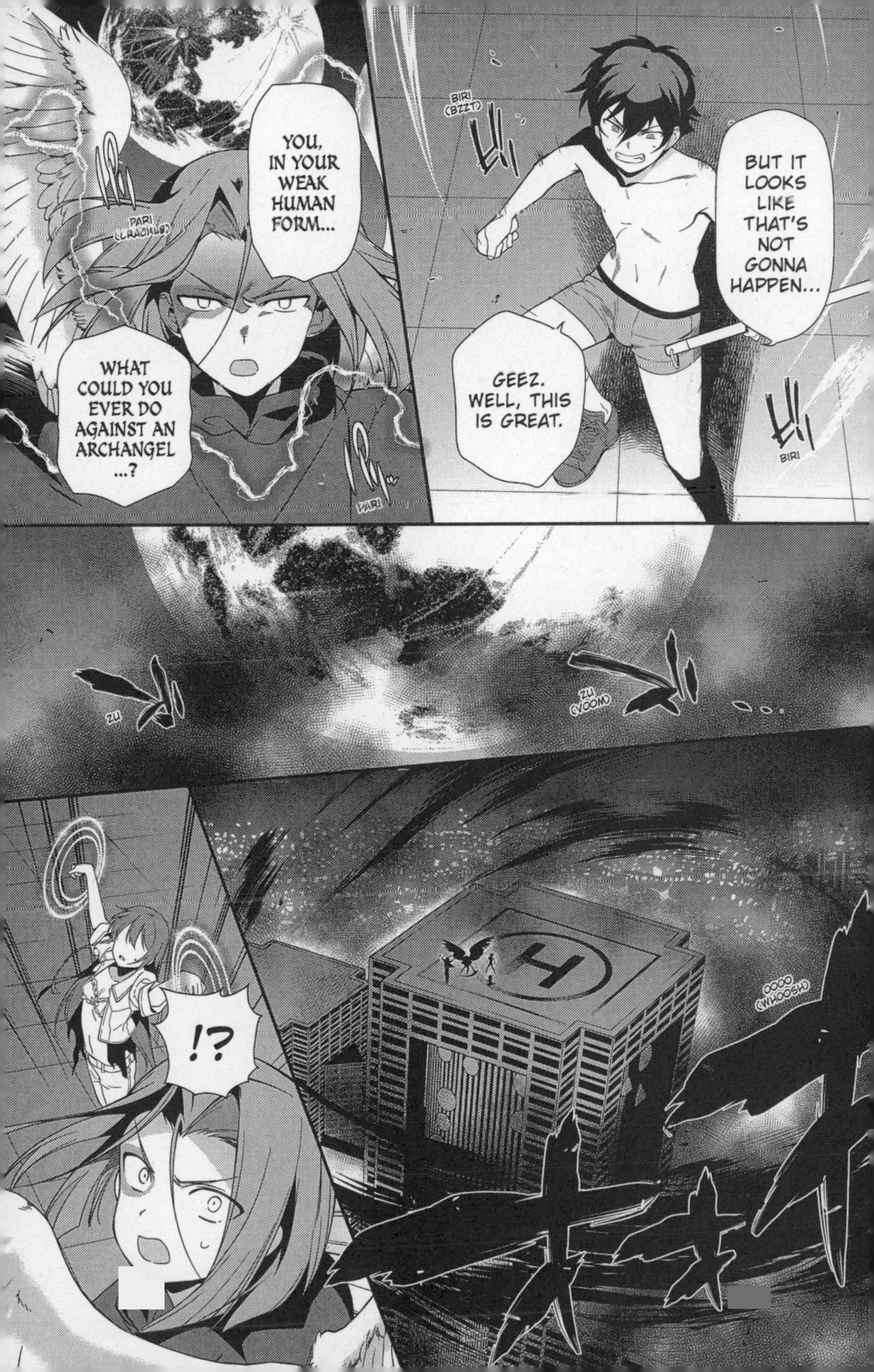
BIRI (BZZT)
BUT IT LOOKS LIKE THAT'S NOT GONNA HAPPEN...
GEEZ. WELL, THIS IS GREAT.
BIRI
YOU, IN YOUR WEAK HUMAN FORM...
PARI (CRACKLE)
WHAT COULD YOU EVER DO AGAINST AN ARCHANGEL ...?
PARI
ZU (VOOM)
ZU
OOOO (WHOOSH)
!?

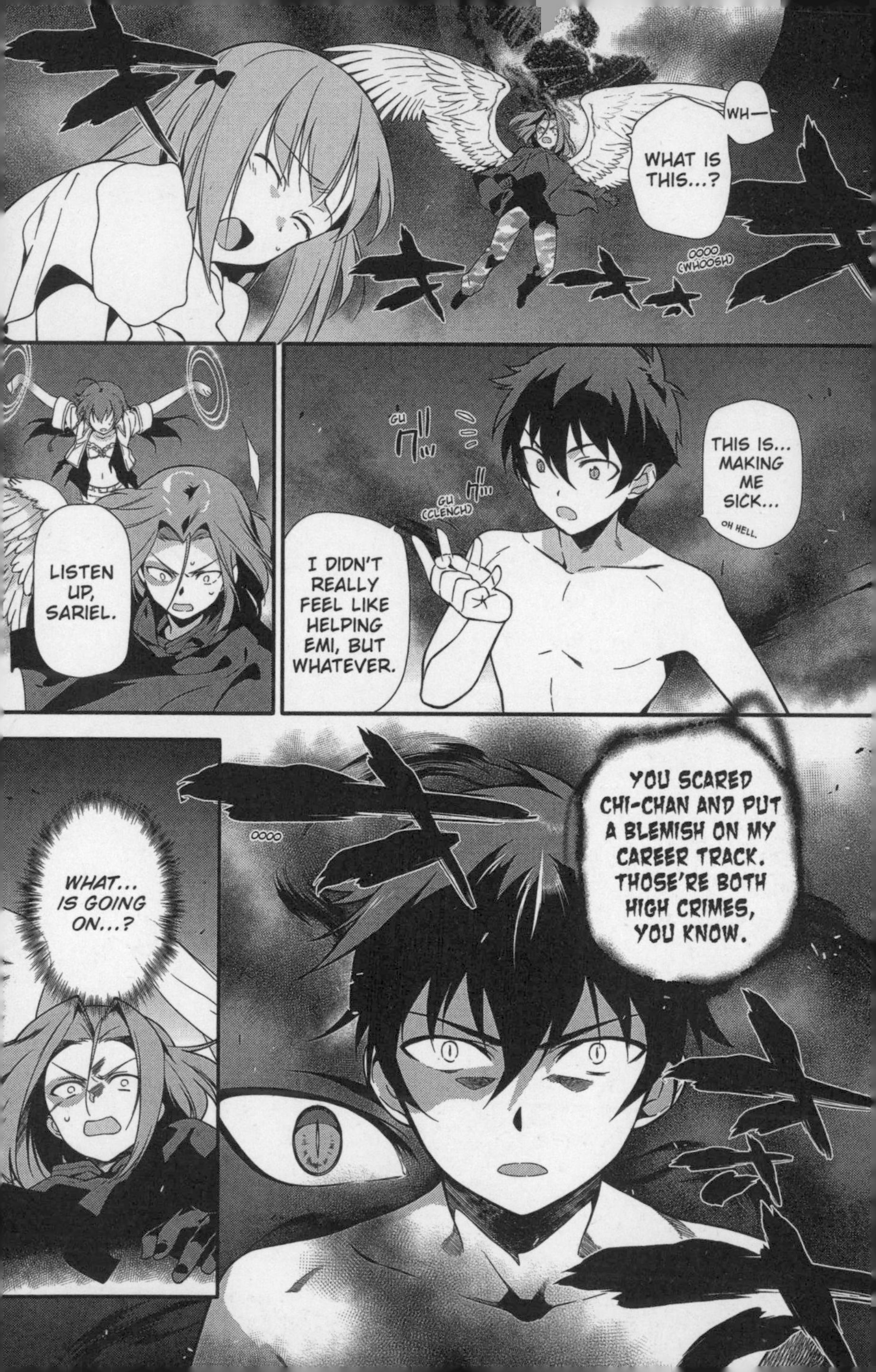
WH—
WHAT IS THIS...?
OOOO (WHOOSH)
GU
THIS IS... MAKING ME SICK...
OH HELL.
GU (CLENCH)
I DIDN'T REALLY FEEL LIKE HELPING EMI, BUT WHATEVER.
LISTEN UP, SARIEL.
YOU SCARED CHI-CHAN AND PUT A BLEMISH ON MY CAREER TRACK. THOSE'RE BOTH HIGH CRIMES, YOU KNOW.
OOOO
WHAT... IS GOING ON...?

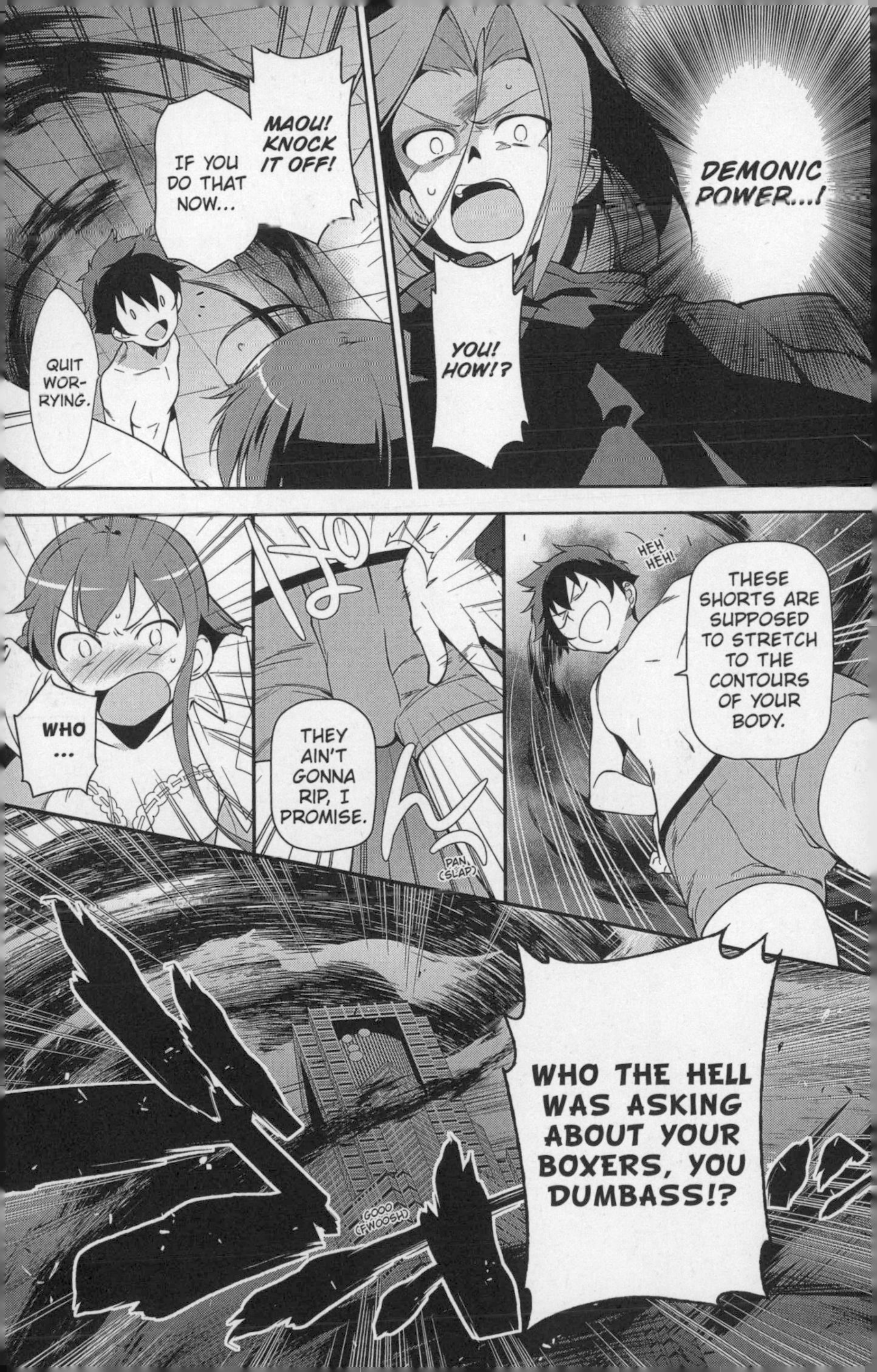
DEMONIC POWER...!
MAOU! KNOCK IT OFF!
YOU! HOW!?
IF YOU DO THAT NOW...
QUIT WOR-RYING.
HEH HEH!
THESE SHORTS ARE SUPPOSED TO STRETCH TO THE CONTOURS OF YOUR BODY.
THEY AIN'T GONNA RIP, I PROMISE.
PAN (SLAP)
WHO ...
WHO THE HELL WAS ASKING ABOUT YOUR BOXERS, YOU DUMBASS!?
GOOO (FWOOSH)

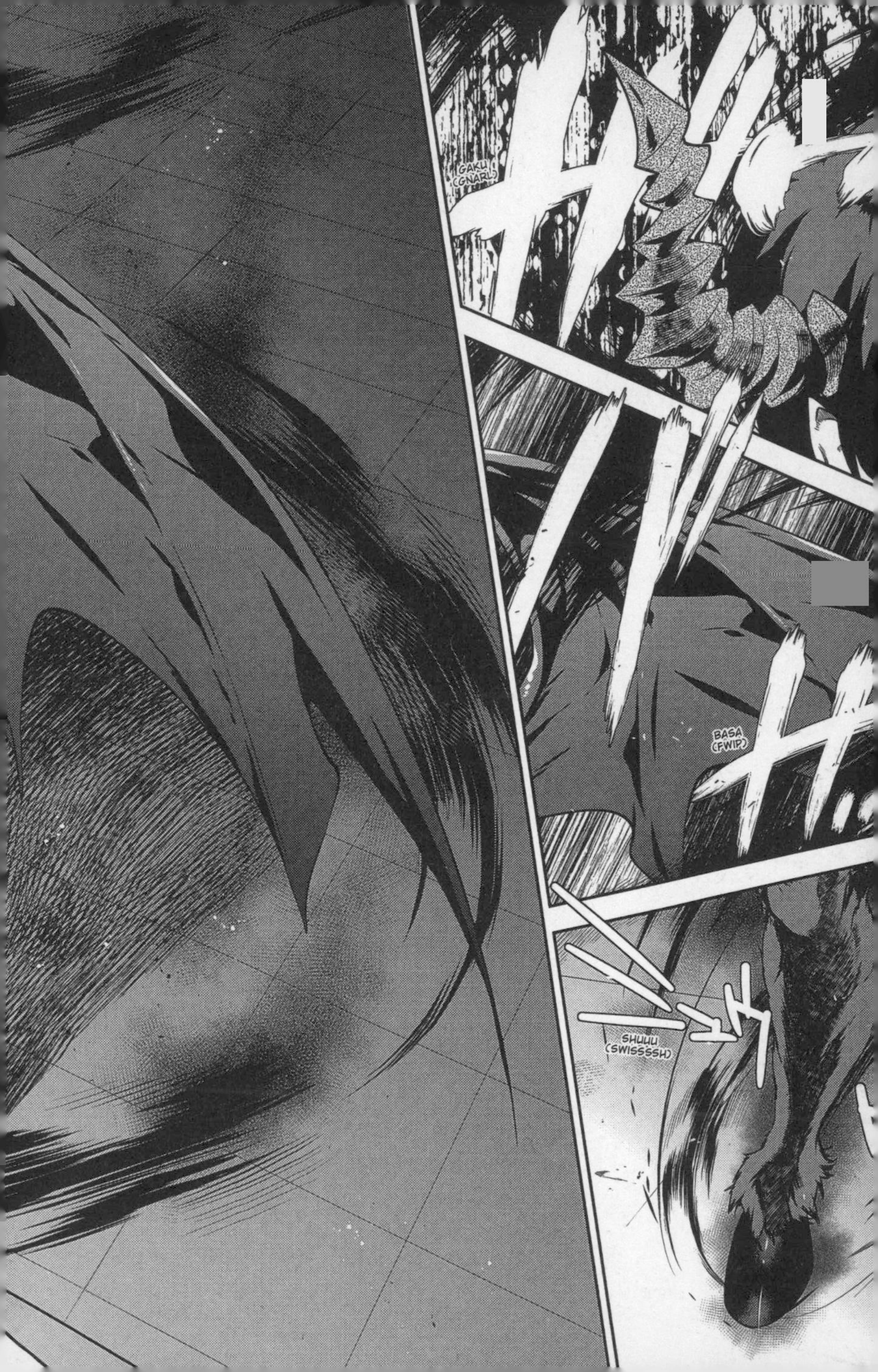
GAKU (GNARL)
BASA (FWIP)
SHUUU (SWISSSSH)

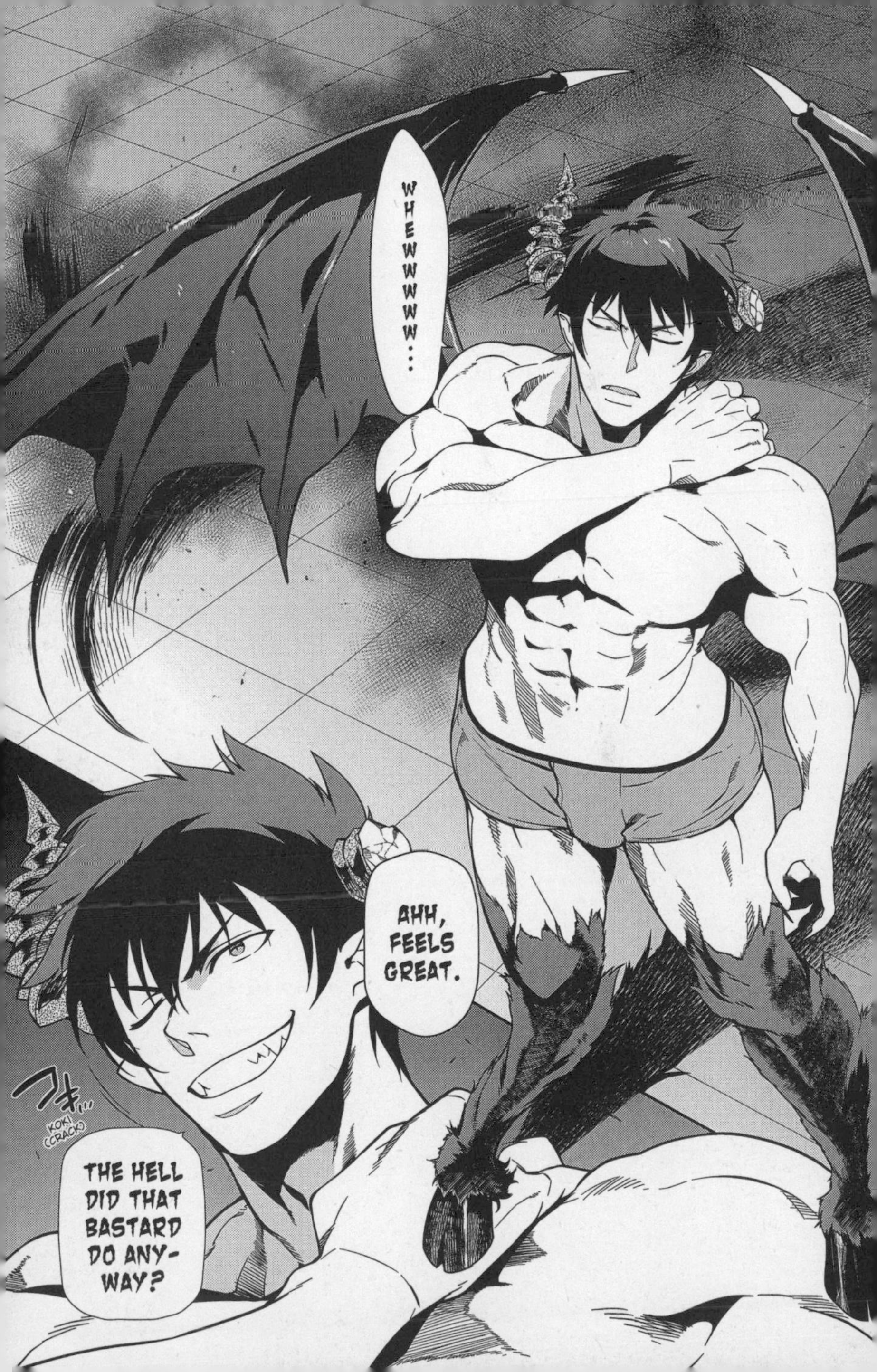
WHEWWWWW...
AHH, FEELS GREAT.
KOKI (CRACK)
THE HELL DID THAT BASTARD DO ANY-WAY?

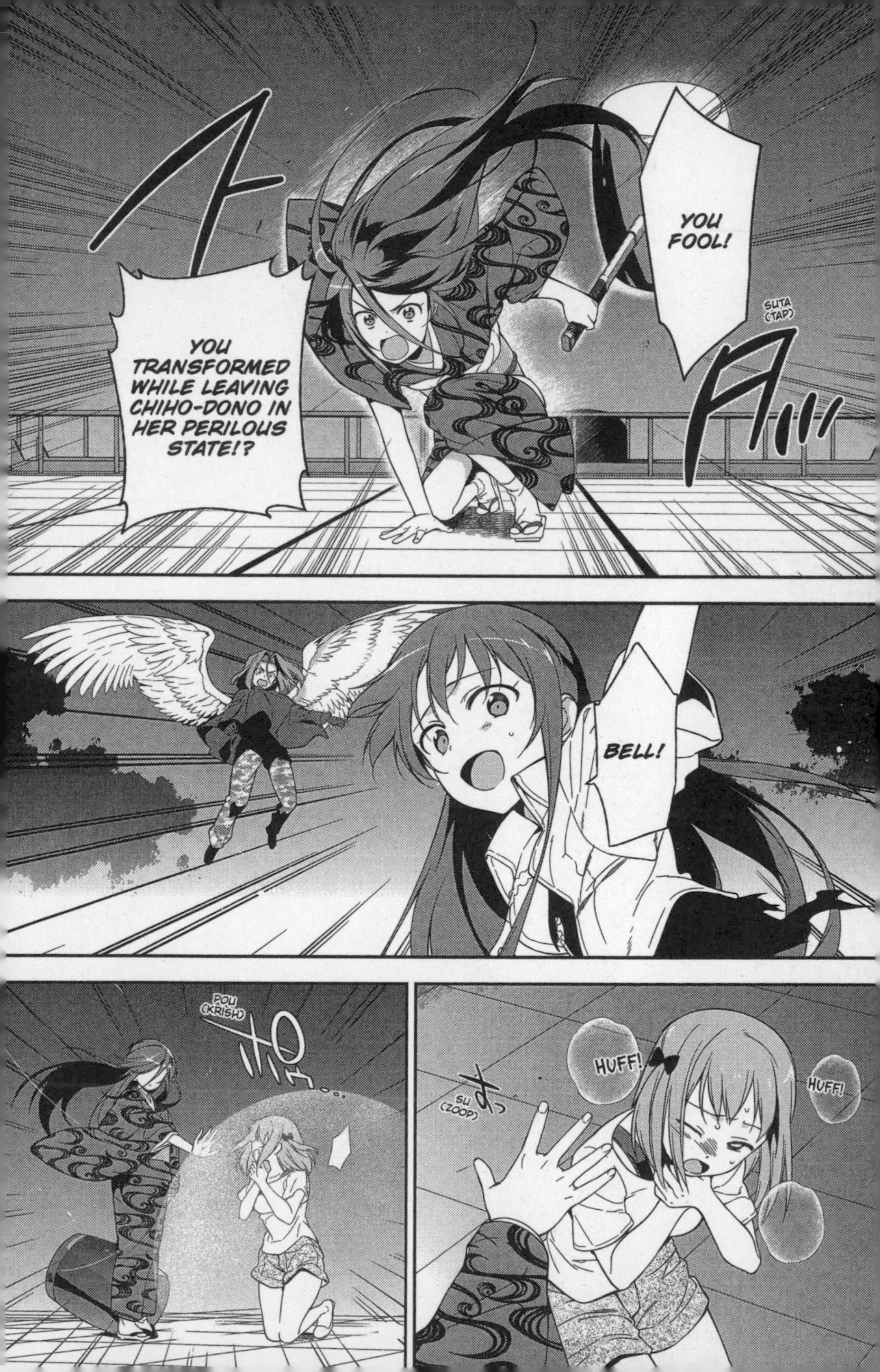
YOU FOOL!
SUTA (TAP)
YOU TRANSFORMED WHILE LEAVING CHIHO-DONO IN HER PERILOUS STATE!?
BELL!
HUFF! HUFF!
SU (ZOOP)
POU (KRISH)

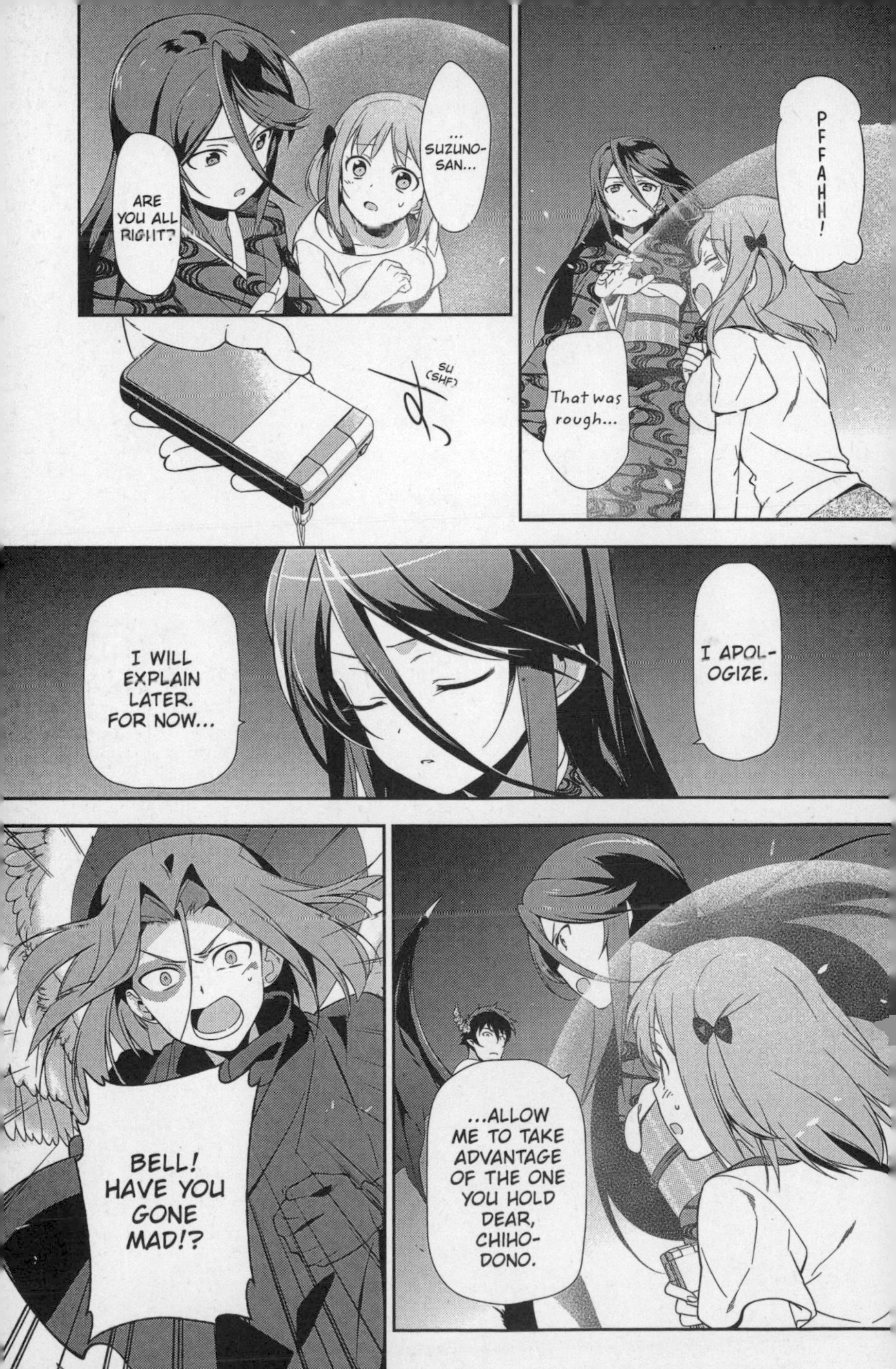
PFFAHH!
That was rough...
...SUZUNO-SAN...
ARE YOU ALL RIGHT?
SU (SHF)
I APOLOGIZE.
I WILL EXPLAIN LATER. FOR NOW...
...ALLOW ME TO TAKE ADVANTAGE OF THE ONE YOU HOLD DEAR, CHIHO-DONO.
BELL! HAVE YOU GONE MAD!?

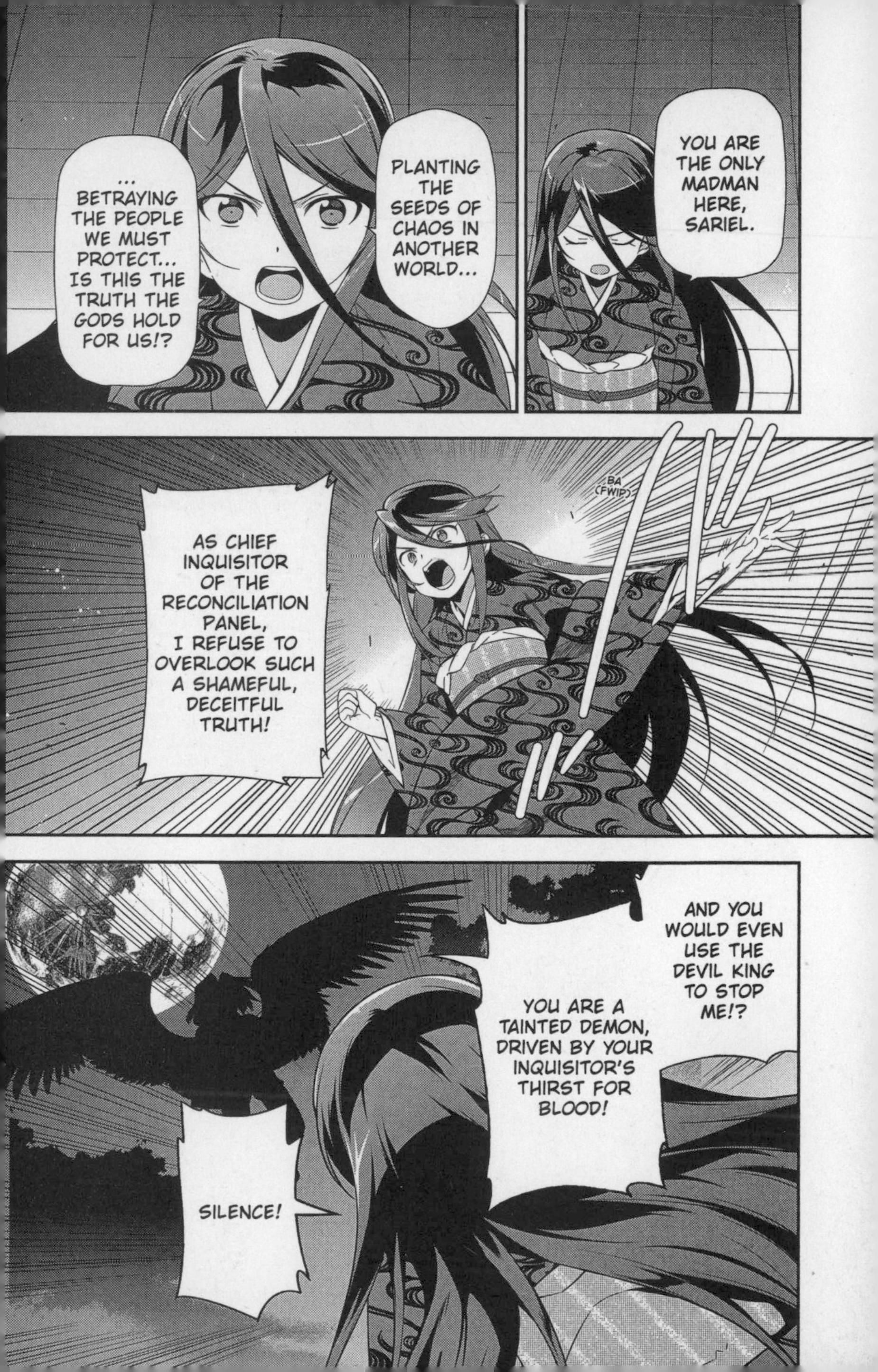
YOU ARE THE ONLY MADMAN HERE, SARIEL.
PLANTING THE SEEDS OF CHAOS IN ANOTHER WORLD...
... BETRAYING THE PEOPLE WE MUST PROTECT... IS THIS THE TRUTH THE GODS HOLD FOR US!?
BA (FWIP)
AS CHIEF INQUISITOR OF THE RECONCILIATION PANEL, I REFUSE TO OVERLOOK SUCH A SHAMEFUL, DECEITFUL TRUTH!
AND YOU WOULD EVEN USE THE DEVIL KING TO STOP ME!?
YOU ARE A TAINTED DEMON, DRIVEN BY YOUR INQUISITOR'S THIRST FOR BLOOD!
SILENCE!

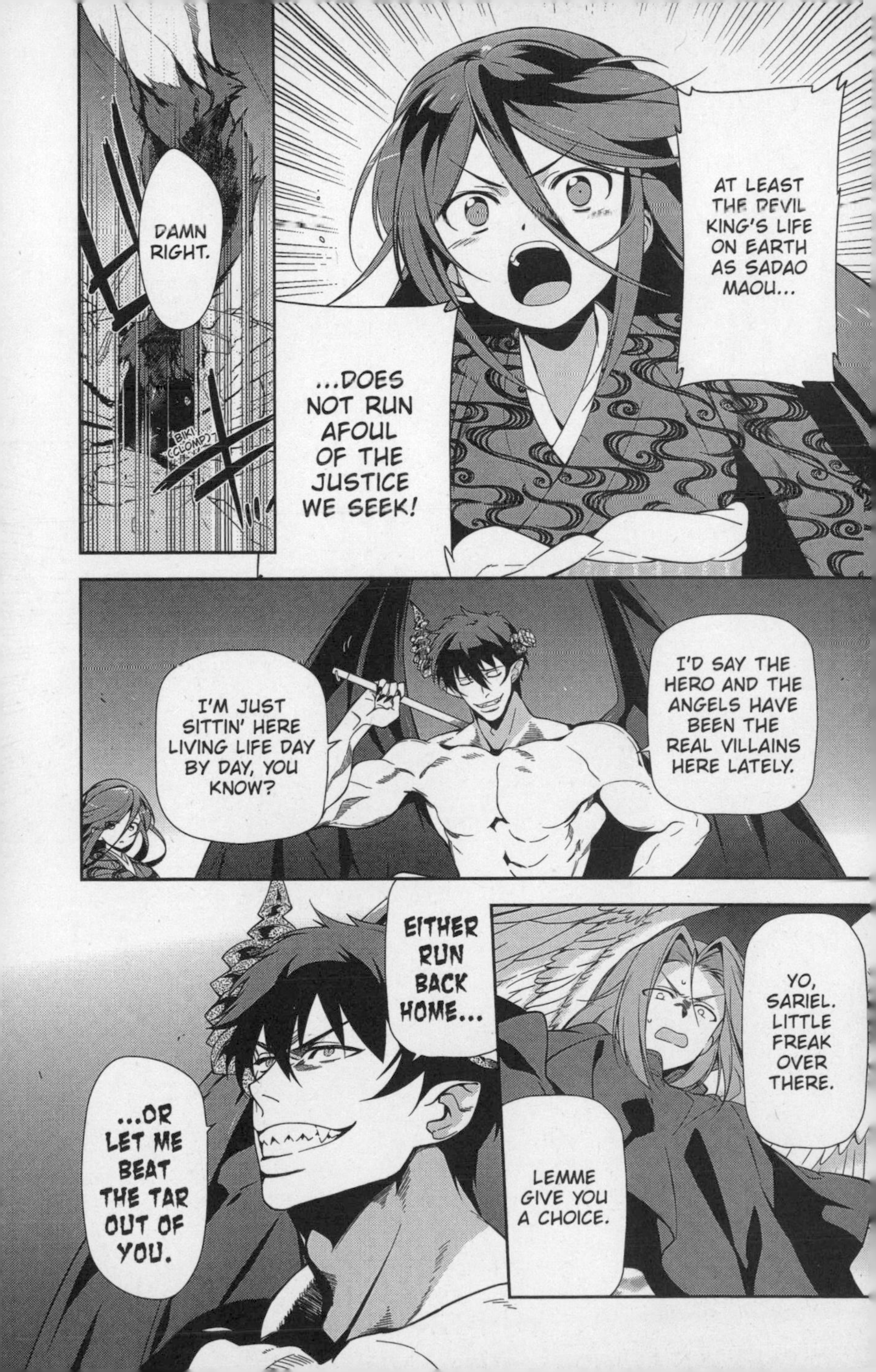
AT LEAST THE DEVIL KING'S LIFE ON EARTH AS SADAO MAOU...
...DOES NOT RUN AFOUL OF THE JUSTICE WE SEEK!
DAMN RIGHT.
BIKI (CLOMP)
I'D SAY THE HERO AND THE ANGELS HAVE BEEN THE REAL VILLAINS HERE LATELY.
I'M JUST SITTIN' HERE LIVING LIFE DAY BY DAY, YOU KNOW?
YO, SARIEL. LITTLE FREAK OVER THERE.
LEMME GIVE YOU A CHOICE.
EITHER RUN BACK HOME...
...OR LET ME BEAT THE TAR OUT OF YOU.

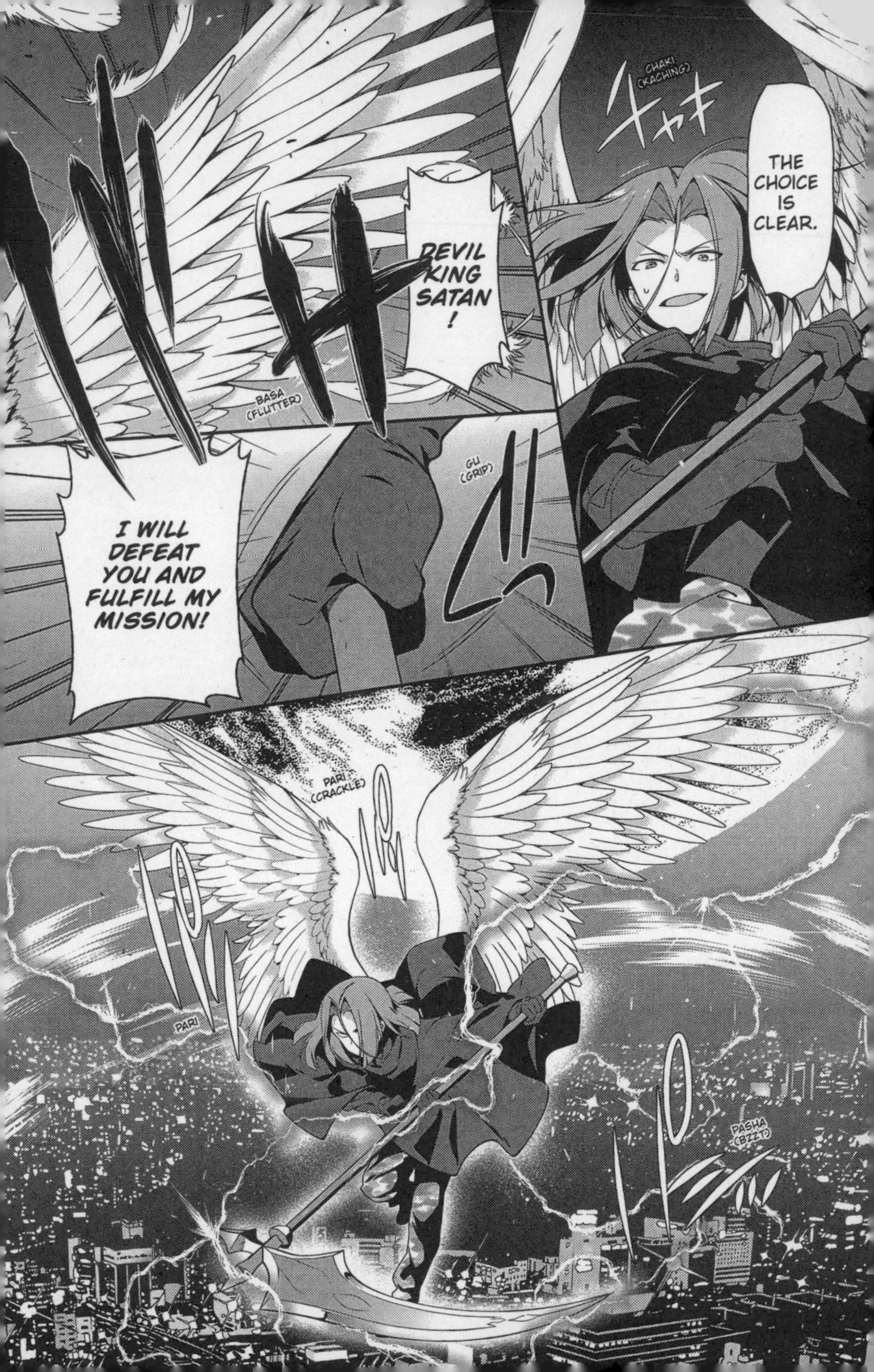
CHAKI (KACHING)
THE CHOICE IS CLEAR.
DEVIL KING SATAN!
BASA (FLUTTER)
GU (GRIP)
I WILL DEFEAT YOU AND FULFILL MY MISSION!
PARI (CRACKLE)
PARI
PASHA (BZZT)

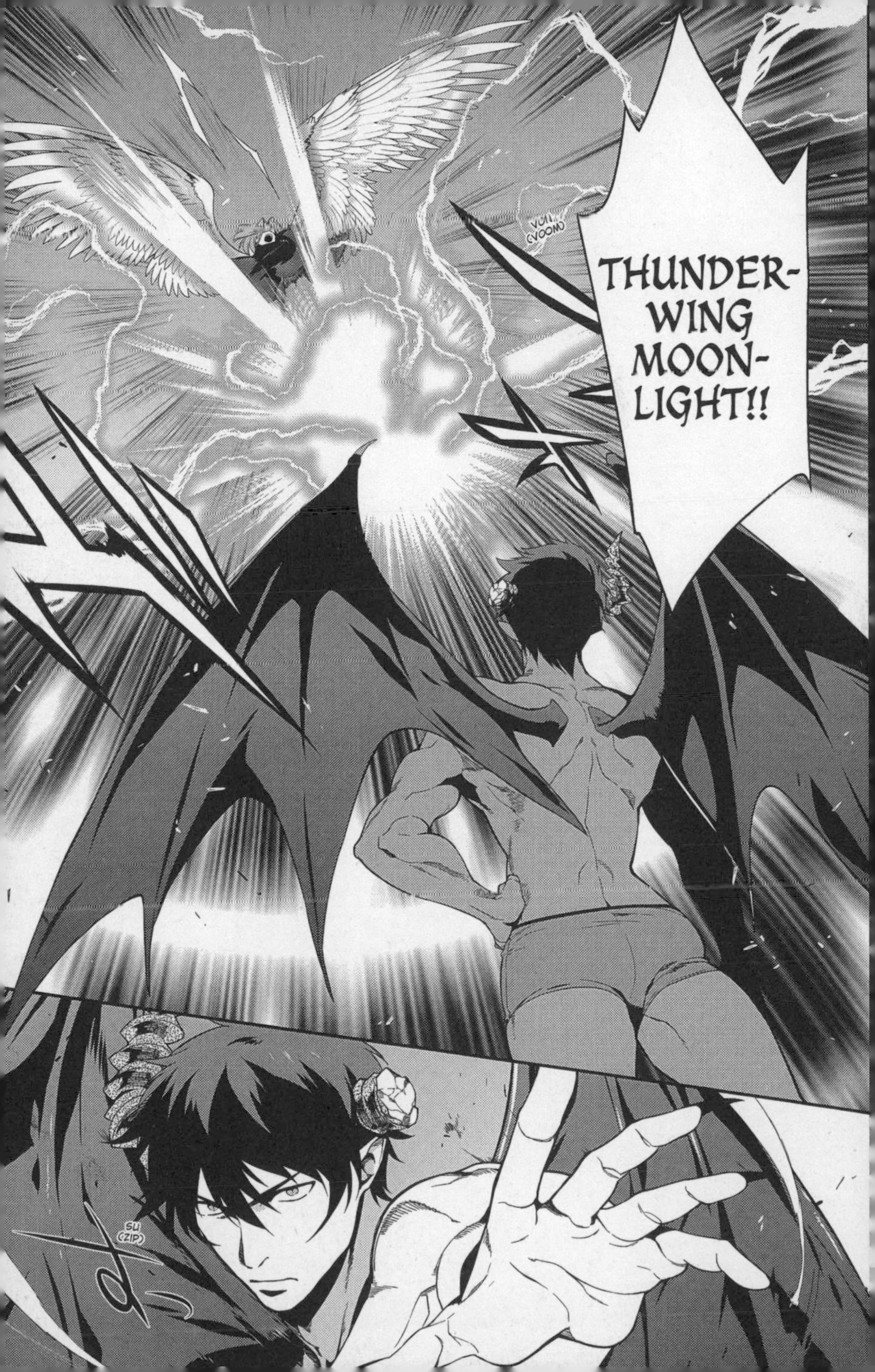
THUNDER-WING MOON-LIGHT!!
VUI (VOOM)
SU (ZIP)

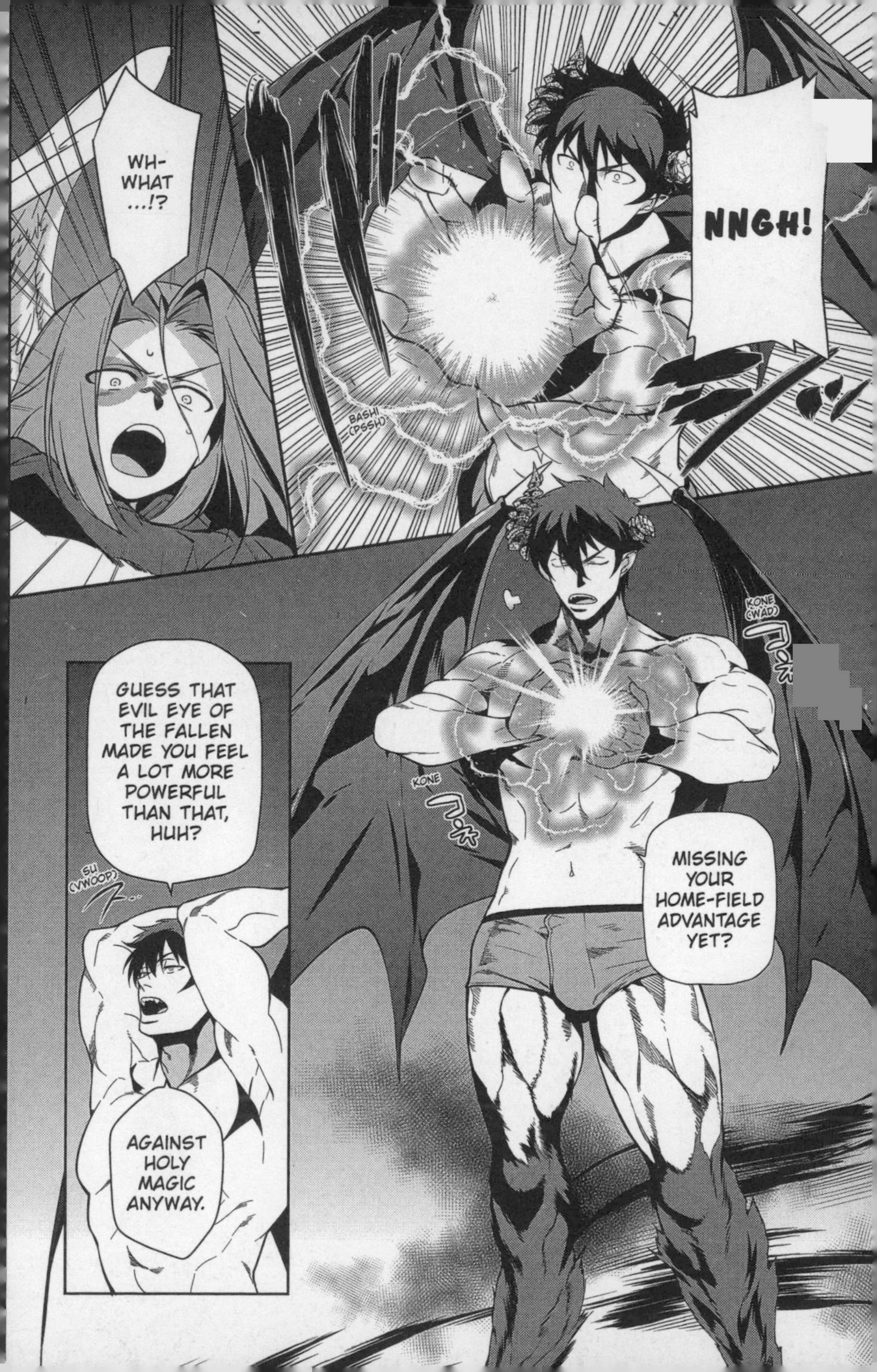
NNGH!
WH-WHAT ...!?
BASHI (PSSH)
KONE (WAD)
KONE
MISSING YOUR HOME-FIELD ADVANTAGE YET?
GUESS THAT EVIL EYE OF THE FALLEN MADE YOU FEEL A LOT MORE POWERFUL THAN THAT, HUH?
SU (VWOOP)
AGAINST HOLY MAGIC ANYWAY.

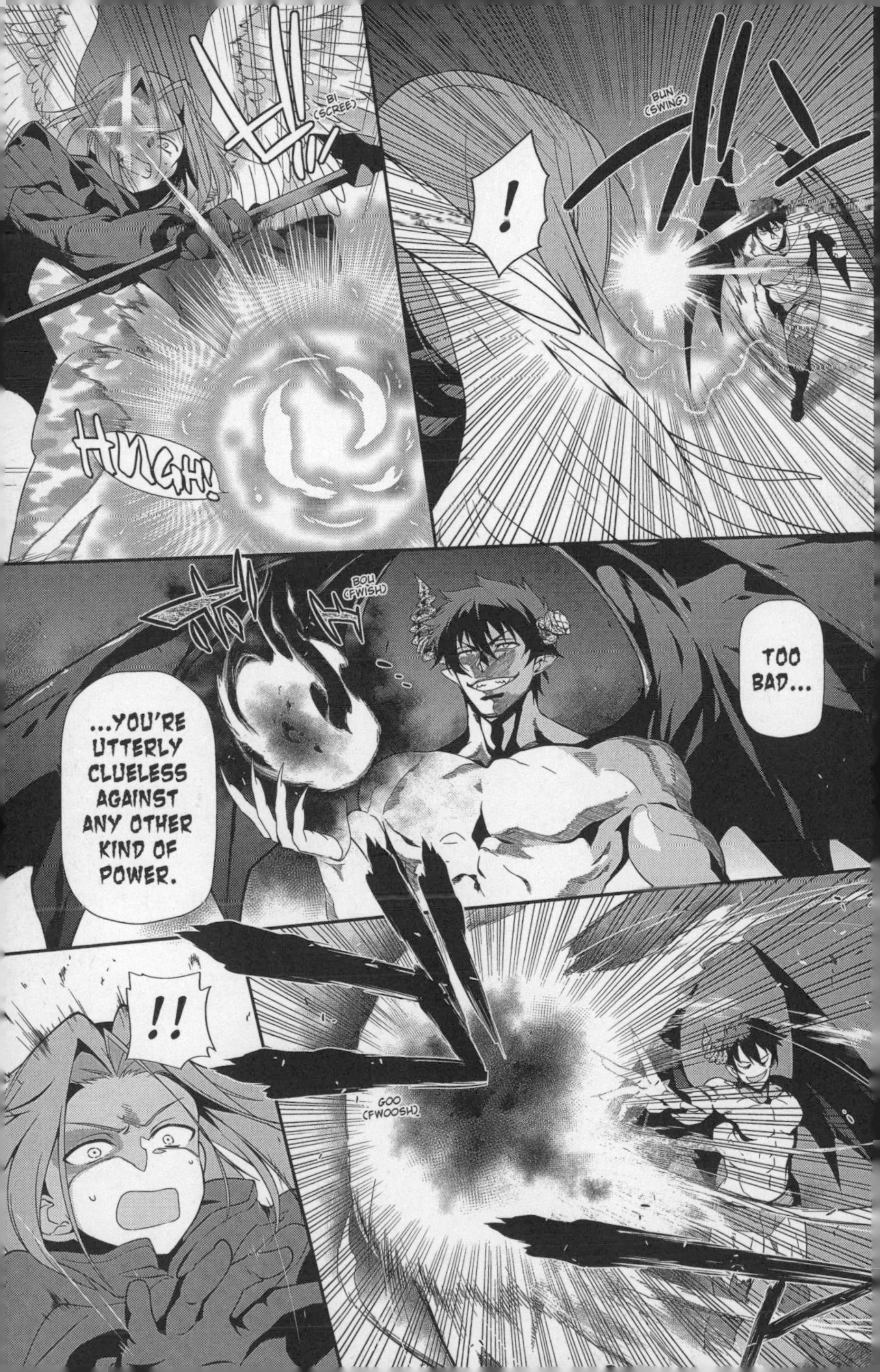
BUN (SWING)
!
BI (SCREE)
HUNGH!
TOO BAD...
BOU (FWISH)
...YOU'RE UTTERLY CLUELESS AGAINST ANY OTHER KIND OF POWER.
GOO (FWOOSH)
!!

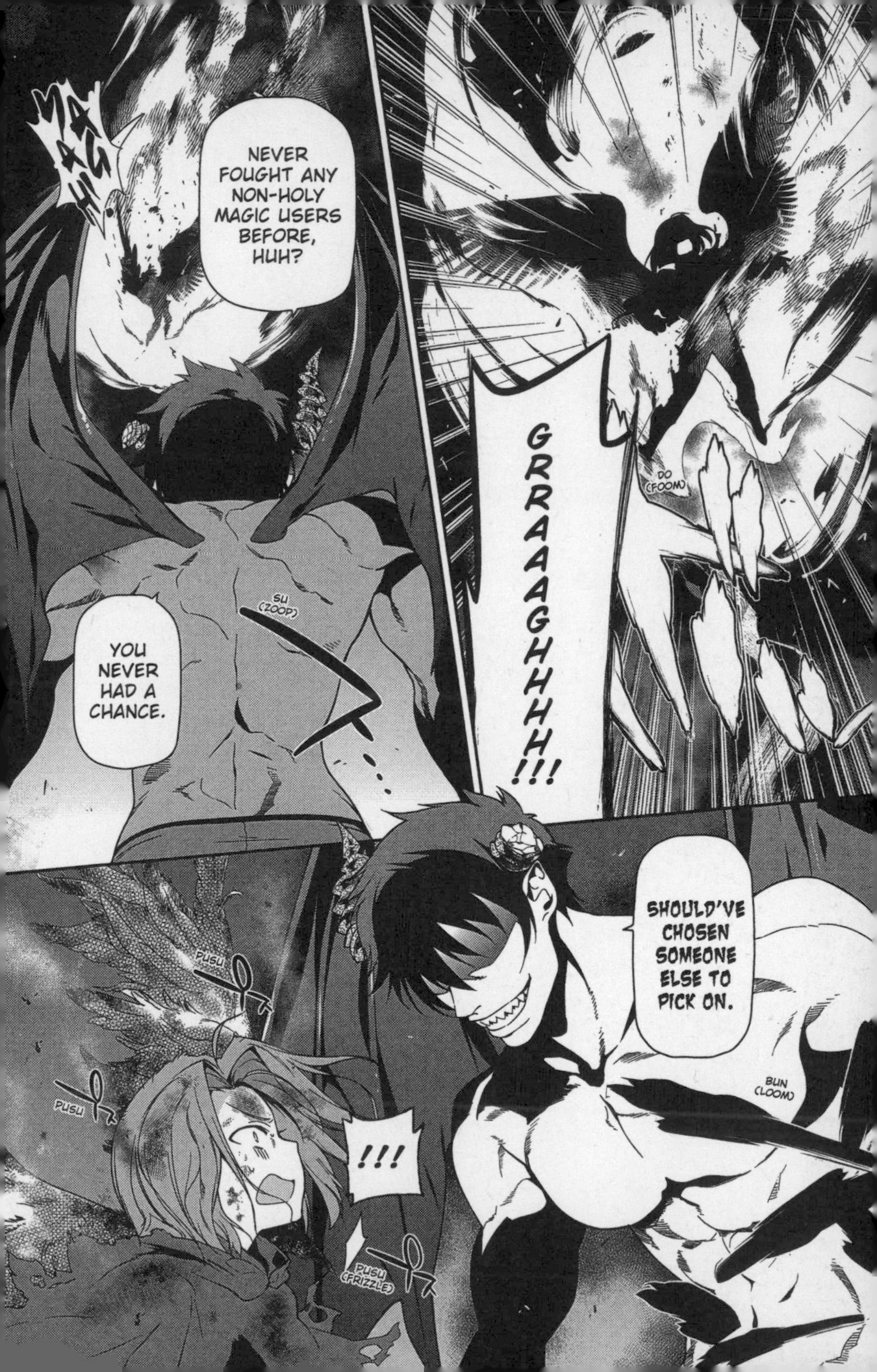
GRRAAAAGHHHHH!!!
DO (FOOM)
MAAGH!
NEVER FOUGHT ANY NON-HOLY MAGIC USERS BEFORE, HUH?
SU (ZOOP)
YOU NEVER HAD A CHANCE.
...
SHOULD'VE CHOSEN SOMEONE ELSE TO PICK ON.
BUN (LOOM)
PUSU
!!!
PUSU
PUSU (FRIZZLE)

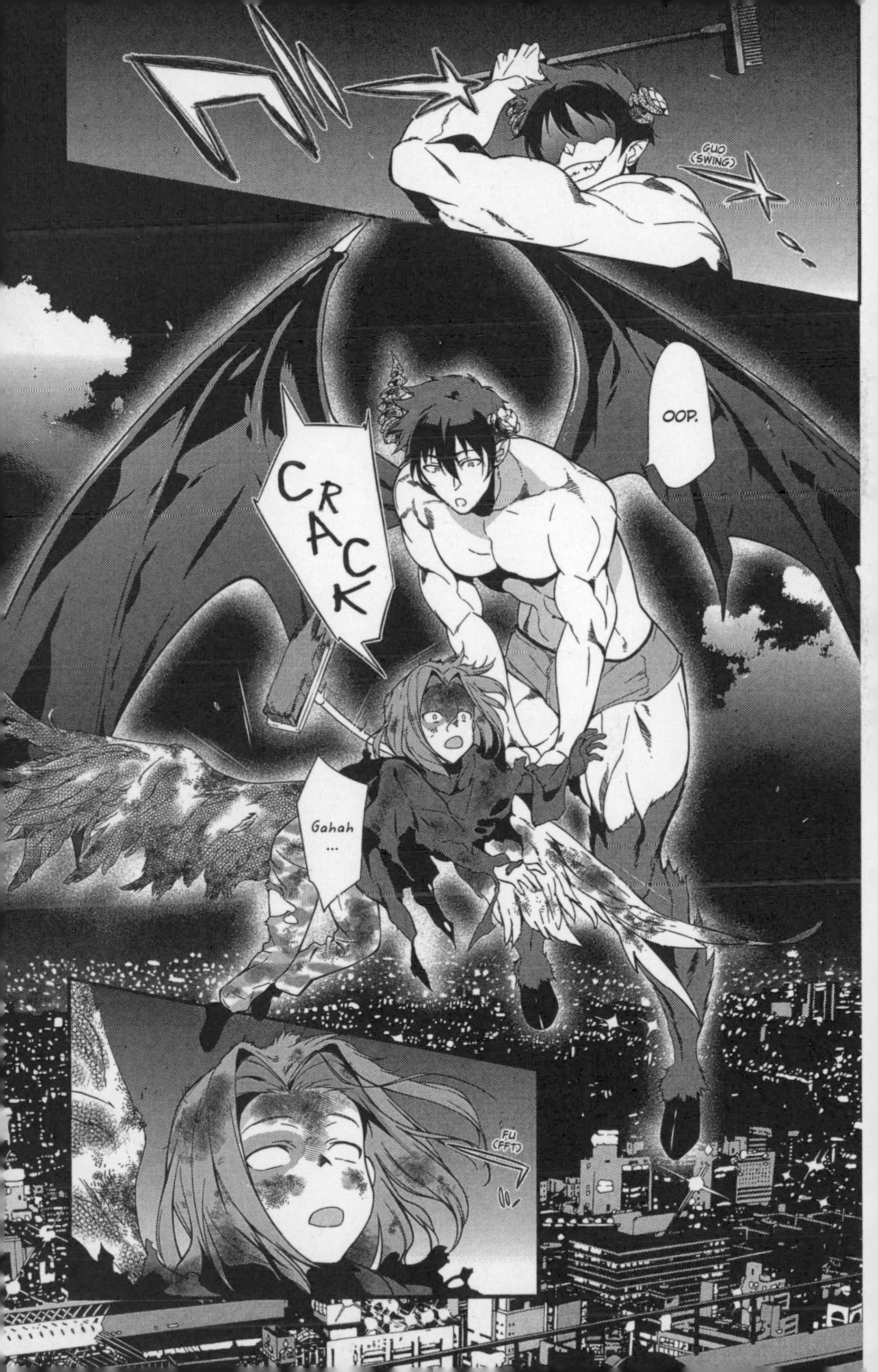
GUO (SWING)
OOP.
CRACK
Gahah ...
FU (FFT)

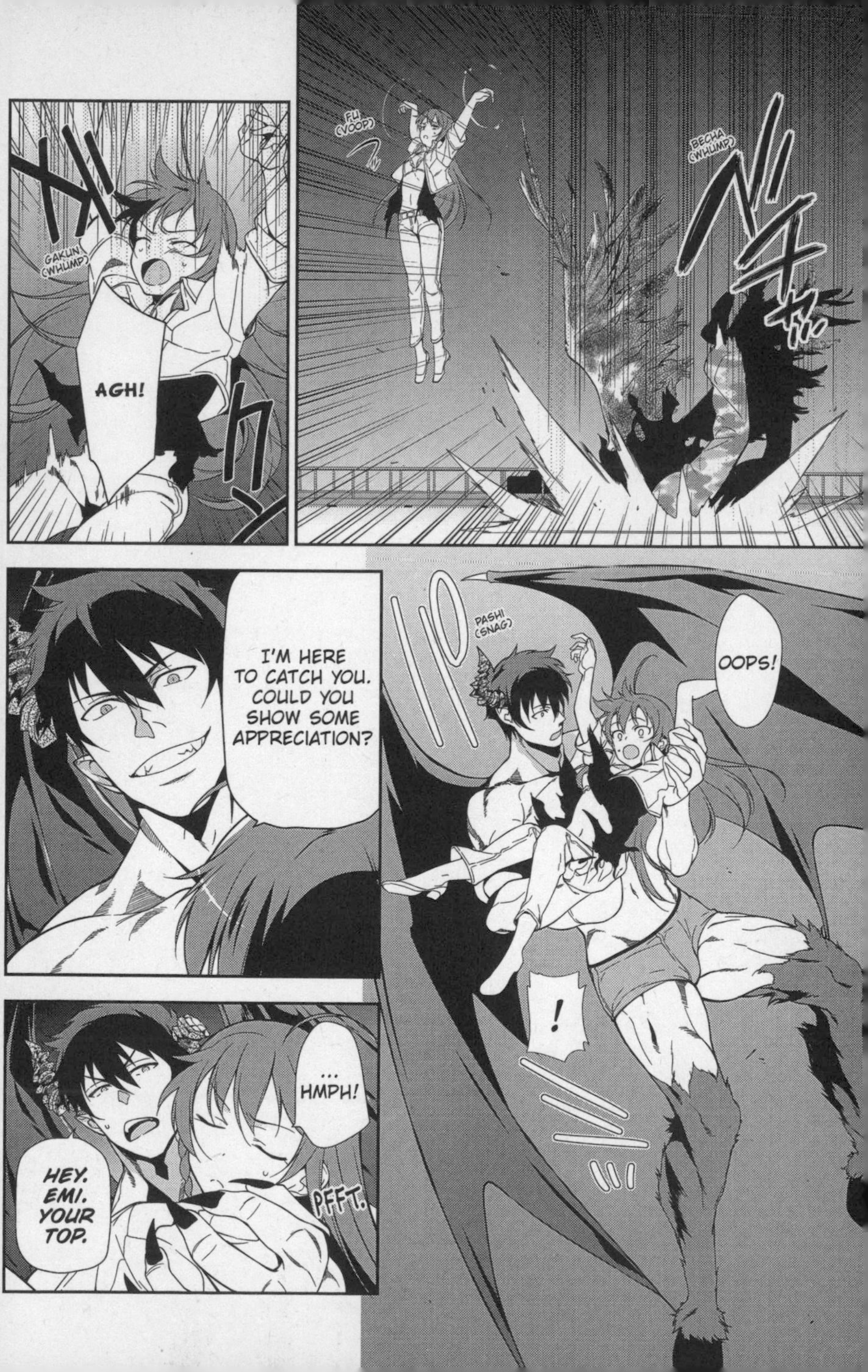
BECHA (WHUMP)
FU (VOOP)
GAKUN (WHUMP)
AGH!
OOPS!
PASHI (SNAG)
!
I'M HERE TO CATCH YOU. COULD YOU SHOW SOME APPRECIATION?
... HMPH!
PFFT.
HEY. EMI. YOUR TOP.

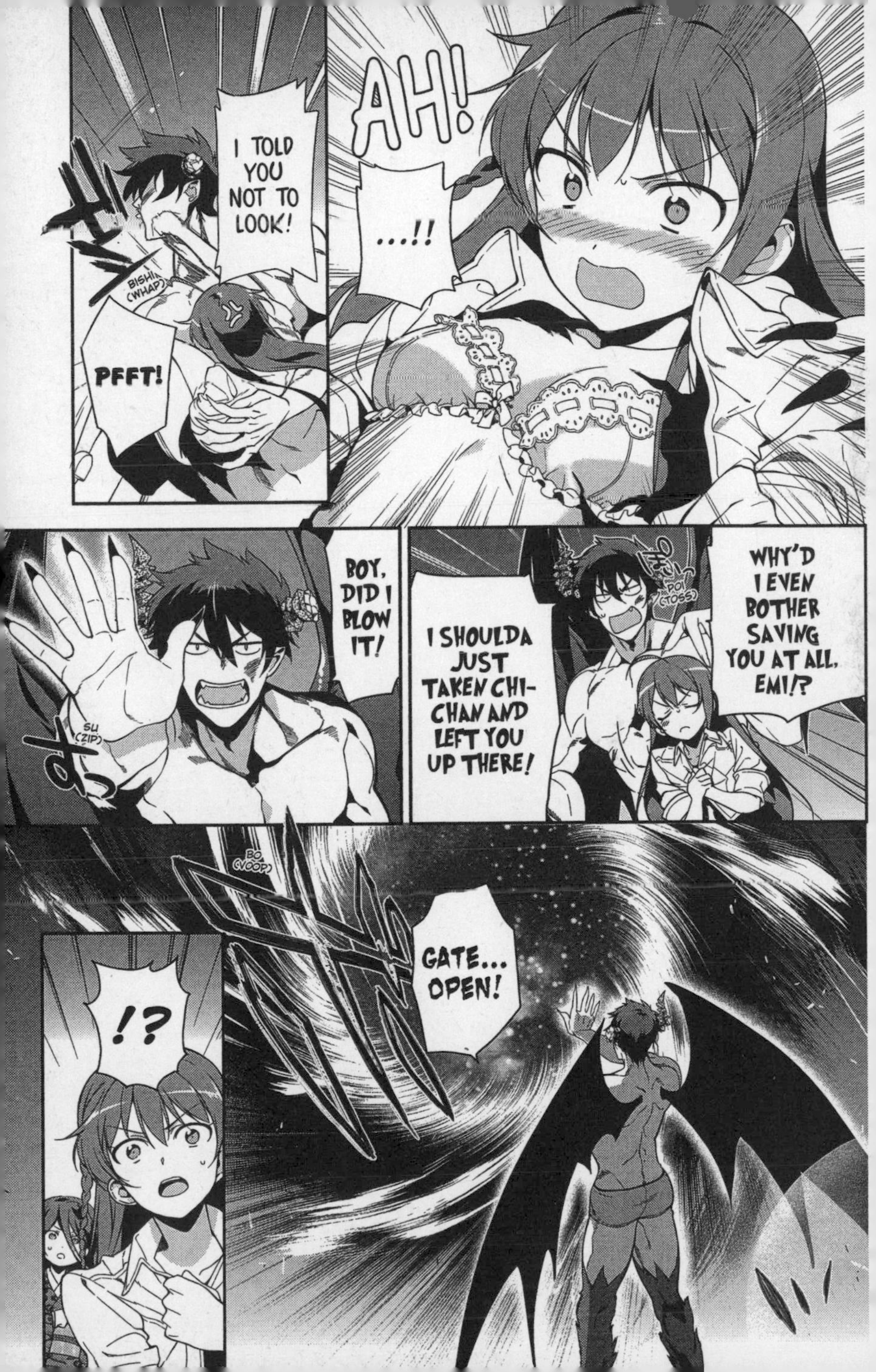
AH!
...!!
I TOLD YOU NOT TO LOOK!
BISHI (WHAP)
PFFT!
WHY'D I EVEN BOTHER SAVING YOU AT ALL, EMI!?
POI (TOSS)
I SHOULDA JUST TAKEN CHI-CHAN AND LEFT YOU UP THERE!
BOY, DID I BLOW IT!
SU (ZIP)
GATE... OPEN!
BO (VOOP)
!?

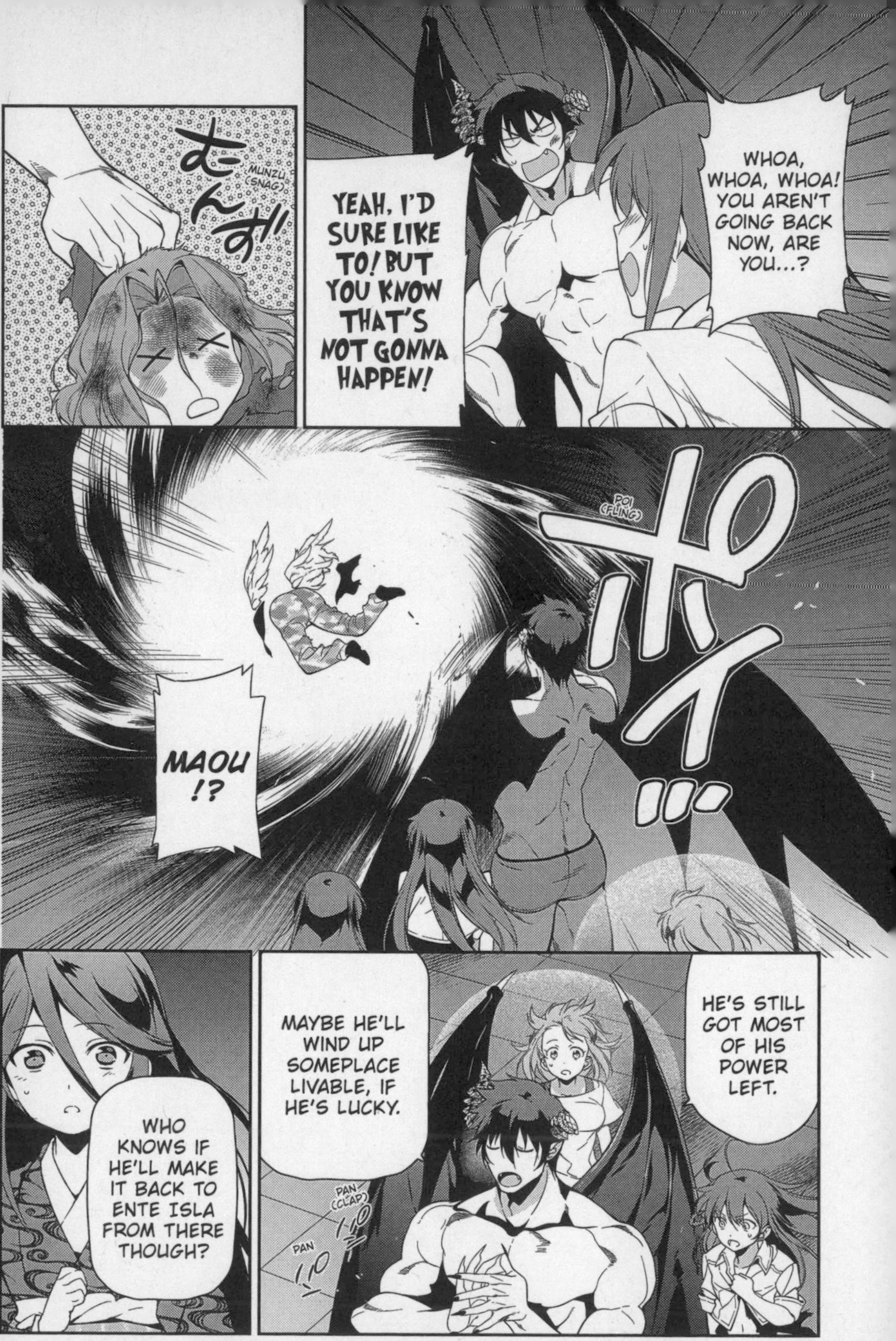
WHOA, WHOA, WHOA! YOU AREN'T GOING BACK NOW, ARE YOU...?
YEAH, I'D SURE LIKE TO! BUT YOU KNOW THAT'S NOT GONNA HAPPEN!
むんず
MUNZU (SNAG)
ポイ
POI (FLING)
MAOU!?
HE'S STILL GOT MOST OF HIS POWER LEFT.
MAYBE HE'LL WIND UP SOMEPLACE LIVABLE, IF HE'S LUCKY.
PAN (CLAP)
PAN
WHO KNOWS IF HE'LL MAKE IT BACK TO ENTE ISLA FROM THERE THOUGH?

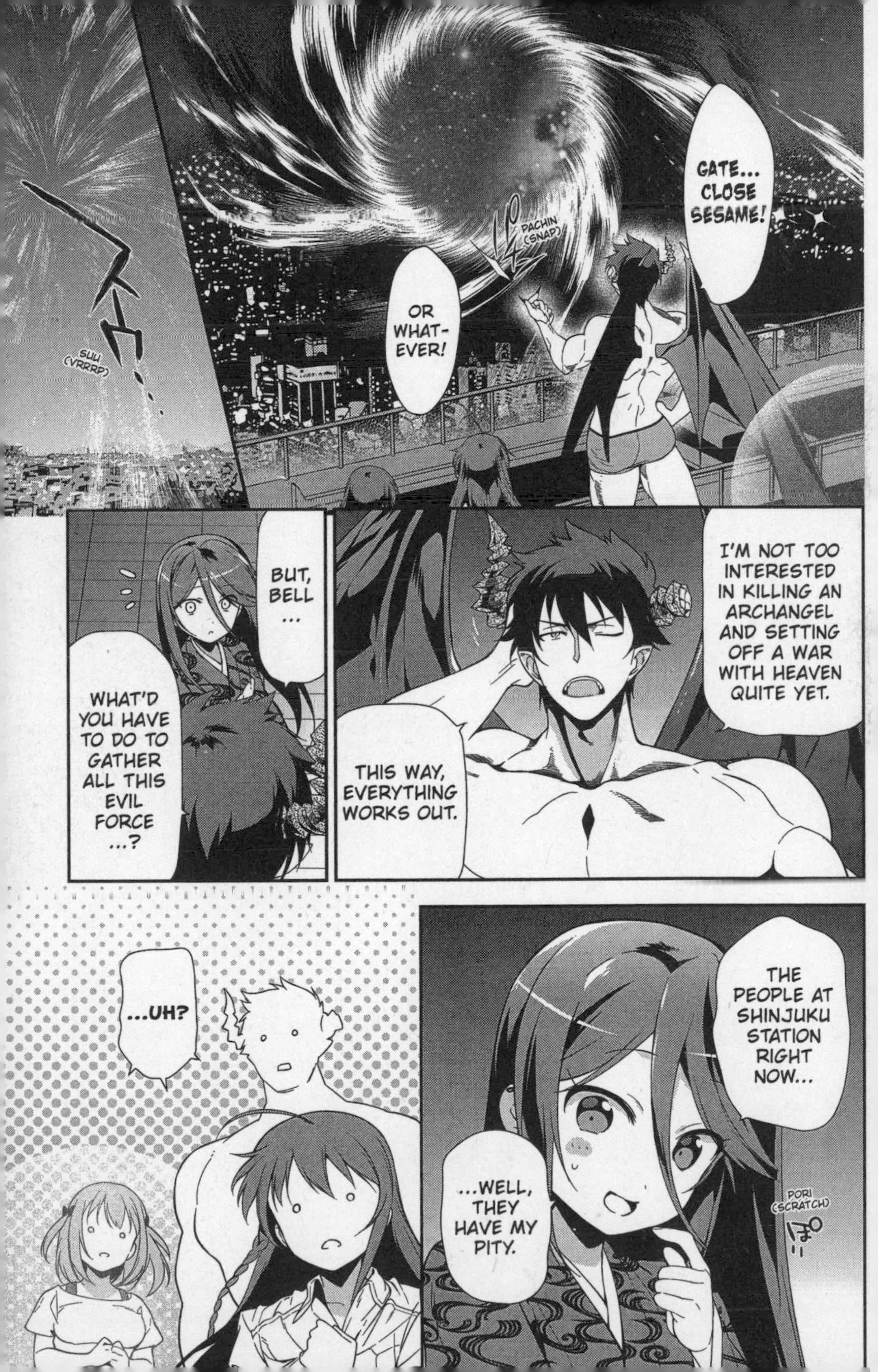
GATE... CLOSE SESAME!
PACHIN (SNAP)
OR WHAT-EVER!
SUU (VRRRP)
I'M NOT TOO INTERESTED IN KILLING AN ARCHANGEL AND SETTING OFF A WAR WITH HEAVEN QUITE YET.
THIS WAY, EVERYTHING WORKS OUT.
BUT, BELL ...
WHAT'D YOU HAVE TO DO TO GATHER ALL THIS EVIL FORCE ...?
THE PEOPLE AT SHINJUKU STATION RIGHT NOW...
PORI (SCRATCH)
...WELL, THEY HAVE MY PITY.
...UH?

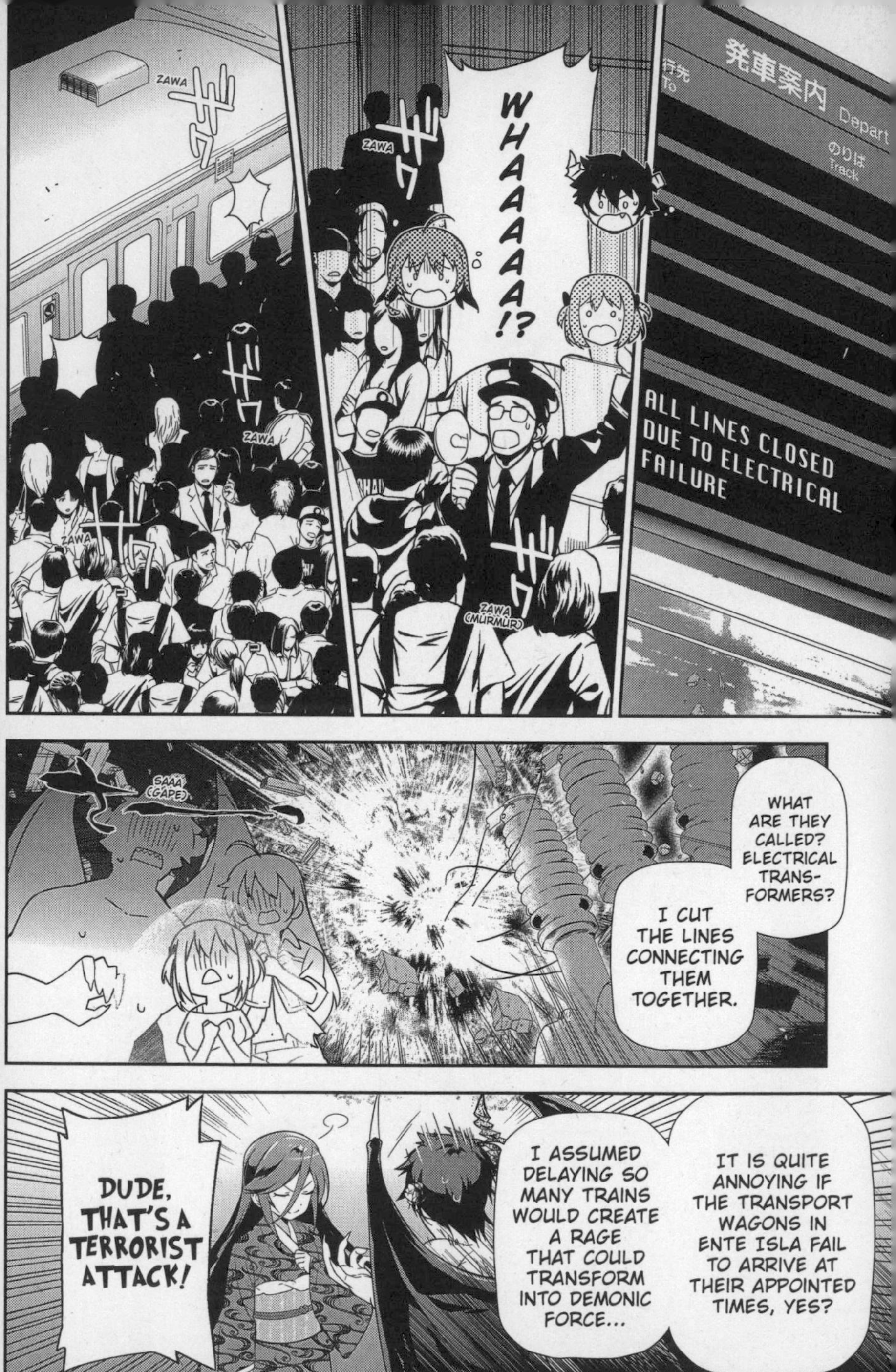
発車案内
行先
To
Depart
のりば
Track
ALL LINES CLOSED DUE TO ELECTRICAL FAILURE
WHAAAAAA!?
ZAWA
ZAWA (MURMUR)
ZAWA
ZAWA
ZAWA
WHAT ARE THEY CALLED? ELECTRICAL TRANS-FORMERS?
I CUT THE LINES CONNECTING THEM TOGETHER.
SAAA (GAPE)
IT IS QUITE ANNOYING IF THE TRANSPORT WAGONS IN ENTE ISLA FAIL TO ARRIVE AT THEIR APPOINTED TIMES, YES?
I ASSUMED DELAYING SO MANY TRAINS WOULD CREATE A RAGE THAT COULD TRANSFORM INTO DEMONIC FORCE...
DUDE, THAT'S A TERRORIST ATTACK!

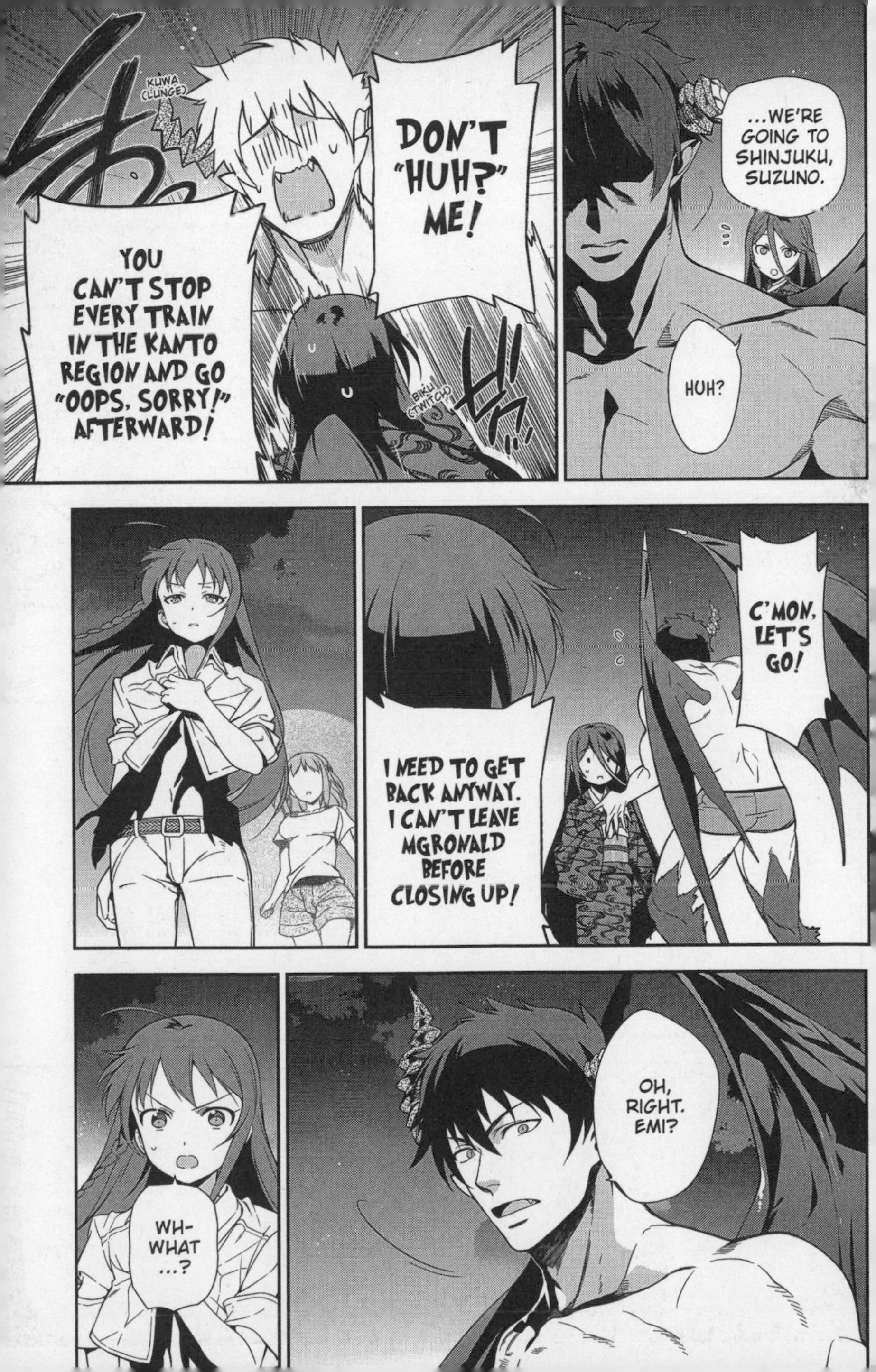
...WE'RE GOING TO SHINJUKU, SUZUNO.
HUH?
DON'T "HUH?" ME!
KUWA (LUNGE)
YOU CAN'T STOP EVERY TRAIN IN THE KANTO REGION AND GO "OOPS, SORRY!" AFTERWARD!
BIKU (TWITCH)
C'MON, LET'S GO!
I NEED TO GET BACK ANYWAY. I CAN'T LEAVE MGRONALD BEFORE CLOSING UP!
OH, RIGHT. EMI?
WH-WHAT...?

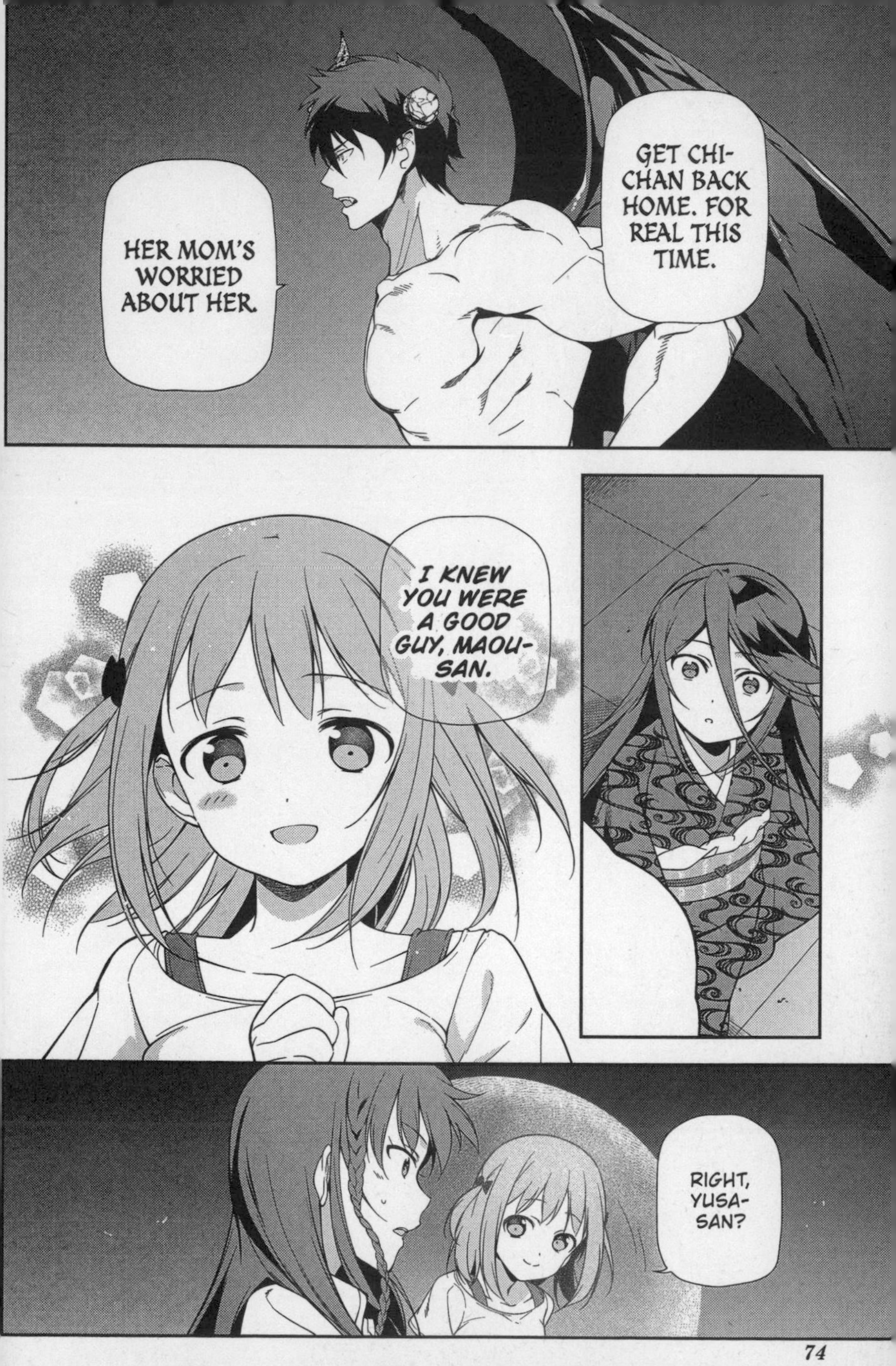
GET CHI-CHAN BACK HOME. FOR REAL THIS TIME.
HER MOM'S WORRIED ABOUT HER.
I KNEW YOU WERE A GOOD GUY, MAOU-SAN.
RIGHT, YUSA-SAN?

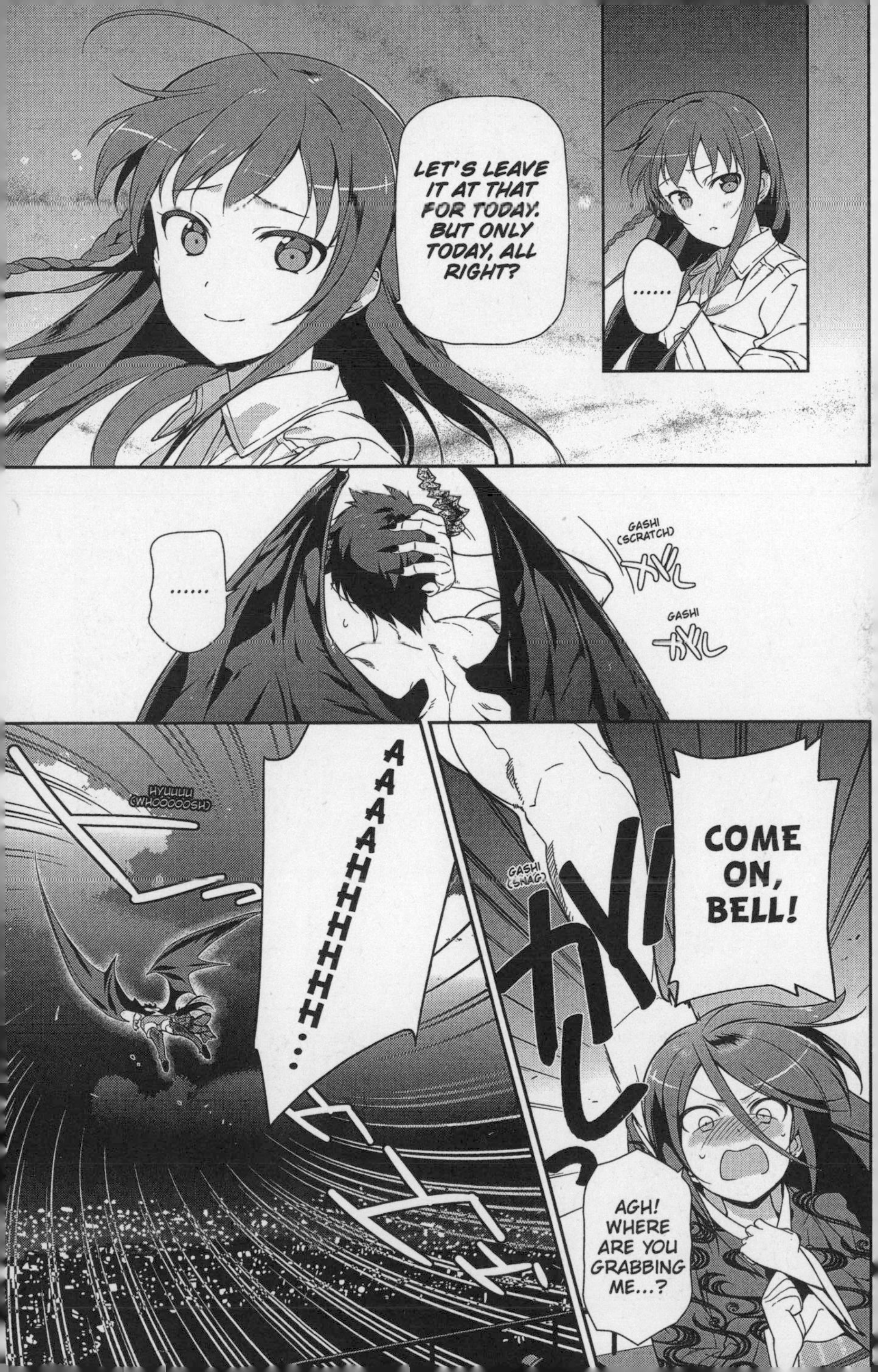
......
LET'S LEAVE IT AT THAT FOR TODAY. BUT ONLY TODAY, ALL RIGHT?
GASHI (SCRATCH)
GASHI
......
COME ON, BELL!
GASHI (SNAG)
AGH! WHERE ARE YOU GRABBING ME...?
HYUUUU (WHOOOOOSH)
AAAAHHHHHH...

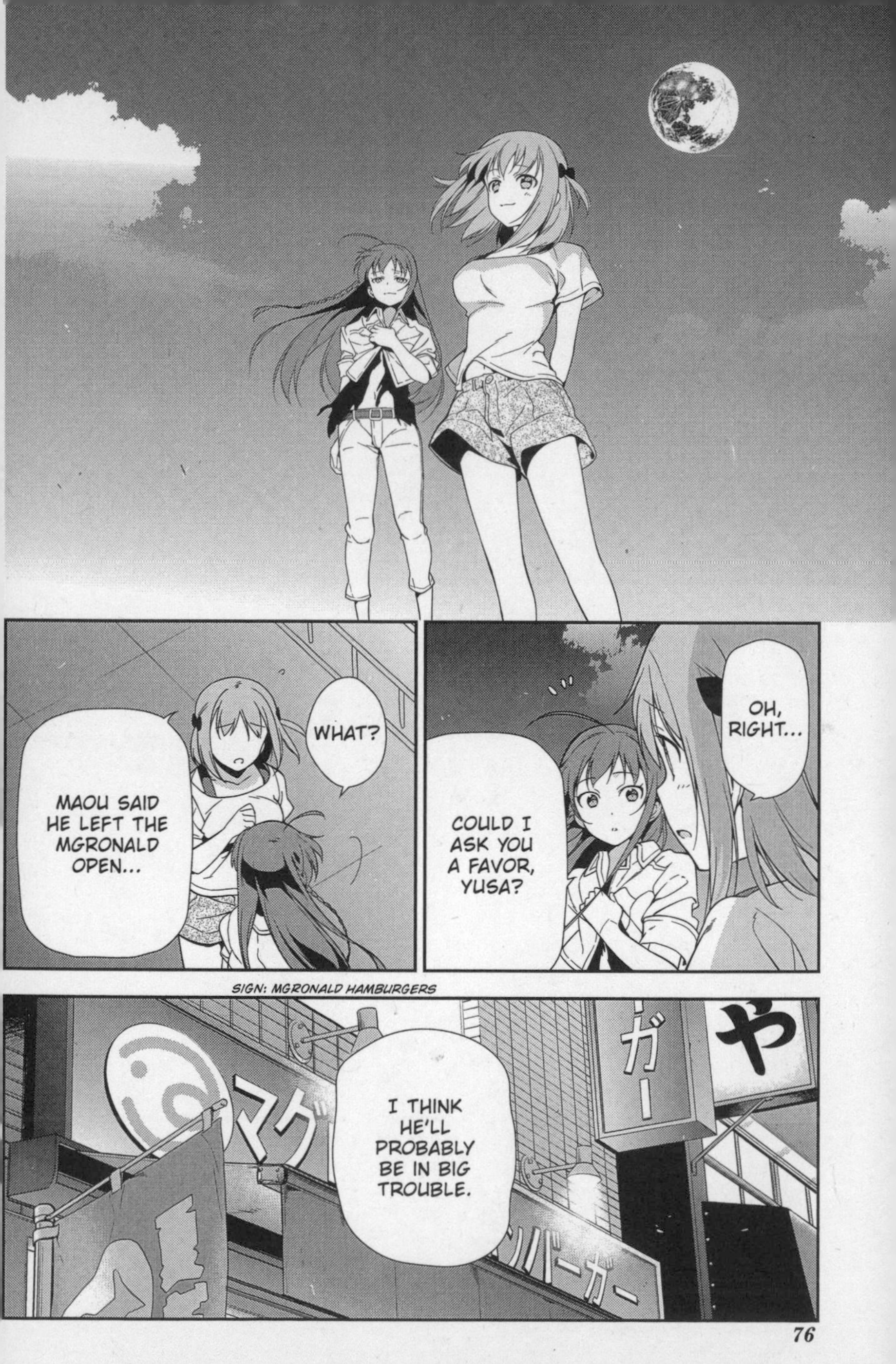
OH, RIGHT...
COULD I ASK YOU A FAVOR, YUSA?
WHAT?
MAOU SAID HE LEFT THE MGRONALD OPEN...
SIGN: MGRONALD HAMBURGERS
I THINK HE'LL PROBABLY BE IN BIG TROUBLE.

Emi
Yusa

THE DEVIL IS A PART-TIMER!

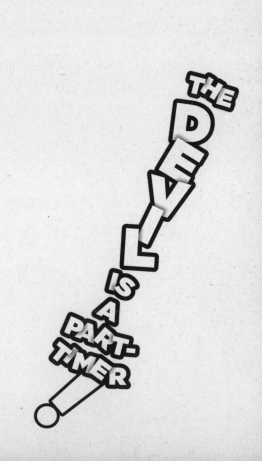

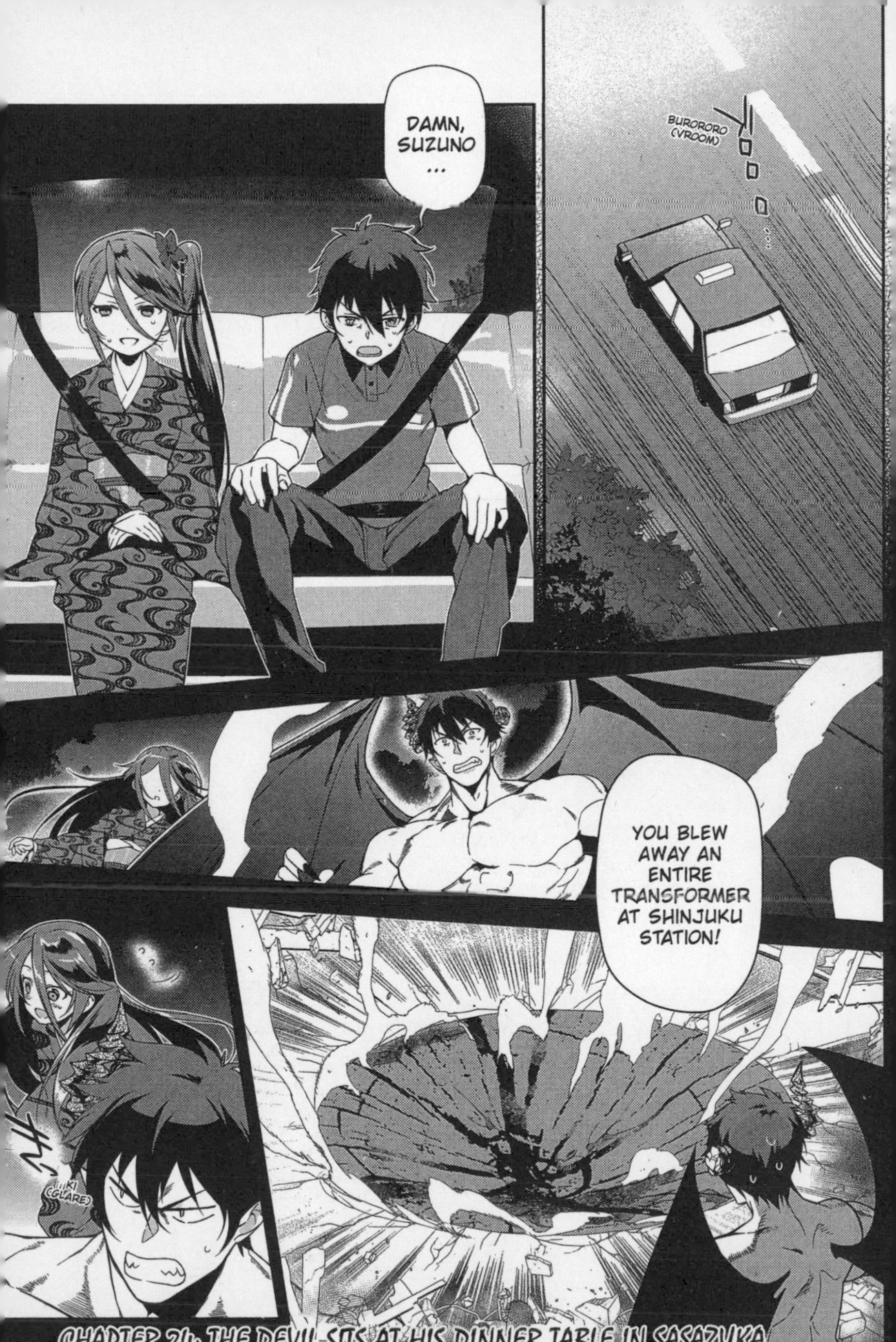
BURORORO (VROOM)
DAMN, SUZUNO ...
YOU BLEW AWAY AN ENTIRE TRANSFORMER AT SHINJUKU STATION!
KI (GLARE)

CHAPTER 24: THE DEVIL SITS AT HIS DINNER TABLE IN SASAZUKA

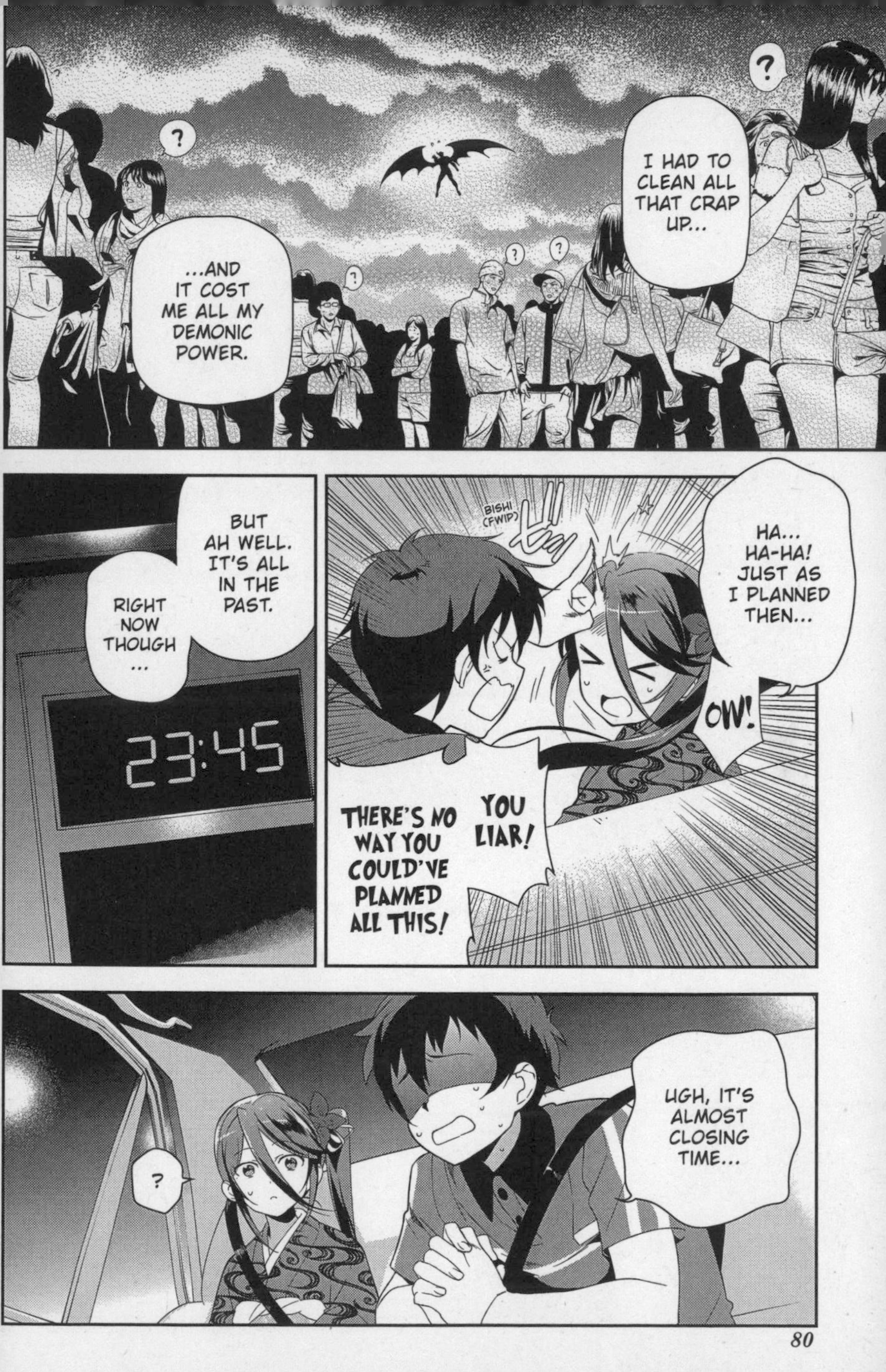
?
I HAD TO CLEAN ALL THAT CRAP UP...
?
?
?
?
...AND IT COST ME ALL MY DEMONIC POWER.
HA... HA-HA! JUST AS I PLANNED THEN...
BISHI (FWIP)
OW!
YOU LIAR!
THERE'S NO WAY YOU COULD'VE PLANNED ALL THIS!
BUT AH WELL. IT'S ALL IN THE PAST.
RIGHT NOW THOUGH...
23:45
UGH, IT'S ALMOST CLOSING TIME...
?

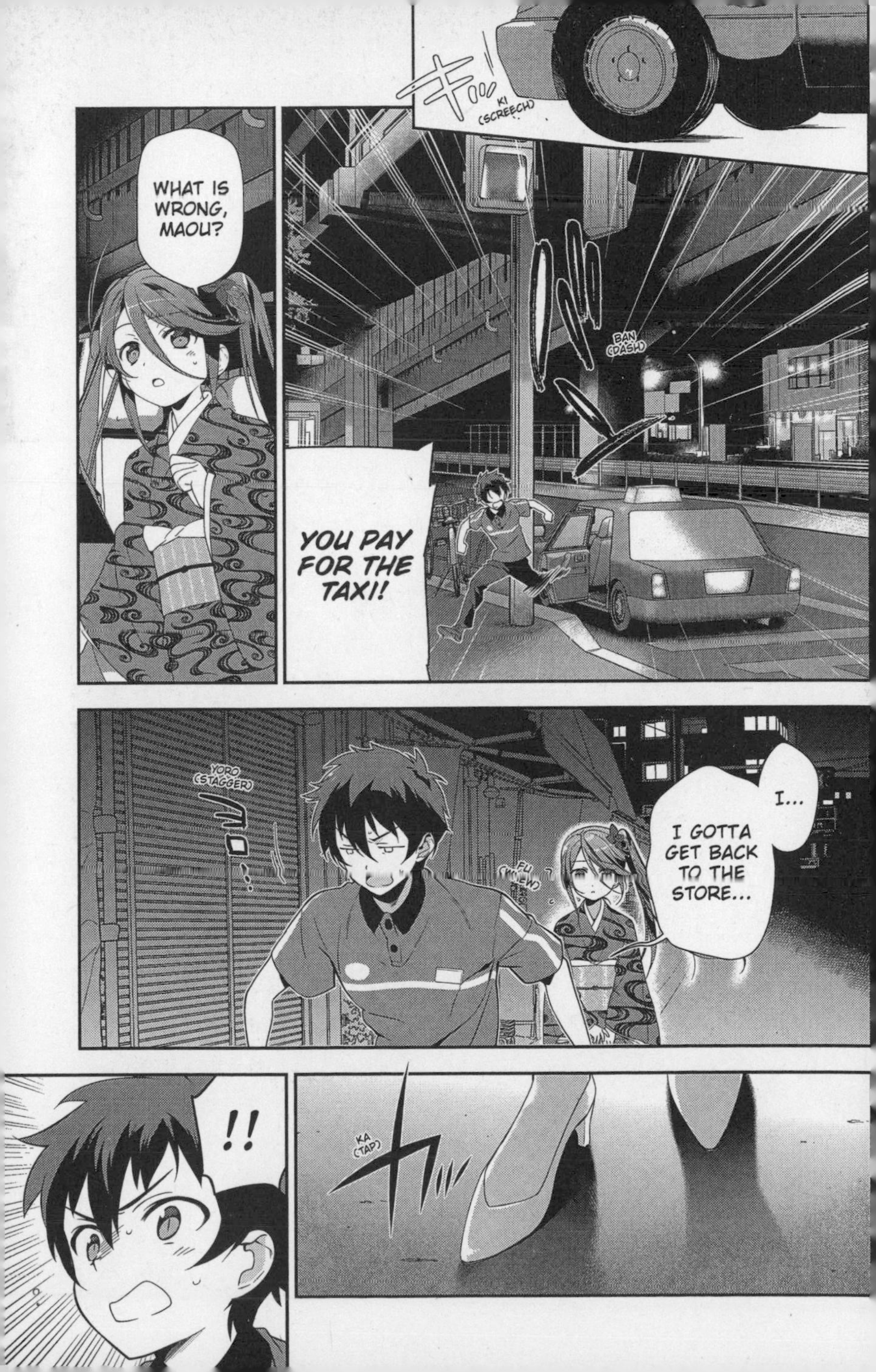
KI (SCREECH)
BAN (DASH)
YOU PAY FOR THE TAXI!
WHAT IS WRONG, MAOU?
I...
I GOTTA GET BACK TO THE STORE...
FU (WHEW)
YORO (STAGGER)
KA (TAP)
!!

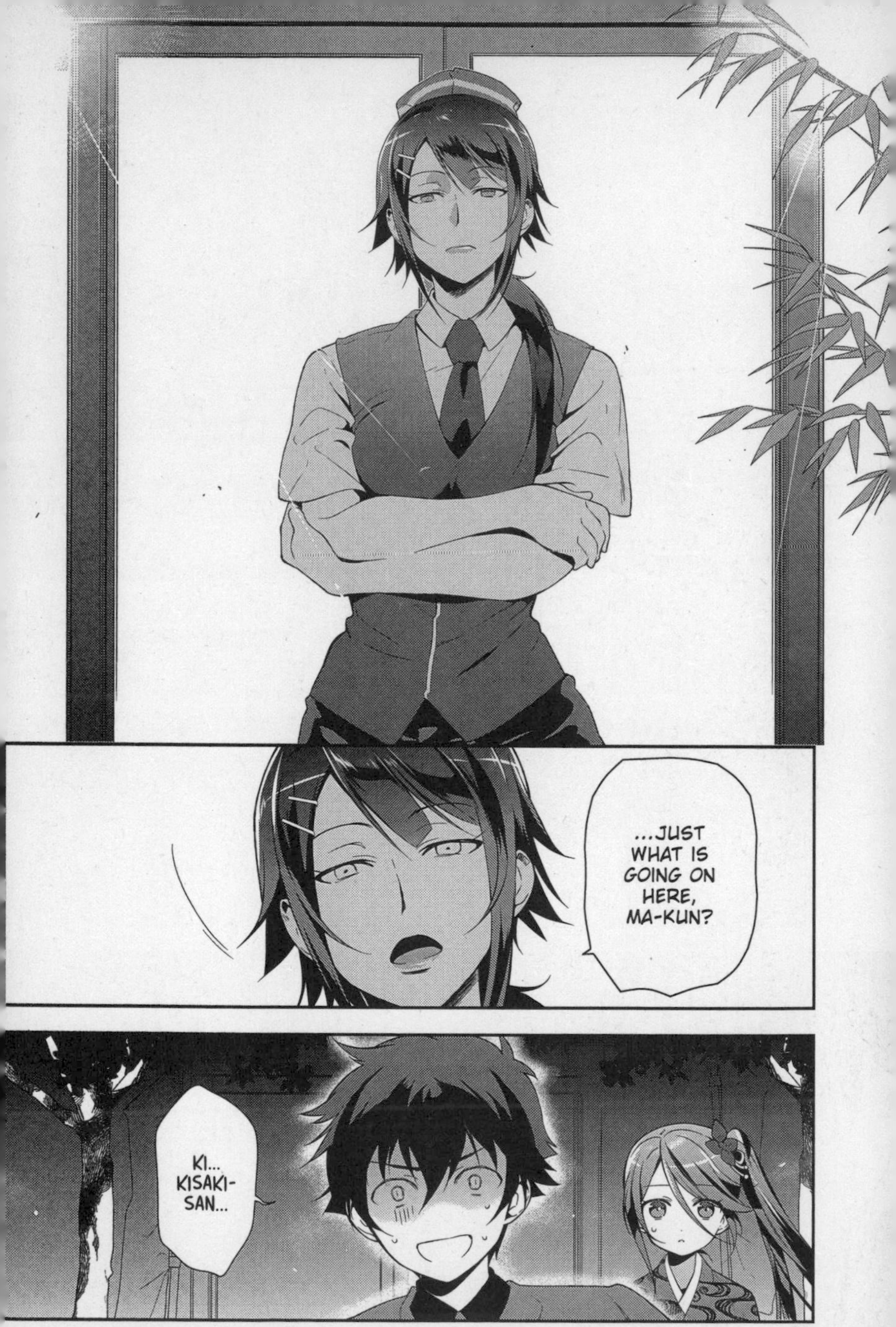
...JUST WHAT IS GOING ON HERE, MA-KUN?
KI... KISAKI-SAN...

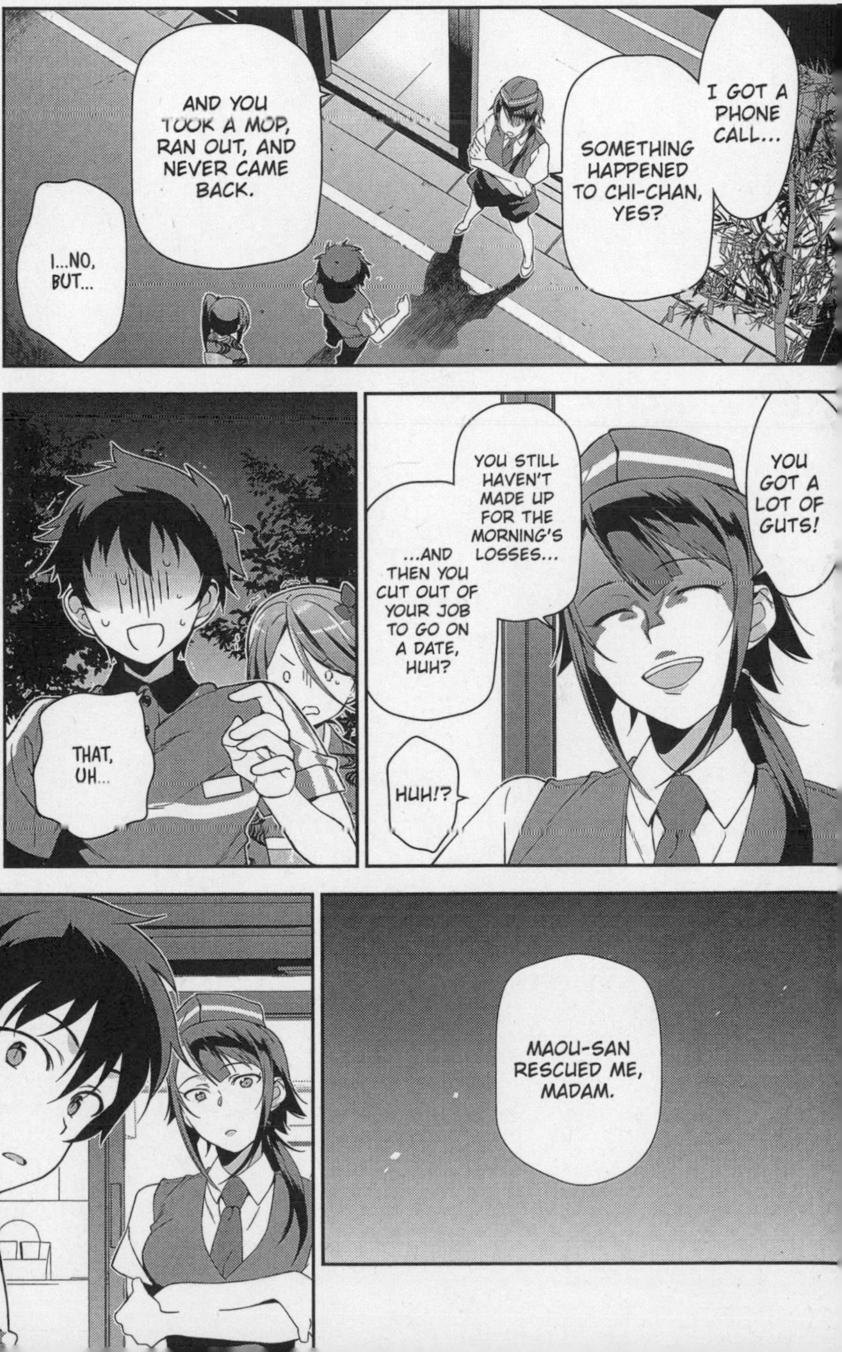
I GOT A PHONE CALL...
SOMETHING HAPPENED TO CHI-CHAN, YES?
AND YOU TOOK A MOP, RAN OUT, AND NEVER CAME BACK.
I...NO, BUT...
YOU GOT A LOT OF GUTS!
YOU STILL HAVEN'T MADE UP FOR THE MORNING'S LOSSES...
...AND THEN YOU CUT OUT OF YOUR JOB TO GO ON A DATE, HUH?
HUH!?
THAT, UH...
MAOU-SAN RESCUED ME, MADAM.

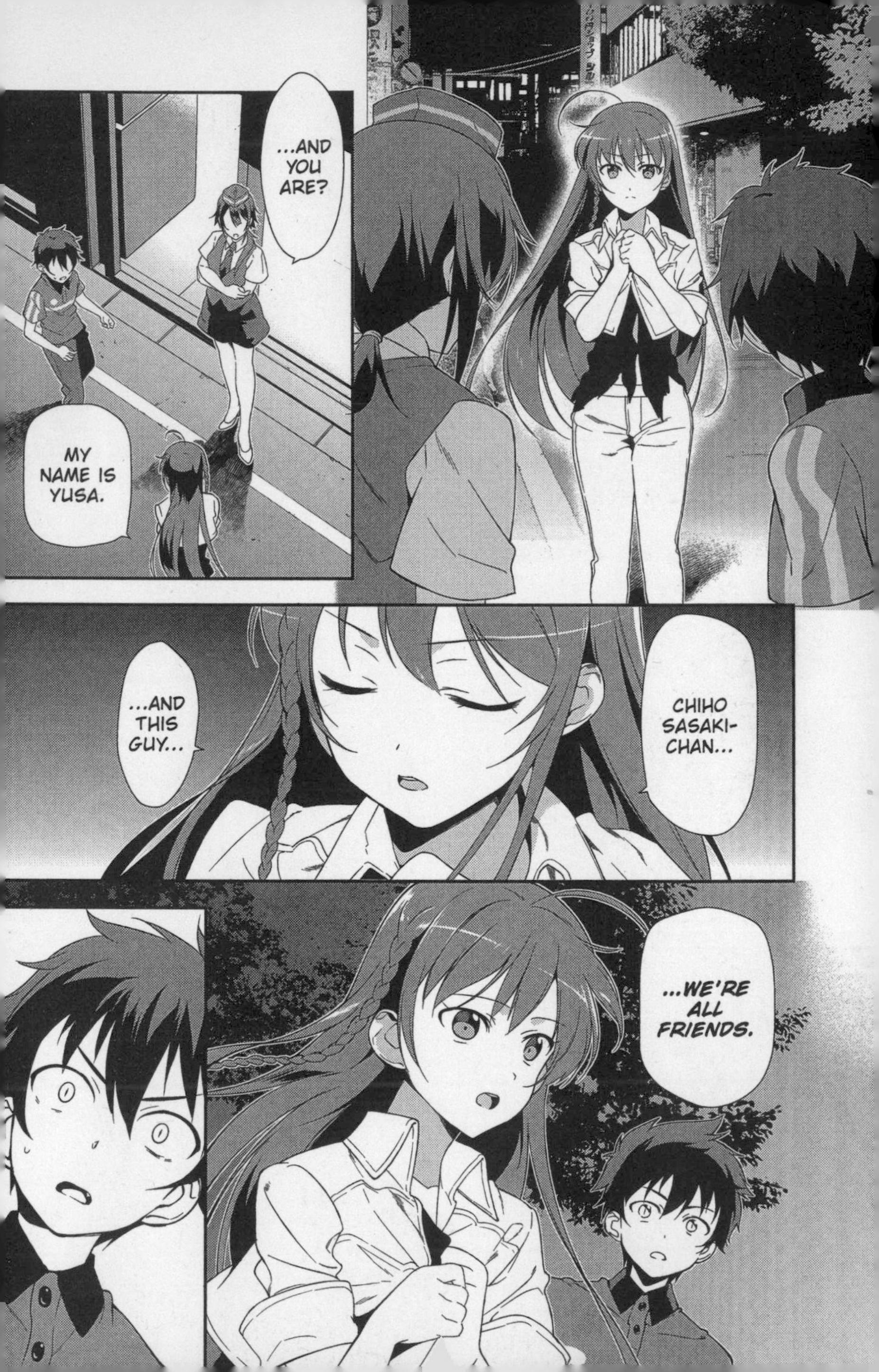
...AND YOU ARE?
MY NAME IS YUSA.
CHIHO SASAKI-CHAN...
...AND THIS GUY...
...WE'RE ALL FRIENDS.

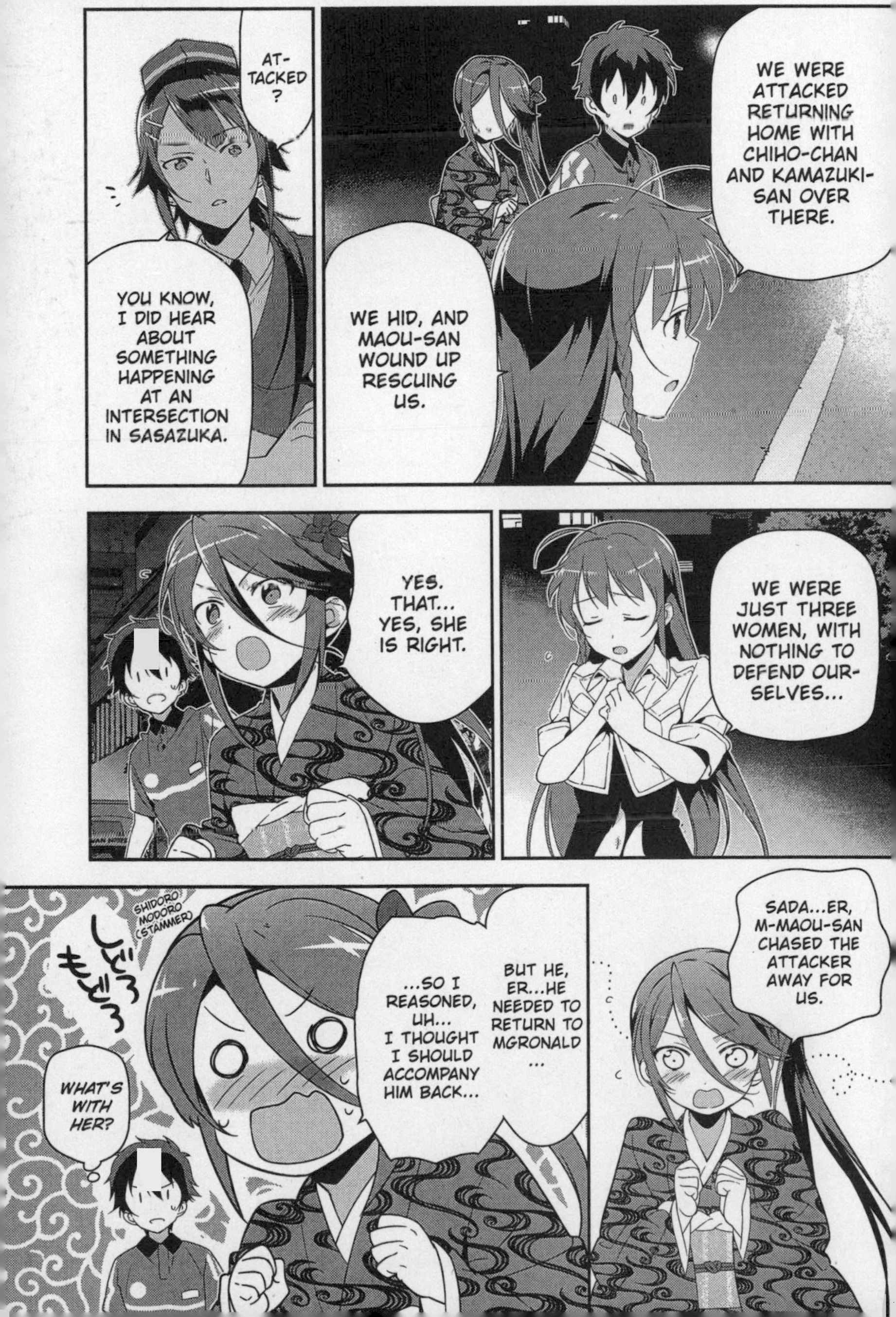
WE WERE ATTACKED RETURNING HOME WITH CHIHO-CHAN AND KAMAZUKI-SAN OVER THERE.
WE HID, AND MAOU-SAN WOUND UP RESCUING US.
AT-TACKED?
YOU KNOW, I DID HEAR ABOUT SOMETHING HAPPENING AT AN INTERSECTION IN SASAZUKA.
WE WERE JUST THREE WOMEN, WITH NOTHING TO DEFEND OURSELVES...
YES. THAT... YES, SHE IS RIGHT.
SADA...ER, M-MAOU-SAN CHASED THE ATTACKER AWAY FOR US.
BUT HE, ER...HE NEEDED TO RETURN TO MGRONALD...
...SO I REASONED, UH... I THOUGHT I SHOULD ACCOMPANY HIM BACK...
しどろもどろ
SHIDORO MODORO (STAMMER)
WHAT'S WITH HER?

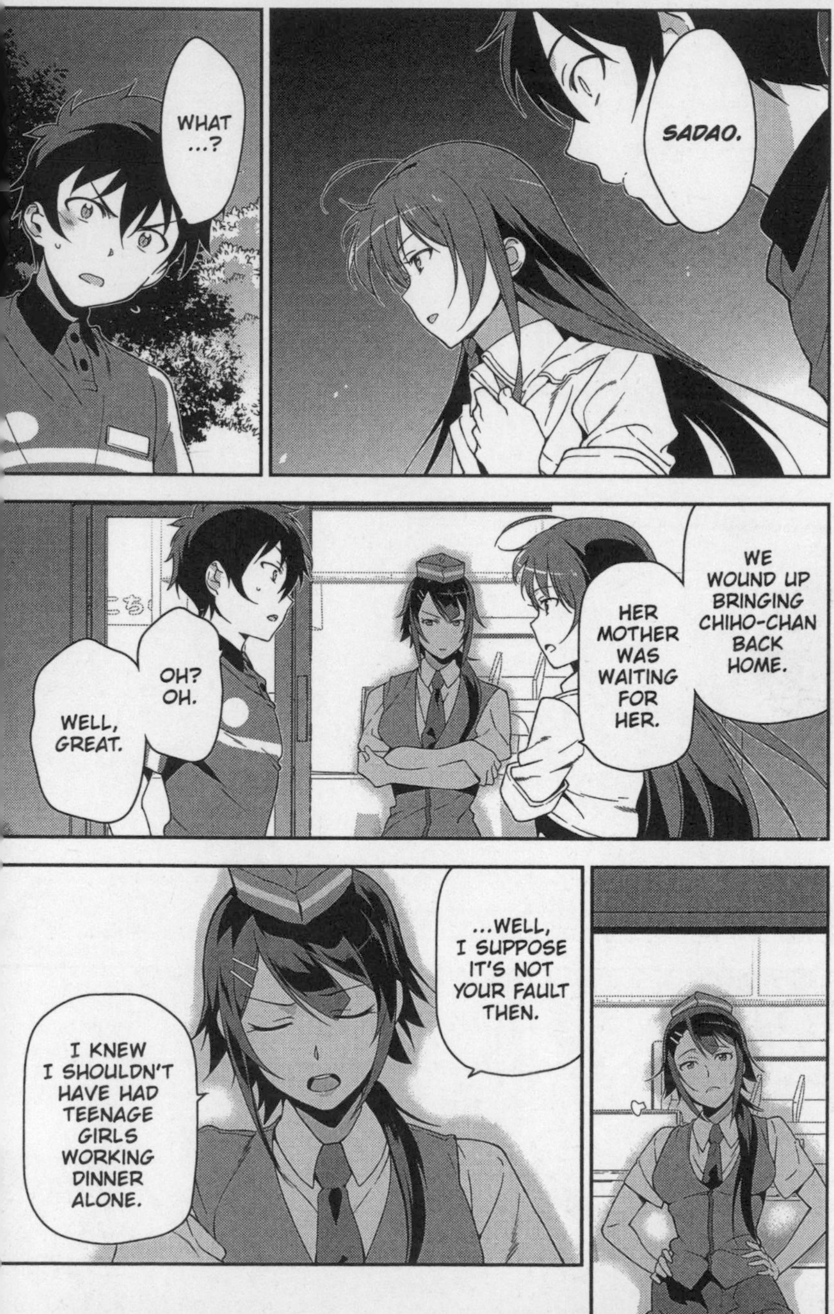
SADAO.
WHAT ...?
WE WOUND UP BRINGING CHIHO-CHAN BACK HOME.
HER MOTHER WAS WAITING FOR HER.
OH? OH.
WELL, GREAT.
...WELL, I SUPPOSE IT'S NOT YOUR FAULT THEN.
I KNEW I SHOULDN'T HAVE HAD TEENAGE GIRLS WORKING DINNER ALONE.

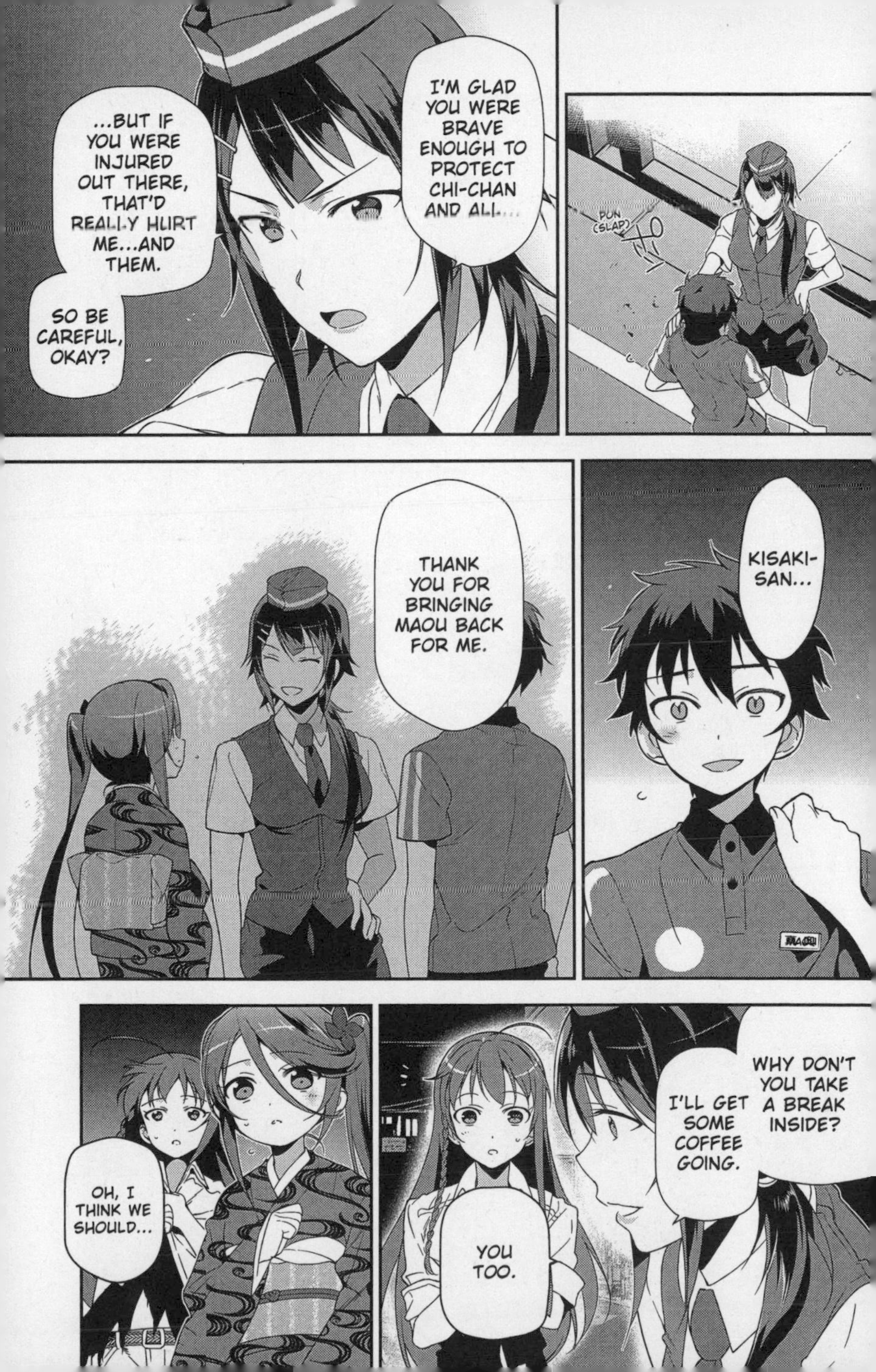
PUN (SLAP)
I'M GLAD YOU WERE BRAVE ENOUGH TO PROTECT CHI-CHAN AND ALL...
...BUT IF YOU WERE INJURED OUT THERE, THAT'D REALLY HURT ME...AND THEM.
SO BE CAREFUL, OKAY?
KISAKI-SAN...
THANK YOU FOR BRINGING MAOU BACK FOR ME.
WHY DON'T YOU TAKE A BREAK INSIDE?
I'LL GET SOME COFFEE GOING.
YOU TOO.
OH, I THINK WE SHOULD...

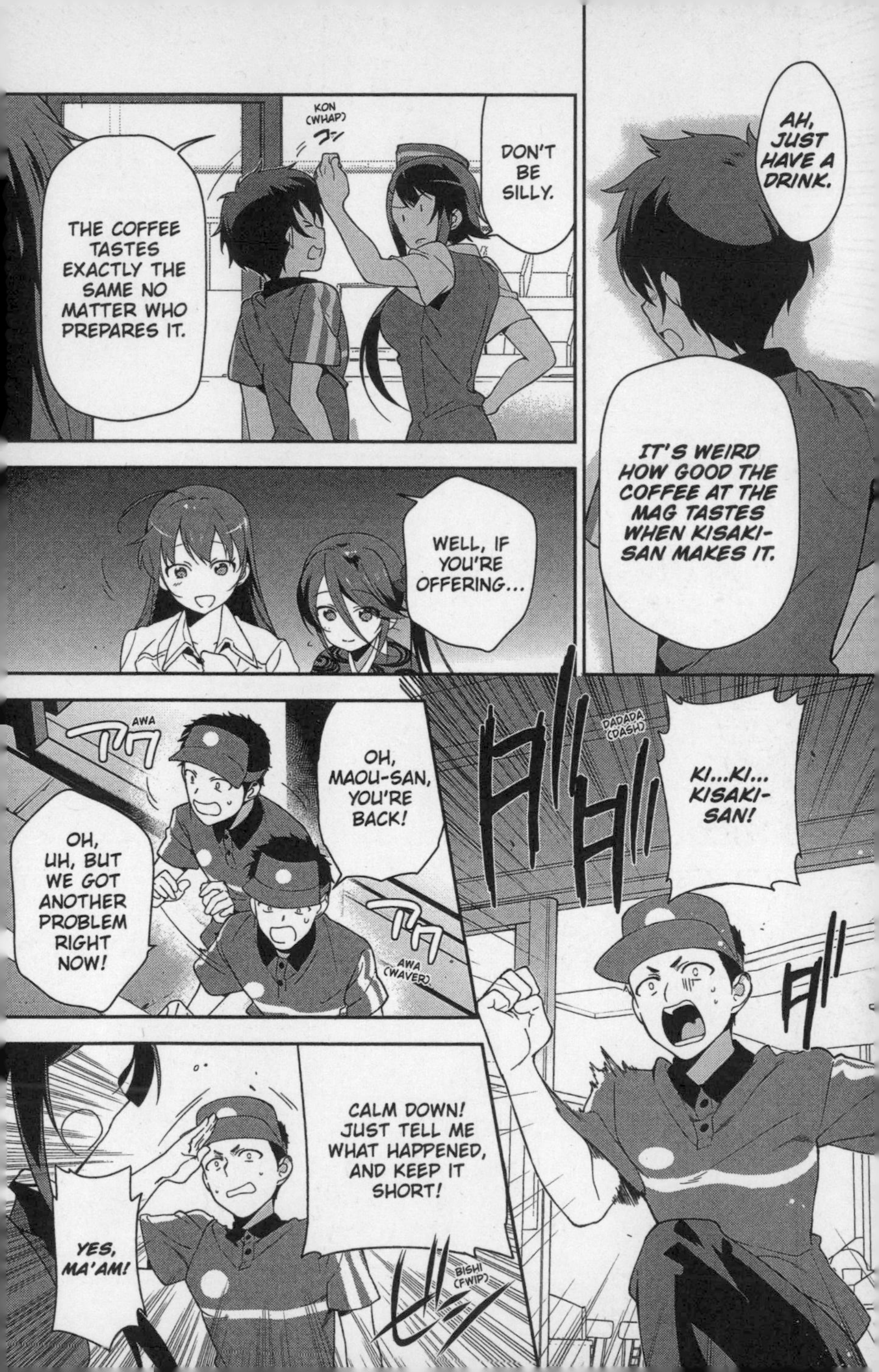
AH, JUST HAVE A DRINK.
IT'S WEIRD HOW GOOD THE COFFEE AT THE MAG TASTES WHEN KISAKI-SAN MAKES IT.
KON (WHAP)
DON'T BE SILLY.
THE COFFEE TASTES EXACTLY THE SAME NO MATTER WHO PREPARES IT.
WELL, IF YOU'RE OFFERING...
DADADA (DASH)
KI...KI... KISAKI-SAN!
AWA
OH, MAOU-SAN, YOU'RE BACK!
OH, UH, BUT WE GOT ANOTHER PROBLEM RIGHT NOW!
AWA (WAVER)
CALM DOWN! JUST TELL ME WHAT HAPPENED, AND KEEP IT SHORT!
YES, MA'AM!
BISHI (FWIP)

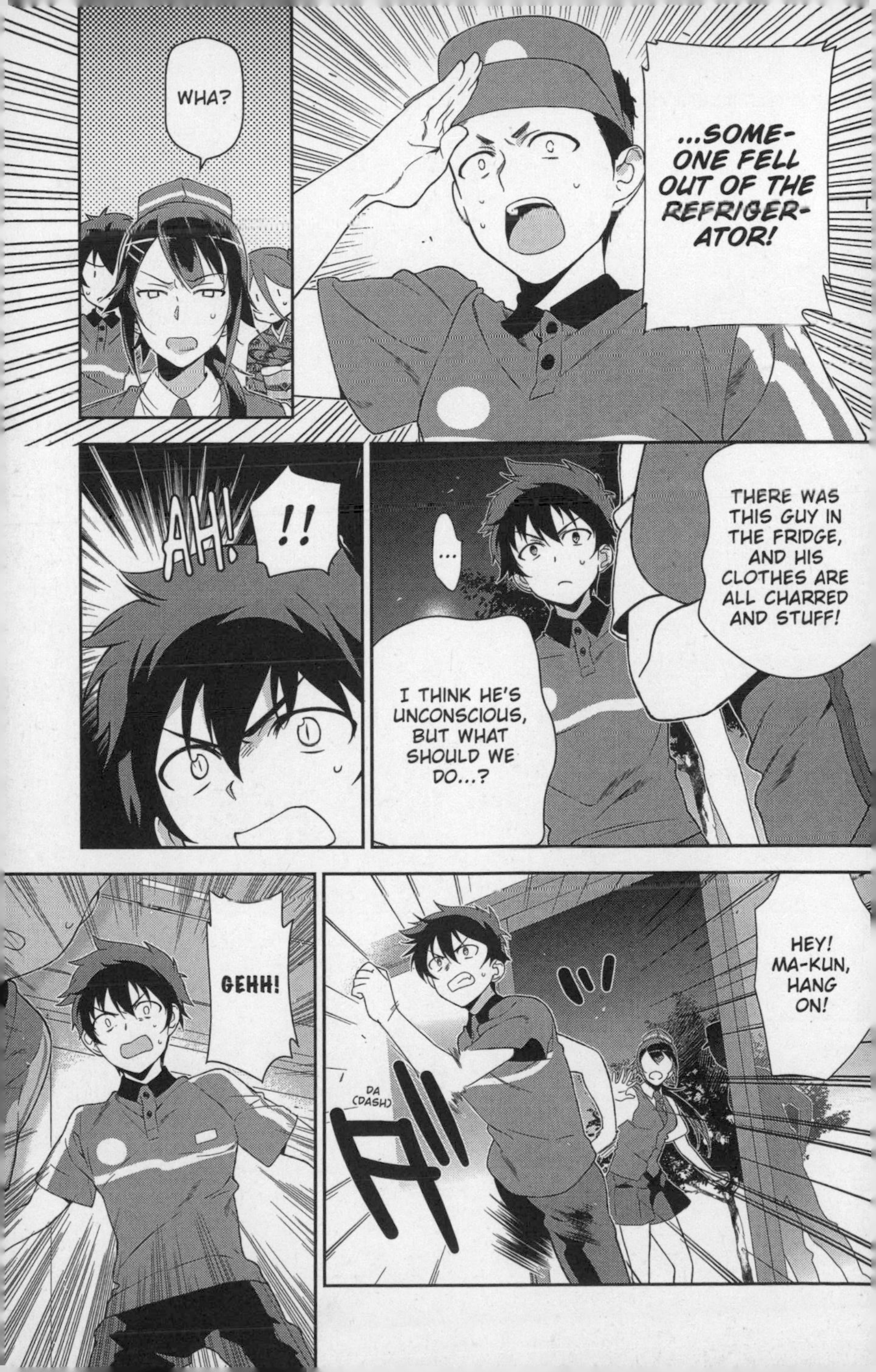
...SOME-ONE FELL OUT OF THE REFRIGER-ATOR!
WHA?
THERE WAS THIS GUY IN THE FRIDGE, AND HIS CLOTHES ARE ALL CHARRED AND STUFF!
...
I THINK HE'S UNCONSCIOUS, BUT WHAT SHOULD WE DO...?
!!
AH!
HEY! MA-KUN, HANG ON!
DA (DASH)
GEHH!

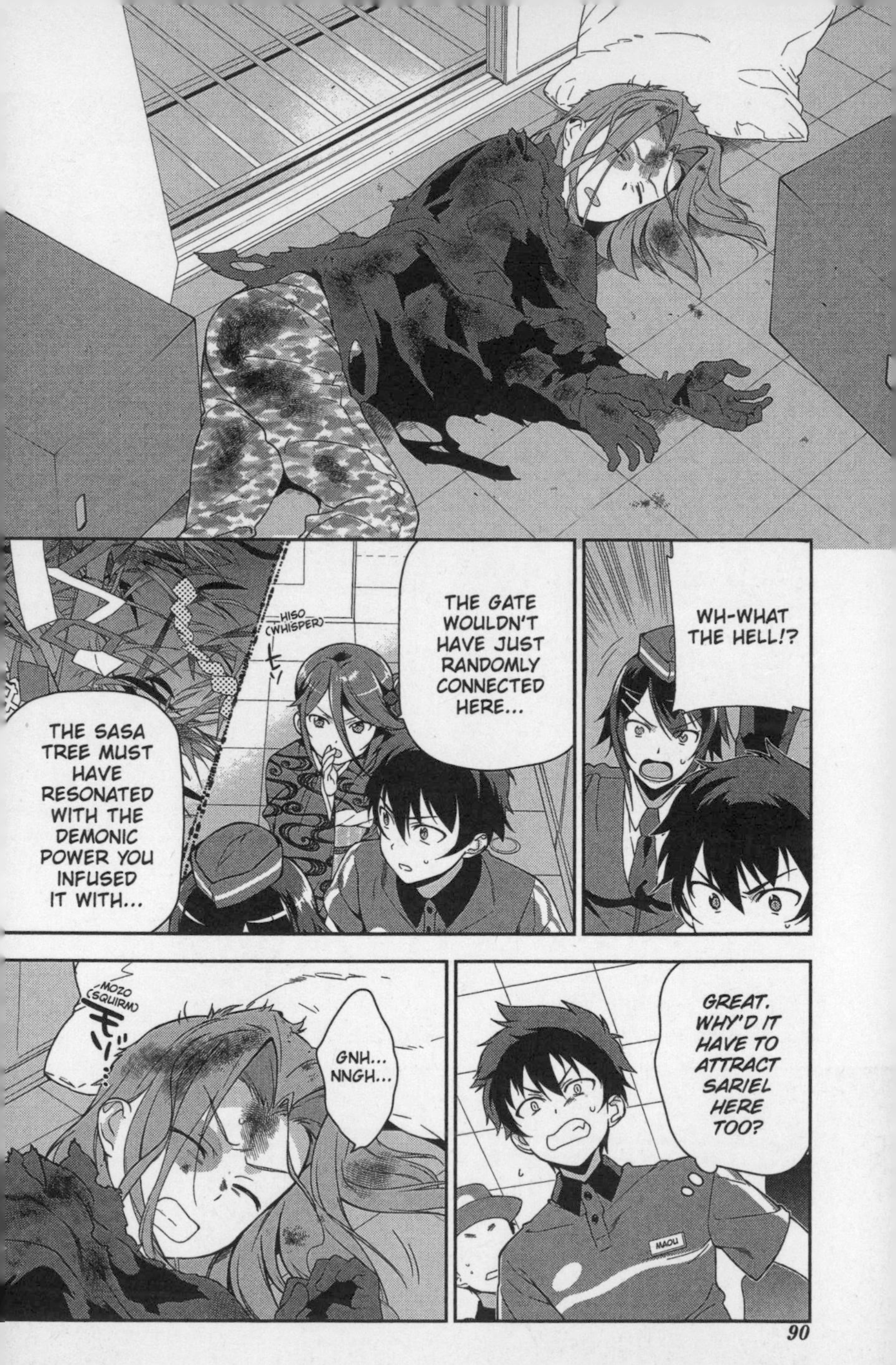
WH-WHAT THE HELL!?
THE GATE WOULDN'T HAVE JUST RANDOMLY CONNECTED HERE...
HISO (WHISPER)
THE SASA TREE MUST HAVE RESONATED WITH THE DEMONIC POWER YOU INFUSED IT WITH...
GREAT. WHY'D IT HAVE TO ATTRACT SARIEL HERE TOO?
MAOU
GNH... NNGH...
MOZO (SQUIRM)

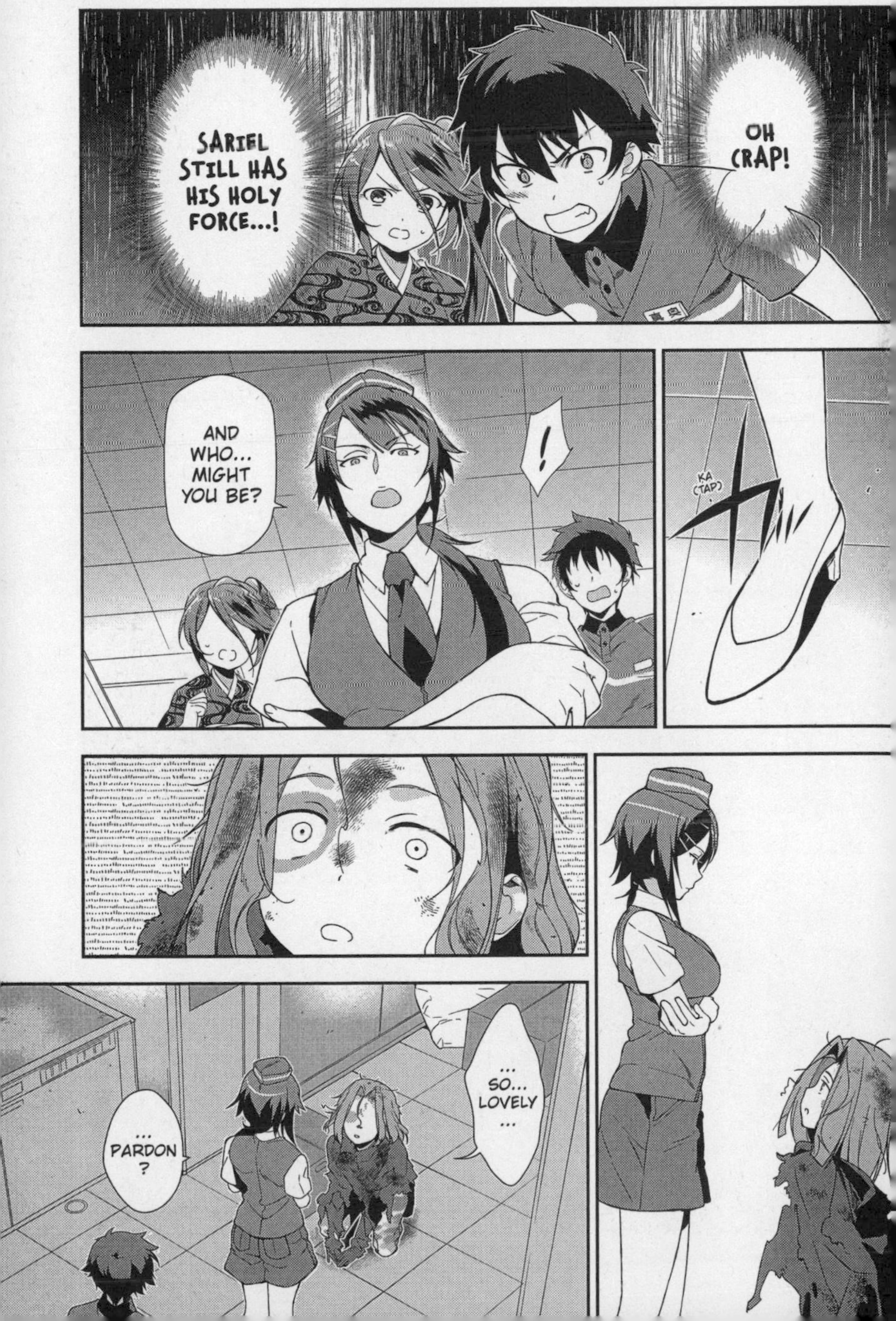
OH CRAP!
SARIEL STILL HAS HIS HOLY FORCE...!
KA (TAP)
!
AND WHO... MIGHT YOU BE?
... SO... LOVELY ...
... PARDON ?

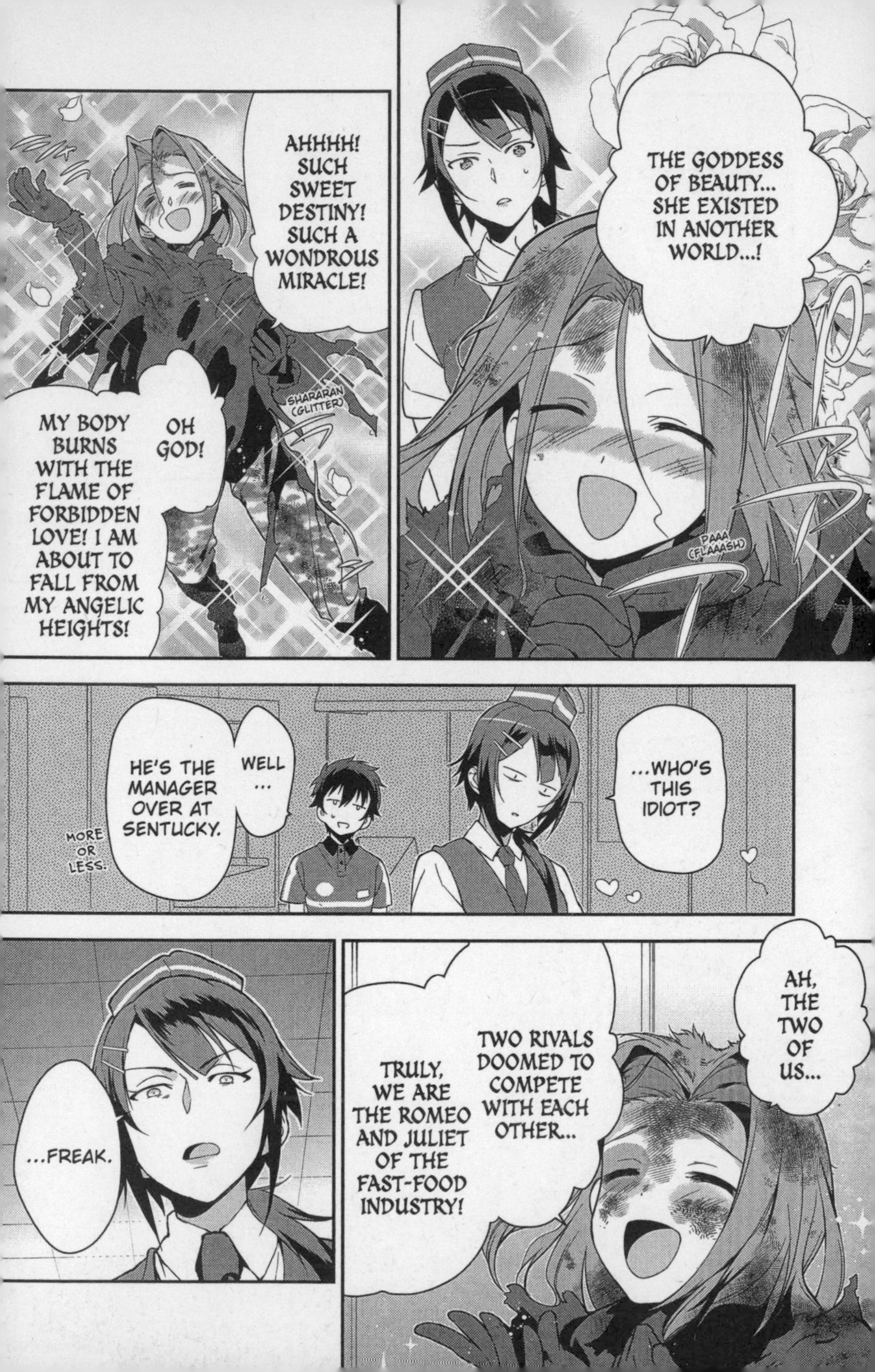
THE GODDESS OF BEAUTY... SHE EXISTED IN ANOTHER WORLD...!
PAAA (FLAAASH)
AHHHH! SUCH SWEET DESTINY! SUCH A WONDROUS MIRACLE!
SHARARAN (GLITTER)
OH GOD!
MY BODY BURNS WITH THE FLAME OF FORBIDDEN LOVE! I AM ABOUT TO FALL FROM MY ANGELIC HEIGHTS!
...WHO'S THIS IDIOT?
WELL...
HE'S THE MANAGER OVER AT SENTUCKY.
MORE OR LESS.
AH, THE TWO OF US...
TWO RIVALS DOOMED TO COMPETE WITH EACH OTHER...
TRULY, WE ARE THE ROMEO AND JULIET OF THE FAST-FOOD INDUSTRY!
...FREAK.

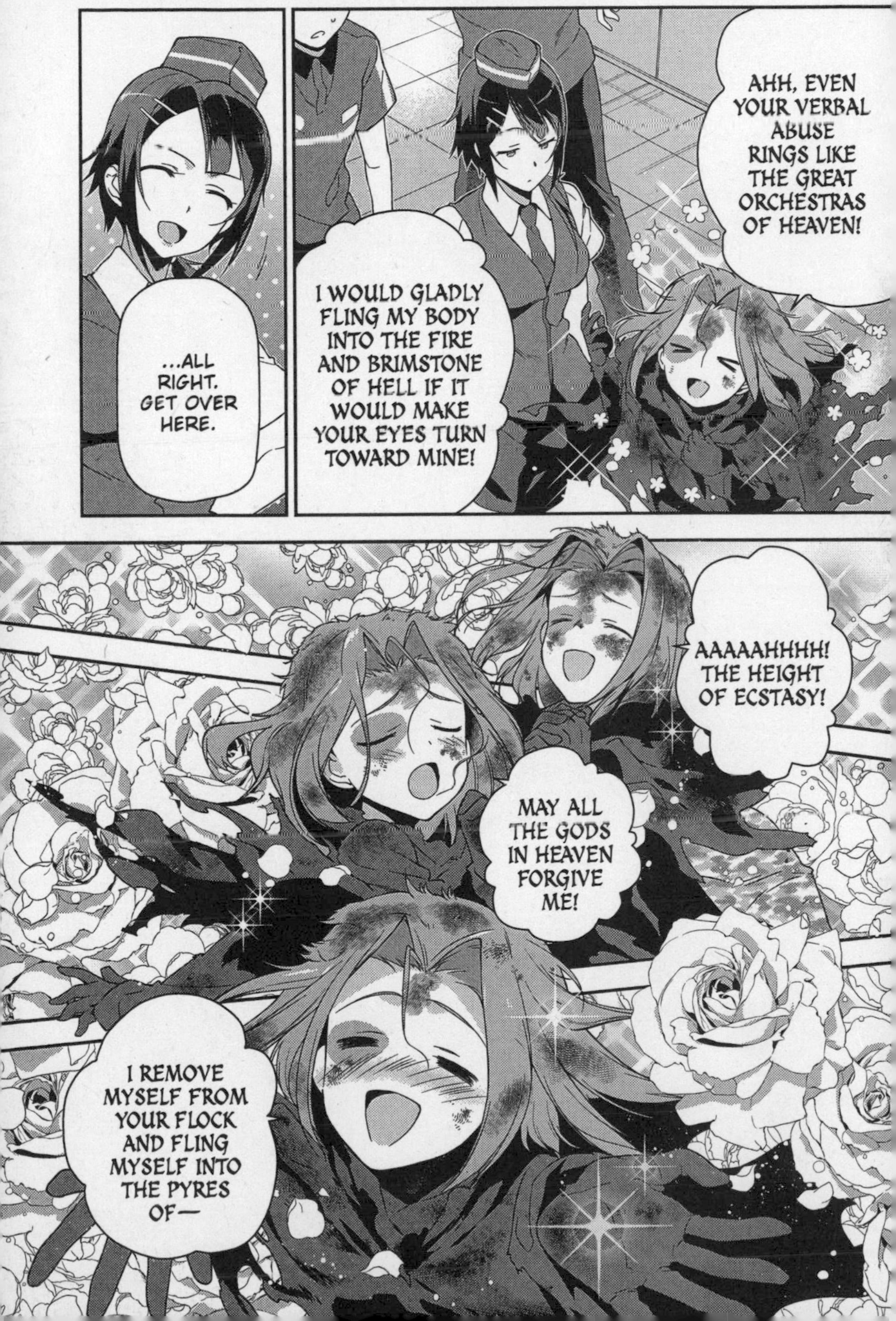
AHH, EVEN YOUR VERBAL ABUSE RINGS LIKE THE GREAT ORCHESTRAS OF HEAVEN!
I WOULD GLADLY FLING MY BODY INTO THE FIRE AND BRIMSTONE OF HELL IF IT WOULD MAKE YOUR EYES TURN TOWARD MINE!
...ALL RIGHT. GET OVER HERE.
AAAAAHHHH! THE HEIGHT OF ECSTASY!
MAY ALL THE GODS IN HEAVEN FORGIVE ME!
I REMOVE MYSELF FROM YOUR FLOCK AND FLING MYSELF INTO THE PYRES OF—

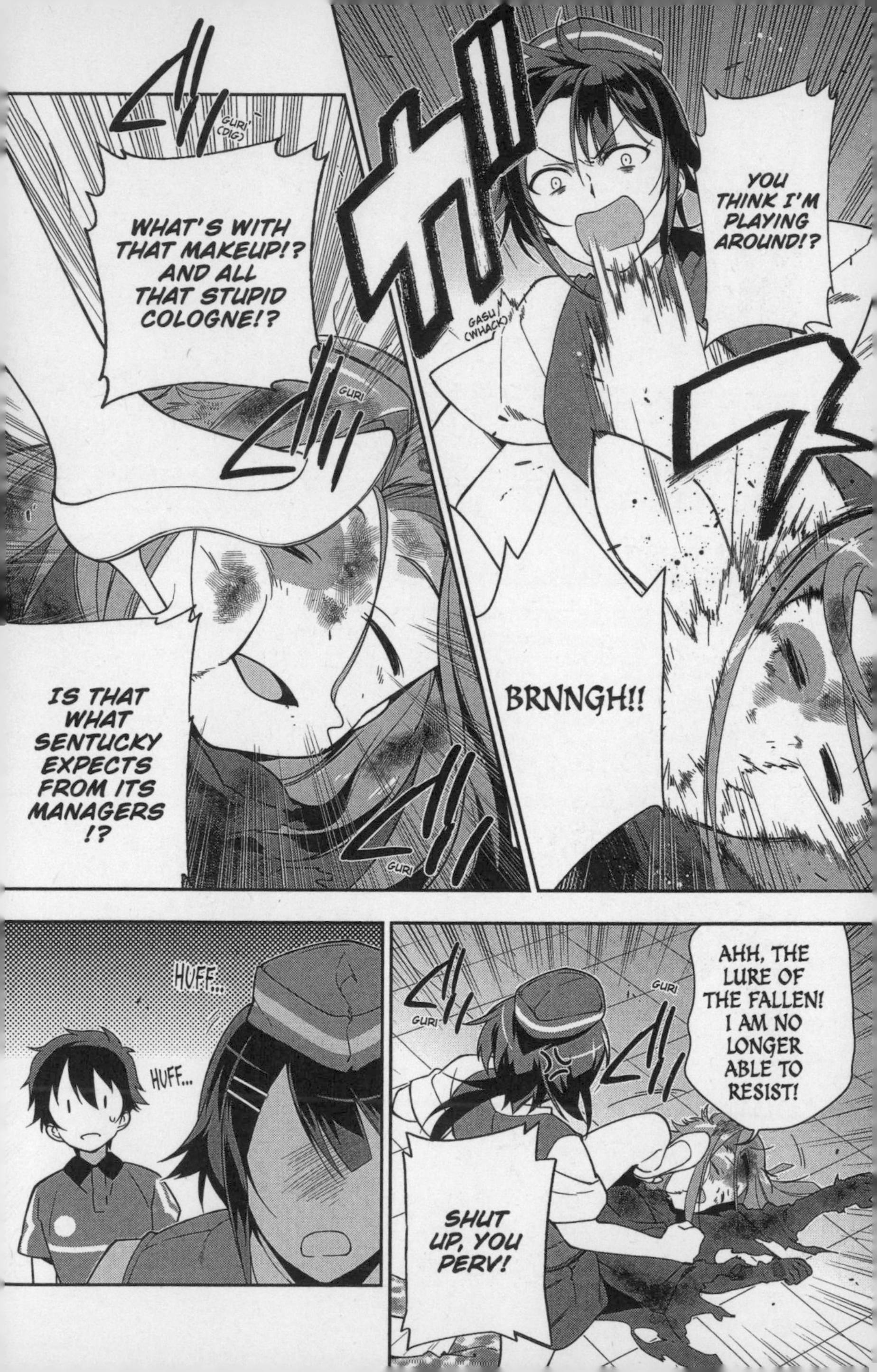
YOU THINK I'M PLAYING AROUND!?
GASU (WHACK)
BRNNGH!!
GURI' (DIG)
WHAT'S WITH THAT MAKEUP!? AND ALL THAT STUPID COLOGNE!?
GURI
IS THAT WHAT SENTUCKY EXPECTS FROM ITS MANAGERS!?
GURI
GURI
GURI
AHH, THE LURE OF THE FALLEN! I AM NO LONGER ABLE TO RESIST!
SHUT UP, YOU PERV!
HUFF...
HUFF...

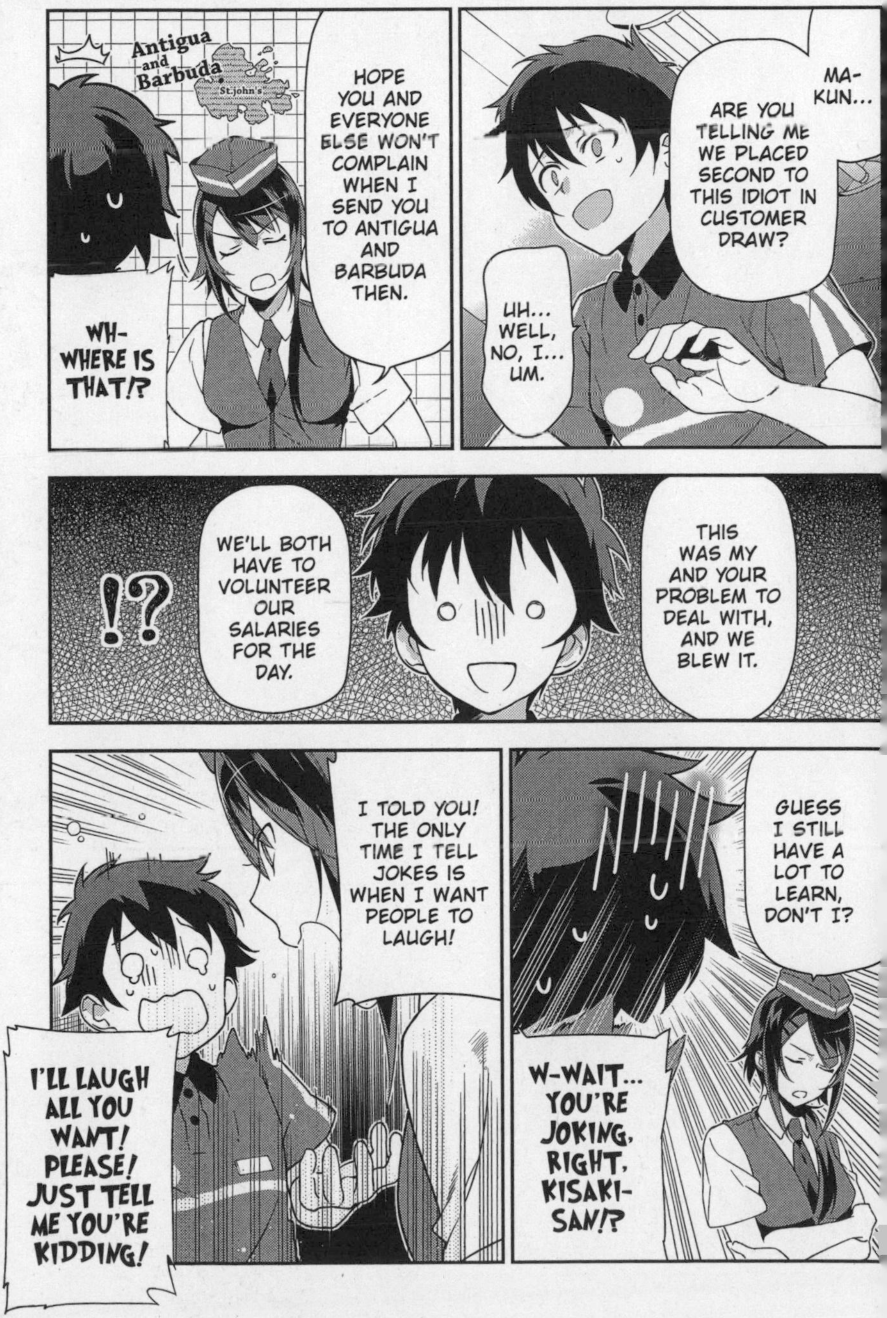
MA-KUN...
ARE YOU TELLING ME WE PLACED SECOND TO THIS IDIOT IN CUSTOMER DRAW?
UH... WELL, NO, I... UM.
Antigua and Barbuda
St.john's
HOPE YOU AND EVERYONE ELSE WON'T COMPLAIN WHEN I SEND YOU TO ANTIGUA AND BARBUDA THEN.
WH- WHERE IS THAT!?
THIS WAS MY AND YOUR PROBLEM TO DEAL WITH, AND WE BLEW IT.
WE'LL BOTH HAVE TO VOLUNTEER OUR SALARIES FOR THE DAY.
!?
GUESS I STILL HAVE A LOT TO LEARN, DON'T I?
W-WAIT... YOU'RE JOKING, RIGHT, KISAKI-SAN!?
I TOLD YOU! THE ONLY TIME I TELL JOKES IS WHEN I WANT PEOPLE TO LAUGH!
I'LL LAUGH ALL YOU WANT! PLEASE! JUST TELL ME YOU'RE KIDDING!

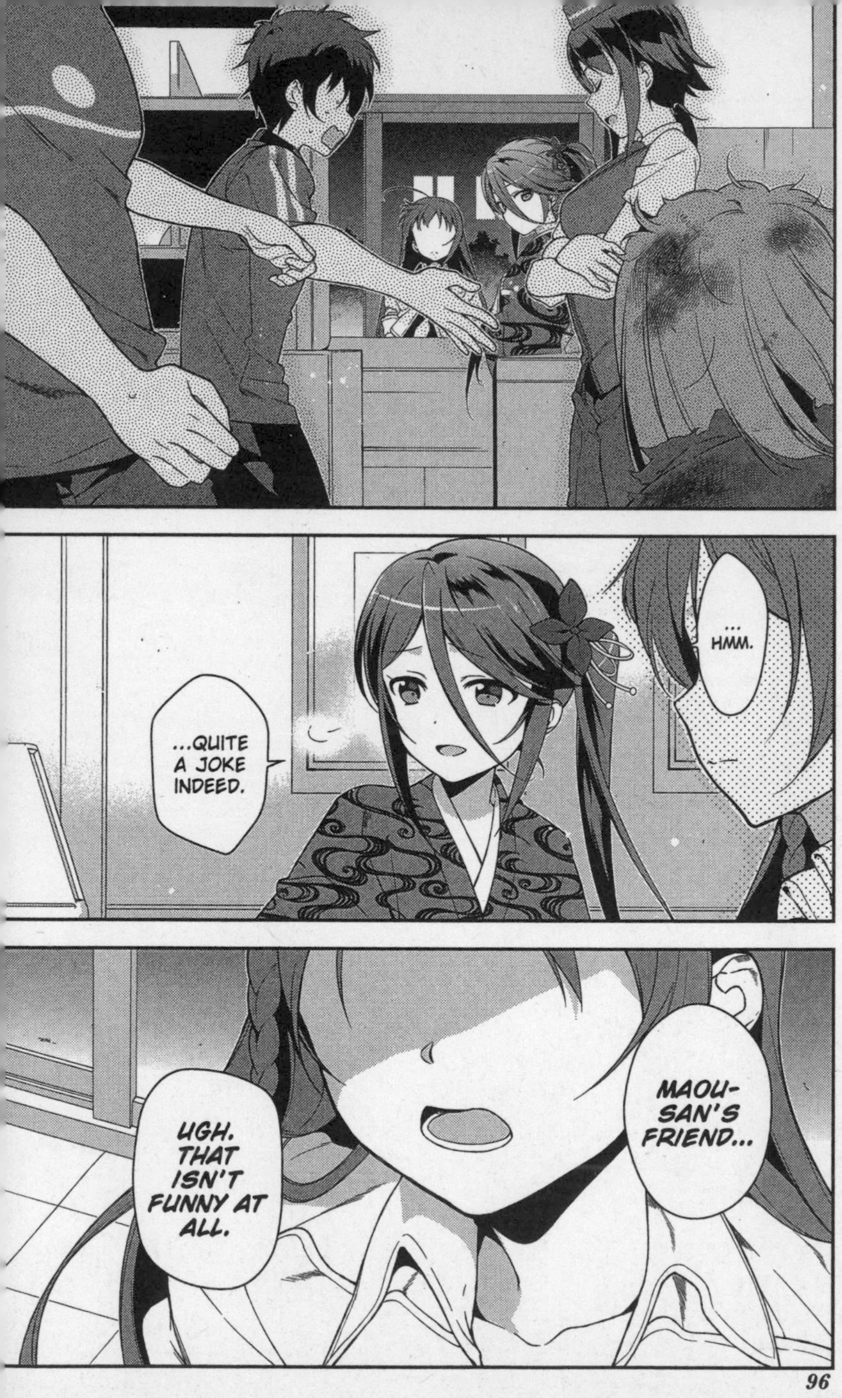

...HMM.
...QUITE A JOKE INDEED.
MAOU-SAN'S FRIEND...
UGH. THAT ISN'T FUNNY AT ALL.

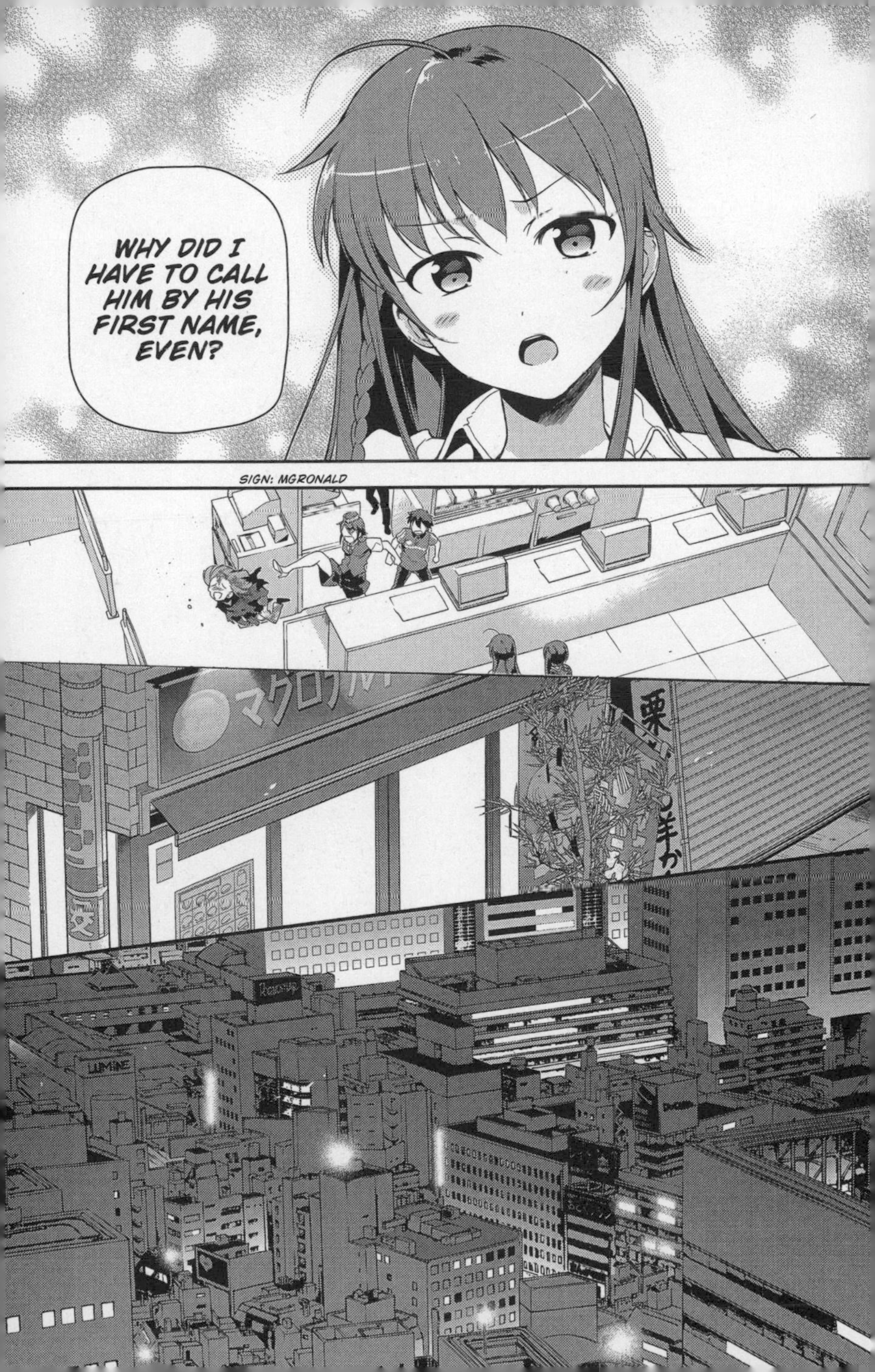
WHY DID I HAVE TO CALL HIM BY HIS FIRST NAME, EVEN?
SIGN: MGRONALD

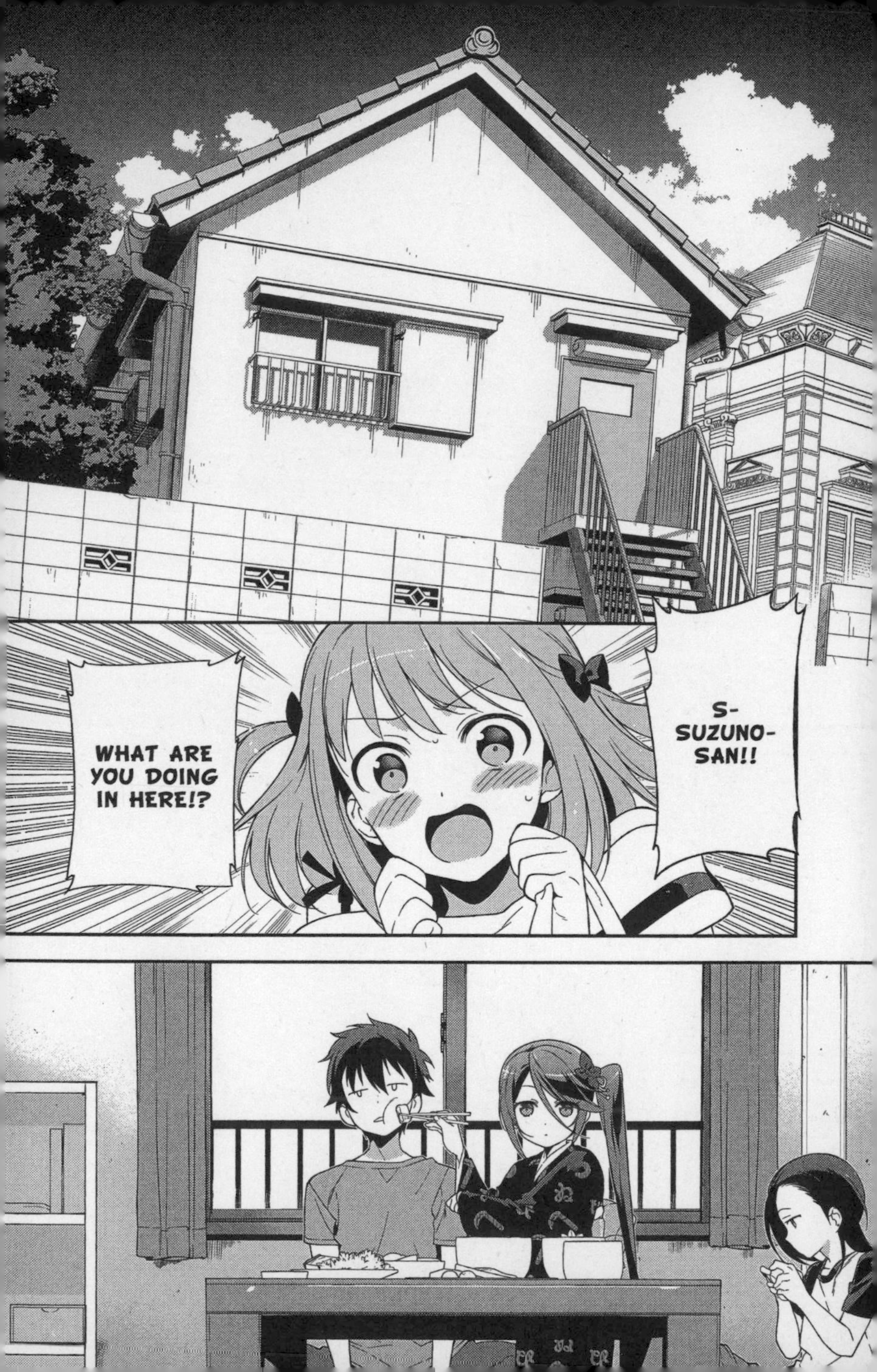
S-SUZUNO-SAN!!
WHAT ARE YOU DOING IN HERE!?

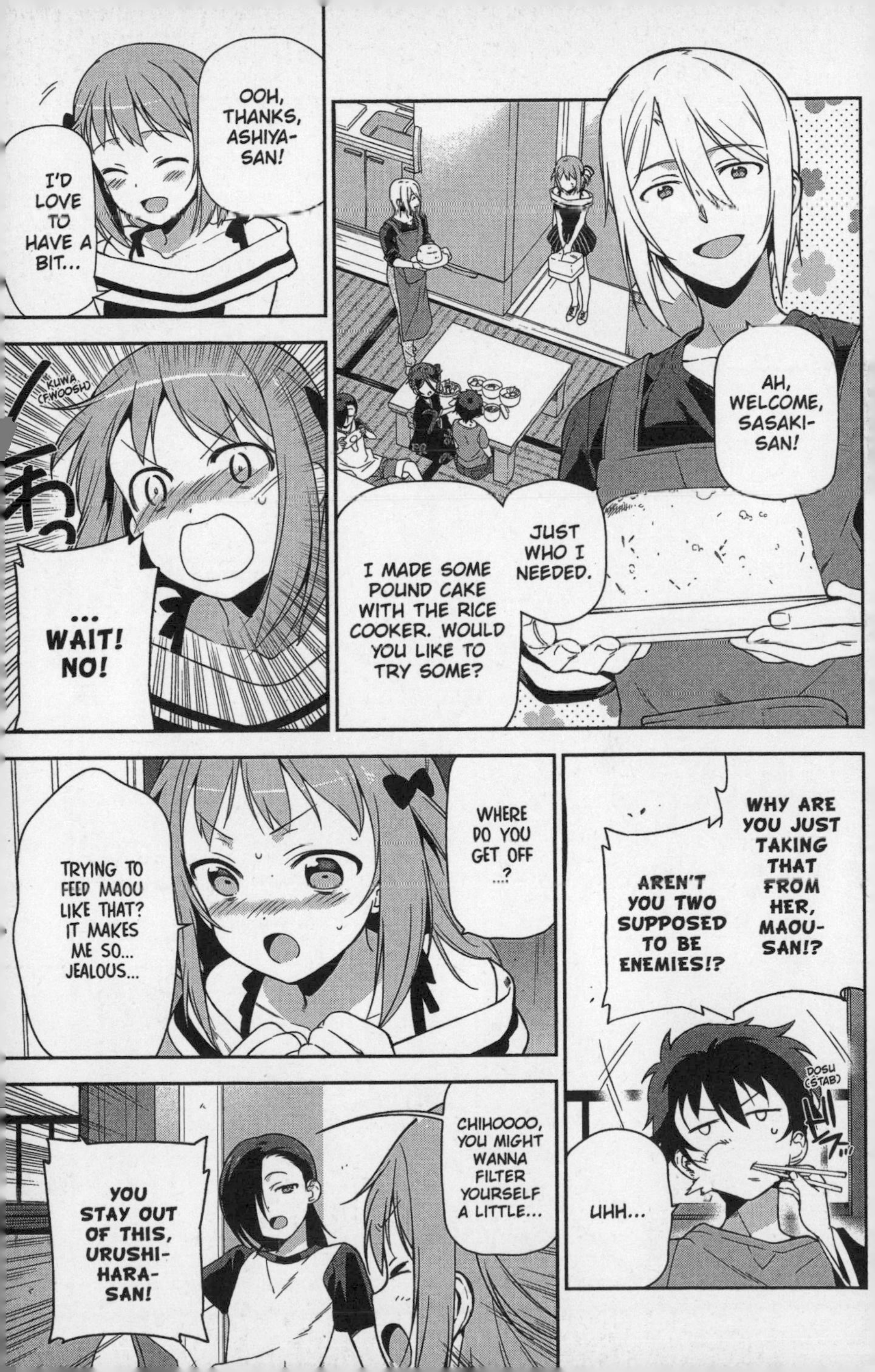
AH, WELCOME, SASAKI-SAN!
JUST WHO I NEEDED.
I MADE SOME POUND CAKE WITH THE RICE COOKER. WOULD YOU LIKE TO TRY SOME?
OOH, THANKS, ASHIYA-SAN!
I'D LOVE TO HAVE A BIT...
KUWA (FWOOSH)
...WAIT! NO!
WHY ARE YOU JUST TAKING THAT FROM HER, MAOU-SAN!?
AREN'T YOU TWO SUPPOSED TO BE ENEMIES!?
DOSU (STAB)
UHH...
WHERE DO YOU GET OFF ...?
TRYING TO FEED MAOU LIKE THAT? IT MAKES ME SO... JEALOUS...
CHIHOOOO, YOU MIGHT WANNA FILTER YOURSELF A LITTLE...
YOU STAY OUT OF THIS, URUSHIHARA-SAN!

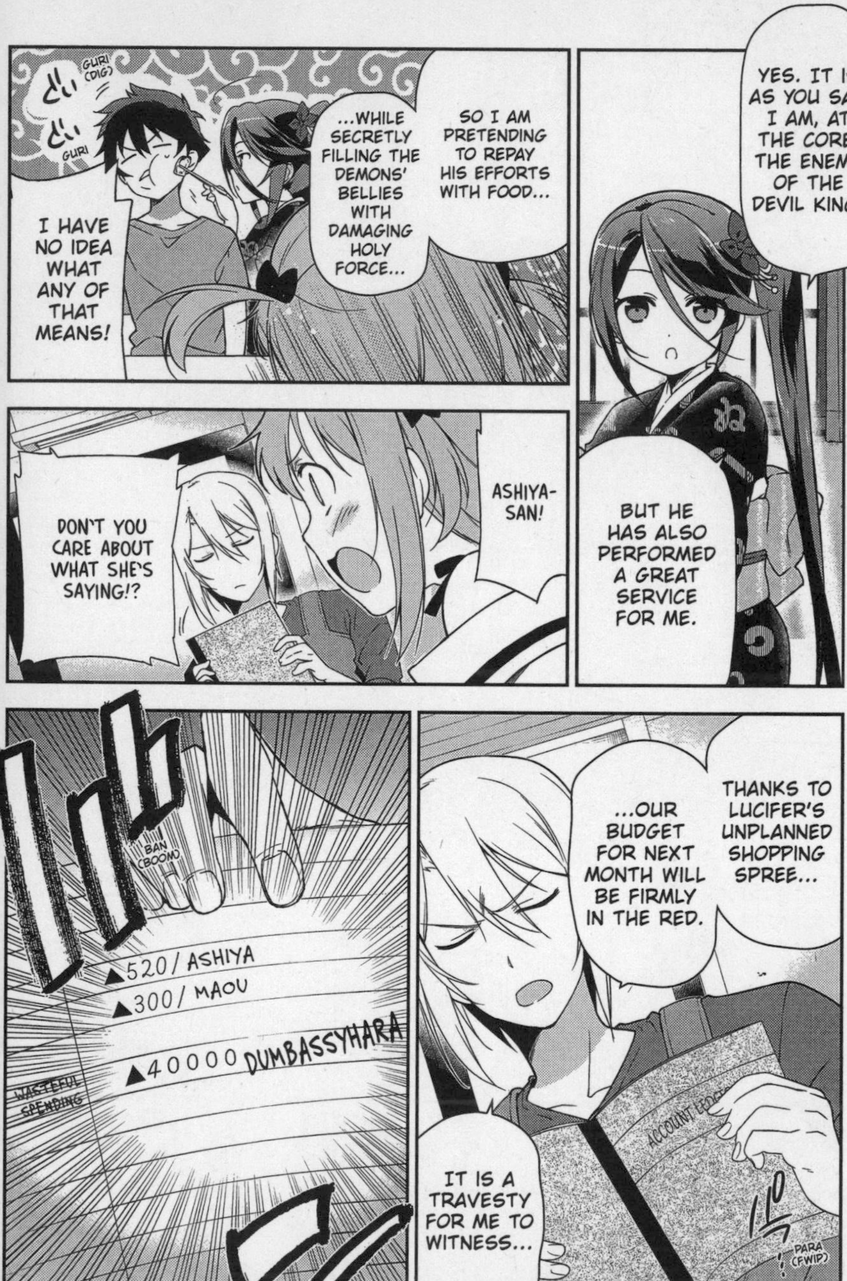
YES. IT IS AS YOU SAY. I AM, AT THE CORE, THE ENEMY OF THE DEVIL KING.
BUT HE HAS ALSO PERFORMED A GREAT SERVICE FOR ME.
SO I AM PRETENDING TO REPAY HIS EFFORTS WITH FOOD...
...WHILE SECRETLY FILLING THE DEMONS' BELLIES WITH DAMAGING HOLY FORCE...
GURI (DIG)
GURI
I HAVE NO IDEA WHAT ANY OF THAT MEANS!
ASHIYA-SAN!
DON'T YOU CARE ABOUT WHAT SHE'S SAYING!?
THANKS TO LUCIFER'S UNPLANNED SHOPPING SPREE...
...OUR BUDGET FOR NEXT MONTH WILL BE FIRMLY IN THE RED.
ACCOUNT LEDGE
IT IS A TRAVESTY FOR ME TO WITNESS...
PARA (FWIP)
BAN (BOOM)
▲520/ ASHIYA
▲300/ MAOU
▲40000 DUMBASSYHARA
WASTEFUL SPENDING

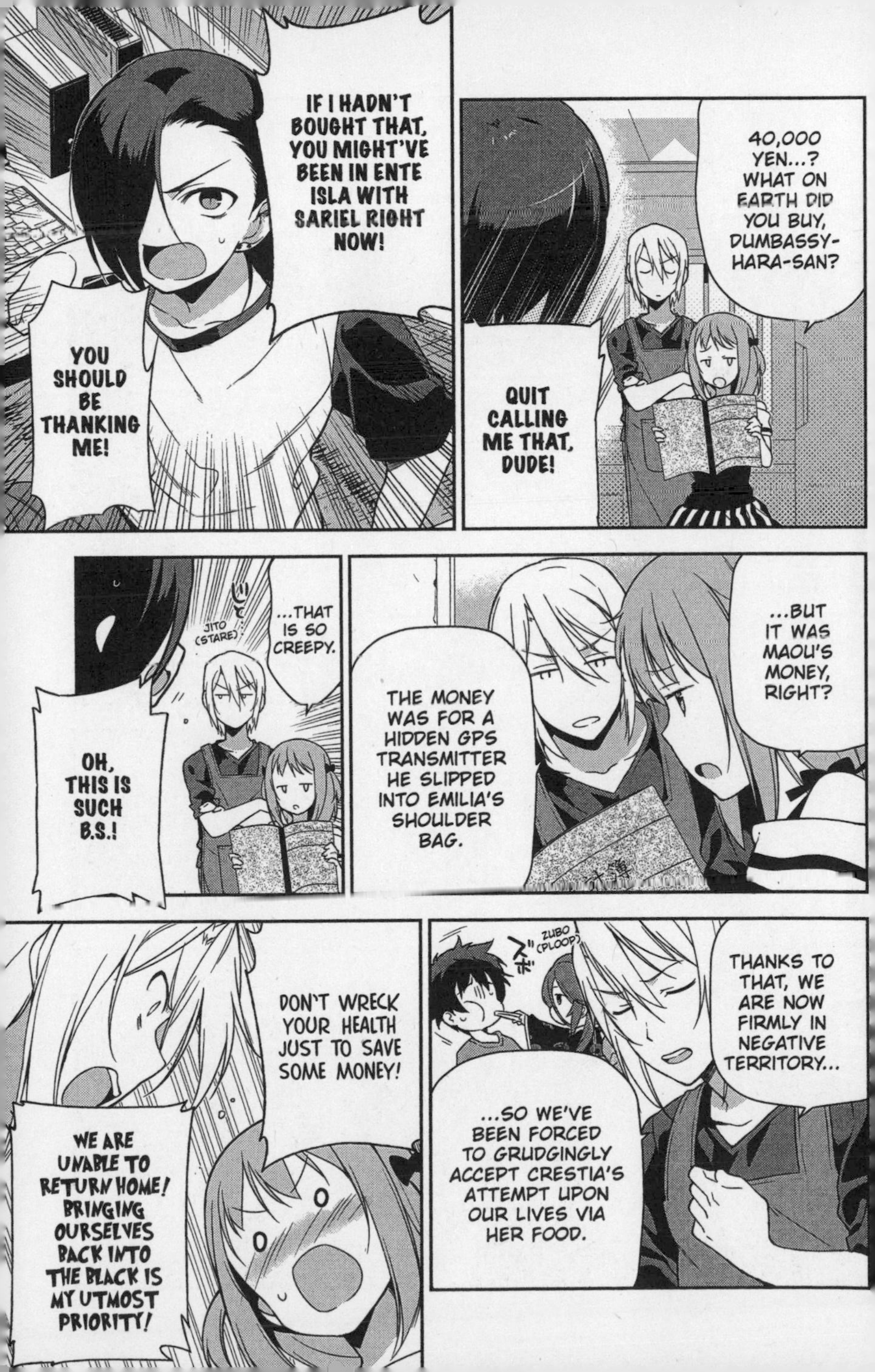
40,000 YEN...? WHAT ON EARTH DID YOU BUY, DUMBASSY-HARA-SAN?
QUIT CALLING ME THAT, DUDE!
IF I HADN'T BOUGHT THAT, YOU MIGHT'VE BEEN IN ENTE ISLA WITH SARIEL RIGHT NOW!
YOU SHOULD BE THANKING ME!
...BUT IT WAS MAOU'S MONEY, RIGHT?
THE MONEY WAS FOR A HIDDEN GPS TRANSMITTER HE SLIPPED INTO EMILIA'S SHOULDER BAG.
...THAT IS SO CREEPY.
JITO (STARE)
OH, THIS IS SUCH B.S.!
THANKS TO THAT, WE ARE NOW FIRMLY IN NEGATIVE TERRITORY...
ズボ
ZUBO (PLOOP)
...SO WE'VE BEEN FORCED TO GRUDGINGLY ACCEPT CRESTIA'S ATTEMPT UPON OUR LIVES VIA HER FOOD.
DON'T WRECK YOUR HEALTH JUST TO SAVE SOME MONEY!
WE ARE UNABLE TO RETURN HOME! BRINGING OURSELVES BACK INTO THE BLACK IS MY UTMOST PRIORITY!

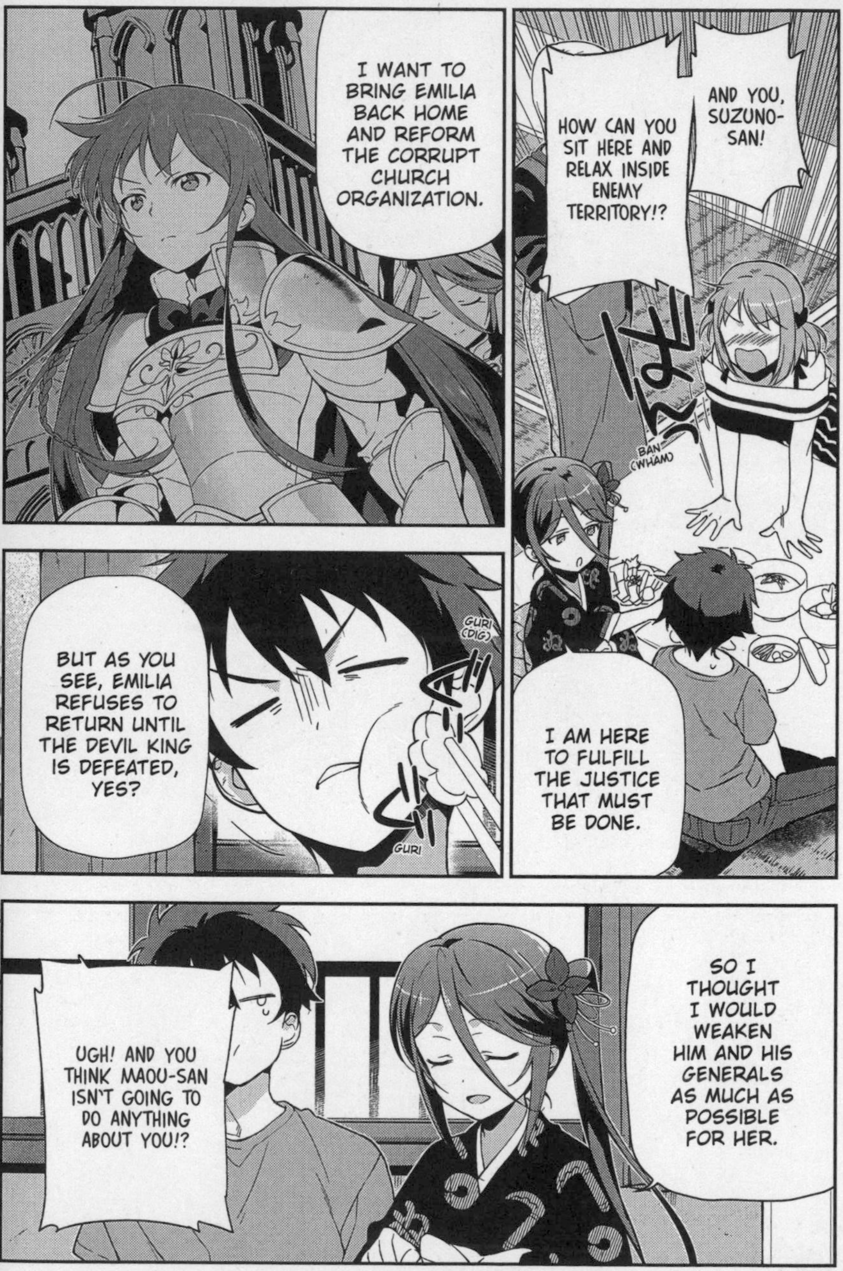
AND YOU, SUZUNO-SAN!
HOW CAN YOU SIT HERE AND RELAX INSIDE ENEMY TERRITORY!?
BAN (WHAM)
I AM HERE TO FULFILL THE JUSTICE THAT MUST BE DONE.
I WANT TO BRING EMILIA BACK HOME AND REFORM THE CORRUPT CHURCH ORGANIZATION.
GURI (DIG)
BUT AS YOU SEE, EMILIA REFUSES TO RETURN UNTIL THE DEVIL KING IS DEFEATED, YES?
GURI
SO I THOUGHT I WOULD WEAKEN HIM AND HIS GENERALS AS MUCH AS POSSIBLE FOR HER.
UGH! AND YOU THINK MAOU-SAN ISN'T GOING TO DO ANYTHING ABOUT YOU!?

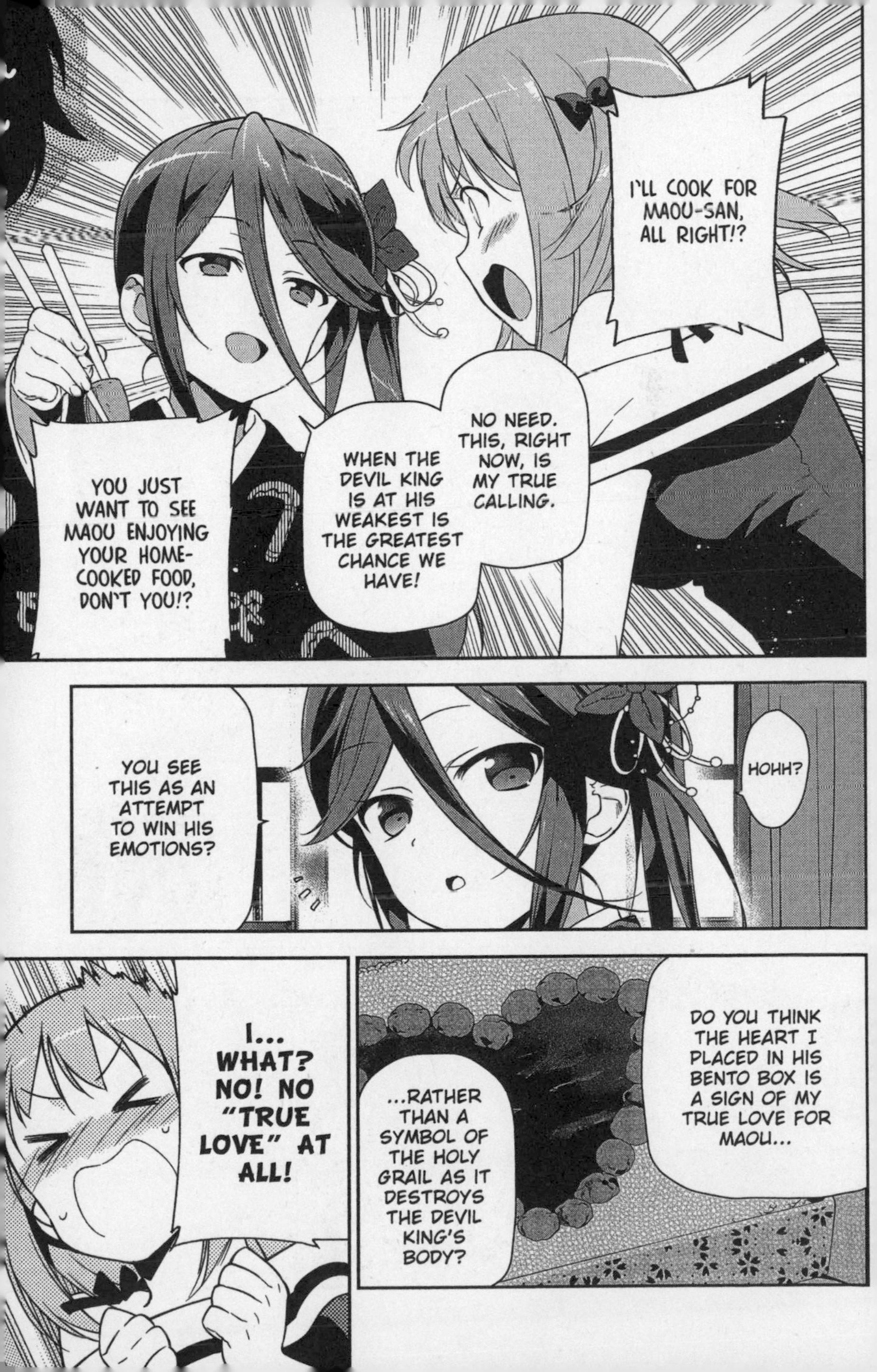
I'LL COOK FOR MAOU-SAN, ALL RIGHT!?
NO NEED. THIS, RIGHT NOW, IS MY TRUE CALLING.
WHEN THE DEVIL KING IS AT HIS WEAKEST IS THE GREATEST CHANCE WE HAVE!
YOU JUST WANT TO SEE MAOU ENJOYING YOUR HOME-COOKED FOOD, DON'T YOU!?
HOHH?
YOU SEE THIS AS AN ATTEMPT TO WIN HIS EMOTIONS?
DO YOU THINK THE HEART I PLACED IN HIS BENTO BOX IS A SIGN OF MY TRUE LOVE FOR MAOU...
...RATHER THAN A SYMBOL OF THE HOLY GRAIL AS IT DESTROYS THE DEVIL KING'S BODY?
I... WHAT? NO! NO "TRUE LOVE" AT ALL!

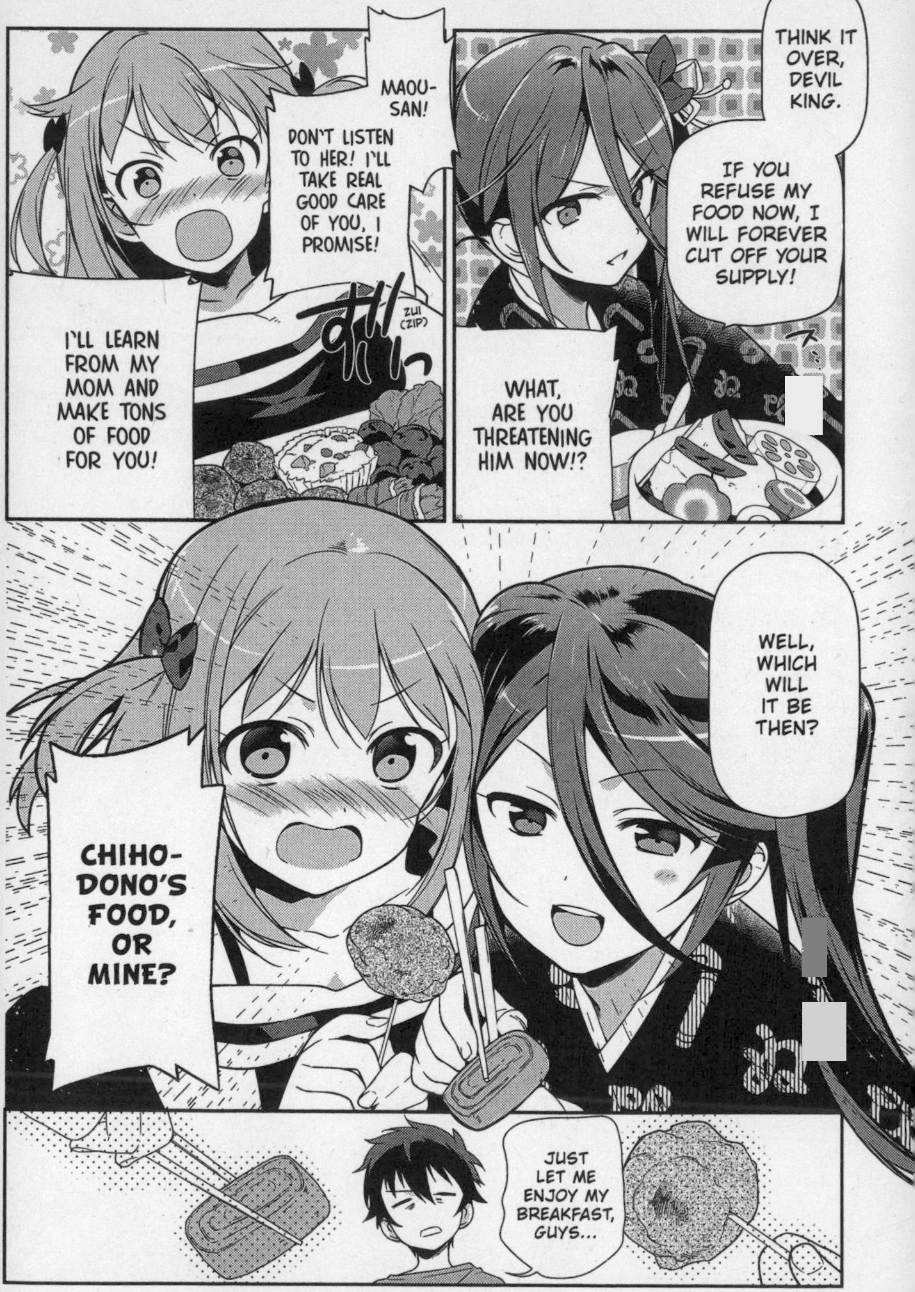
THINK IT OVER, DEVIL KING.
IF YOU REFUSE MY FOOD NOW, I WILL FOREVER CUT OFF YOUR SUPPLY!
WHAT, ARE YOU THREATENING HIM NOW!?
MAOU-SAN!
DON'T LISTEN TO HER! I'LL TAKE REAL GOOD CARE OF YOU, I PROMISE!
ZUI (ZIP)
I'LL LEARN FROM MY MOM AND MAKE TONS OF FOOD FOR YOU!
WELL, WHICH WILL IT BE THEN?
CHIHO-DONO'S FOOD, OR MINE?
JUST LET ME ENJOY MY BREAKFAST, GUYS...

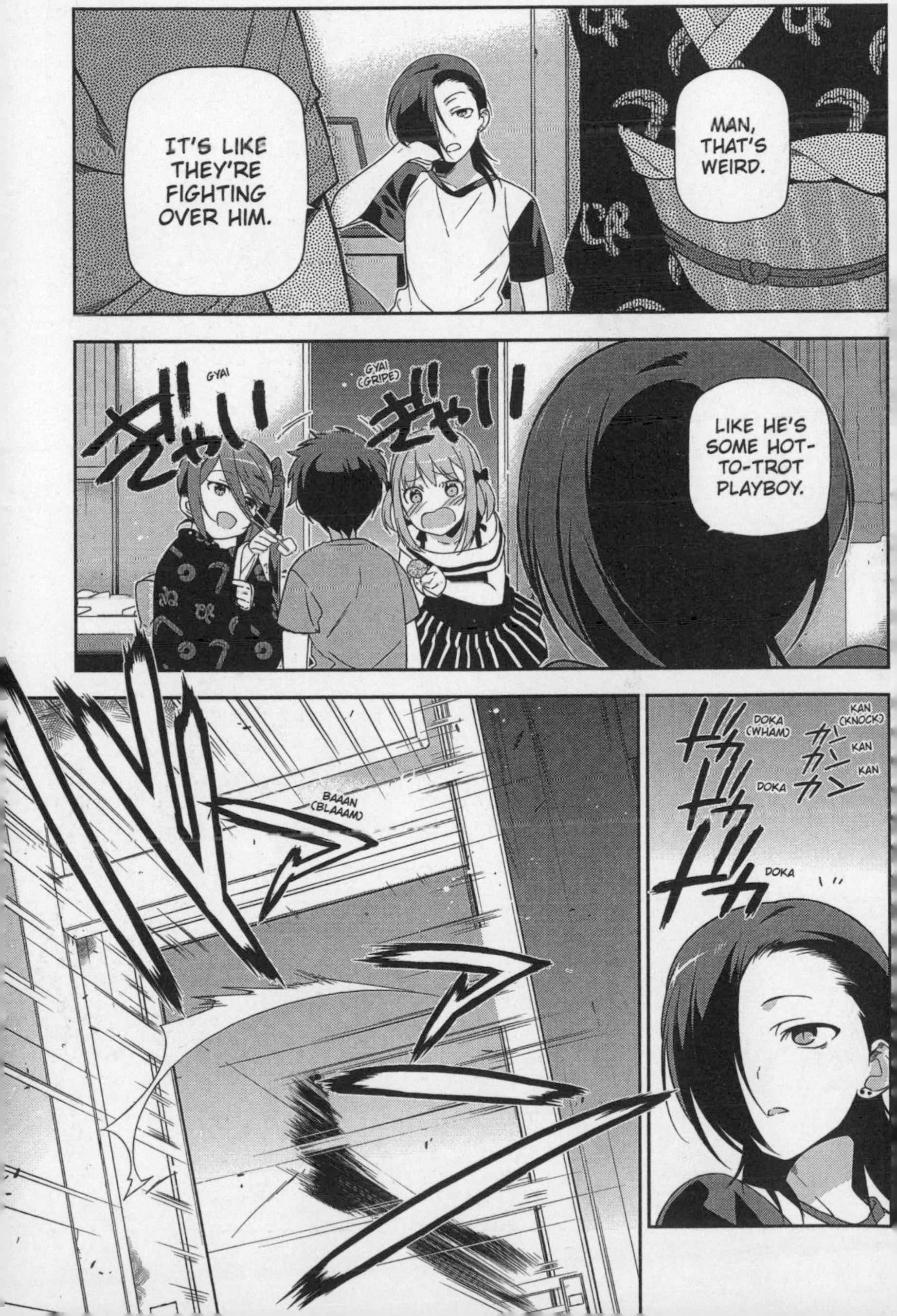
MAN, THAT'S WEIRD.
IT'S LIKE THEY'RE FIGHTING OVER HIM.
LIKE HE'S SOME HOT-TO-TROT PLAYBOY.
GYAI (GRIPE)
GYAI
KAN (KNOCK)
KAN
KAN
DOKA (WHAM)
DOKA
DOKA
BAAAN (BLAAAM)

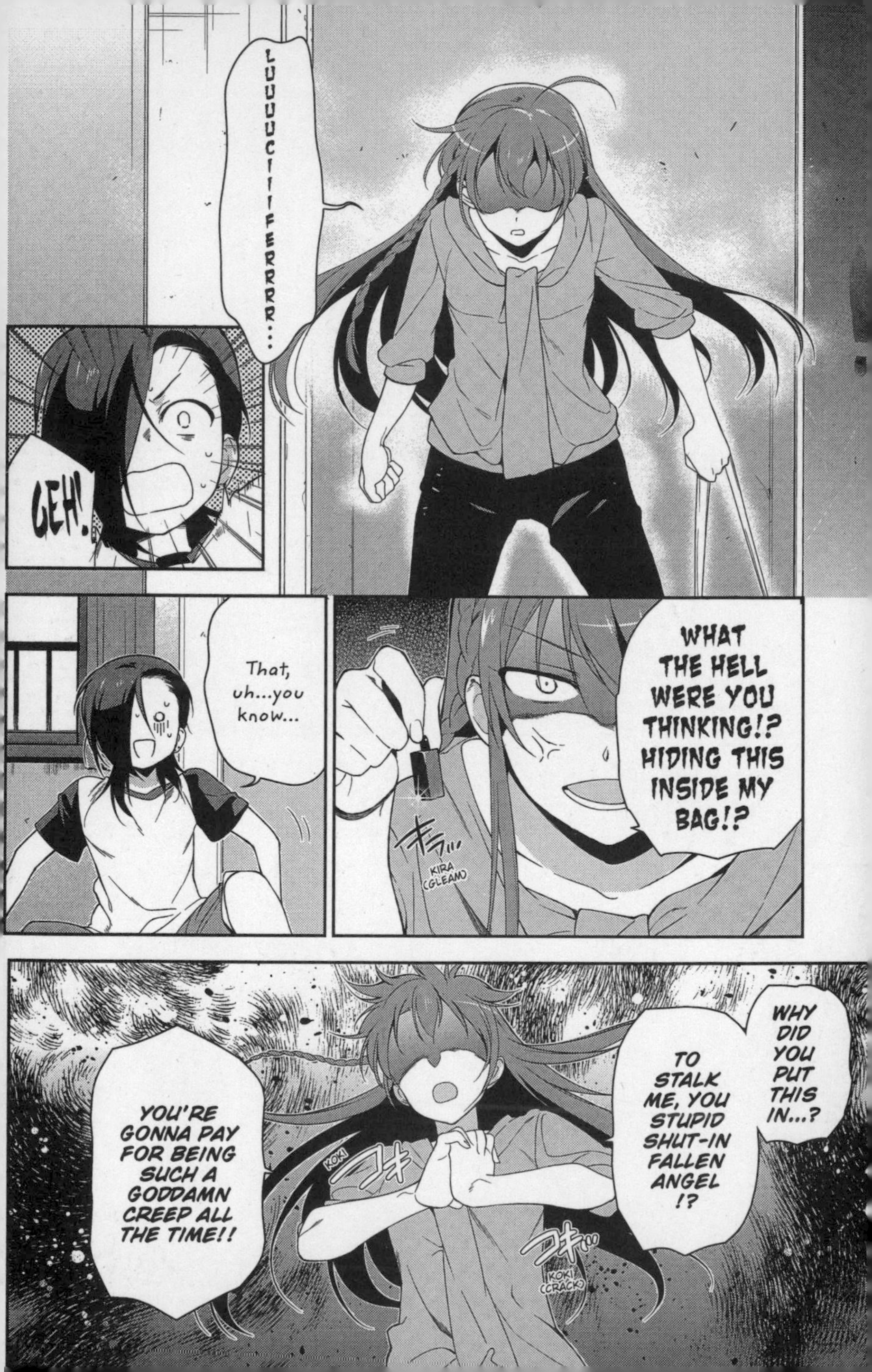
LUUUUCIIIFERRRR...
GEH!
WHAT THE HELL WERE YOU THINKING!? HIDING THIS INSIDE MY BAG!?
KIRA (GLEAM)
That, uh...you know...
WHY DID YOU PUT THIS IN...?
TO STALK ME, YOU STUPID SHUT-IN FALLEN ANGEL!?
KOKI
YOU'RE GONNA PAY FOR BEING SUCH A GODDAMN CREEP ALL THE TIME!!
KOKI (CRACK)

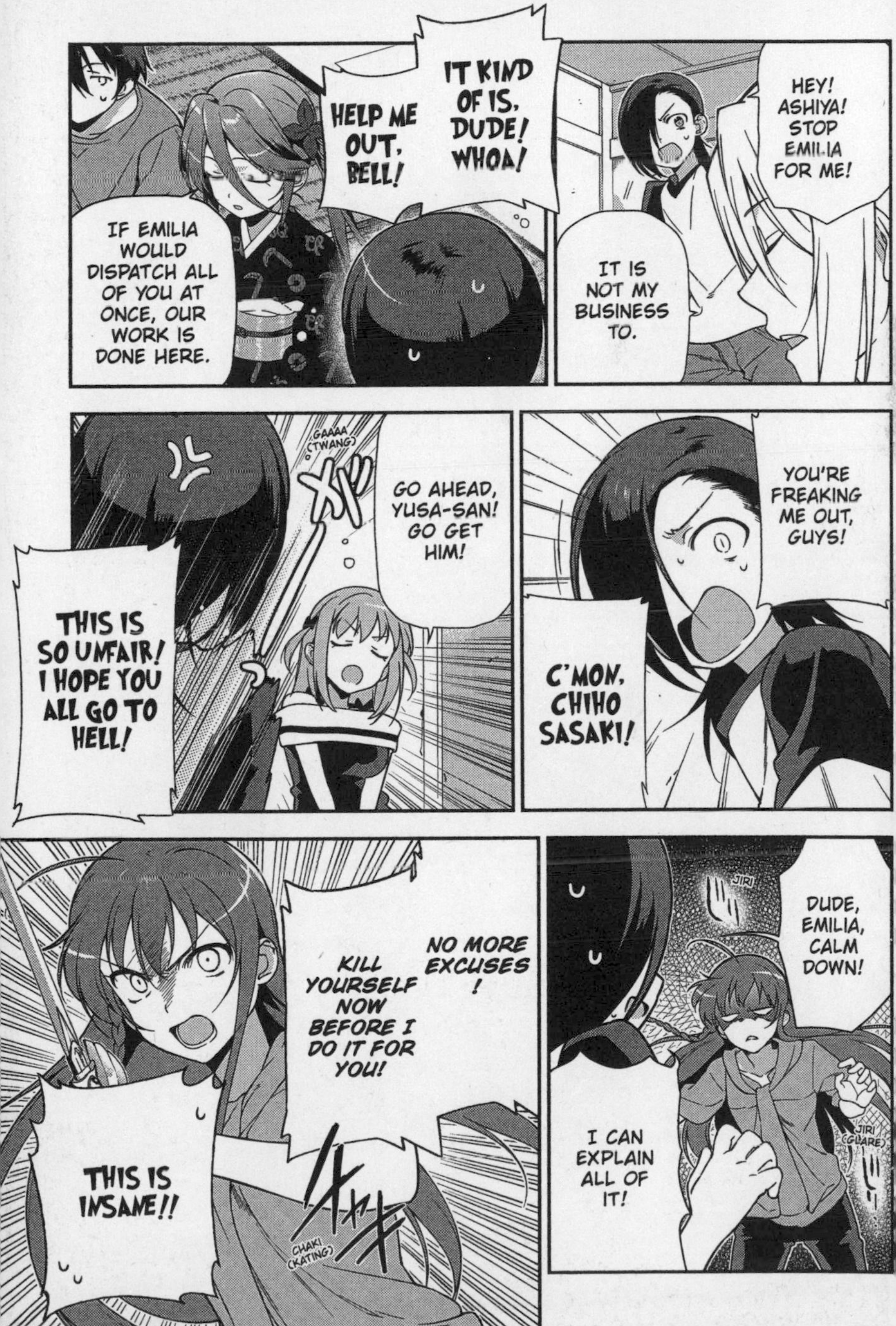
HEY! ASHIYA! STOP EMILIA FOR ME!
IT IS NOT MY BUSINESS TO.
IT KIND OF IS, DUDE! WHOA!
HELP ME OUT, BELL!
IF EMILIA WOULD DISPATCH ALL OF YOU AT ONCE, OUR WORK IS DONE HERE.
YOU'RE FREAKING ME OUT, GUYS!
C'MON, CHIHO SASAKI!
GAAAA (TWANG)
GO AHEAD, YUSA-SAN! GO GET HIM!
THIS IS SO UNFAIR! I HOPE YOU ALL GO TO HELL!
JIRI
DUDE, EMILIA, CALM DOWN!
JIRI (GLARE)
I CAN EXPLAIN ALL OF IT!
NO MORE EXCUSES!
KILL YOURSELF NOW BEFORE I DO IT FOR YOU!
CHAKI (KATING)
THIS IS INSANE!!

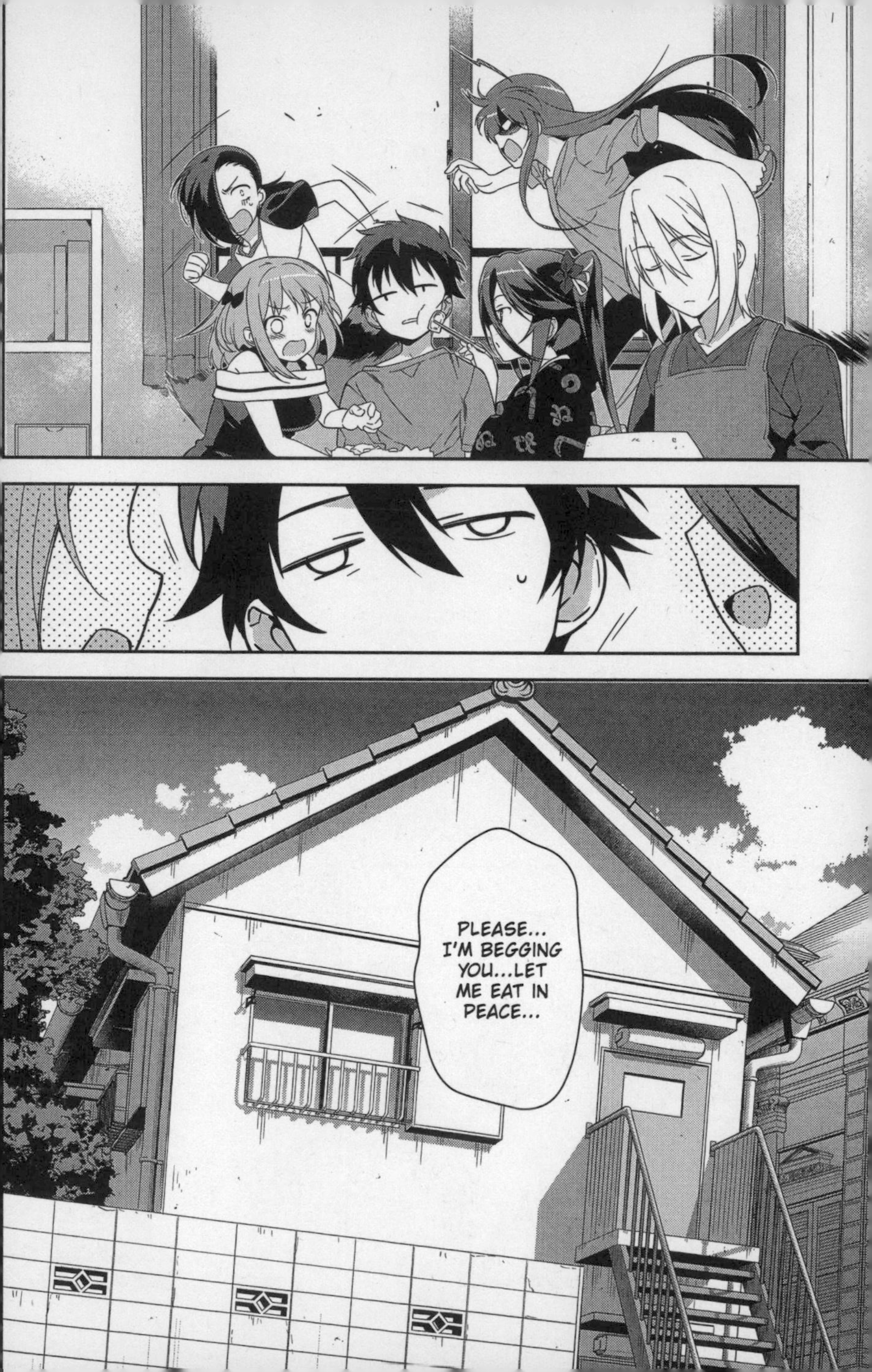
PLEASE... I'M BEGGING YOU...LET ME EAT IN PEACE...

Sadao
Maou

THE DEVIL IS A PART-TIMER!

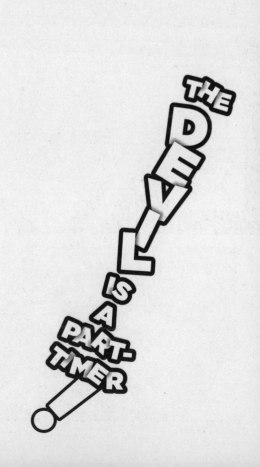

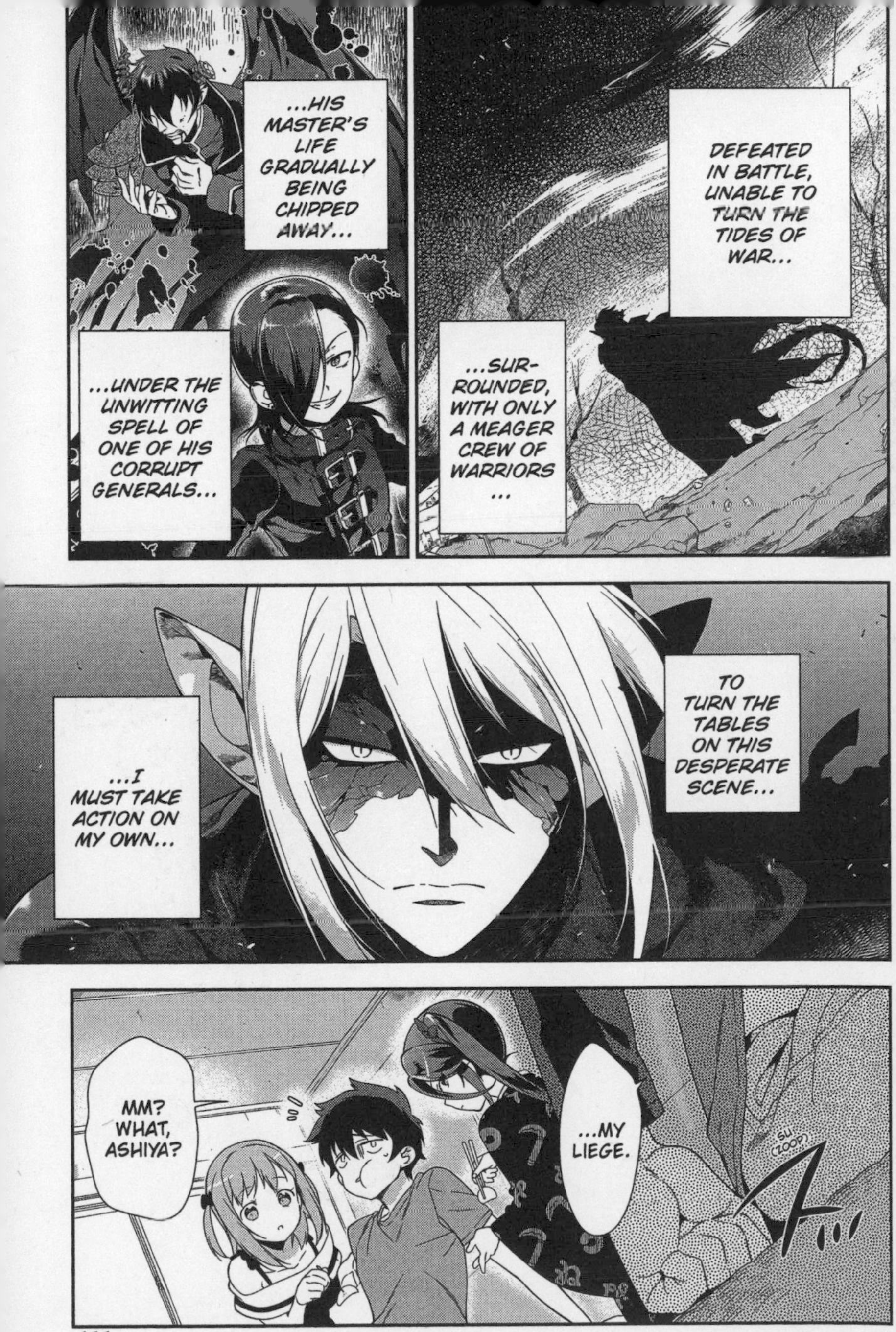
DEFEATED IN BATTLE, UNABLE TO TURN THE TIDES OF WAR...
...SURROUNDED, WITH ONLY A MEAGER CREW OF WARRIORS ...
...HIS MASTER'S LIFE GRADUALLY BEING CHIPPED AWAY...
...UNDER THE UNWITTING SPELL OF ONE OF HIS CORRUPT GENERALS...
TO TURN THE TABLES ON THIS DESPERATE SCENE...
...I MUST TAKE ACTION ON MY OWN...
SU (ZOOP)
...MY LIEGE.
MM? WHAT, ASHIYA?

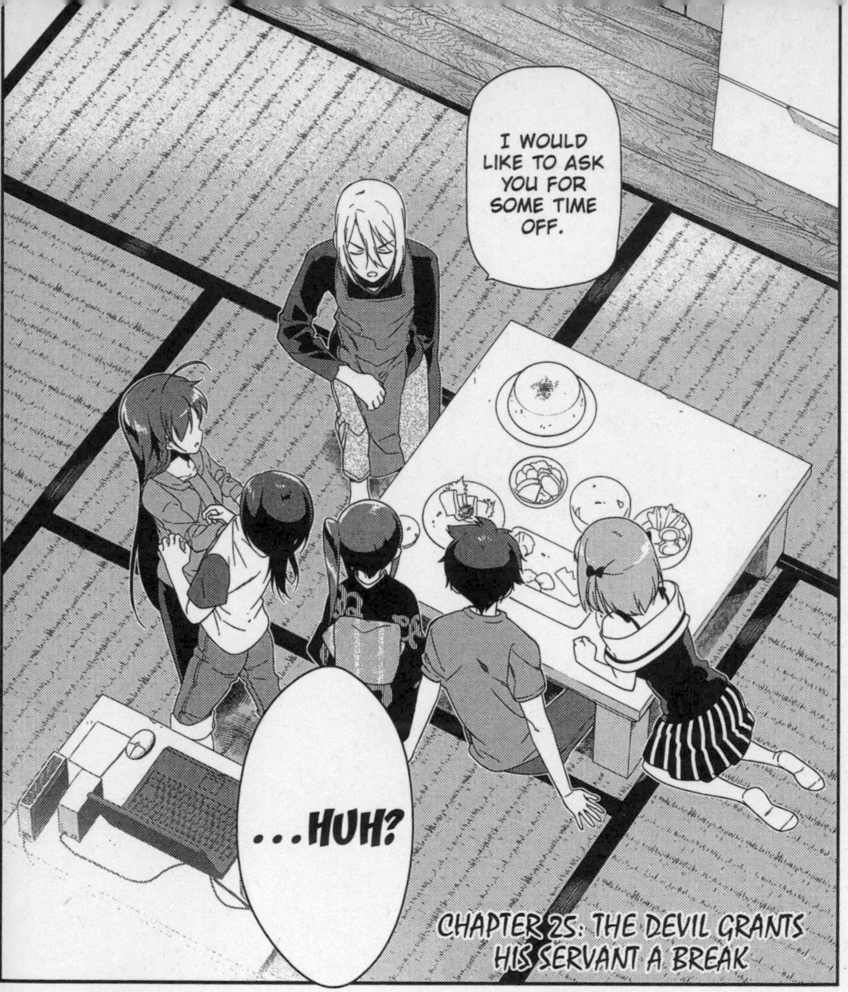
I WOULD LIKE TO ASK YOU FOR SOME TIME OFF.
...HUH?
CHAPTER 25: THE DEVIL GRANTS HIS SERVANT A BREAK

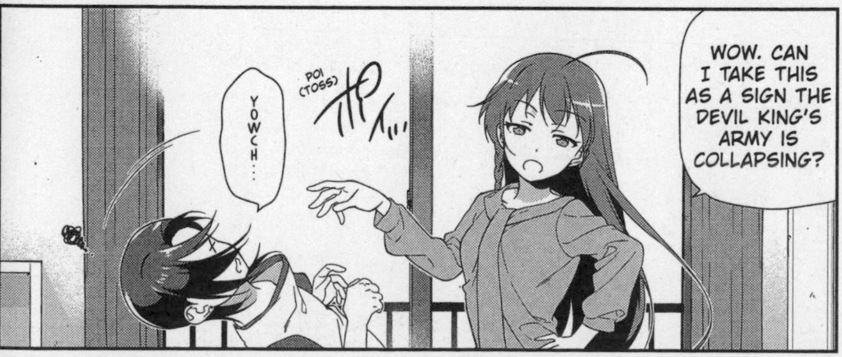
WOW. CAN I TAKE THIS AS A SIGN THE DEVIL KING'S ARMY IS COLLAPSING?
POI (TOSS)
YOWCH...

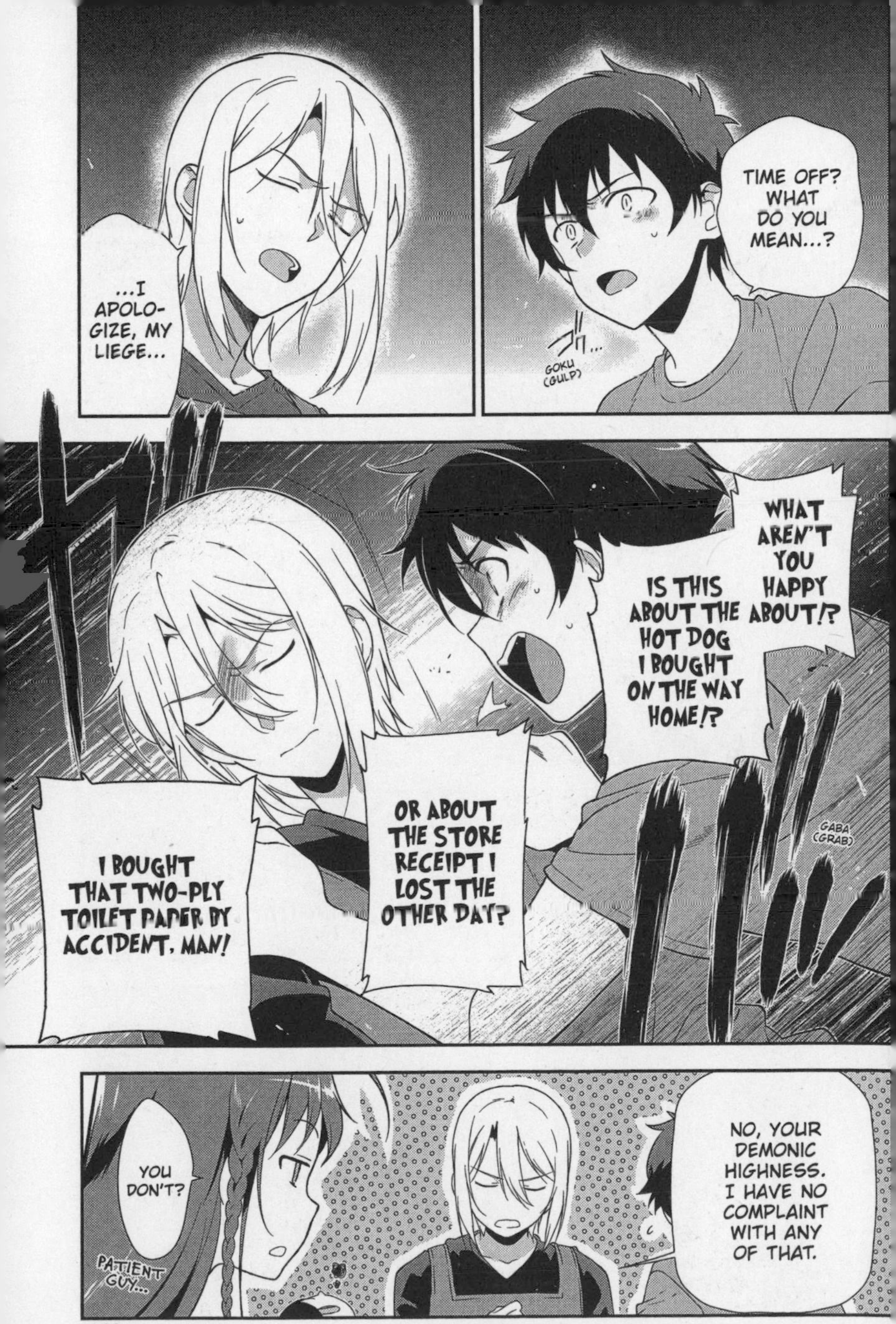
TIME OFF? WHAT DO YOU MEAN...?
GOKU (GULP)
...I APOLOGIZE, MY LIEGE...
WHAT AREN'T YOU HAPPY ABOUT!?
IS THIS ABOUT THE HOT DOG I BOUGHT ON THE WAY HOME!?
GABA (GRAB)
OR ABOUT THE STORE RECEIPT I LOST THE OTHER DAY?
I BOUGHT THAT TWO-PLY TOILET PAPER BY ACCIDENT, MAN!
NO, YOUR DEMONIC HIGHNESS. I HAVE NO COMPLAINT WITH ANY OF THAT.
YOU DON'T?
PATIENT GUY...

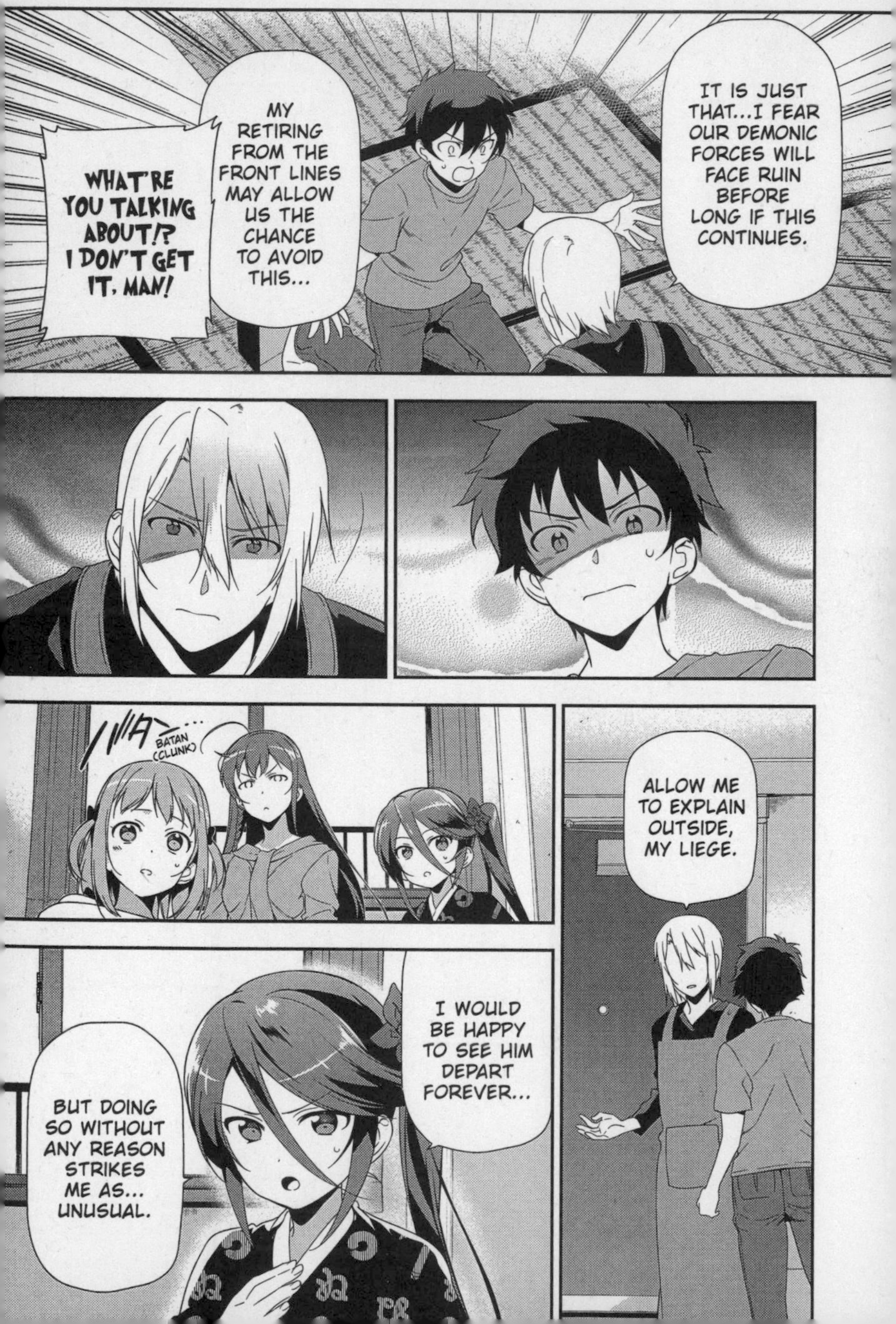
IT IS JUST THAT...I FEAR OUR DEMONIC FORCES WILL FACE RUIN BEFORE LONG IF THIS CONTINUES.
MY RETIRING FROM THE FRONT LINES MAY ALLOW US THE CHANCE TO AVOID THIS...
WHAT'RE YOU TALKING ABOUT!? I DON'T GET IT, MAN!
ALLOW ME TO EXPLAIN OUTSIDE, MY LIEGE.
BATAN (CLUNK)
I WOULD BE HAPPY TO SEE HIM DEPART FOREVER...
BUT DOING SO WITHOUT ANY REASON STRIKES ME AS... UNUSUAL.

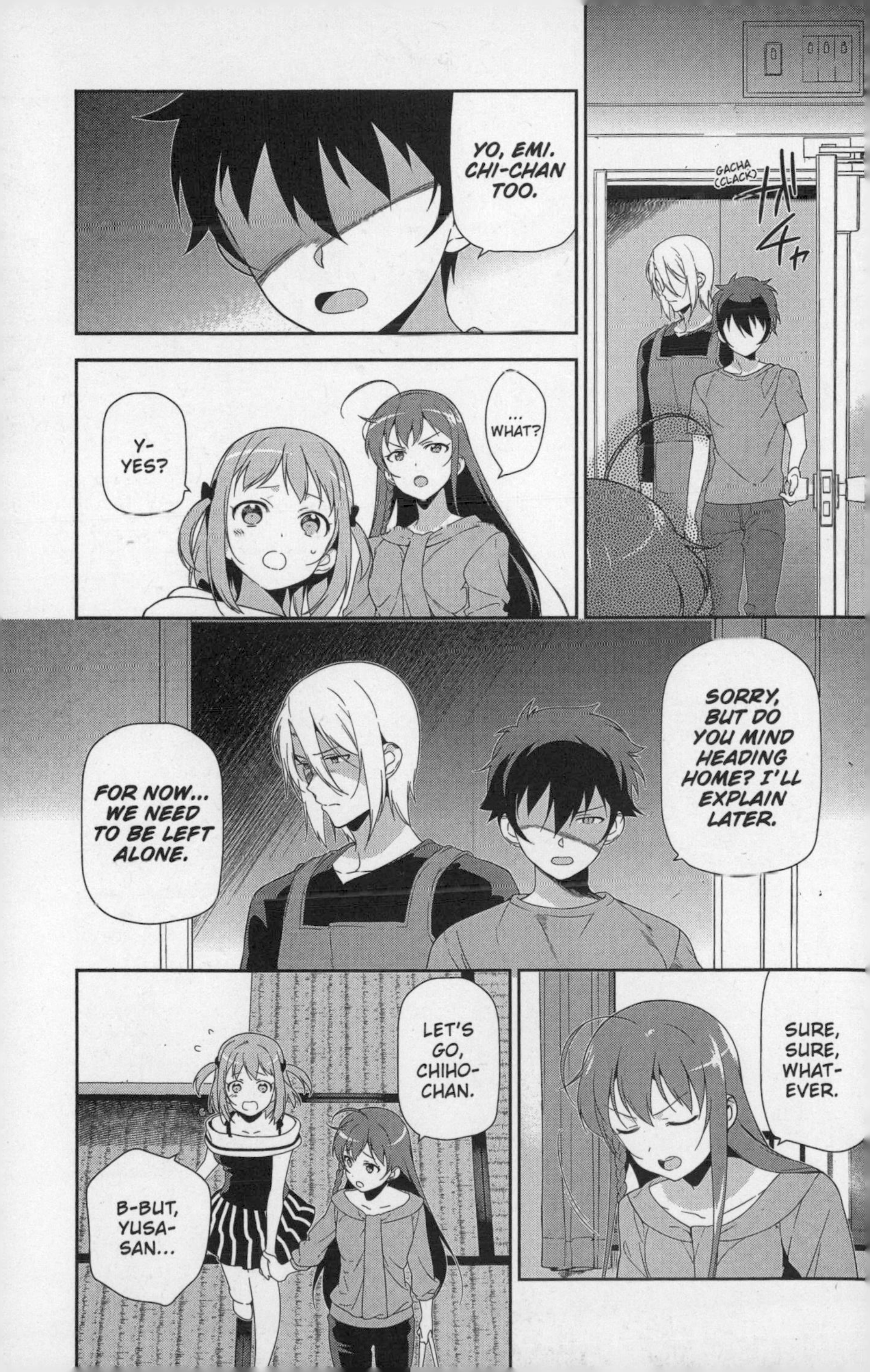
GACHA (CLACK)
YO, EMI. CHI-CHAN TOO.
... WHAT?
Y- YES?
SORRY, BUT DO YOU MIND HEADING HOME? I'LL EXPLAIN LATER.
FOR NOW... WE NEED TO BE LEFT ALONE.
SURE, SURE, WHAT-EVER.
LET'S GO, CHIHO-CHAN.
B-BUT, YUSA-SAN...

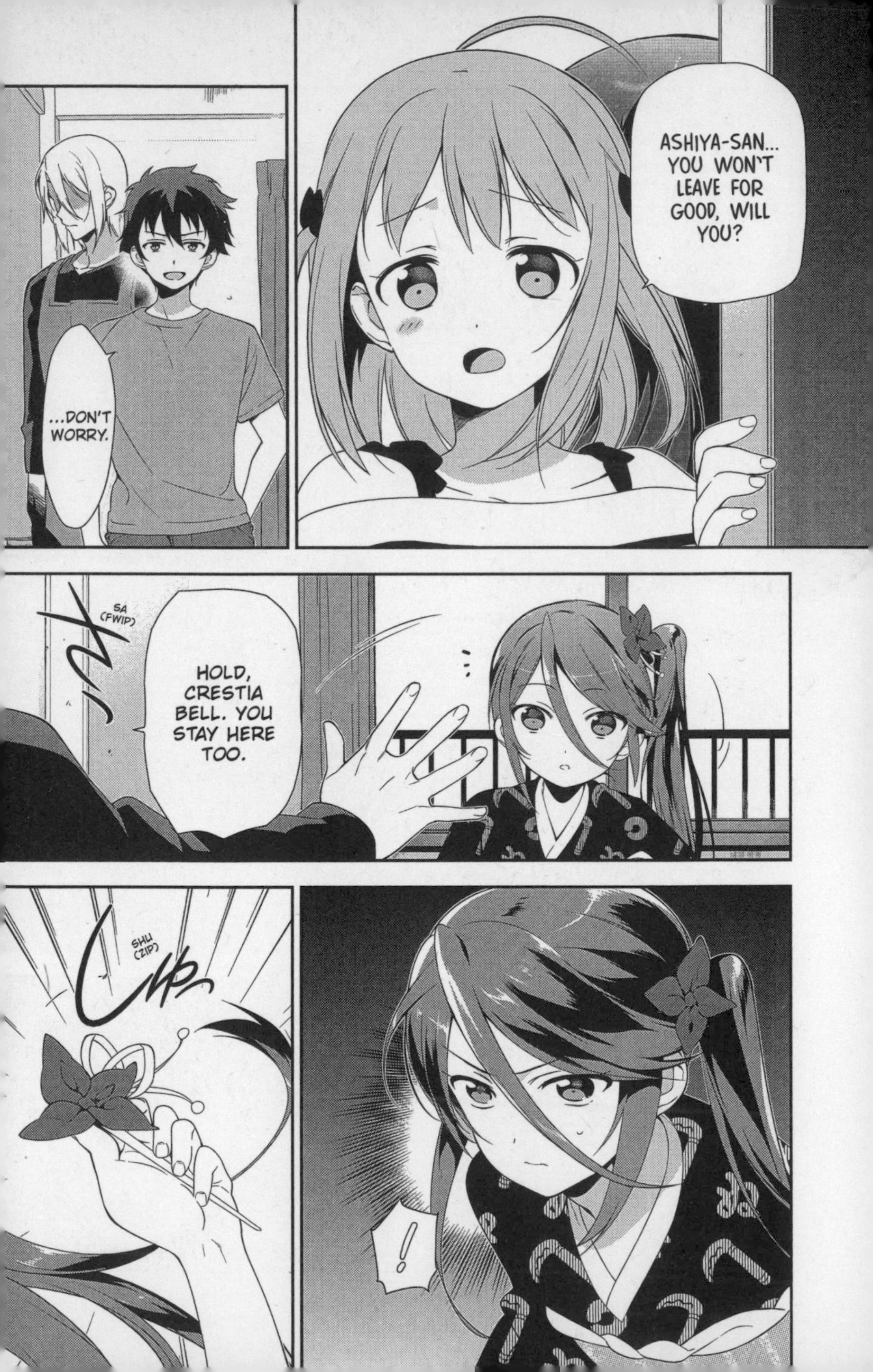
ASHIYA-SAN... YOU WON'T LEAVE FOR GOOD, WILL YOU?
...DON'T WORRY.
HOLD, CRESTIA BELL. YOU STAY HERE TOO.
SA (FWIP)
!
SHU (ZIP)

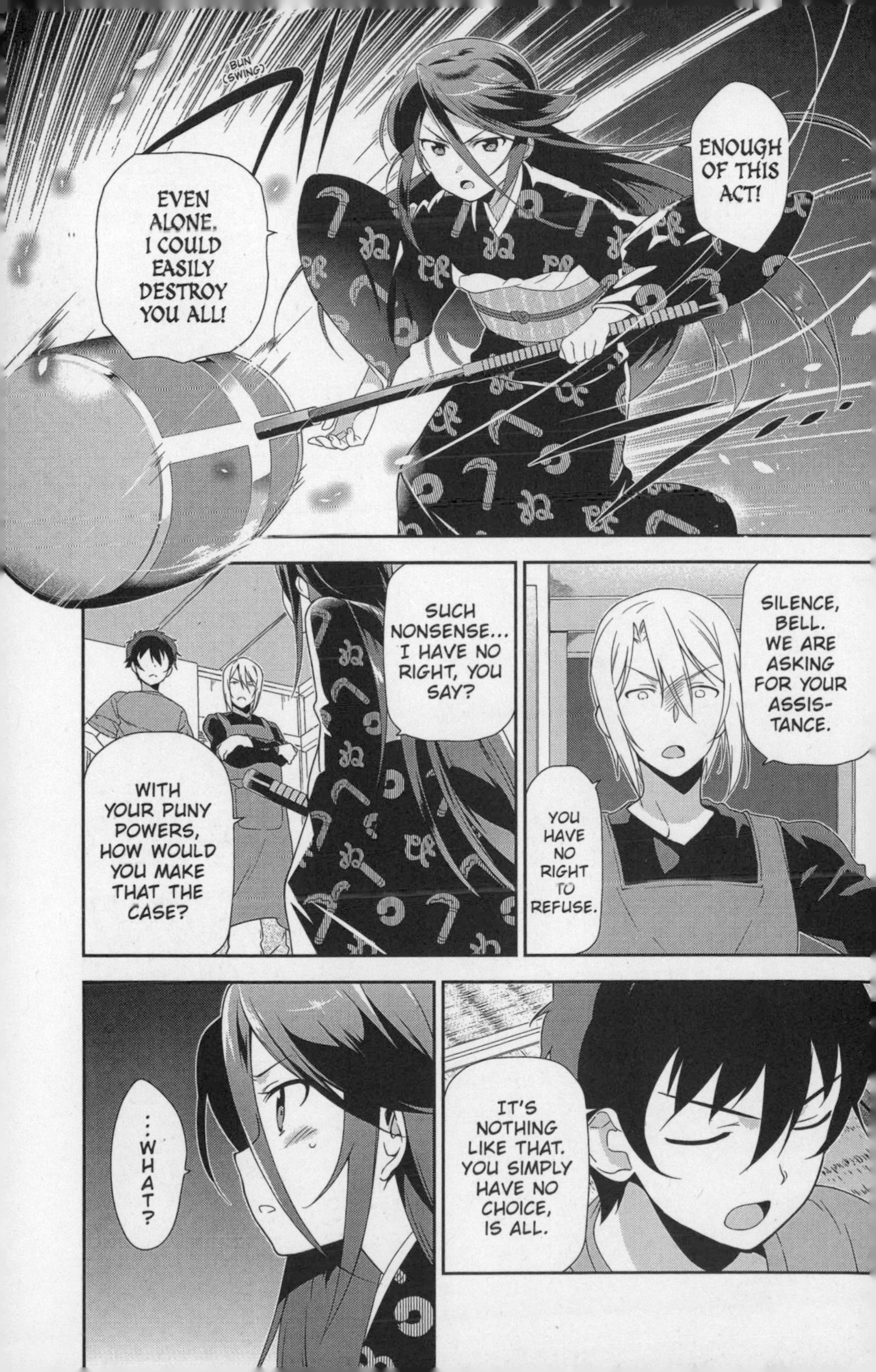
ENOUGH OF THIS ACT!
BUN (SWING)
EVEN ALONE, I COULD EASILY DESTROY YOU ALL!
SILENCE, BELL. WE ARE ASKING FOR YOUR ASSIS-TANCE.
YOU HAVE NO RIGHT TO REFUSE.
SUCH NONSENSE... I HAVE NO RIGHT, YOU SAY?
WITH YOUR PUNY POWERS, HOW WOULD YOU MAKE THAT THE CASE?
IT'S NOTHING LIKE THAT. YOU SIMPLY HAVE NO CHOICE, IS ALL.
...WHAT?

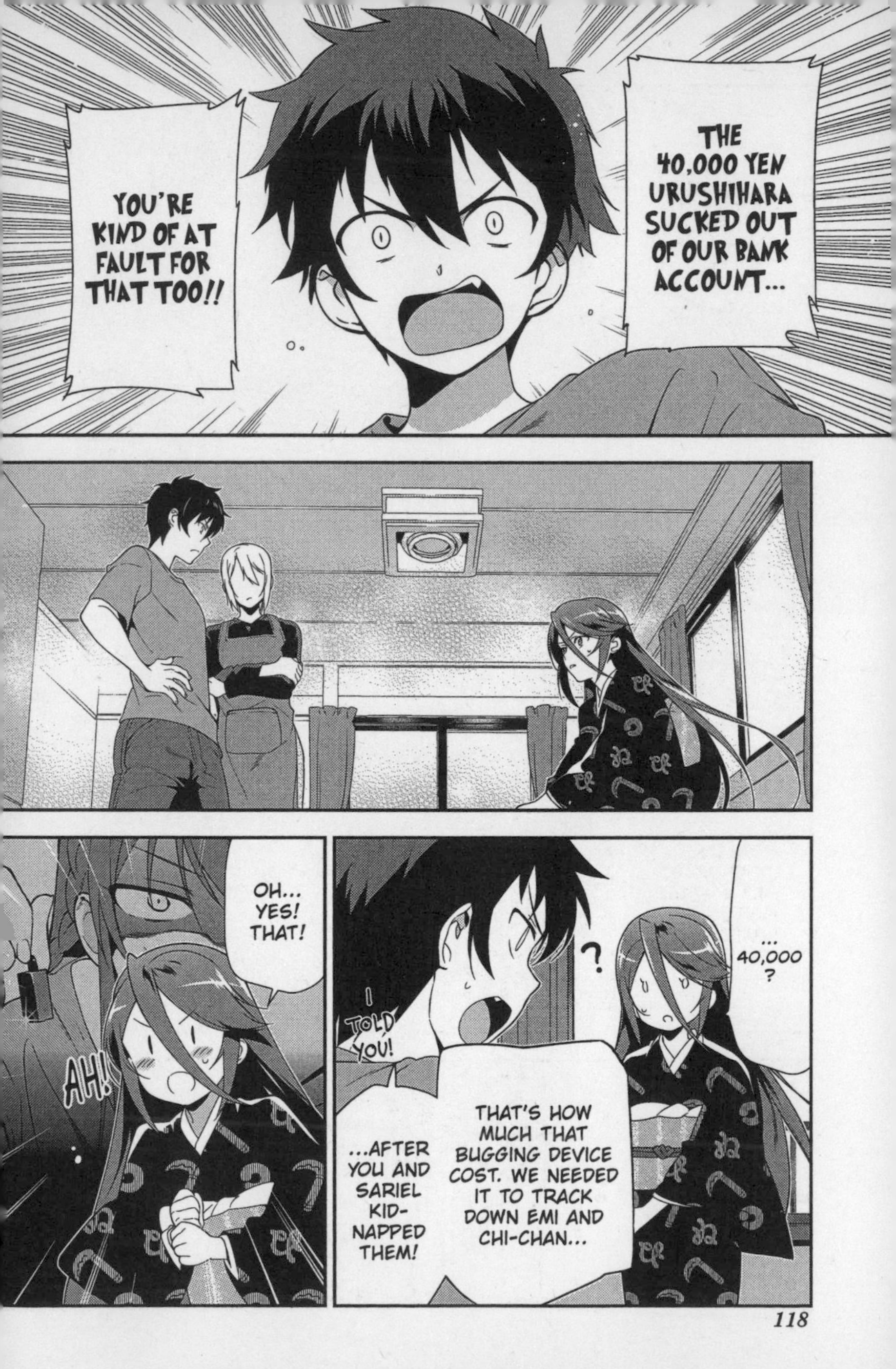
THE 40,000 YEN URUSHIHARA SUCKED OUT OF OUR BANK ACCOUNT...
YOU'RE KIND OF AT FAULT FOR THAT TOO!!
...40,000?
?
I TOLD YOU!
THAT'S HOW MUCH THAT BUGGING DEVICE COST. WE NEEDED IT TO TRACK DOWN EMI AND CHI-CHAN...
...AFTER YOU AND SARIEL KID-NAPPED THEM!
OH... YES! THAT!
AH!

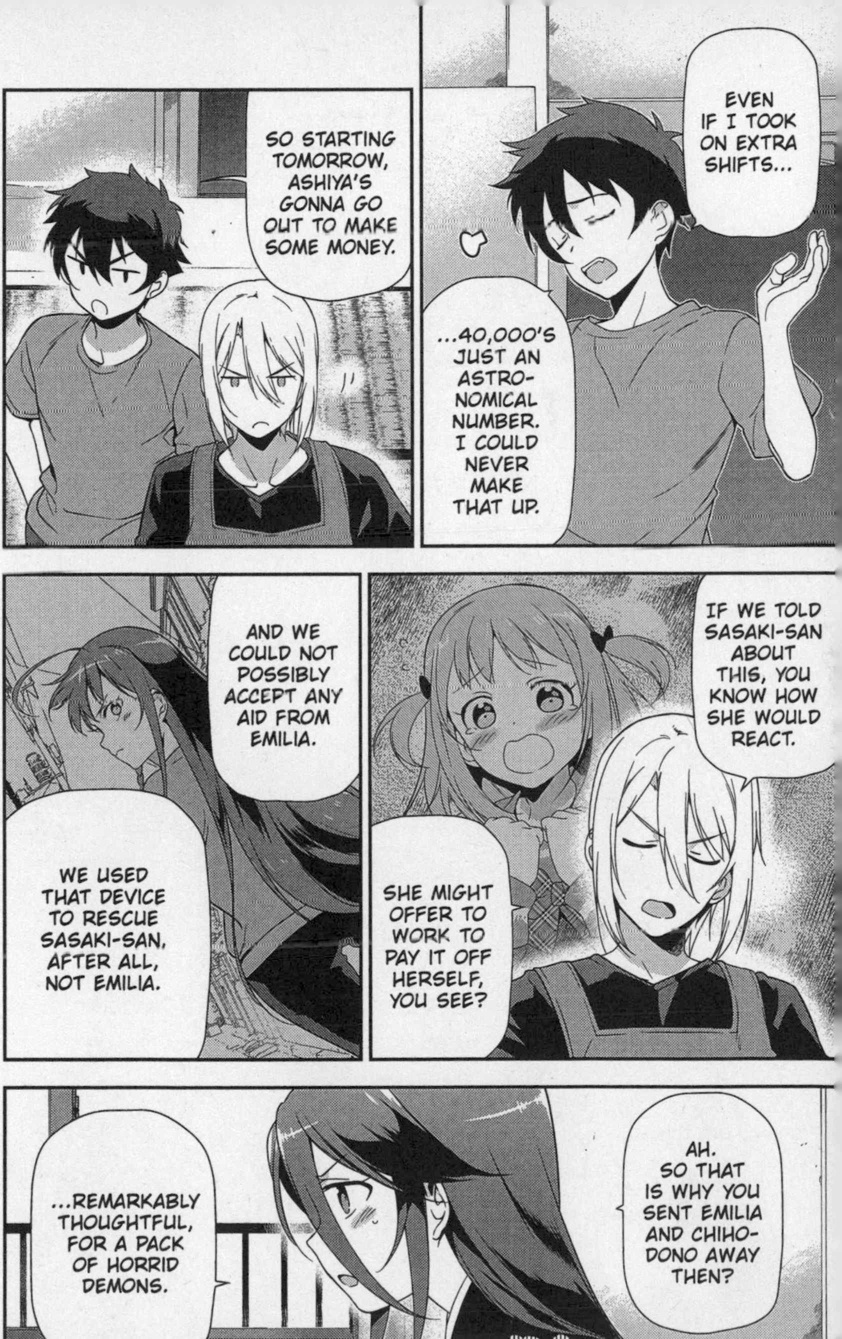
EVEN IF I TOOK ON EXTRA SHIFTS...
...40,000'S JUST AN ASTRONOMICAL NUMBER. I COULD NEVER MAKE THAT UP.
SO STARTING TOMORROW, ASHIYA'S GONNA GO OUT TO MAKE SOME MONEY.
IF WE TOLD SASAKI-SAN ABOUT THIS, YOU KNOW HOW SHE WOULD REACT.
SHE MIGHT OFFER TO WORK TO PAY IT OFF HERSELF, YOU SEE?
AND WE COULD NOT POSSIBLY ACCEPT ANY AID FROM EMILIA.
WE USED THAT DEVICE TO RESCUE SASAKI-SAN, AFTER ALL, NOT EMILIA.
AH. SO THAT IS WHY YOU SENT EMILIA AND CHIHO-DONO AWAY THEN?
...REMARKABLY THOUGHTFUL, FOR A PACK OF HORRID DEMONS.

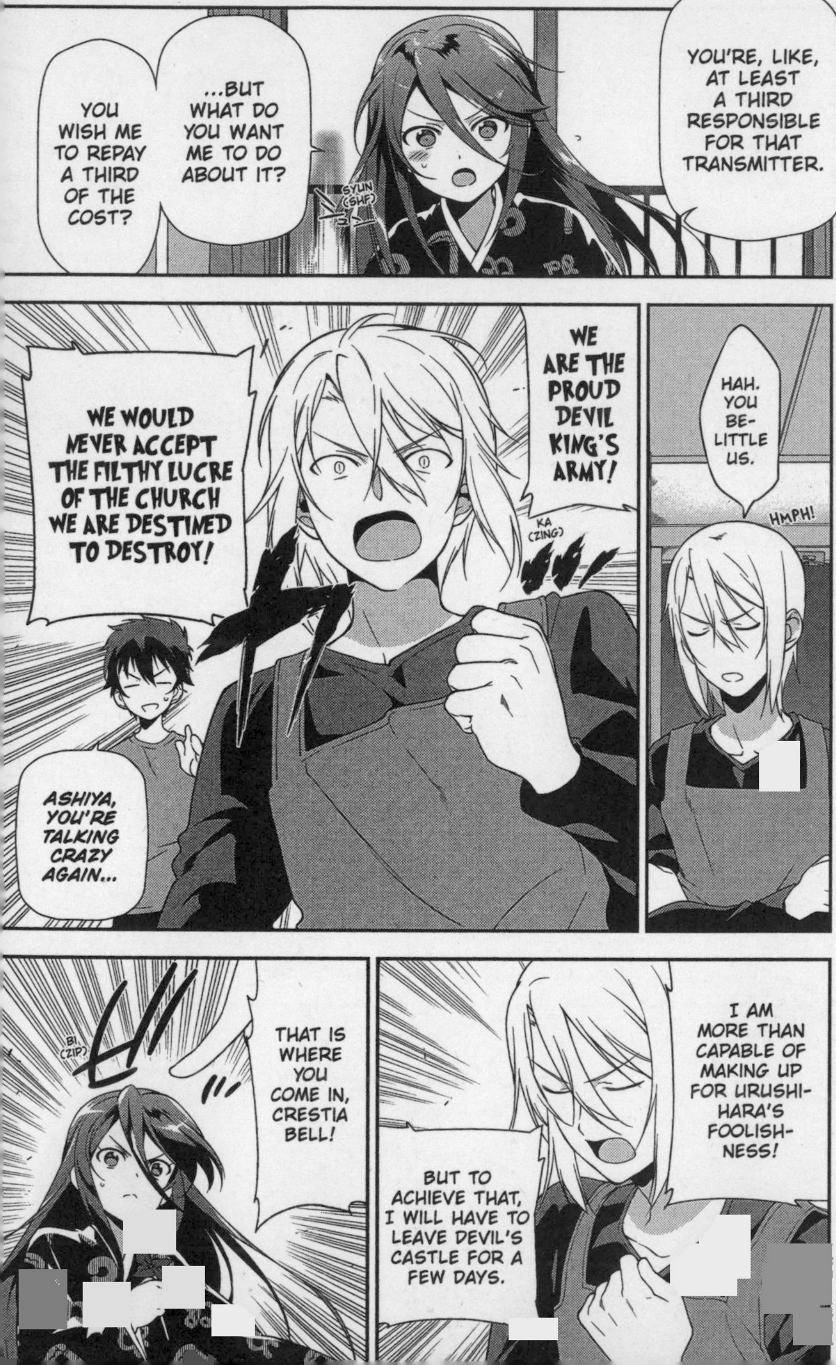
YOU'RE, LIKE, AT LEAST A THIRD RESPONSIBLE FOR THAT TRANSMITTER.
...BUT WHAT DO YOU WANT ME TO DO ABOUT IT?
SYUN (SHF)
YOU WISH ME TO REPAY A THIRD OF THE COST?
HAH. YOU BE-LITTLE US.
HMPH!
WE ARE THE PROUD DEVIL KING'S ARMY!
KA (ZING)
WE WOULD NEVER ACCEPT THE FILTHY LUCRE OF THE CHURCH WE ARE DESTINED TO DESTROY!
ASHIYA, YOU'RE TALKING CRAZY AGAIN...
I AM MORE THAN CAPABLE OF MAKING UP FOR URUSHI-HARA'S FOOLISH-NESS!
BUT TO ACHIEVE THAT, I WILL HAVE TO LEAVE DEVIL'S CASTLE FOR A FEW DAYS.
THAT IS WHERE YOU COME IN, CRESTIA BELL!
BI (ZIP)

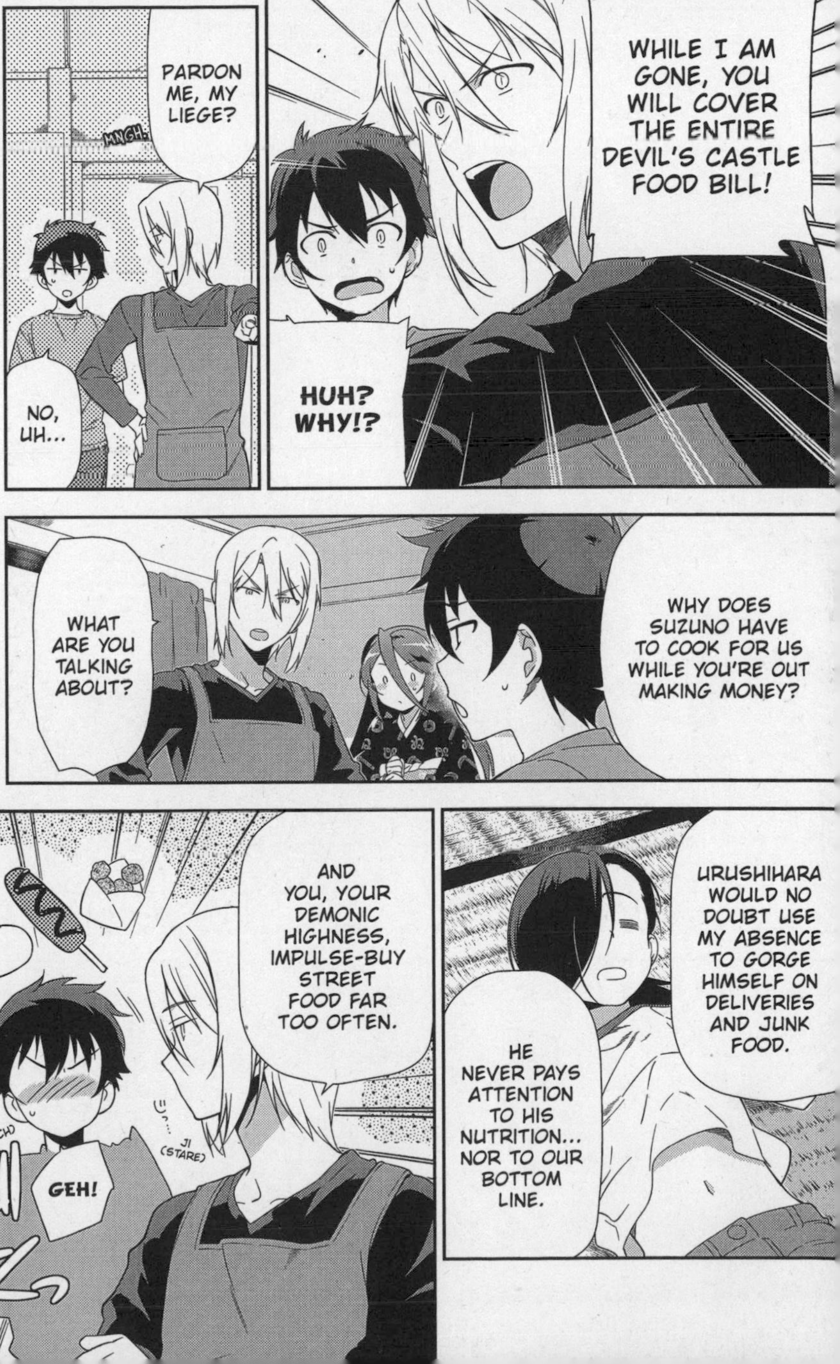
WHILE I AM GONE, YOU WILL COVER THE ENTIRE DEVIL'S CASTLE FOOD BILL!
HUH? WHY!?
PARDON ME, MY LIEGE?
MNGH.
NO, UH...
WHY DOES SUZUNO HAVE TO COOK FOR US WHILE YOU'RE OUT MAKING MONEY?
WHAT ARE YOU TALKING ABOUT?
URUSHIHARA WOULD NO DOUBT USE MY ABSENCE TO GORGE HIMSELF ON DELIVERIES AND JUNK FOOD.
HE NEVER PAYS ATTENTION TO HIS NUTRITION... NOR TO OUR BOTTOM LINE.
AND YOU, YOUR DEMONIC HIGHNESS, IMPULSE-BUY STREET FOOD FAR TOO OFTEN.
JI (STARE)
GIKU (TWITCH)
GEH!

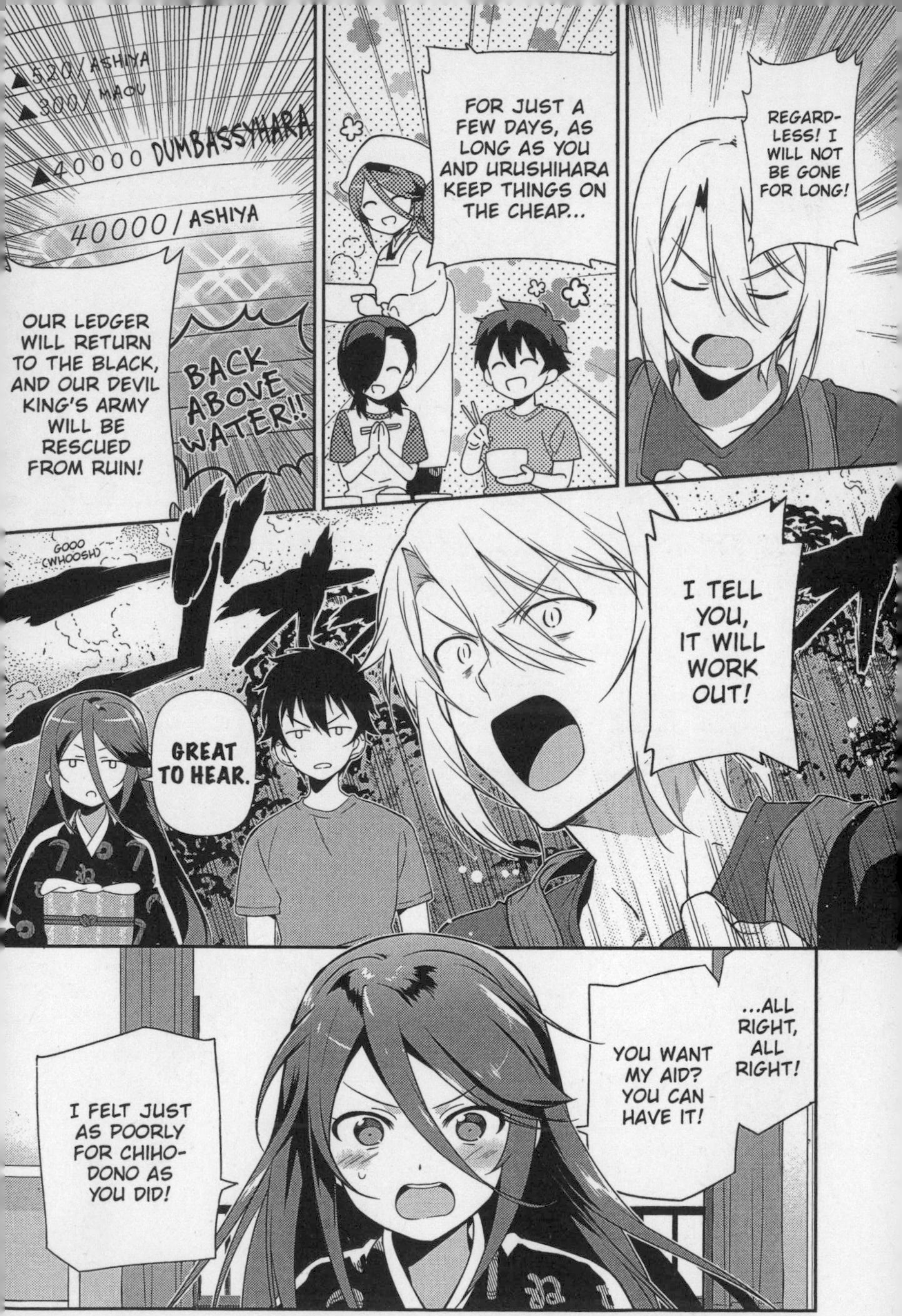
REGARDLESS! I WILL NOT BE GONE FOR LONG!
FOR JUST A FEW DAYS, AS LONG AS YOU AND URUSHIHARA KEEP THINGS ON THE CHEAP...
▲520/ ASHIYA
▲300/ MAOU
▲40000 DUMBASSYHARA
40000/ ASHIYA
OUR LEDGER WILL RETURN TO THE BLACK, AND OUR DEVIL KING'S ARMY WILL BE RESCUED FROM RUIN!
BACK ABOVE WATER!!
I TELL YOU, IT WILL WORK OUT!
GREAT TO HEAR.
GOOO (WHOOSH)
...ALL RIGHT, ALL RIGHT!
YOU WANT MY AID? YOU CAN HAVE IT!
I FELT JUST AS POORLY FOR CHIHO-DONO AS YOU DID!

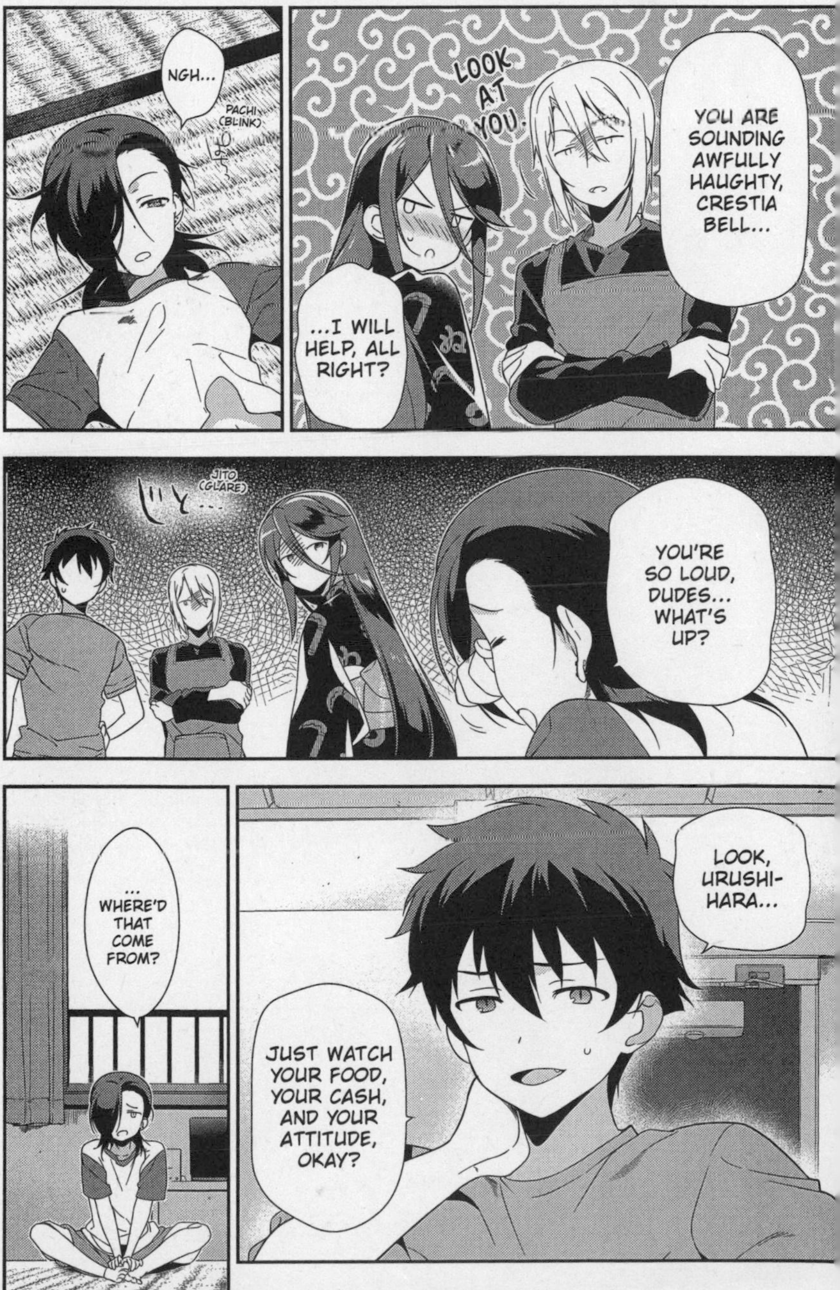
YOU ARE SOUNDING AWFULLY HAUGHTY, CRESTIA BELL...
LOOK AT YOU.
...I WILL HELP, ALL RIGHT?
NGH...
PACHI (BLINK)
YOU'RE SO LOUD, DUDES... WHAT'S UP?
JITO (GLARE)
LOOK, URUSHI-HARA...
JUST WATCH YOUR FOOD, YOUR CASH, AND YOUR ATTITUDE, OKAY?
...WHERE'D THAT COME FROM?

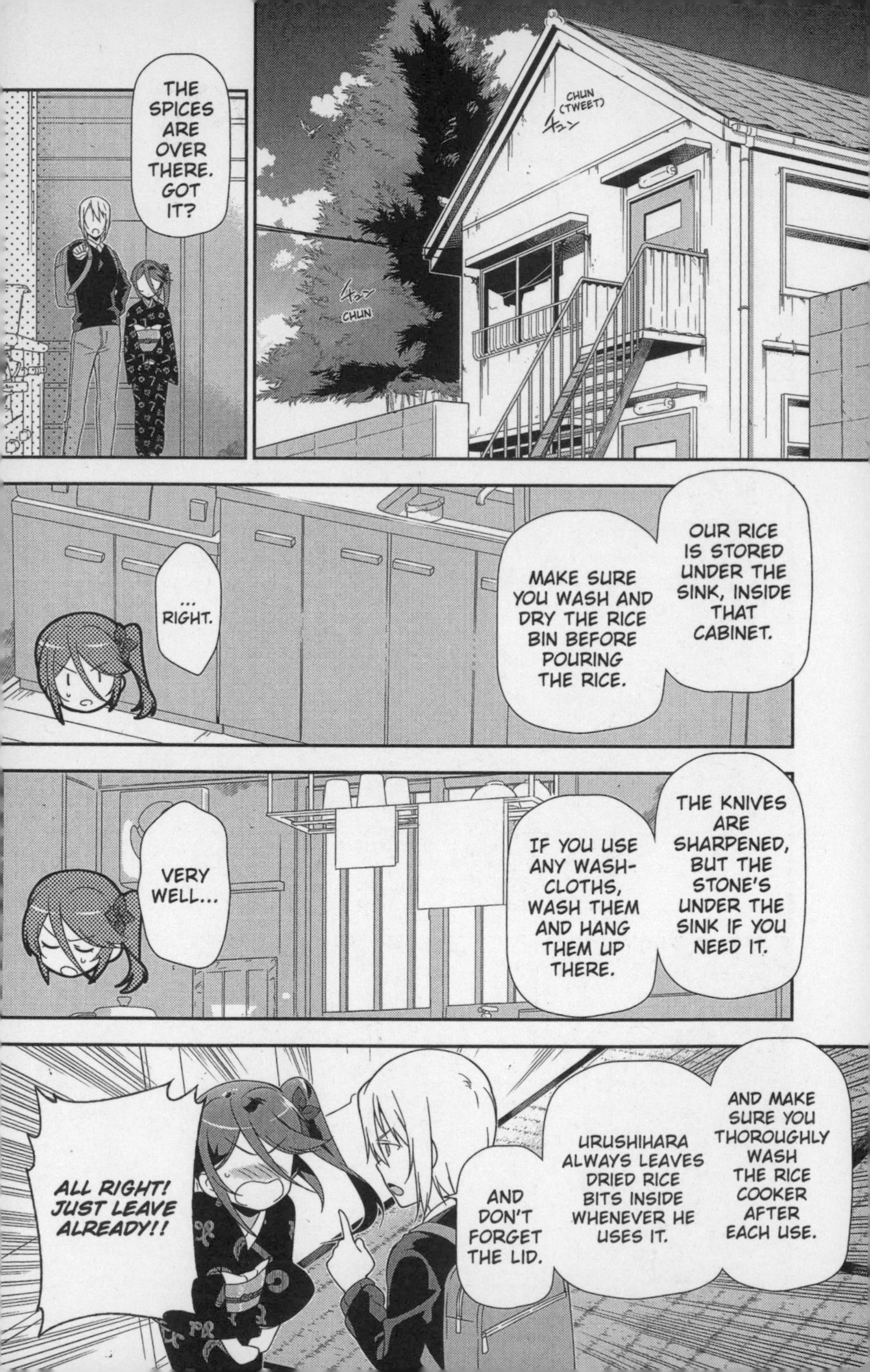
CHUN (TWEET)
CHUN
THE SPICES ARE OVER THERE. GOT IT?
OUR RICE IS STORED UNDER THE SINK, INSIDE THAT CABINET.
MAKE SURE YOU WASH AND DRY THE RICE BIN BEFORE POURING THE RICE.
... RIGHT.
THE KNIVES ARE SHARPENED, BUT THE STONE'S UNDER THE SINK IF YOU NEED IT.
IF YOU USE ANY WASH-CLOTHS, WASH THEM AND HANG THEM UP THERE.
VERY WELL...
AND MAKE SURE YOU THOROUGHLY WASH THE RICE COOKER AFTER EACH USE.
URUSHIHARA ALWAYS LEAVES DRIED RICE BITS INSIDE WHENEVER HE USES IT.
AND DON'T FORGET THE LID.
ALL RIGHT! JUST LEAVE ALREADY!!

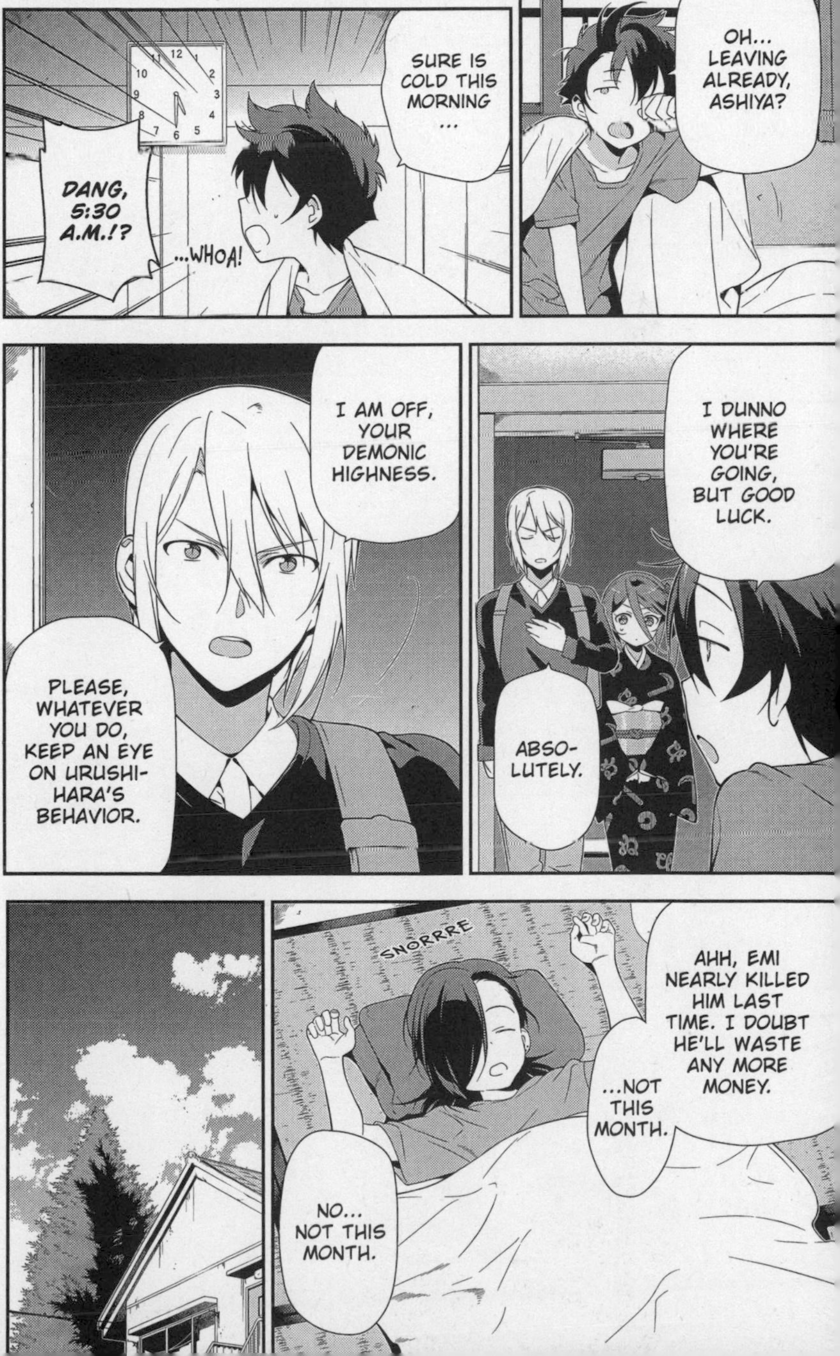
OH... LEAVING ALREADY, ASHIYA?
SURE IS COLD THIS MORNING ...
...WHOA!
DANG, 5:30 A.M.!?
I DUNNO WHERE YOU'RE GOING, BUT GOOD LUCK.
ABSO-LUTELY.
I AM OFF, YOUR DEMONIC HIGHNESS.
PLEASE, WHATEVER YOU DO, KEEP AN EYE ON URUSHI-HARA'S BEHAVIOR.
SNORRRE
AHH, EMI NEARLY KILLED HIM LAST TIME. I DOUBT HE'LL WASTE ANY MORE MONEY.
...NOT THIS MONTH.
NO... NOT THIS MONTH.

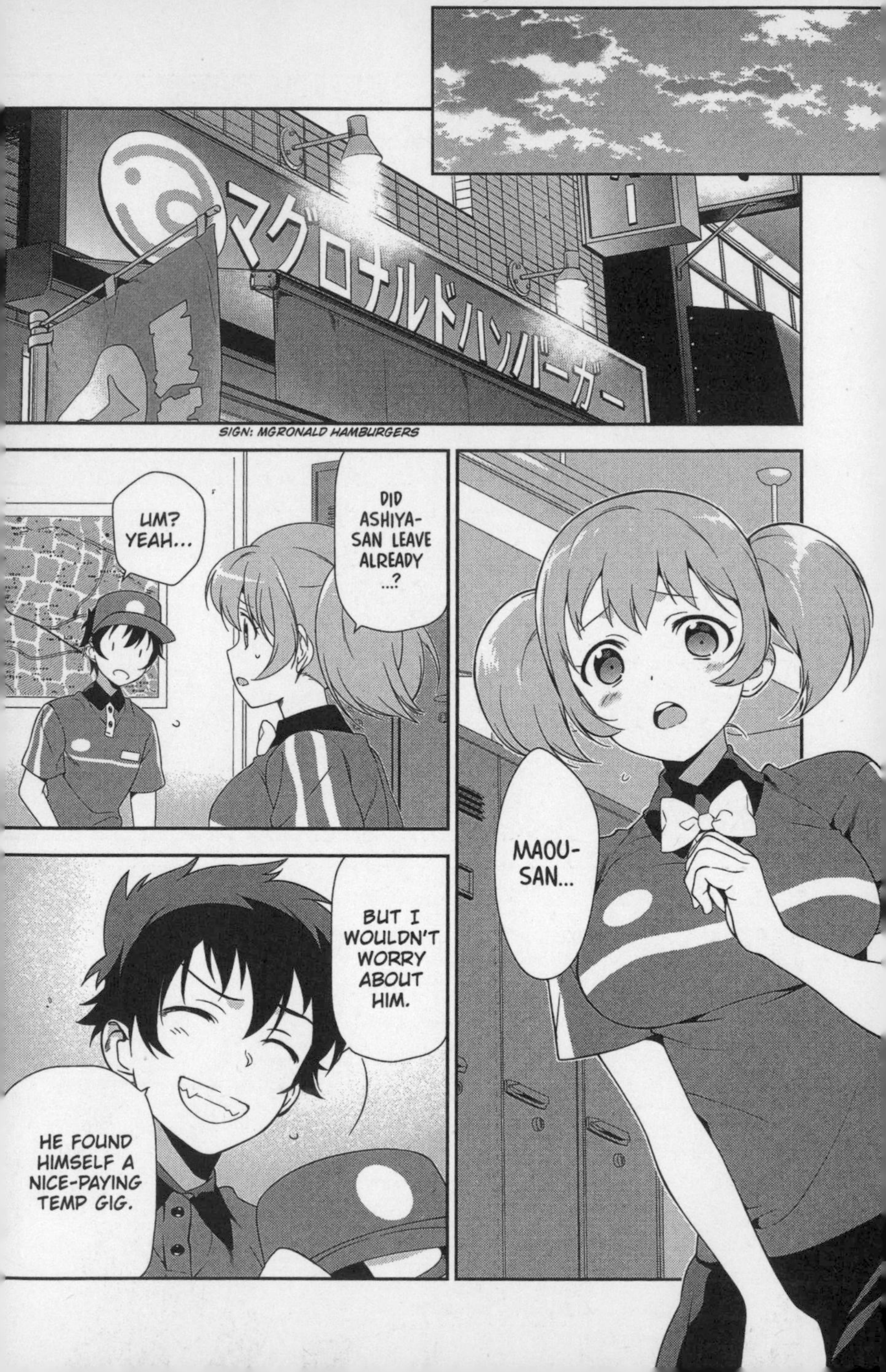
マグロナルドハンバーガー
SIGN: MGRONALD HAMBURGERS
MAOU-SAN...
DID ASHIYA-SAN LEAVE ALREADY ...?
UM? YEAH...
BUT I WOULDN'T WORRY ABOUT HIM.
HE FOUND HIMSELF A NICE-PAYING TEMP GIG.

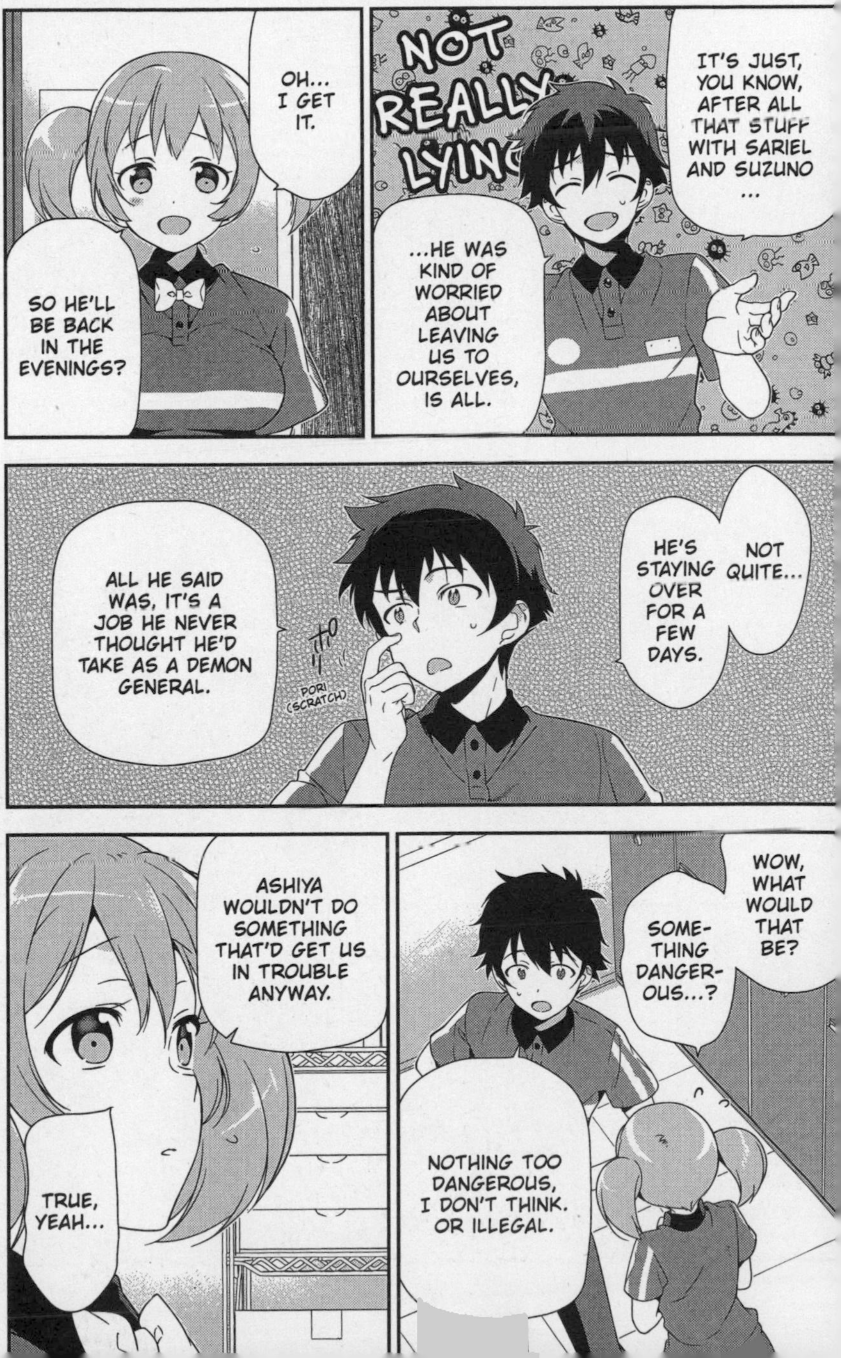
IT'S JUST, YOU KNOW, AFTER ALL THAT STUFF WITH SARIEL AND SUZUNO ...
NOT REALLY LYIN
...HE WAS KIND OF WORRIED ABOUT LEAVING US TO OURSELVES, IS ALL.
OH... I GET IT.
SO HE'LL BE BACK IN THE EVENINGS?
NOT QUITE...
HE'S STAYING OVER FOR A FEW DAYS.
PORI (SCRATCH)
ALL HE SAID WAS, IT'S A JOB HE NEVER THOUGHT HE'D TAKE AS A DEMON GENERAL.
WOW, WHAT WOULD THAT BE?
SOME-THING DANGER-OUS...?
NOTHING TOO DANGEROUS, I DON'T THINK. OR ILLEGAL.
ASHIYA WOULDN'T DO SOMETHING THAT'D GET US IN TROUBLE ANYWAY.
TRUE, YEAH...

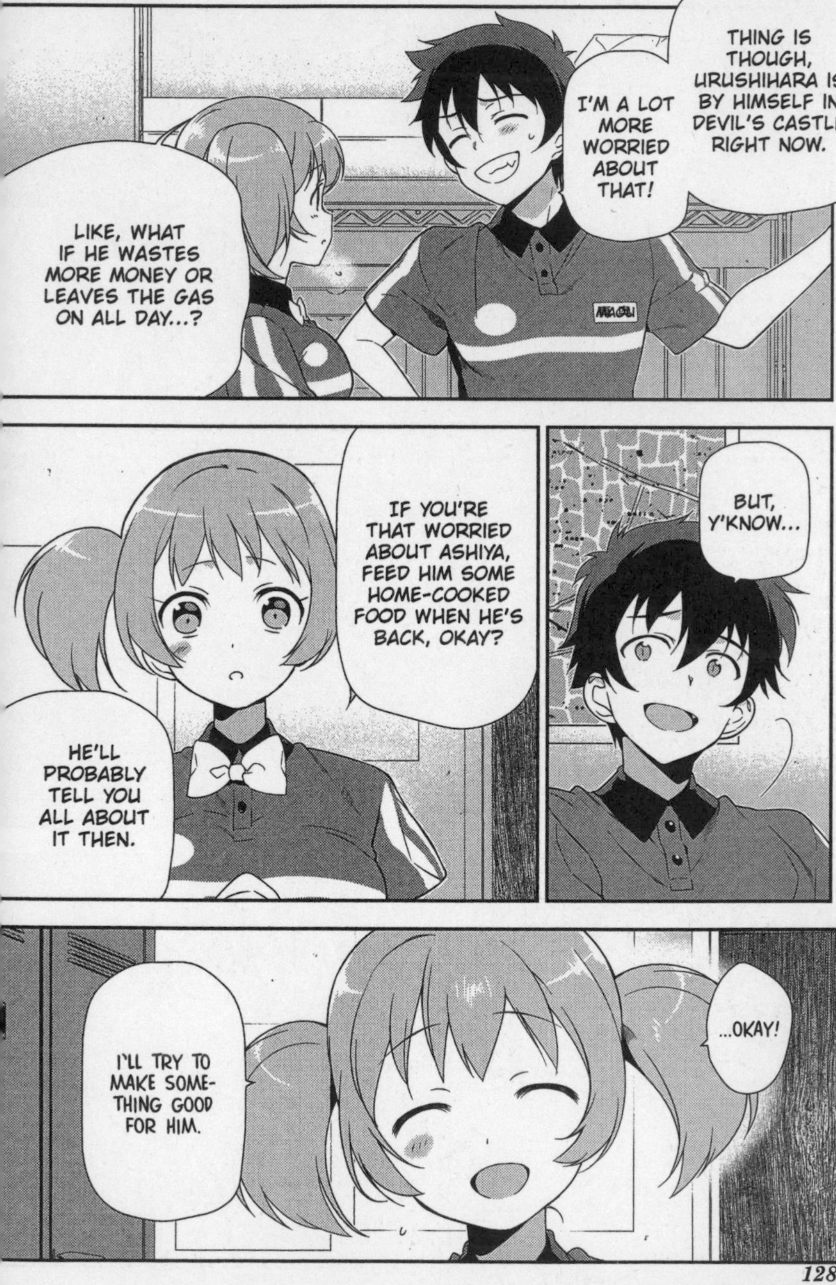
THING IS THOUGH, URUSHIHARA IS BY HIMSELF IN DEVIL'S CASTLE RIGHT NOW.
I'M A LOT MORE WORRIED ABOUT THAT!
LIKE, WHAT IF HE WASTES MORE MONEY OR LEAVES THE GAS ON ALL DAY...?
BUT, Y'KNOW...
IF YOU'RE THAT WORRIED ABOUT ASHIYA, FEED HIM SOME HOME-COOKED FOOD WHEN HE'S BACK, OKAY?
HE'LL PROBABLY TELL YOU ALL ABOUT IT THEN.
...OKAY!
I'LL TRY TO MAKE SOME-THING GOOD FOR HIM.

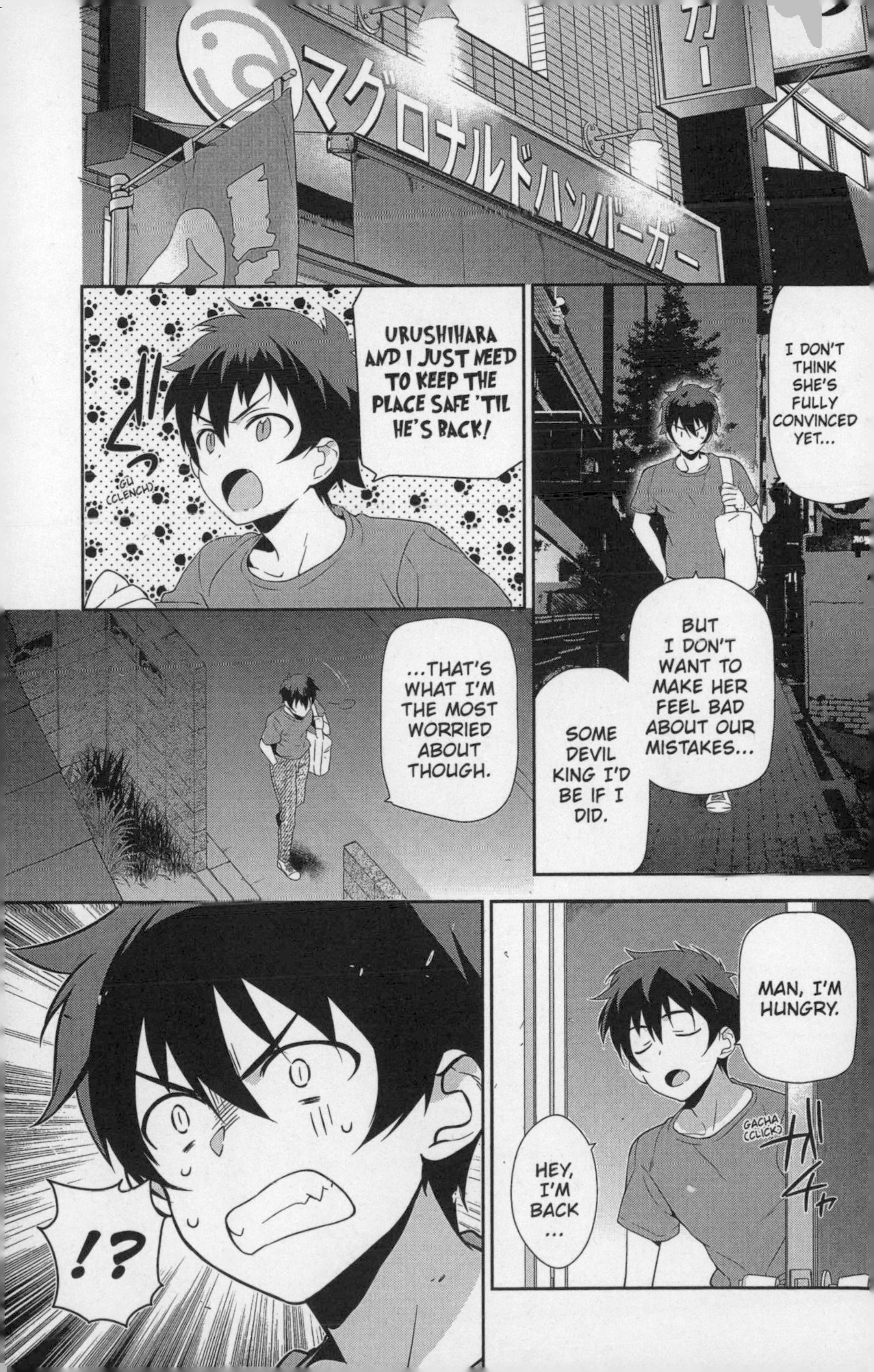

マグロナルドハンバーガー
I DON'T THINK SHE'S FULLY CONVINCED YET...
BUT I DON'T WANT TO MAKE HER FEEL BAD ABOUT OUR MISTAKES...
SOME DEVIL KING I'D BE IF I DID.
URUSHIHARA AND I JUST NEED TO KEEP THE PLACE SAFE 'TIL HE'S BACK!
ぐっ
GU (CLENCH)
...THAT'S WHAT I'M THE MOST WORRIED ABOUT THOUGH.
MAN, I'M HUNGRY.
ガチャ
GACHA (CLICK)
HEY, I'M BACK...
!?

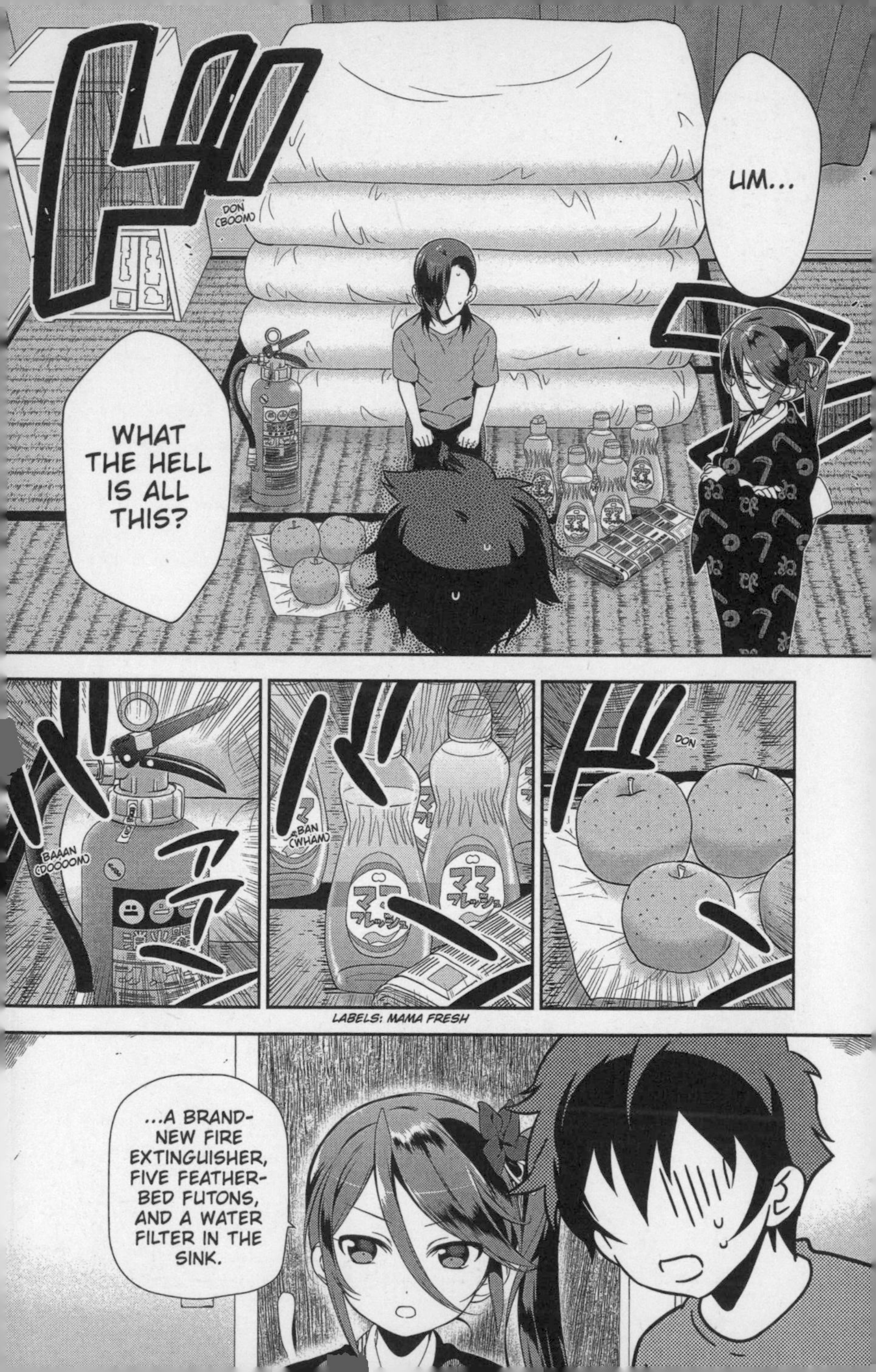
UM...
DON (BOOM)
WHAT THE HELL IS ALL THIS?
DON
BAN (WHAM)
BAAAN (DOOOOM)
LABELS: MAMA FRESH
...A BRAND-NEW FIRE EXTINGUISHER, FIVE FEATHER-BED FUTONS, AND A WATER FILTER IN THE SINK.

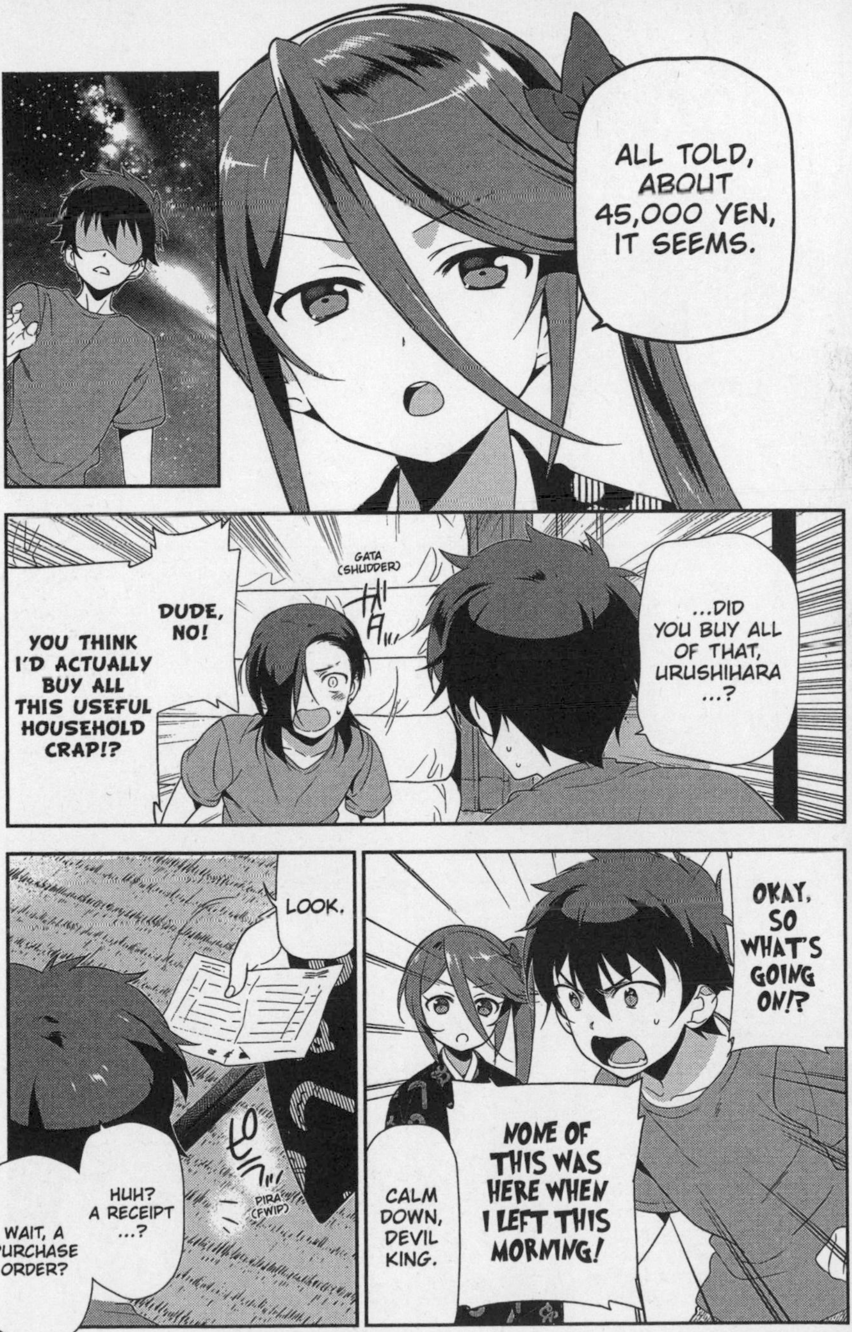
ALL TOLD, ABOUT 45,000 YEN, IT SEEMS.
...DID YOU BUY ALL OF THAT, URUSHIHARA ...?
GATA (SHUDDER)
DUDE, NO!
YOU THINK I'D ACTUALLY BUY ALL THIS USEFUL HOUSEHOLD CRAP!?
OKAY, SO WHAT'S GOING ON!?
NONE OF THIS WAS HERE WHEN I LEFT THIS MORNING!
CALM DOWN, DEVIL KING.
LOOK.
HUH? A RECEIPT ...?
PIRA (FWIP)
WAIT, A PURCHASE ORDER?

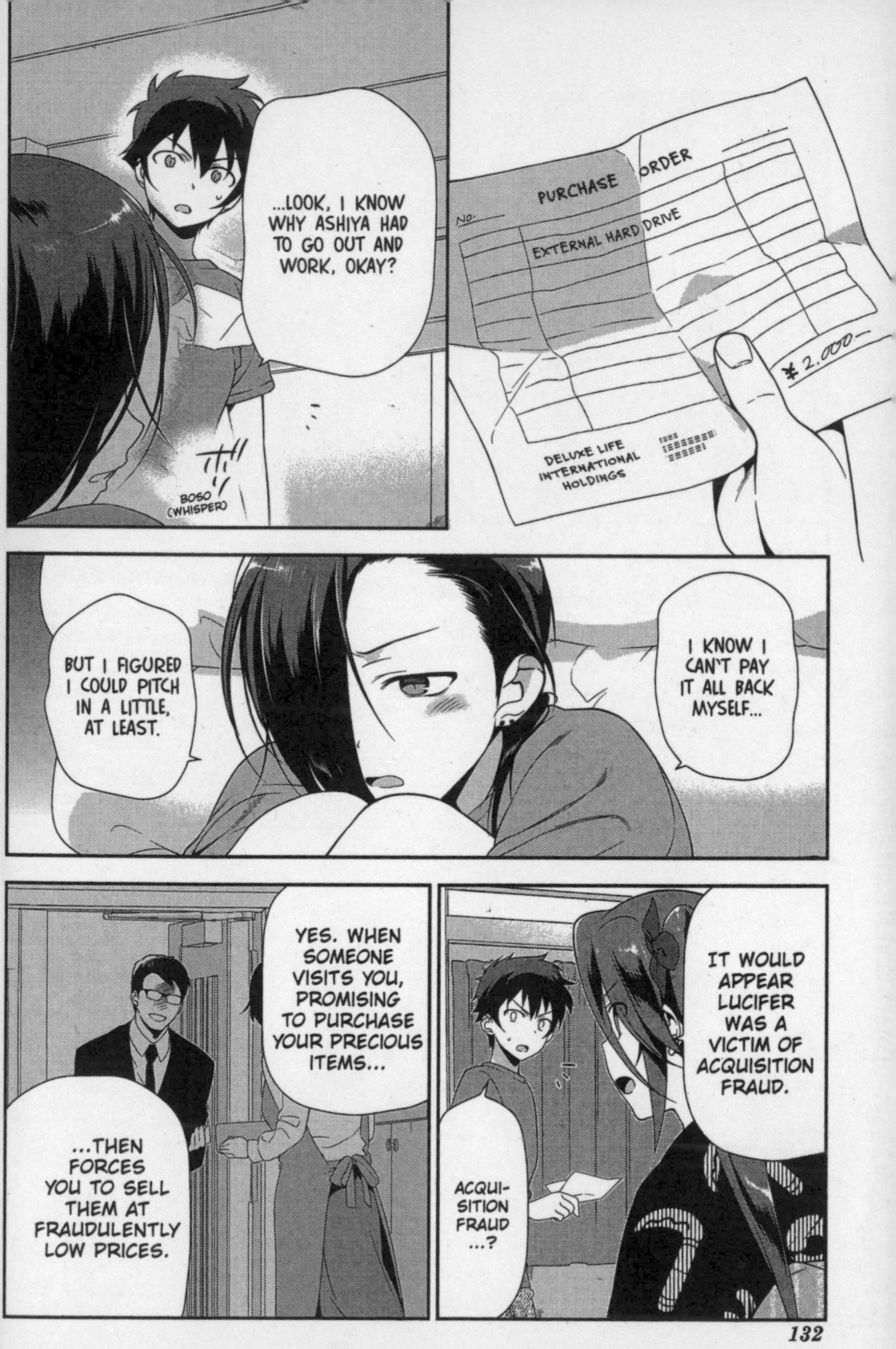
PURCHASE ORDER
NO.
EXTERNAL HARD DRIVE
¥2,000-
DELUXE LIFE INTERNATIONAL HOLDINGS
...LOOK, I KNOW WHY ASHIYA HAD TO GO OUT AND WORK, OKAY?
BOSO (WHISPER)
I KNOW I CAN'T PAY IT ALL BACK MYSELF...
BUT I FIGURED I COULD PITCH IN A LITTLE, AT LEAST.
IT WOULD APPEAR LUCIFER WAS A VICTIM OF ACQUISITION FRAUD.
ACQUISITION FRAUD...?
YES. WHEN SOMEONE VISITS YOU, PROMISING TO PURCHASE YOUR PRECIOUS ITEMS...
...THEN FORCES YOU TO SELL THEM AT FRAUDULENTLY LOW PRICES.

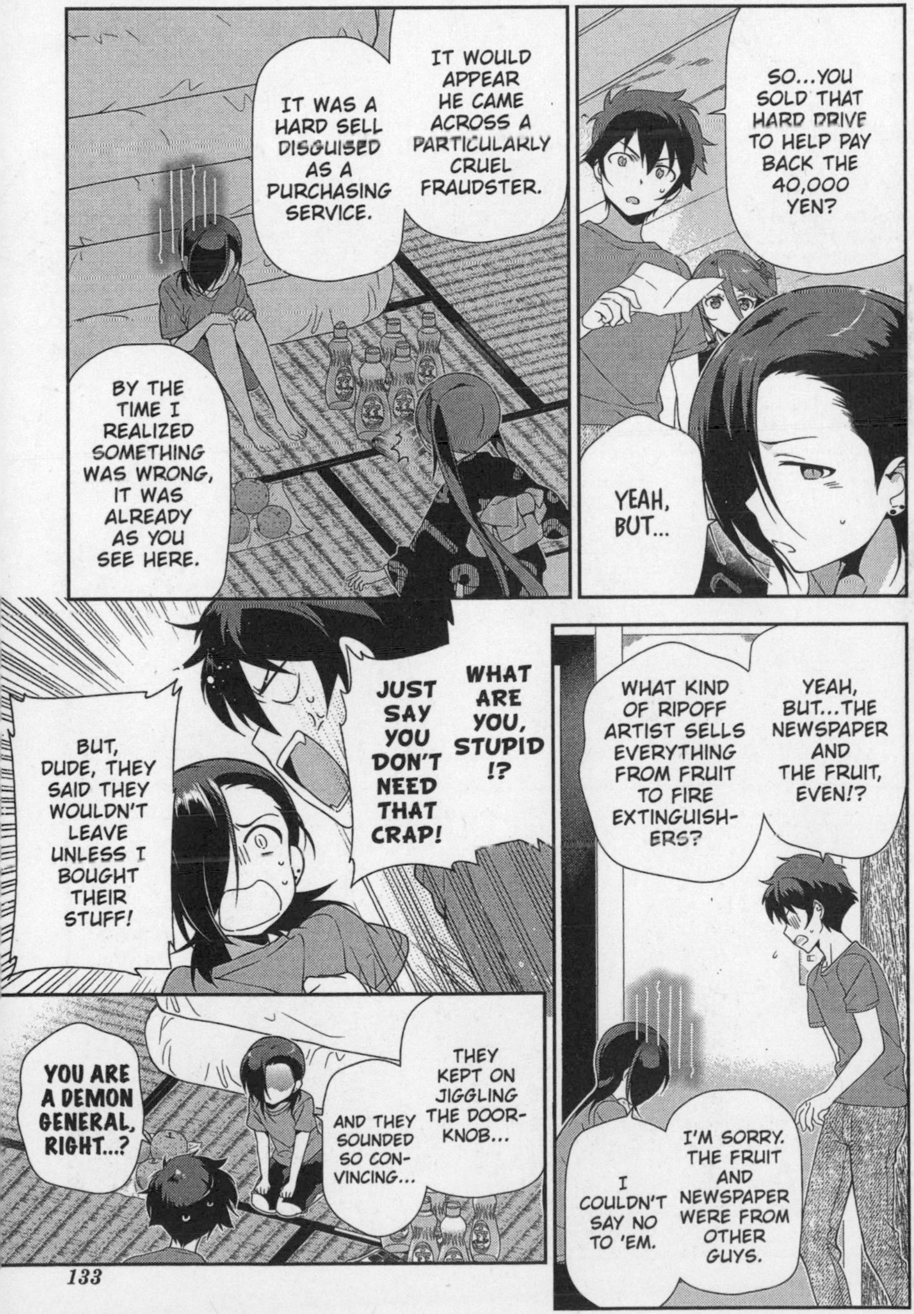
SO...YOU SOLD THAT HARD DRIVE TO HELP PAY BACK THE 40,000 YEN?
YEAH, BUT...
IT WOULD APPEAR HE CAME ACROSS A PARTICULARLY CRUEL FRAUDSTER.
IT WAS A HARD SELL DISGUISED AS A PURCHASING SERVICE.
BY THE TIME I REALIZED SOMETHING WAS WRONG, IT WAS ALREADY AS YOU SEE HERE.
YEAH, BUT...THE NEWSPAPER AND THE FRUIT, EVEN!?
WHAT KIND OF RIPOFF ARTIST SELLS EVERYTHING FROM FRUIT TO FIRE EXTINGUISH-ERS?
I'M SORRY. THE FRUIT AND NEWSPAPER WERE FROM OTHER GUYS.
I COULDN'T SAY NO TO 'EM.
WHAT ARE YOU, STUPID!?
JUST SAY YOU DON'T NEED THAT CRAP!
BUT, DUDE, THEY SAID THEY WOULDN'T LEAVE UNLESS I BOUGHT THEIR STUFF!
THEY KEPT ON JIGGLING THE DOOR-KNOB...
AND THEY SOUNDED SO CON-VINCING...
YOU ARE A DEMON GENERAL, RIGHT...?

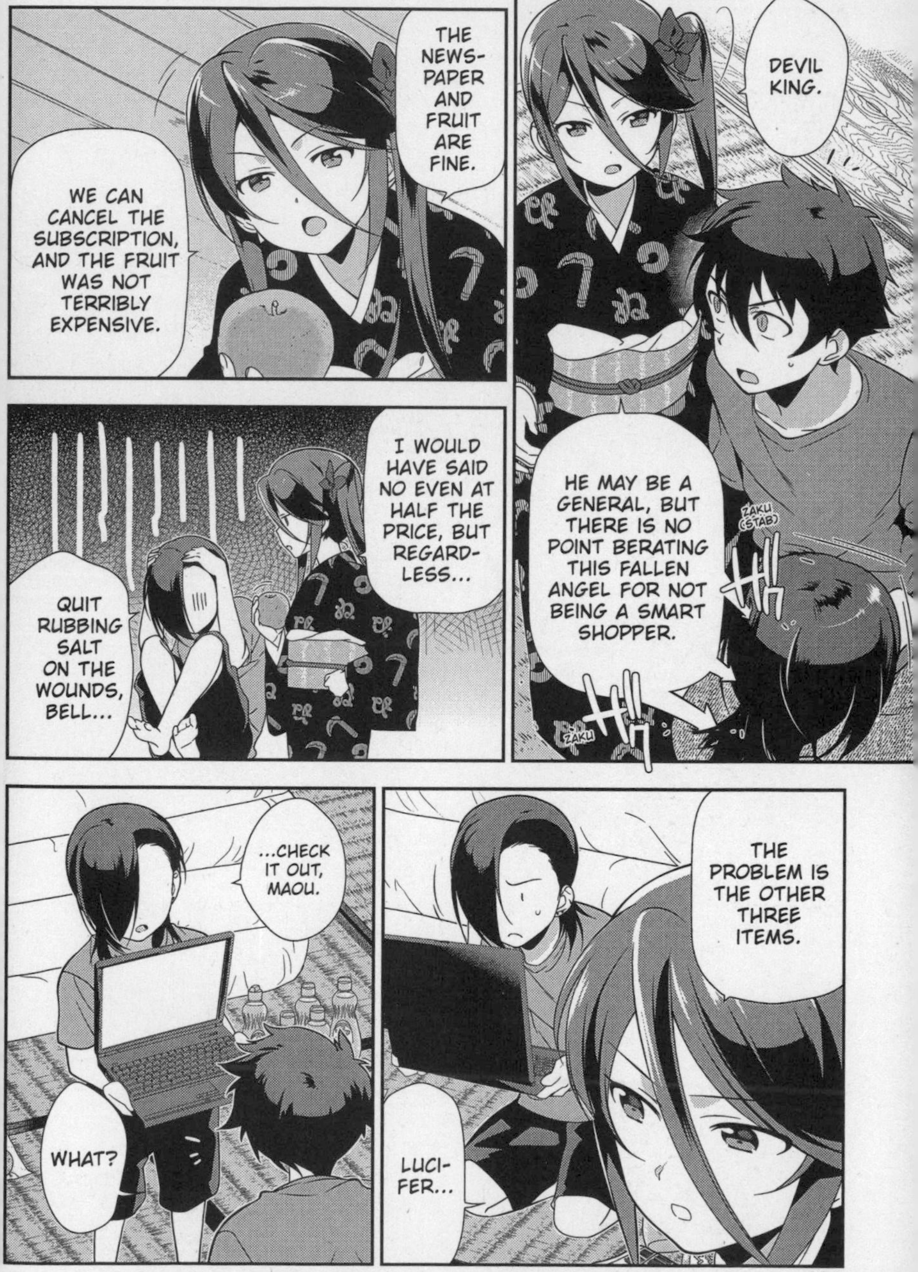
DEVIL KING.
HE MAY BE A GENERAL, BUT THERE IS NO POINT BERATING THIS FALLEN ANGEL FOR NOT BEING A SMART SHOPPER.
ZAKU (STAB)
ZAKU
THE NEWS-PAPER AND FRUIT ARE FINE.
WE CAN CANCEL THE SUBSCRIPTION, AND THE FRUIT WAS NOT TERRIBLY EXPENSIVE.
I WOULD HAVE SAID NO EVEN AT HALF THE PRICE, BUT REGARD-LESS...
QUIT RUBBING SALT ON THE WOUNDS, BELL...
THE PROBLEM IS THE OTHER THREE ITEMS.
LUCI-FER...
...CHECK IT OUT, MAOU.
WHAT?

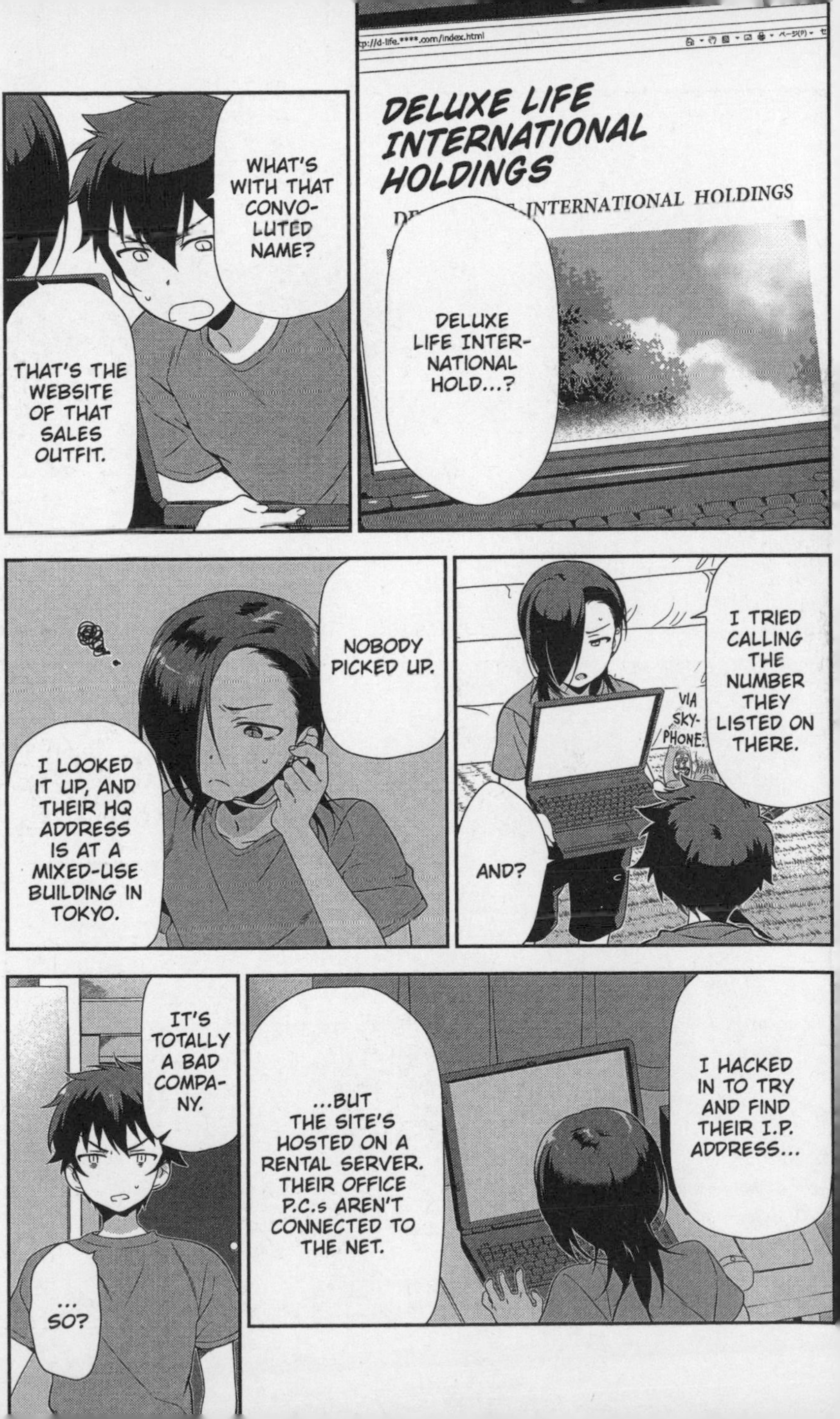

DELUXE LIFE INTERNATIONAL HOLDINGS
DELUXE LIFE INTERNATIONAL HOLD...?
WHAT'S WITH THAT CONVOLUTED NAME?
THAT'S THE WEBSITE OF THAT SALES OUTFIT.
I TRIED CALLING THE NUMBER THEY LISTED ON THERE.
VIA SKY-PHONE.
AND?
NOBODY PICKED UP.
I LOOKED IT UP, AND THEIR HQ ADDRESS IS AT A MIXED-USE BUILDING IN TOKYO.
I HACKED IN TO TRY AND FIND THEIR I.P. ADDRESS...
...BUT THE SITE'S HOSTED ON A RENTAL SERVER. THEIR OFFICE P.C.s AREN'T CONNECTED TO THE NET.
IT'S TOTALLY A BAD COMPANY.
... SO?

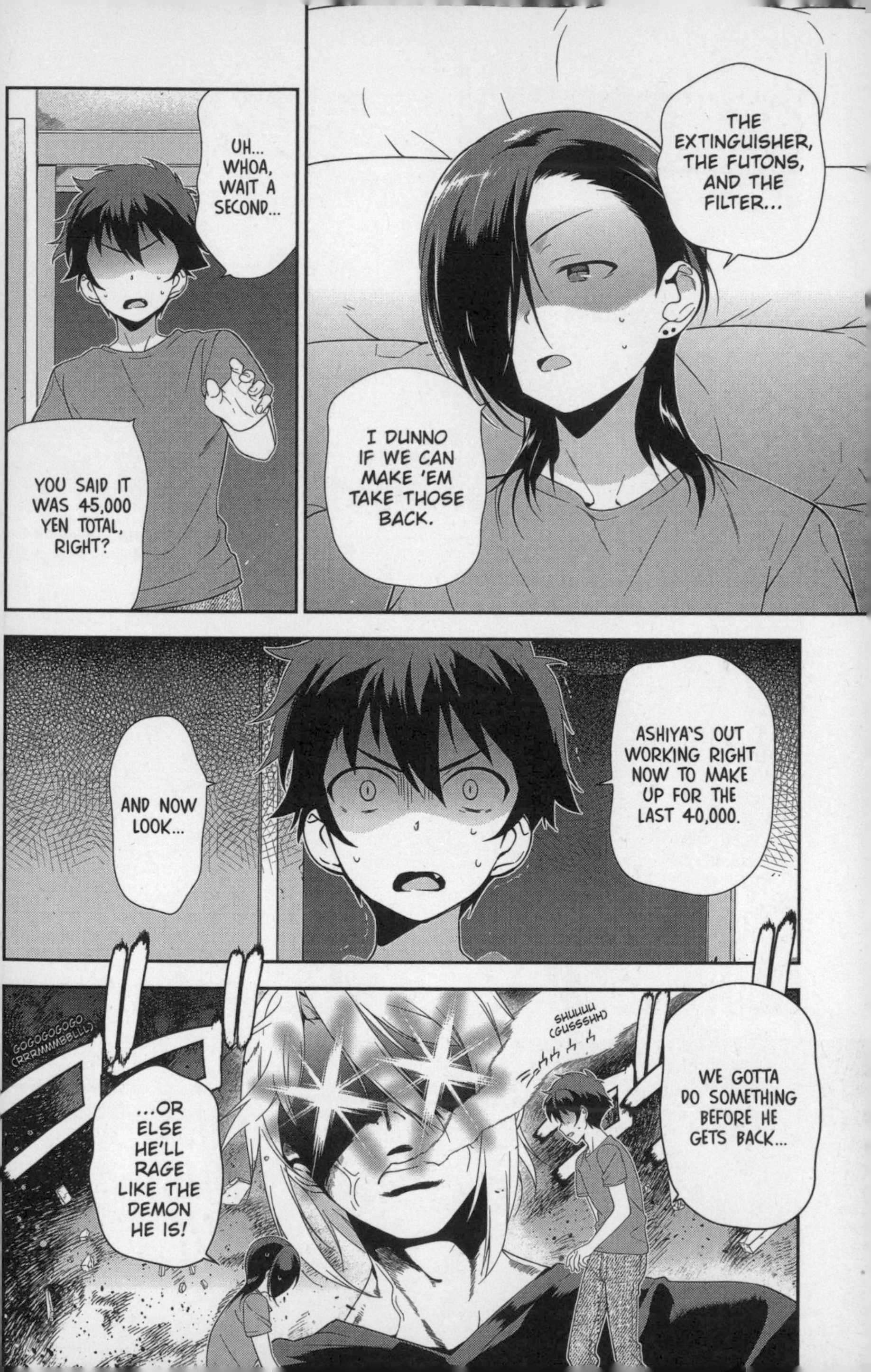
THE EXTINGUISHER, THE FUTONS, AND THE FILTER...
I DUNNO IF WE CAN MAKE 'EM TAKE THOSE BACK.
UH... WHOA, WAIT A SECOND...
YOU SAID IT WAS 45,000 YEN TOTAL, RIGHT?
ASHIYA'S OUT WORKING RIGHT NOW TO MAKE UP FOR THE LAST 40,000.
AND NOW LOOK...
WE GOTTA DO SOMETHING BEFORE HE GETS BACK...
SHUUUU (GUSSSHH)
...OR ELSE HE'LL RAGE LIKE THE DEMON HE IS!
GOGOGOGOGO (RRRUMMMBBLLL)

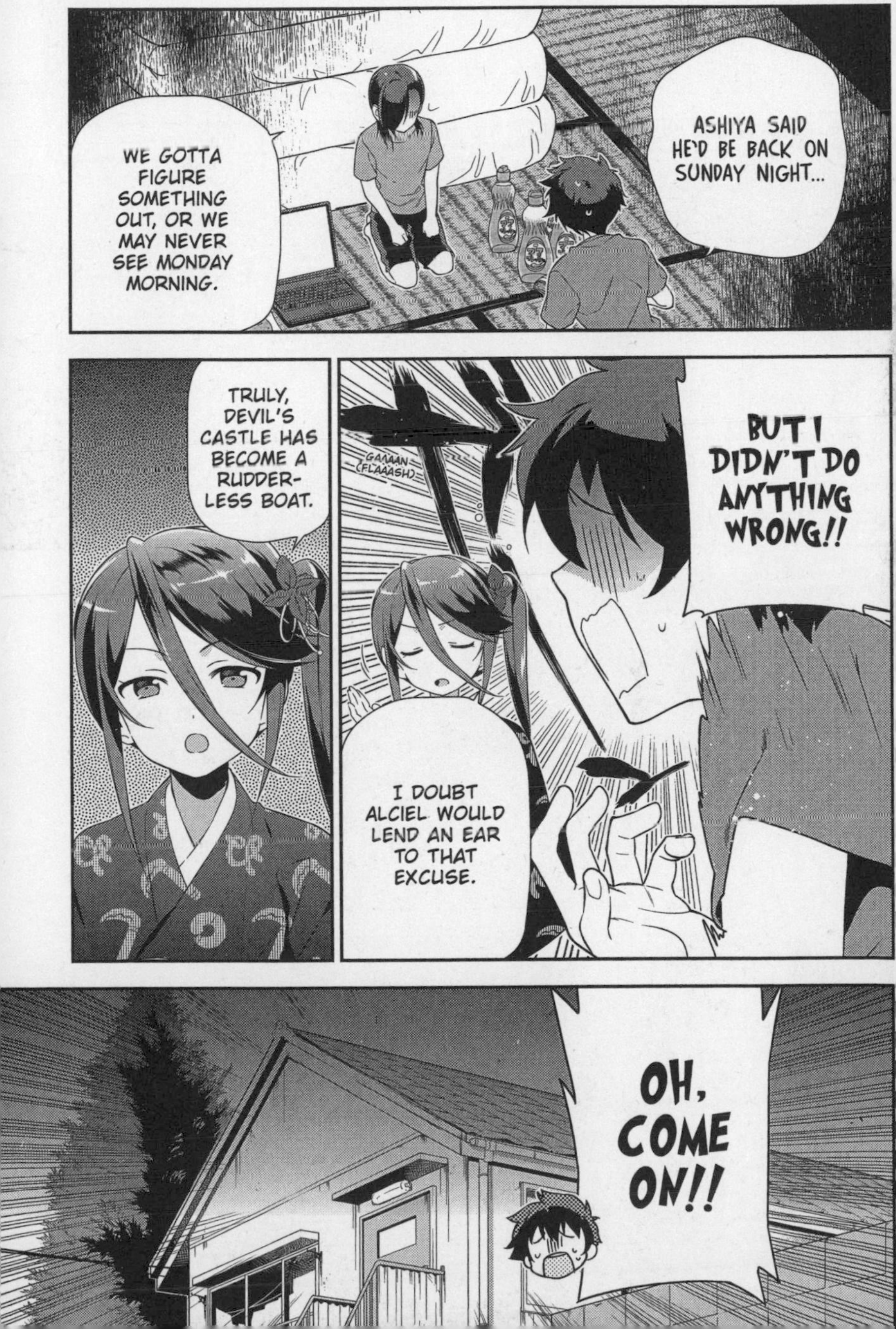
ASHIYA SAID HE'D BE BACK ON SUNDAY NIGHT...
WE GOTTA FIGURE SOMETHING OUT, OR WE MAY NEVER SEE MONDAY MORNING.
BUT I DIDN'T DO ANYTHING WRONG!!
GAAAAN (FLAAASH)
I DOUBT ALCIEL WOULD LEND AN EAR TO THAT EXCUSE.
TRULY, DEVIL'S CASTLE HAS BECOME A RUDDER-LESS BOAT.
OH, COME ON!!

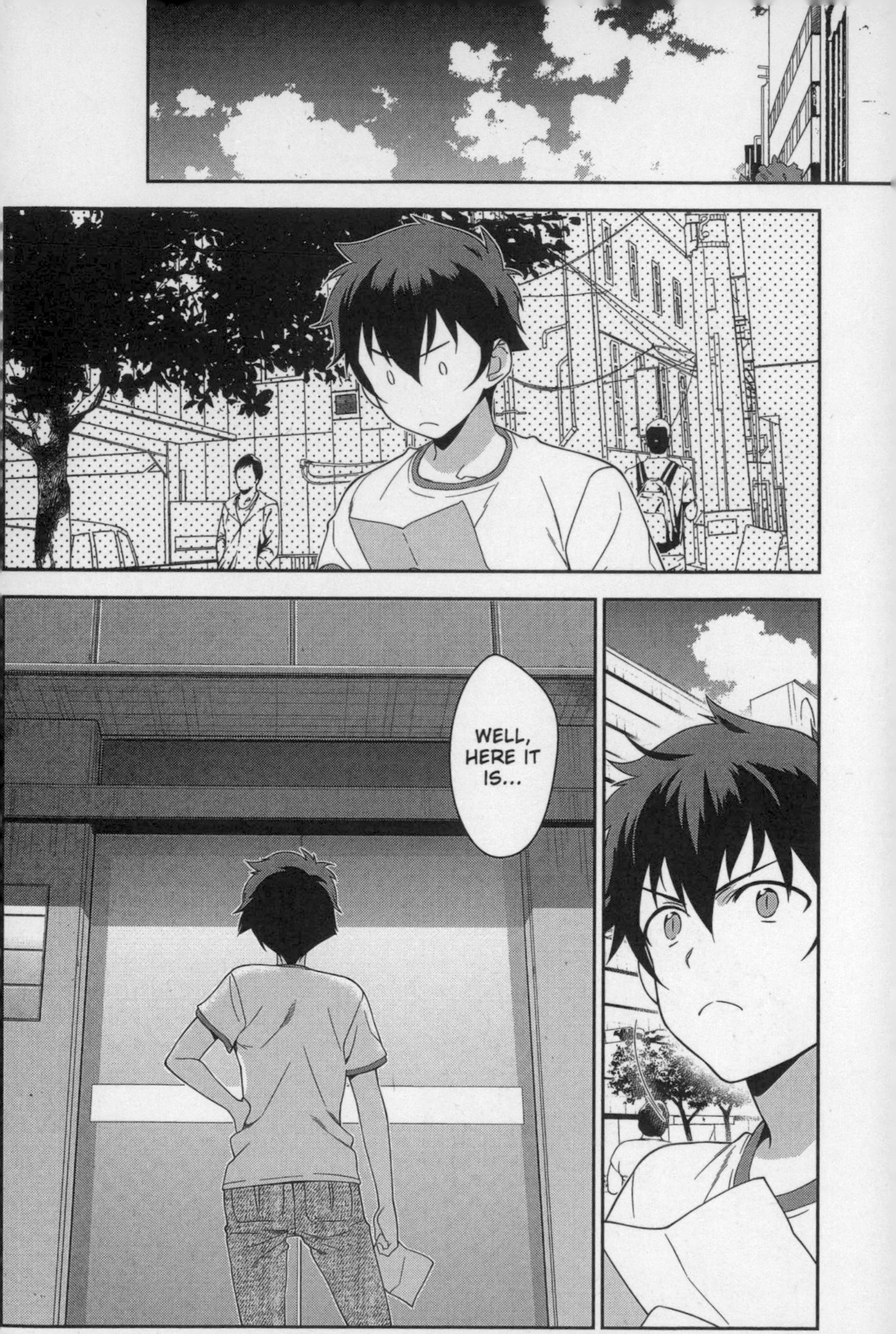
WELL, HERE IT IS...

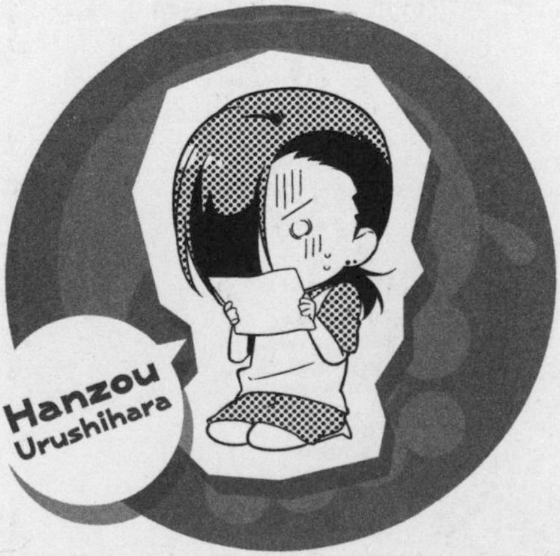
Hanzou
Urushihara

THE DEVIL IS A PART-TIMER!

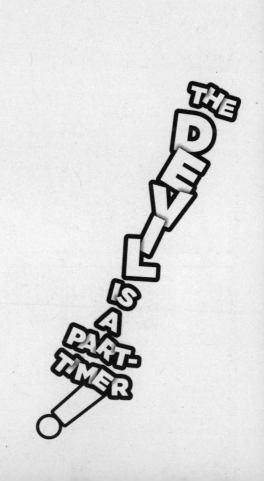

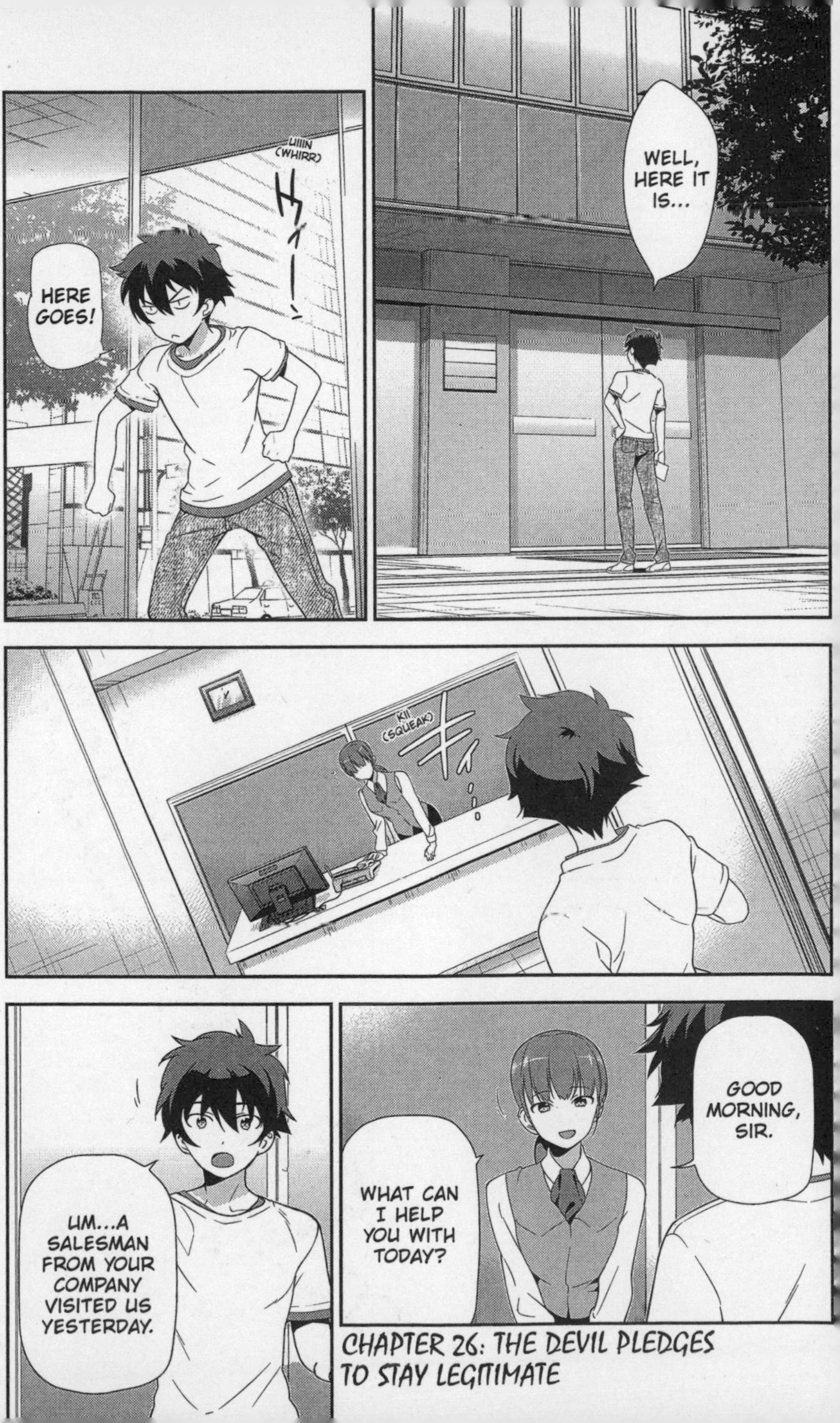
WELL, HERE IT IS...
UIIIN (WHIRR)
HERE GOES!
KII (SQUEAK)
GOOD MORNING, SIR.
WHAT CAN I HELP YOU WITH TODAY?
UM...A SALESMAN FROM YOUR COMPANY VISITED US YESTERDAY.

CHAPTER 26: THE DEVIL PLEDGES TO STAY LEGITIMATE

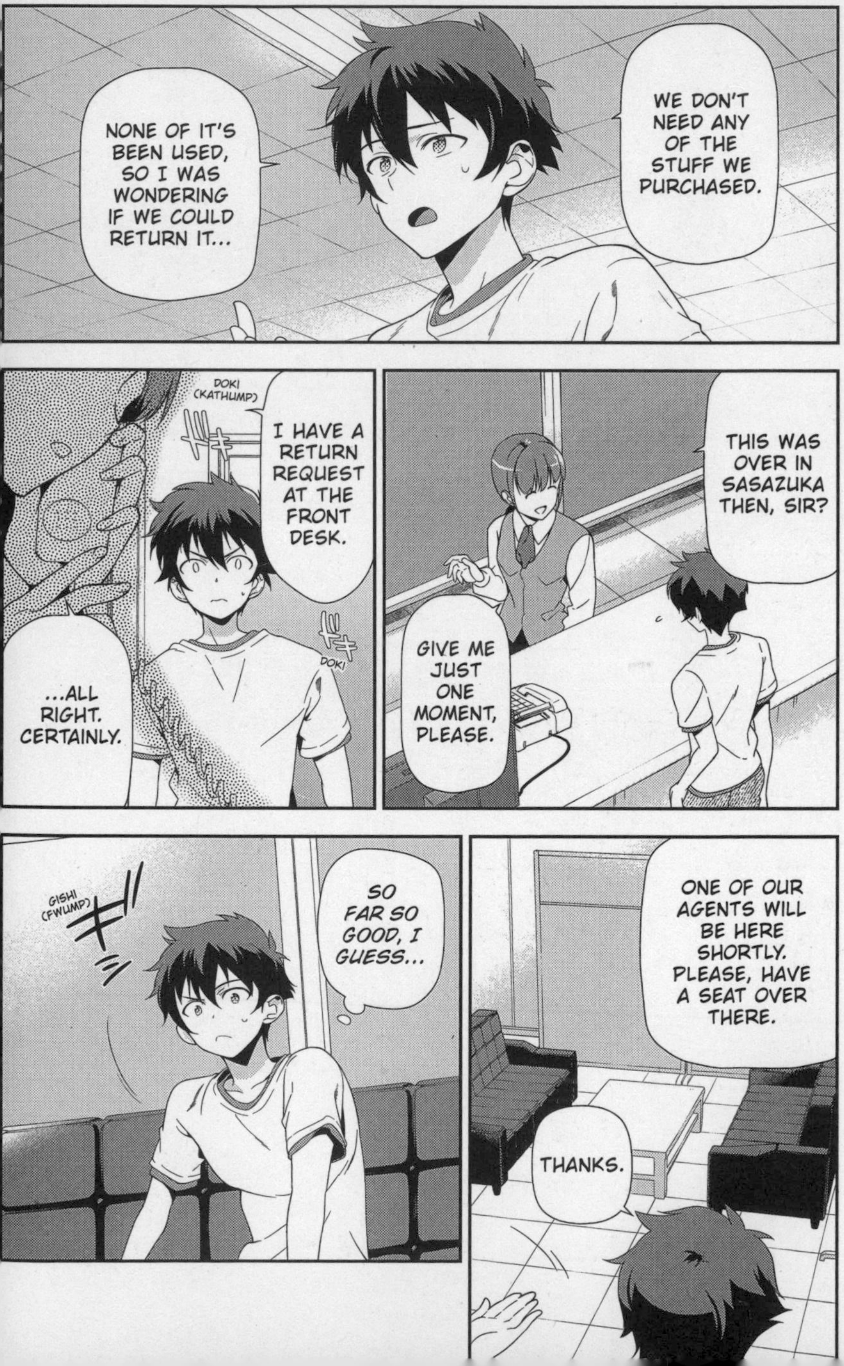
WE DON'T NEED ANY OF THE STUFF WE PURCHASED.
NONE OF IT'S BEEN USED, SO I WAS WONDERING IF WE COULD RETURN IT...
THIS WAS OVER IN SASAZUKA THEN, SIR?
GIVE ME JUST ONE MOMENT, PLEASE.
DOKI (KATHUMP)
I HAVE A RETURN REQUEST AT THE FRONT DESK.
DOKI
...ALL RIGHT. CERTAINLY.
ONE OF OUR AGENTS WILL BE HERE SHORTLY. PLEASE, HAVE A SEAT OVER THERE.
THANKS.
GISHI (FWUMP)
SO FAR SO GOOD, I GUESS...

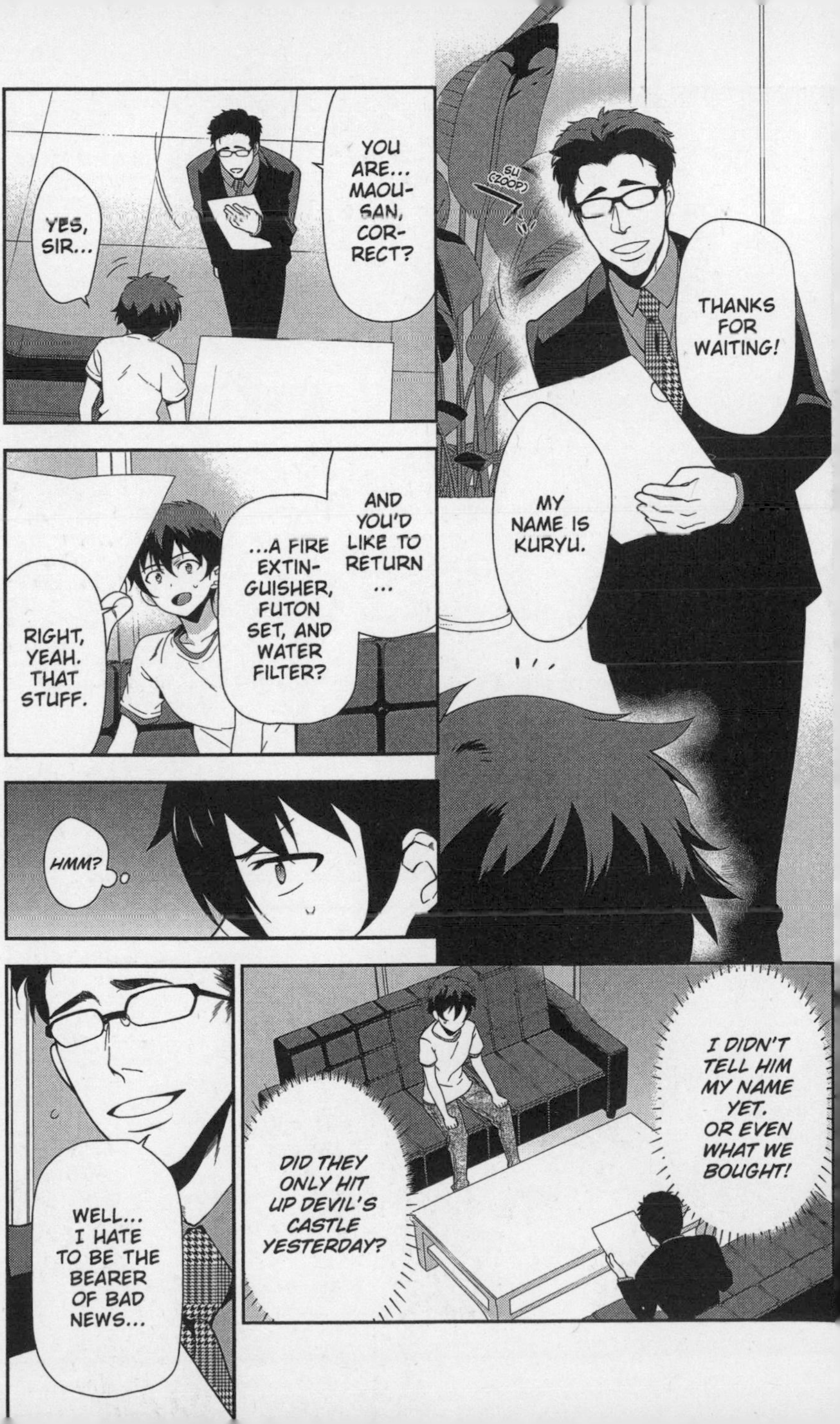
SU (ZOOP)
THANKS FOR WAITING!
MY NAME IS KURYU.
YOU ARE... MAOU-SAN, COR-RECT?
YES, SIR...
AND YOU'D LIKE TO RETURN ...
...A FIRE EXTIN-GUISHER, FUTON SET, AND WATER FILTER?
RIGHT, YEAH. THAT STUFF.
HMM?
I DIDN'T TELL HIM MY NAME YET. OR EVEN WHAT WE BOUGHT!
DID THEY ONLY HIT UP DEVIL'S CASTLE YESTERDAY?
WELL... I HATE TO BE THE BEARER OF BAD NEWS...

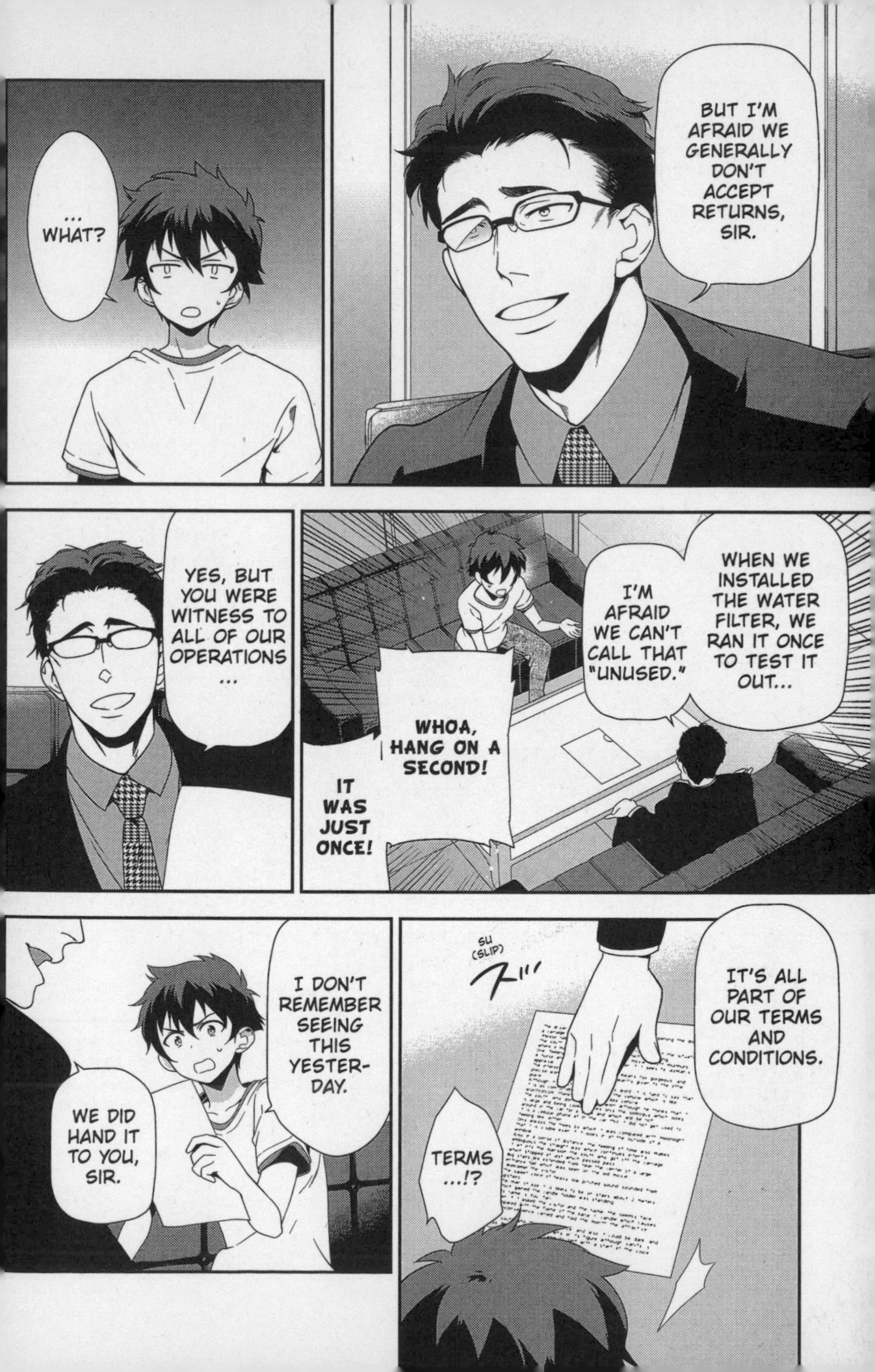
BUT I'M AFRAID WE GENERALLY DON'T ACCEPT RETURNS, SIR.
... WHAT?
WHEN WE INSTALLED THE WATER FILTER, WE RAN IT ONCE TO TEST IT OUT...
I'M AFRAID WE CAN'T CALL THAT "UNUSED."
WHOA, HANG ON A SECOND!
IT WAS JUST ONCE!
YES, BUT YOU WERE WITNESS TO ALL OF OUR OPERATIONS ...
IT'S ALL PART OF OUR TERMS AND CONDITIONS.
SU (SLIP)
TERMS ...!?
I DON'T REMEMBER SEEING THIS YESTER-DAY.
WE DID HAND IT TO YOU, SIR.

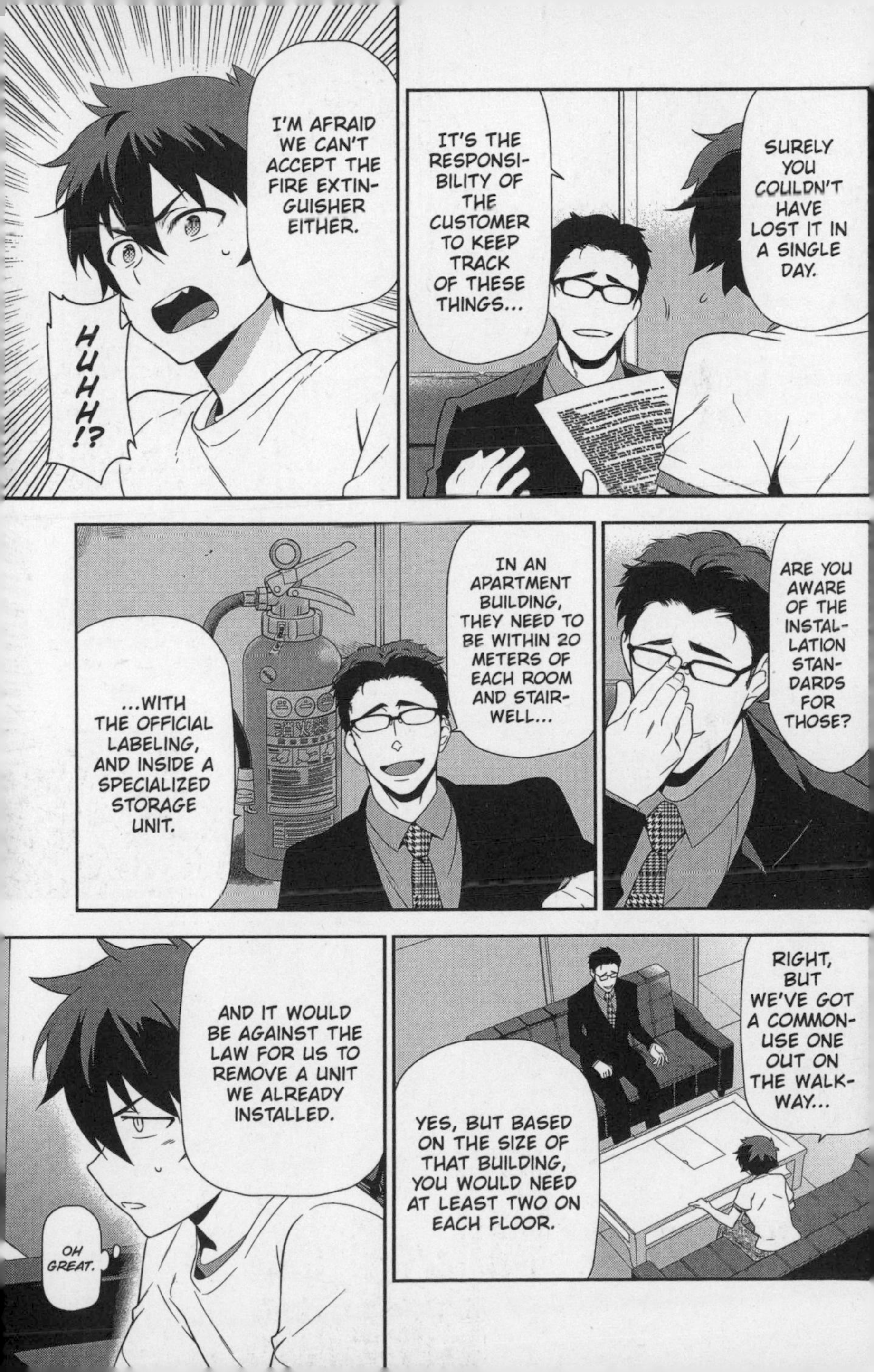

SURELY YOU COULDN'T HAVE LOST IT IN A SINGLE DAY.
IT'S THE RESPONSIBILITY OF THE CUSTOMER TO KEEP TRACK OF THESE THINGS...
I'M AFRAID WE CAN'T ACCEPT THE FIRE EXTINGUISHER EITHER.
HUHHH!?
ARE YOU AWARE OF THE INSTALLATION STANDARDS FOR THOSE?
IN AN APARTMENT BUILDING, THEY NEED TO BE WITHIN 20 METERS OF EACH ROOM AND STAIRWELL...
...WITH THE OFFICIAL LABELING, AND INSIDE A SPECIALIZED STORAGE UNIT.
RIGHT, BUT WE'VE GOT A COMMON-USE ONE OUT ON THE WALKWAY...
YES, BUT BASED ON THE SIZE OF THAT BUILDING, YOU WOULD NEED AT LEAST TWO ON EACH FLOOR.
AND IT WOULD BE AGAINST THE LAW FOR US TO REMOVE A UNIT WE ALREADY INSTALLED.
OH GREAT.

A SET OF SEVEN FEATHER-BED FUTONS, CORRECT?

IF THEY'RE IN UNOPENED, UNUSED CONDITION, WE CAN ACCEPT THOSE.

I THINK I'M STARTING TO GET THIS.

OKAY, WHAT ABOUT THE FUTONS?

	FIRE EXTINGU
1 SET	WATER FILTER
7	FEATHER-BED FUTON (BED ONLY)

Hanyou Urushikara

NO, IT WAS SEVEN.

IT'S WRITTEN RIGHT HERE, SIR.

SU (ZOOP)

...UM, THAT SHOULD BE FIVE.

IF THAT'S THE CASE, EVEN IF THEY'RE UNUSED, WE'D ONLY BE ABLE TO REFUND THE REMAINING FIVE FUTONS AT THEIR USED-GOODS VALUE.

GRR!

THEY MUST'VE DOCTORED THAT RECEIPT...

...I'M AFRAID FIVE FUTONS WOULDN'T BE A FULL SET.

146

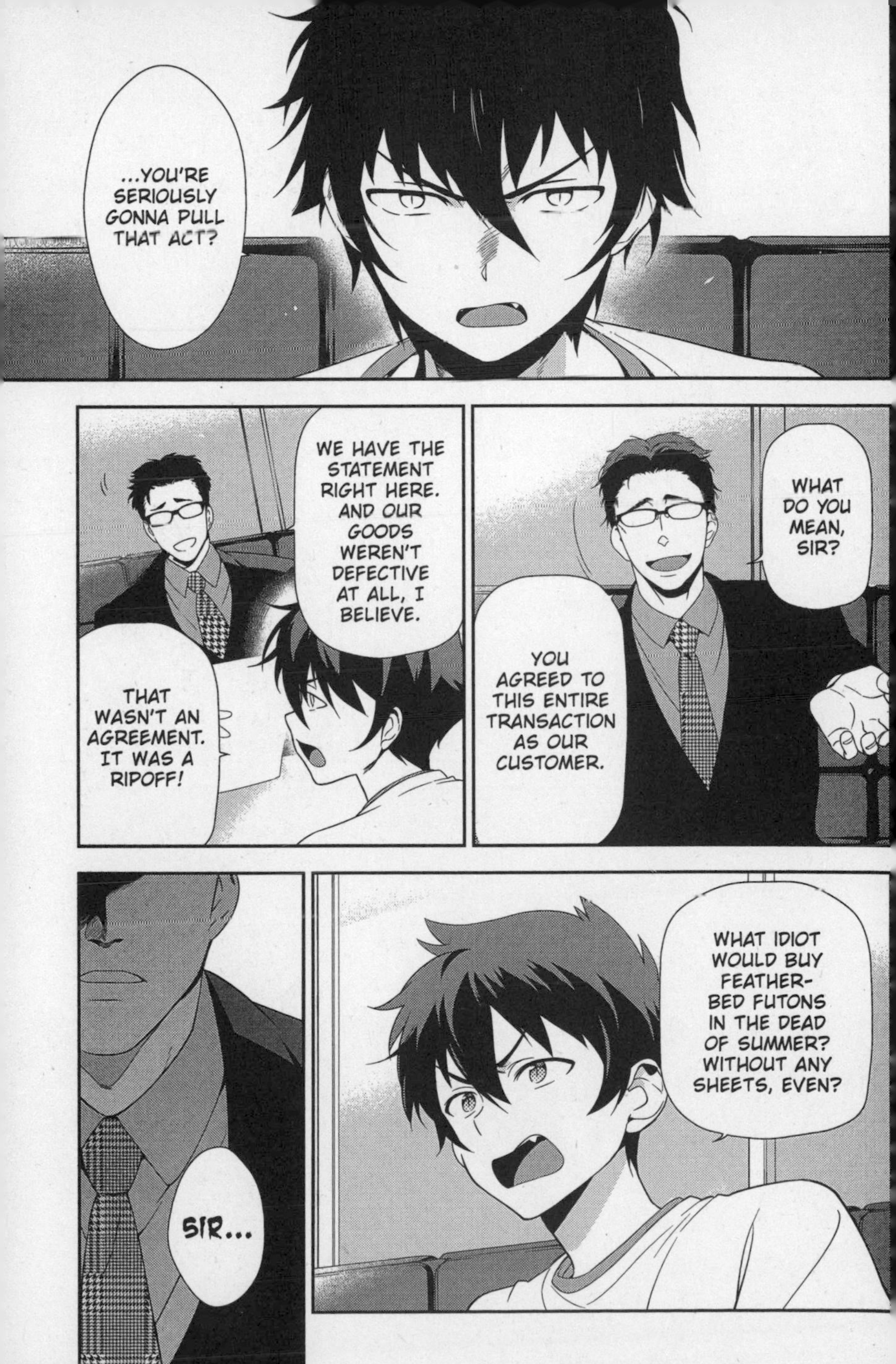
...YOU'RE SERIOUSLY GONNA PULL THAT ACT?
WHAT DO YOU MEAN, SIR?
YOU AGREED TO THIS ENTIRE TRANSACTION AS OUR CUSTOMER.
WE HAVE THE STATEMENT RIGHT HERE. AND OUR GOODS WEREN'T DEFECTIVE AT ALL, I BELIEVE.
THAT WASN'T AN AGREEMENT. IT WAS A RIPOFF!
WHAT IDIOT WOULD BUY FEATHER-BED FUTONS IN THE DEAD OF SUMMER? WITHOUT ANY SHEETS, EVEN?
SIR...

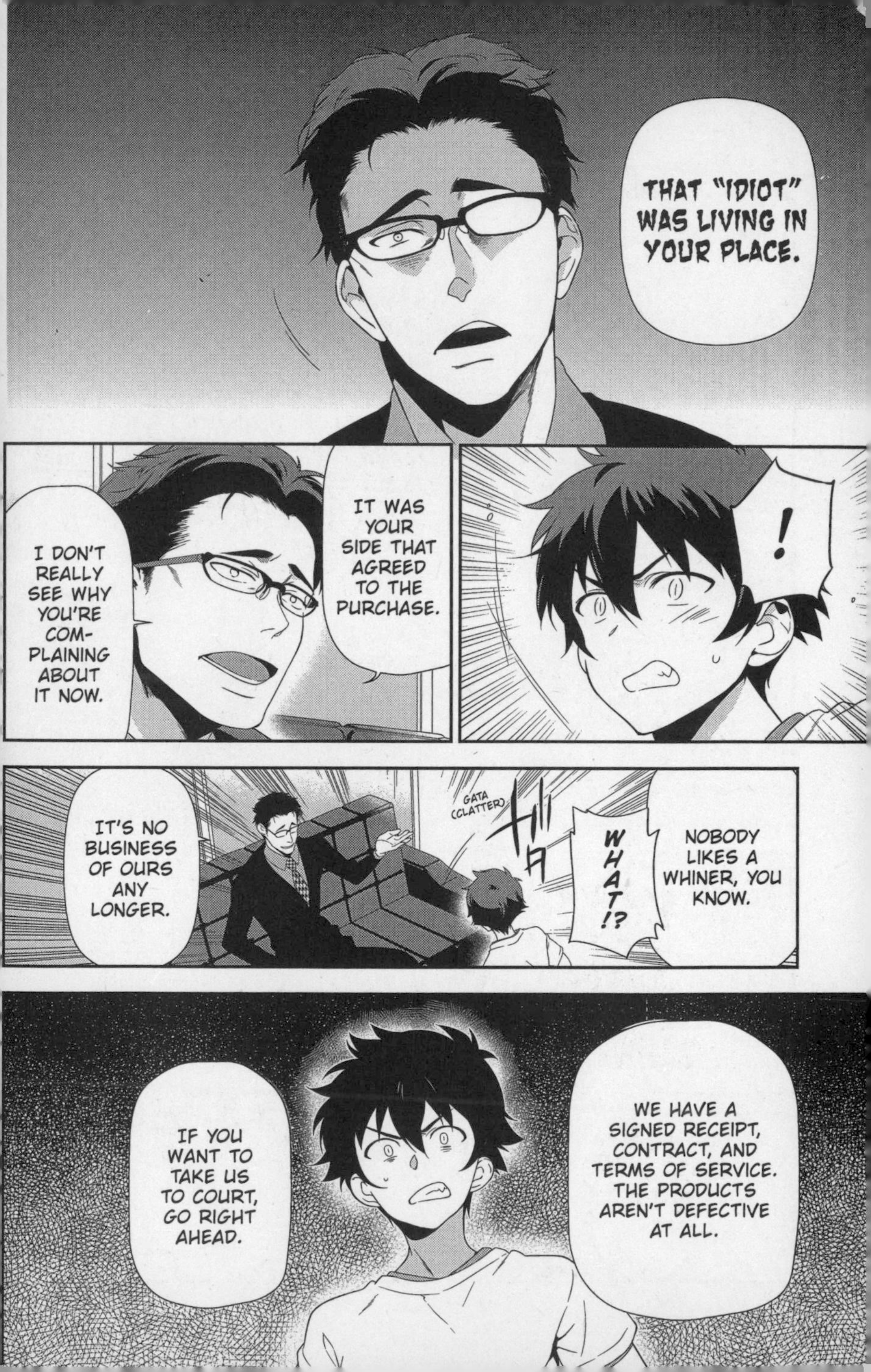
THAT "IDIOT" WAS LIVING IN YOUR PLACE.
!
IT WAS YOUR SIDE THAT AGREED TO THE PURCHASE.
I DON'T REALLY SEE WHY YOU'RE COM-PLAINING ABOUT IT NOW.
NOBODY LIKES A WHINER, YOU KNOW.
WHAT!?
GATA (CLATTER)
IT'S NO BUSINESS OF OURS ANY LONGER.
WE HAVE A SIGNED RECEIPT, CONTRACT, AND TERMS OF SERVICE. THE PRODUCTS AREN'T DEFECTIVE AT ALL.
IF YOU WANT TO TAKE US TO COURT, GO RIGHT AHEAD.

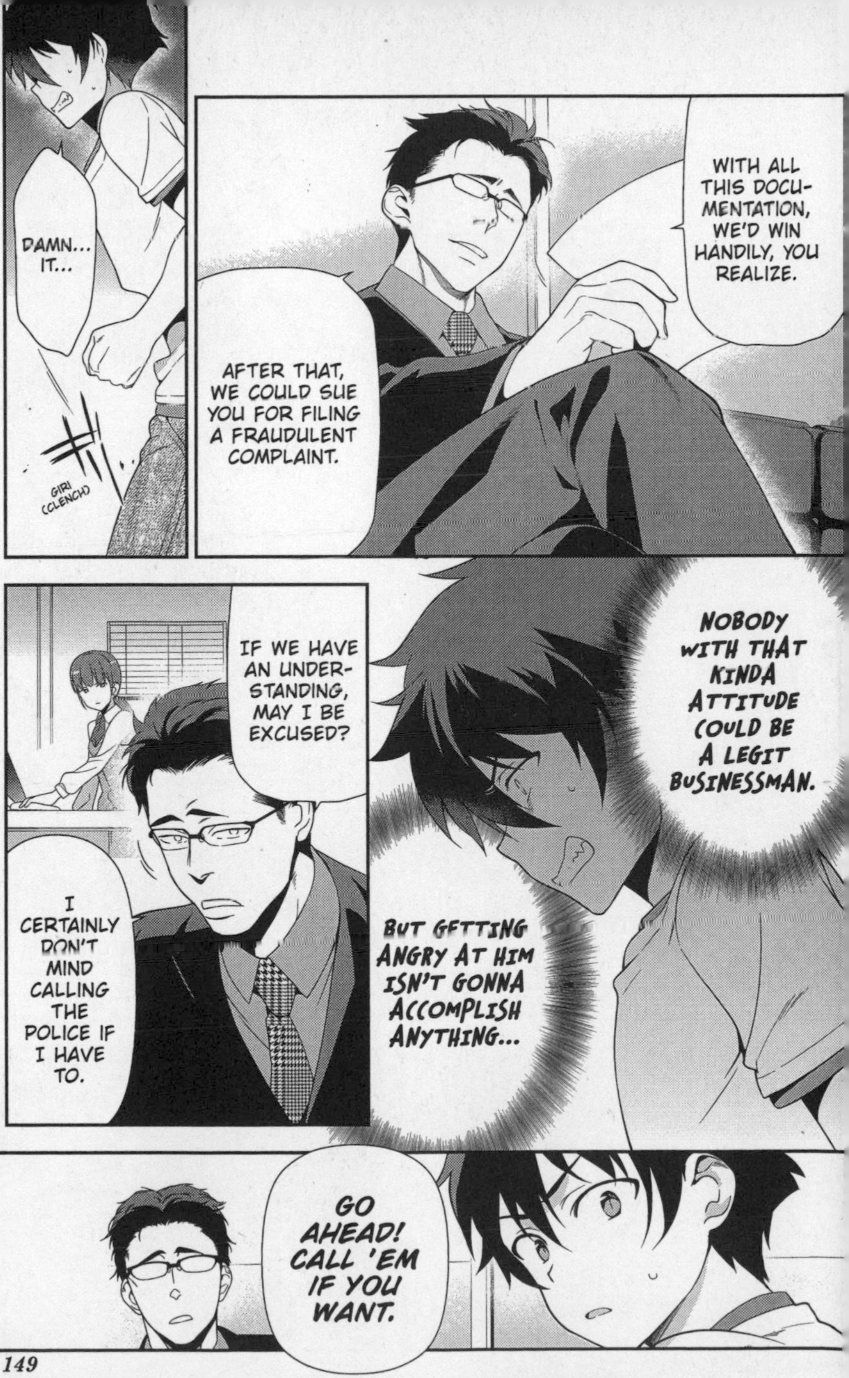
WITH ALL THIS DOCU-MENTATION, WE'D WIN HANDILY, YOU REALIZE.
AFTER THAT, WE COULD SUE YOU FOR FILING A FRAUDULENT COMPLAINT.
DAMN... IT...
GIRI (CLENCH)
NOBODY WITH THAT KINDA ATTITUDE COULD BE A LEGIT BUSINESSMAN.
BUT GETTING ANGRY AT HIM ISN'T GONNA ACCOMPLISH ANYTHING...
IF WE HAVE AN UNDER-STANDING, MAY I BE EXCUSED?
I CERTAINLY DON'T MIND CALLING THE POLICE IF I HAVE TO.
GO AHEAD! CALL 'EM IF YOU WANT.

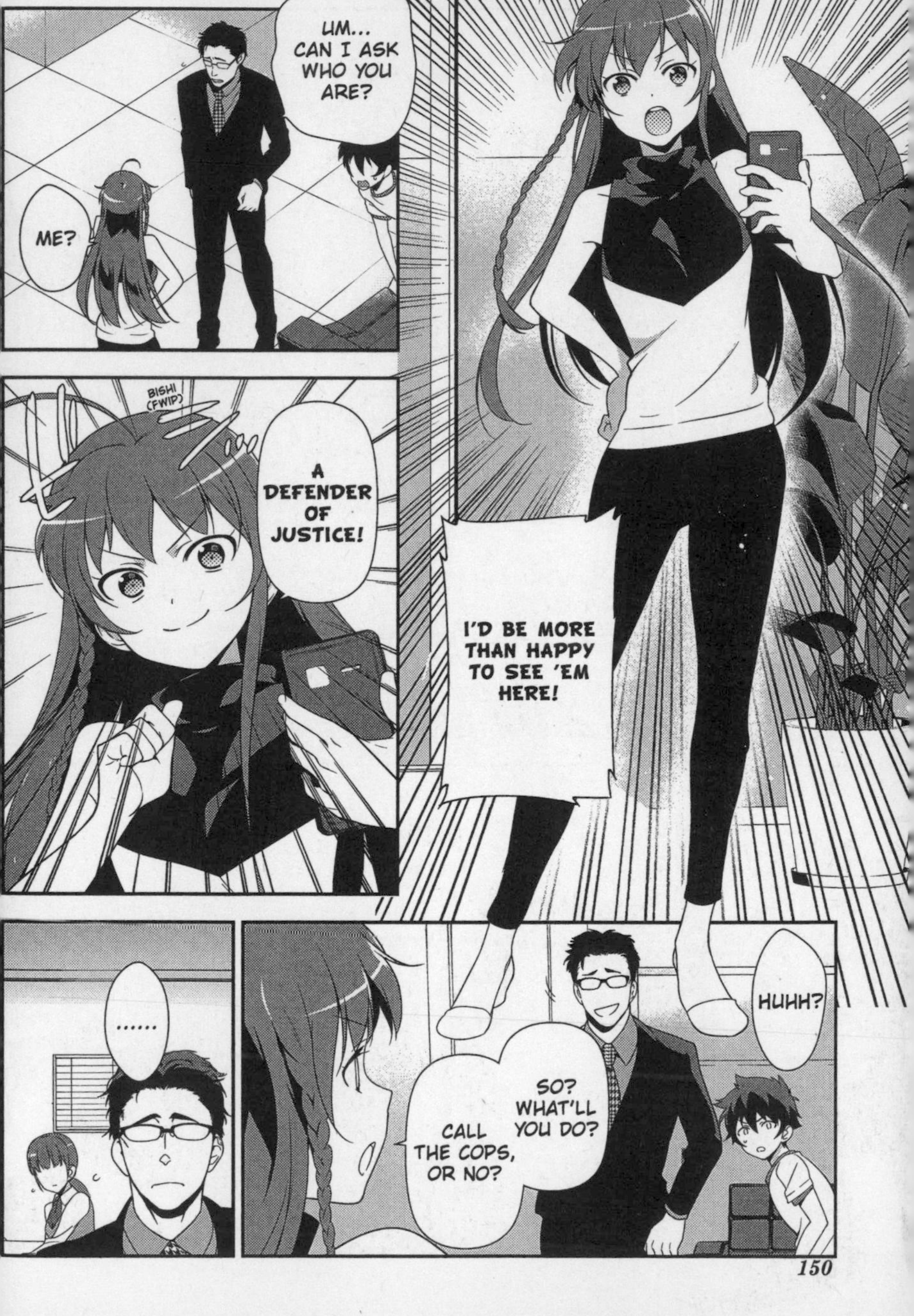
I'D BE MORE THAN HAPPY TO SEE 'EM HERE!
UM... CAN I ASK WHO YOU ARE?
ME?
BISHI (FWIP)
A DEFENDER OF JUSTICE!
HUHH?
SO? WHAT'LL YOU DO?
CALL THE COPS, OR NO?
....

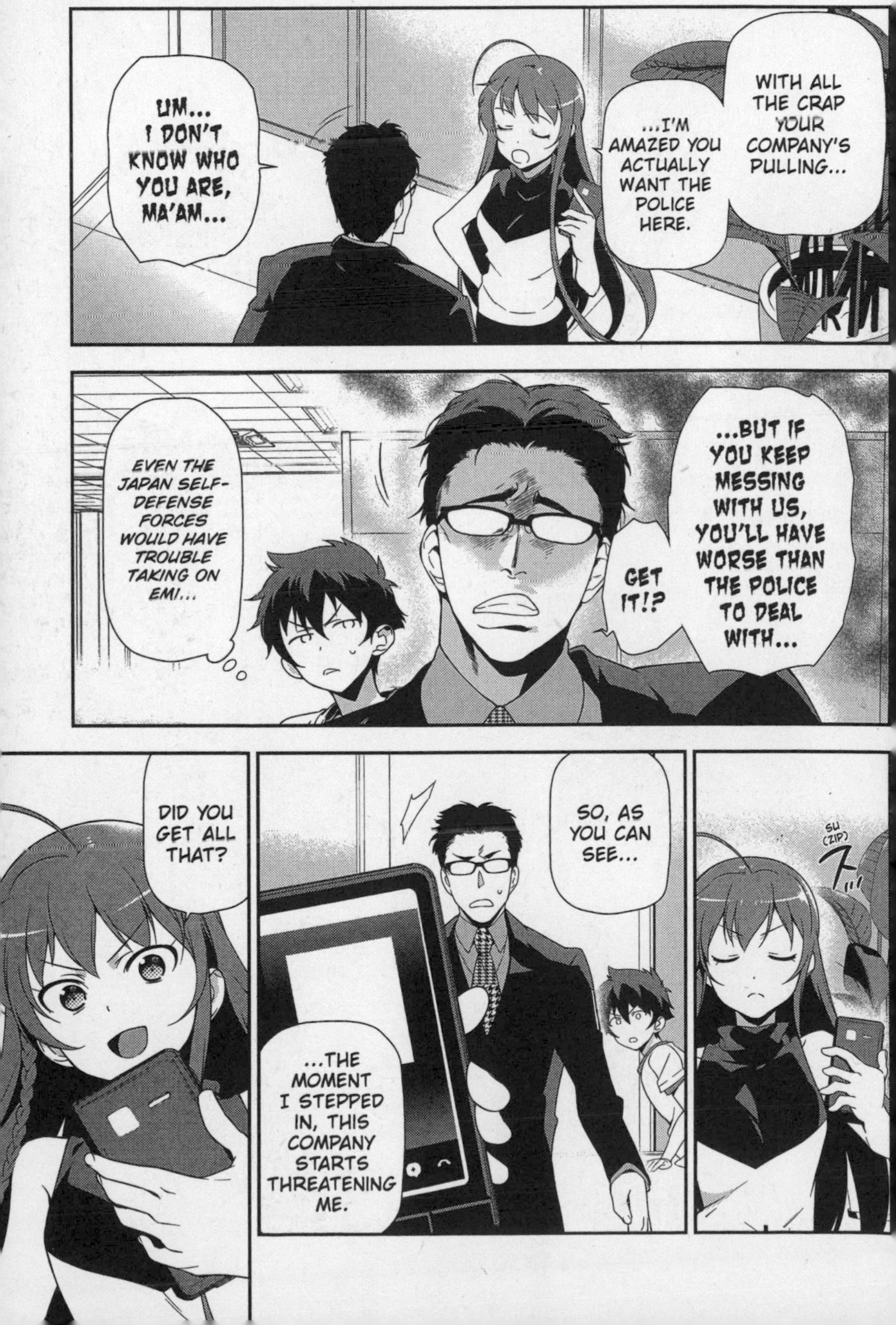
WITH ALL THE CRAP YOUR COMPANY'S PULLING...
...I'M AMAZED YOU ACTUALLY WANT THE POLICE HERE.
UM... I DON'T KNOW WHO YOU ARE, MA'AM...
...BUT IF YOU KEEP MESSING WITH US, YOU'LL HAVE WORSE THAN THE POLICE TO DEAL WITH...
GET IT!?
EVEN THE JAPAN SELF-DEFENSE FORCES WOULD HAVE TROUBLE TAKING ON EMI...
SU (ZIP)
SO, AS YOU CAN SEE...
...THE MOMENT I STEPPED IN, THIS COMPANY STARTS THREATENING ME.
DID YOU GET ALL THAT?

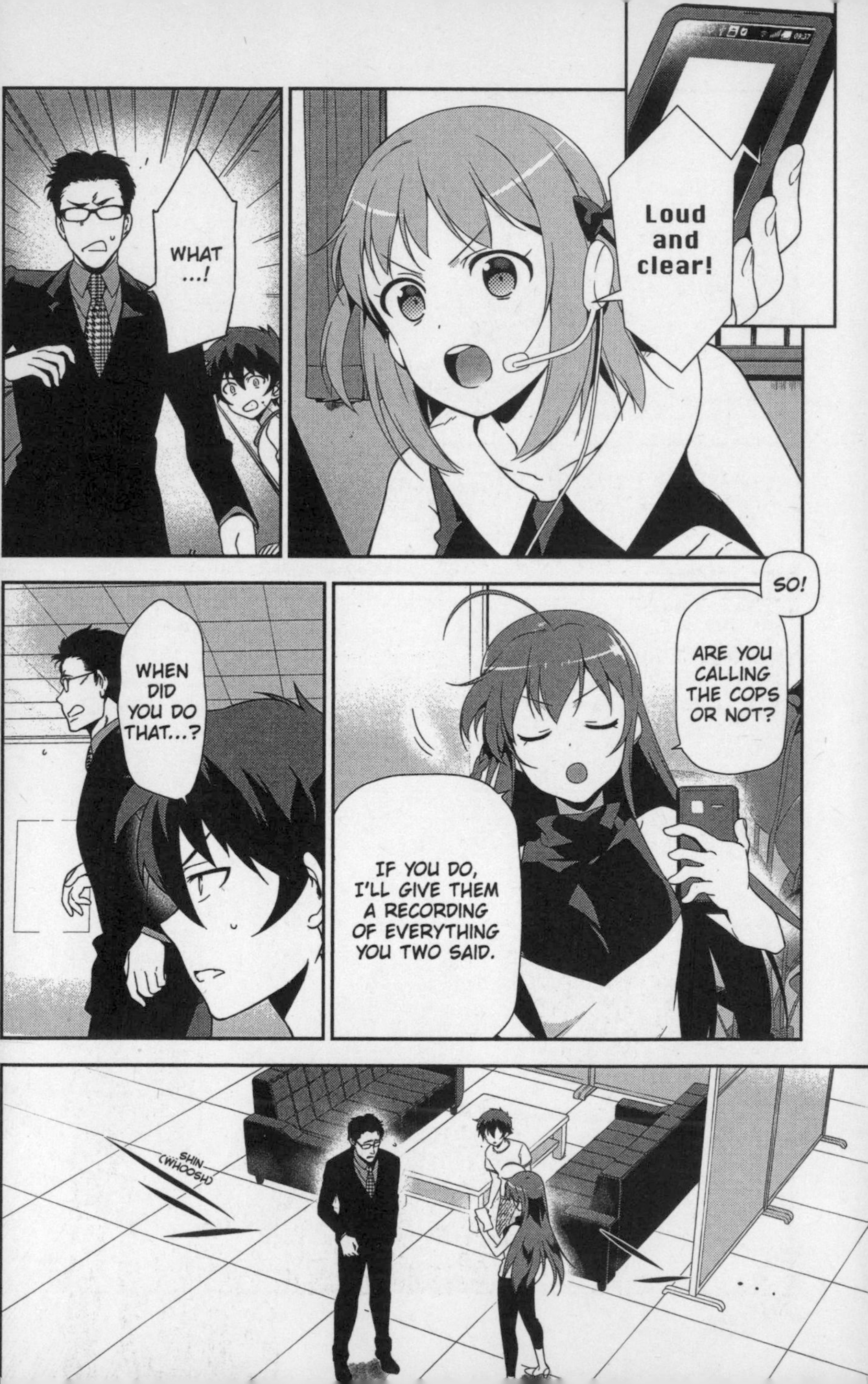
Loud and clear!
WHAT ...!
SO!
ARE YOU CALLING THE COPS OR NOT?
IF YOU DO, I'LL GIVE THEM A RECORDING OF EVERYTHING YOU TWO SAID.
WHEN DID YOU DO THAT...?
SHIN (WHOOSH)
...

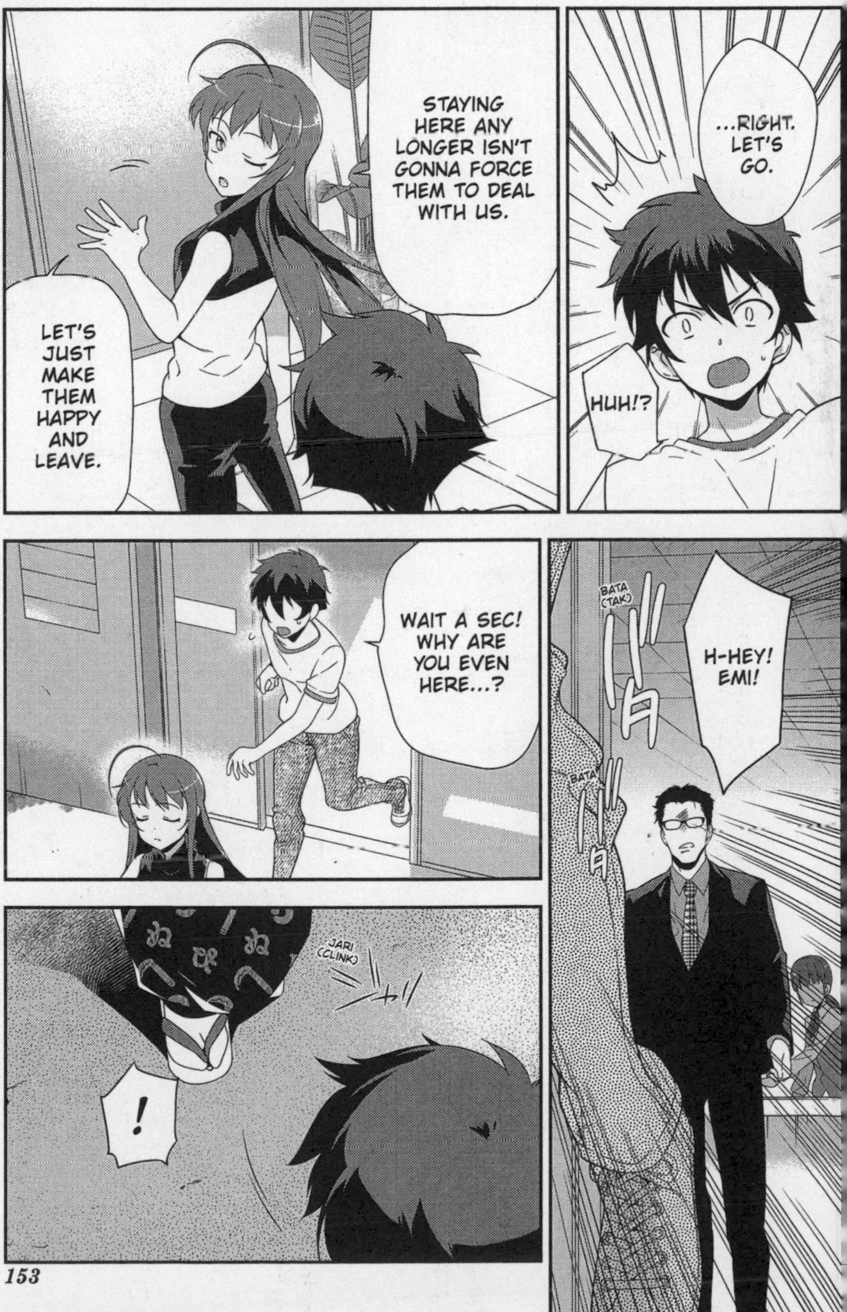
...RIGHT. LET'S GO.
HUH!?
STAYING HERE ANY LONGER ISN'T GONNA FORCE THEM TO DEAL WITH US.
LET'S JUST MAKE THEM HAPPY AND LEAVE.
H-HEY! EMI!
BATA (TAK)
BATA
WAIT A SEC! WHY ARE YOU EVEN HERE...?
JARI (CLINK)
!

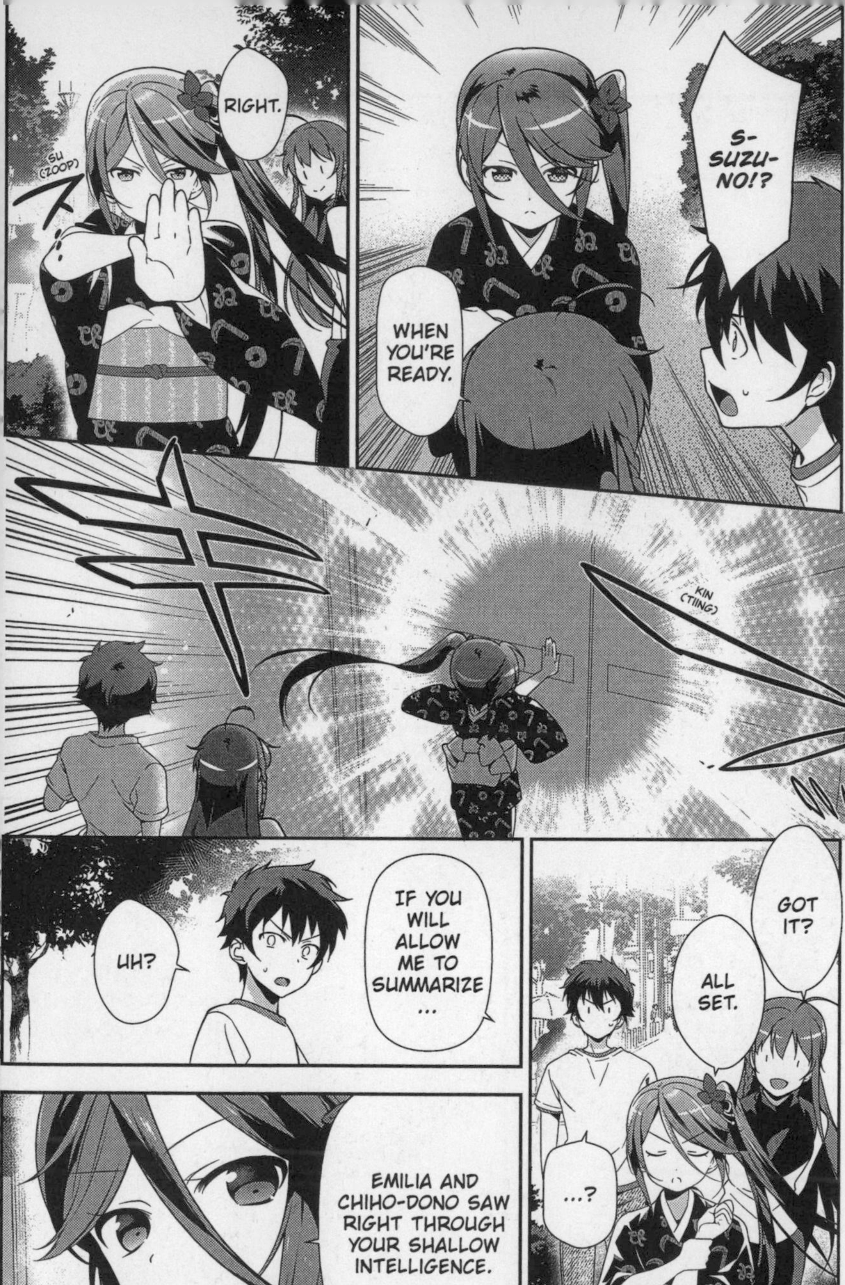
S-SUZUNO!?
WHEN YOU'RE READY.
RIGHT.
SU (ZOOP)
KIN (TIING)
GOT IT?
ALL SET.
...?
IF YOU WILL ALLOW ME TO SUMMARIZE ...
UH?
EMILIA AND CHIHO-DONO SAW RIGHT THROUGH YOUR SHALLOW INTELLIGENCE.

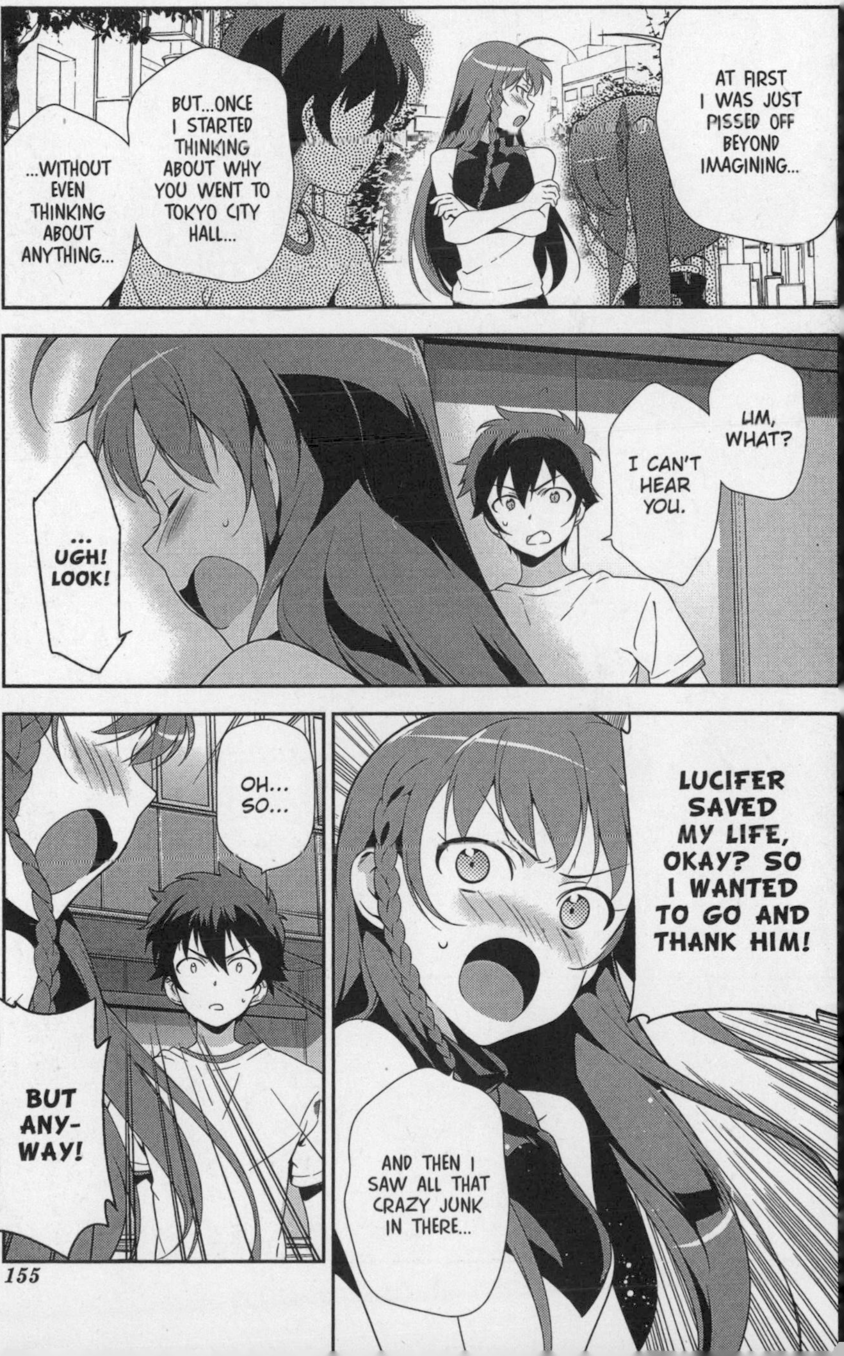
AT FIRST I WAS JUST PISSED OFF BEYOND IMAGINING...
BUT...ONCE I STARTED THINKING ABOUT WHY YOU WENT TO TOKYO CITY HALL...
...WITHOUT EVEN THINKING ABOUT ANYTHING...
UM, WHAT?
I CAN'T HEAR YOU.
... UGH! LOOK!
LUCIFER SAVED MY LIFE, OKAY? SO I WANTED TO GO AND THANK HIM!
AND THEN I SAW ALL THAT CRAZY JUNK IN THERE...
OH... SO...
BUT ANY-WAY!

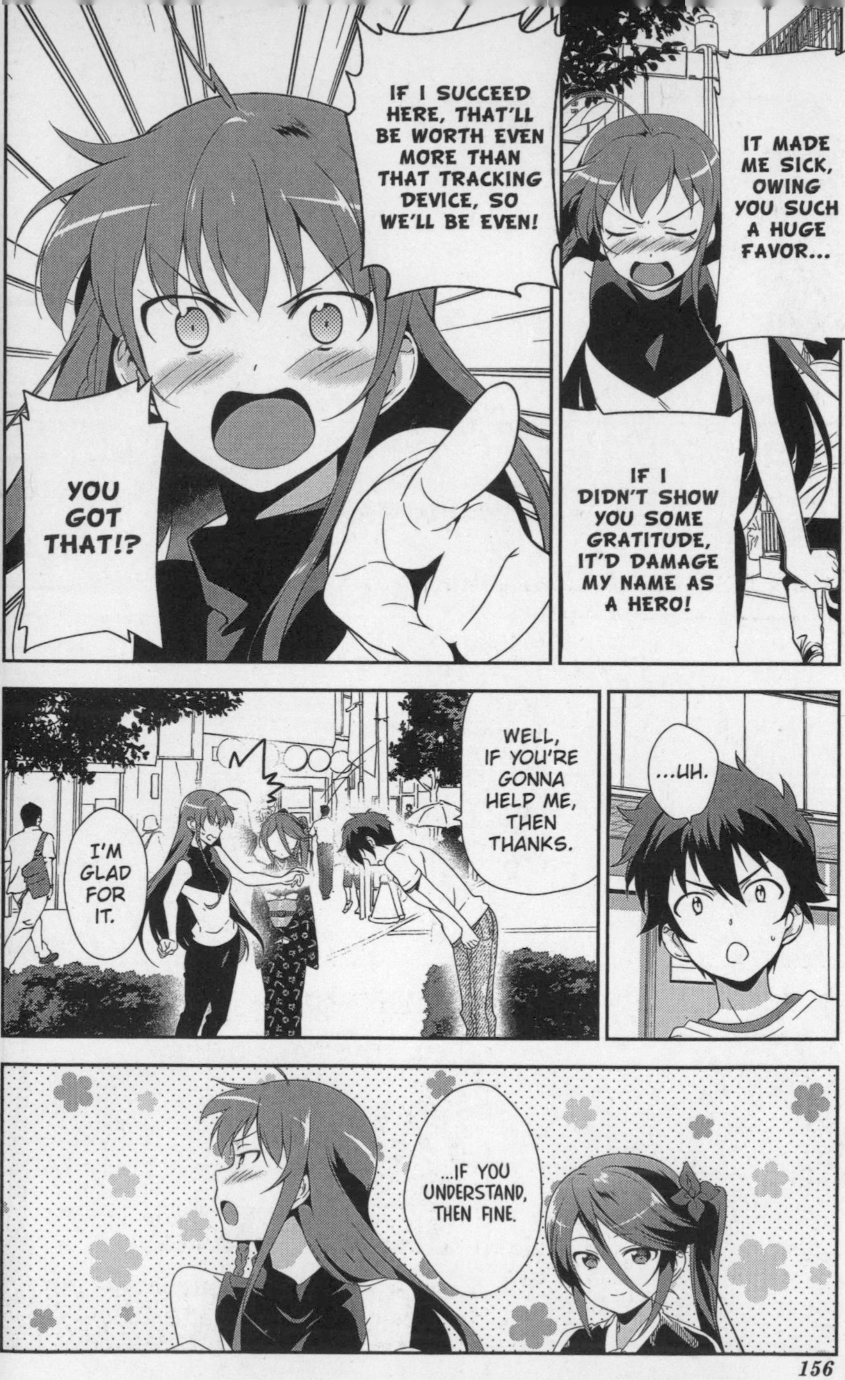
IT MADE ME SICK, OWING YOU SUCH A HUGE FAVOR...
IF I DIDN'T SHOW YOU SOME GRATITUDE, IT'D DAMAGE MY NAME AS A HERO!
IF I SUCCEED HERE, THAT'LL BE WORTH EVEN MORE THAN THAT TRACKING DEVICE, SO WE'LL BE EVEN!
YOU GOT THAT!?
...UH.
WELL, IF YOU'RE GONNA HELP ME, THEN THANKS.
I'M GLAD FOR IT.
...IF YOU UNDERSTAND, THEN FINE.

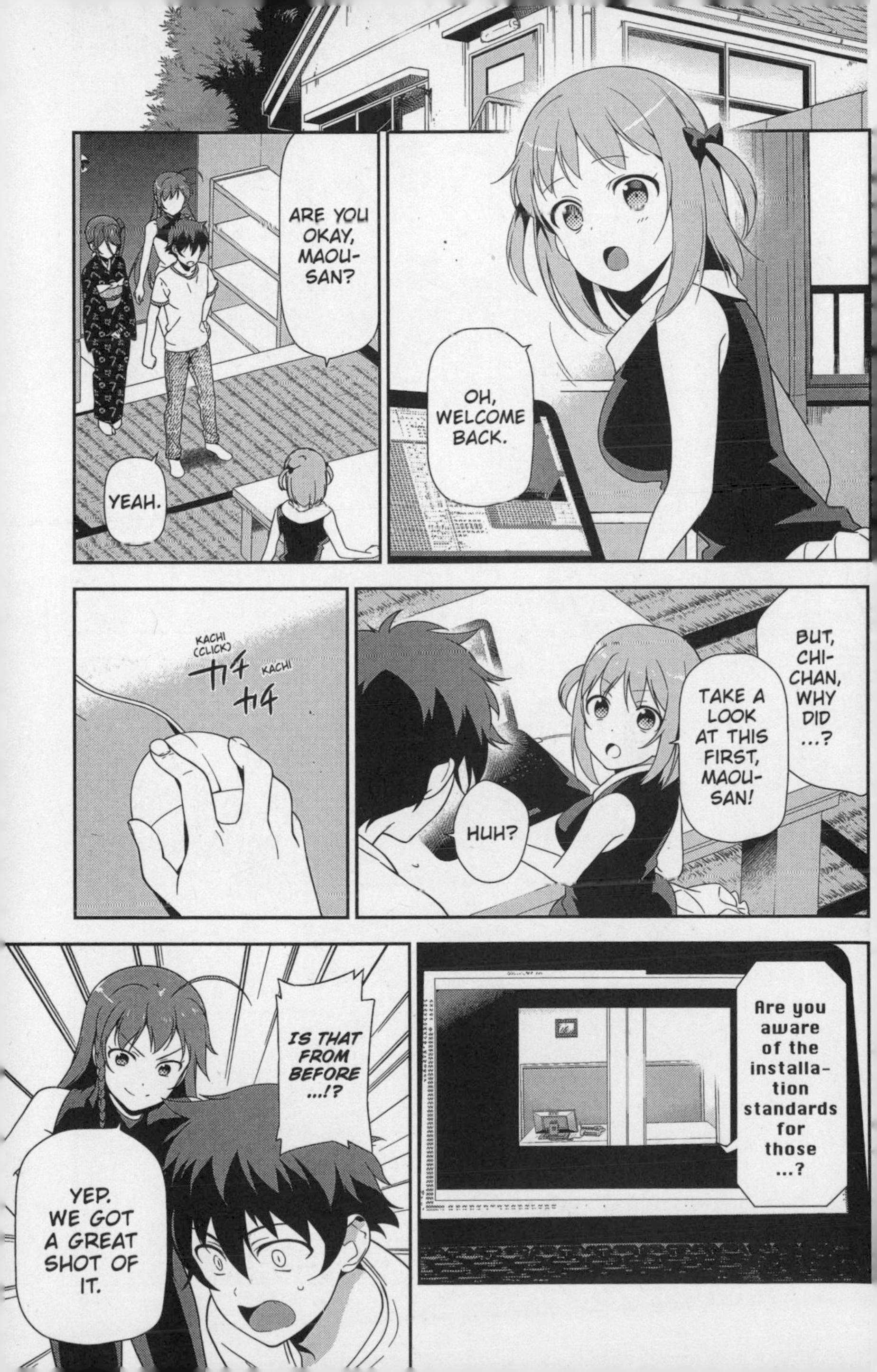
OH, WELCOME BACK.
ARE YOU OKAY, MAOU-SAN?
YEAH.
BUT, CHI-CHAN, WHY DID ...?
TAKE A LOOK AT THIS FIRST, MAOU-SAN!
HUH?
KACHI (CLICK)
カチ
KACHI
カチ
Are you aware of the installation standards for those ...?
IS THAT FROM BEFORE ...!?
YEP. WE GOT A GREAT SHOT OF IT.

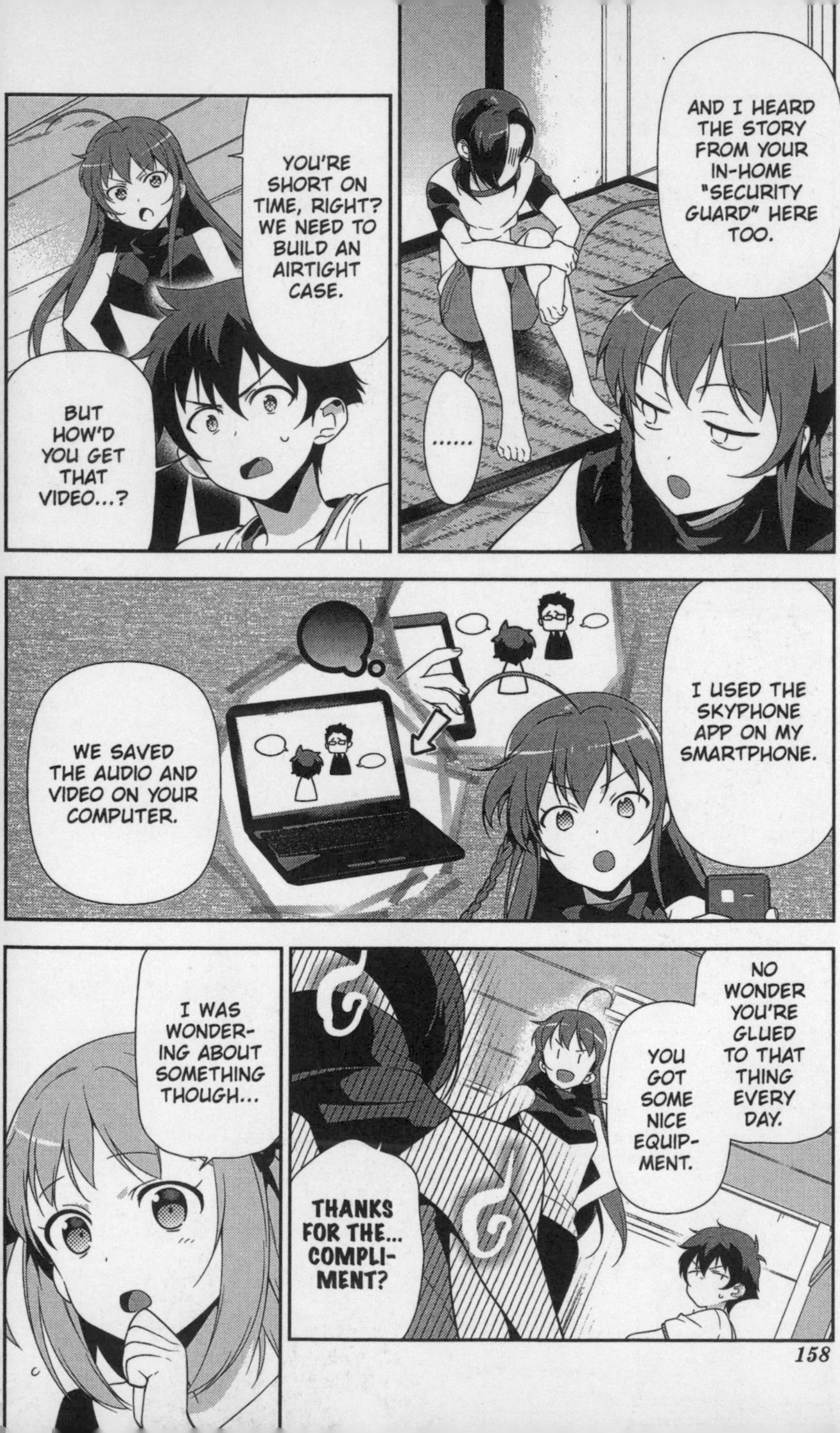
AND I HEARD THE STORY FROM YOUR IN-HOME "SECURITY GUARD" HERE TOO.
......
YOU'RE SHORT ON TIME, RIGHT? WE NEED TO BUILD AN AIRTIGHT CASE.
BUT HOW'D YOU GET THAT VIDEO...?
I USED THE SKYPHONE APP ON MY SMARTPHONE.
WE SAVED THE AUDIO AND VIDEO ON YOUR COMPUTER.
NO WONDER YOU'RE GLUED TO THAT THING EVERY DAY.
YOU GOT SOME NICE EQUIP-MENT.
THANKS FOR THE... COMPLI-MENT?
I WAS WONDER-ING ABOUT SOMETHING THOUGH...

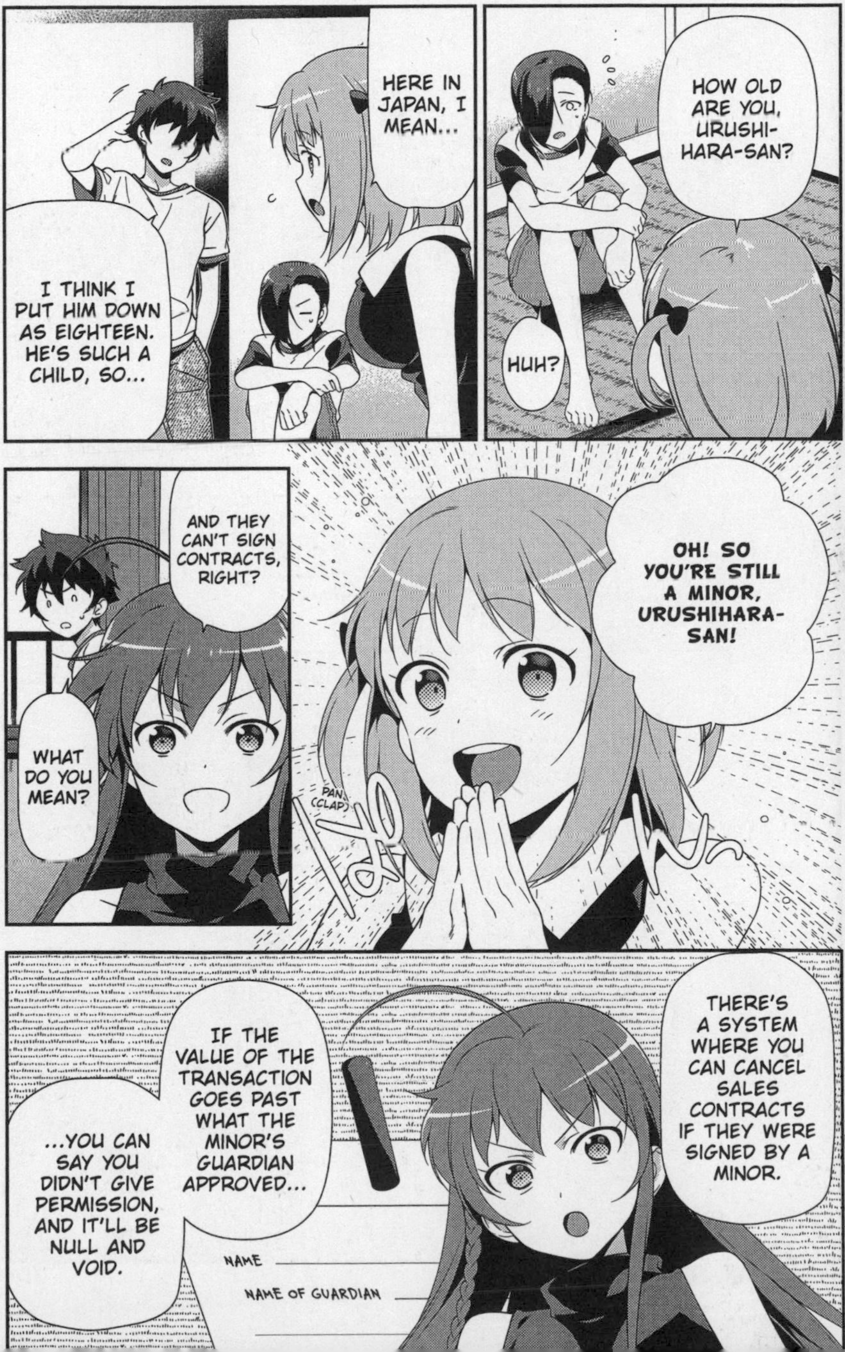
HOW OLD ARE YOU, URUSHIHARA-SAN?
HUH?
HERE IN JAPAN, I MEAN...
I THINK I PUT HIM DOWN AS EIGHTEEN. HE'S SUCH A CHILD, SO...
OH! SO YOU'RE STILL A MINOR, URUSHIHARA-SAN!
PAN (CLAP)
AND THEY CAN'T SIGN CONTRACTS, RIGHT?
WHAT DO YOU MEAN?
THERE'S A SYSTEM WHERE YOU CAN CANCEL SALES CONTRACTS IF THEY WERE SIGNED BY A MINOR.
IF THE VALUE OF THE TRANSACTION GOES PAST WHAT THE MINOR'S GUARDIAN APPROVED...
...YOU CAN SAY YOU DIDN'T GIVE PERMISSION, AND IT'LL BE NULL AND VOID.
NAME
NAME OF GUARDIAN

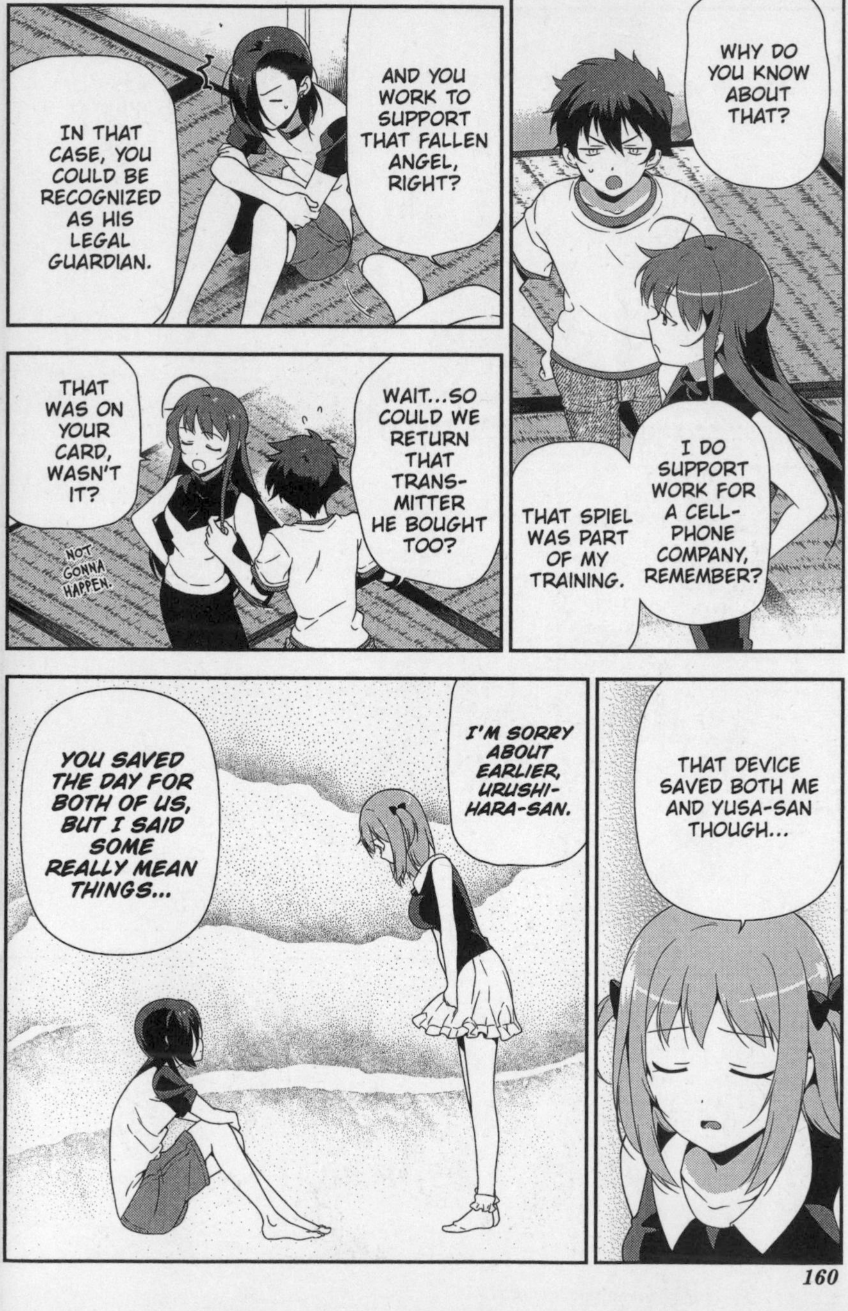
WHY DO YOU KNOW ABOUT THAT?
I DO SUPPORT WORK FOR A CELL-PHONE COMPANY, REMEMBER?
THAT SPIEL WAS PART OF MY TRAINING.
AND YOU WORK TO SUPPORT THAT FALLEN ANGEL, RIGHT?
IN THAT CASE, YOU COULD BE RECOGNIZED AS HIS LEGAL GUARDIAN.
WAIT...SO COULD WE RETURN THAT TRANS-MITTER HE BOUGHT TOO?
THAT WAS ON YOUR CARD, WASN'T IT?
NOT GONNA HAPPEN.
THAT DEVICE SAVED BOTH ME AND YUSA-SAN THOUGH...
I'M SORRY ABOUT EARLIER, URUSHI-HARA-SAN.
YOU SAVED THE DAY FOR BOTH OF US, BUT I SAID SOME REALLY MEAN THINGS...

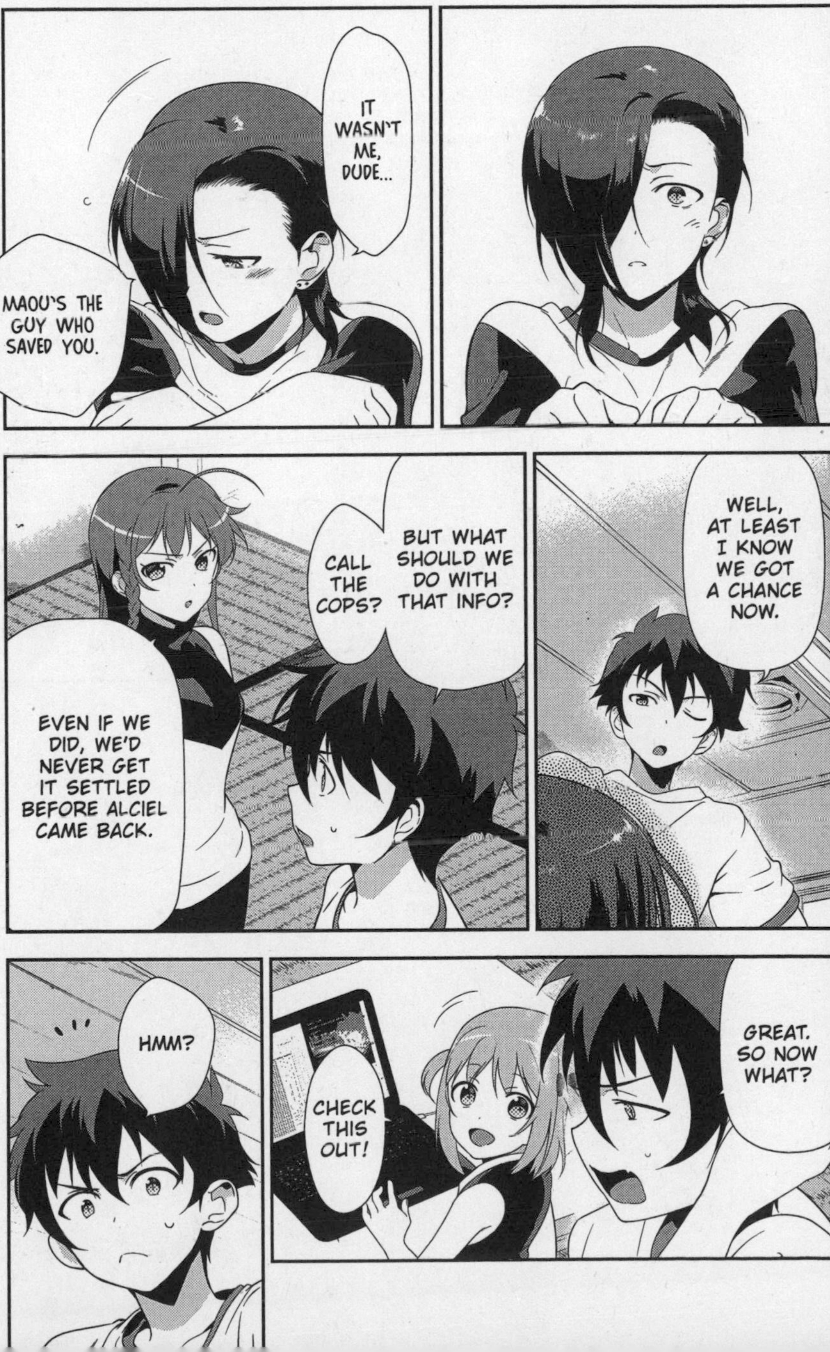
IT WASN'T ME, DUDE...
MAOU'S THE GUY WHO SAVED YOU.
WELL, AT LEAST I KNOW WE GOT A CHANCE NOW.
BUT WHAT SHOULD WE DO WITH THAT INFO?
CALL THE COPS?
EVEN IF WE DID, WE'D NEVER GET IT SETTLED BEFORE ALCIEL CAME BACK.
GREAT. SO NOW WHAT?
CHECK THIS OUT!
HMM?

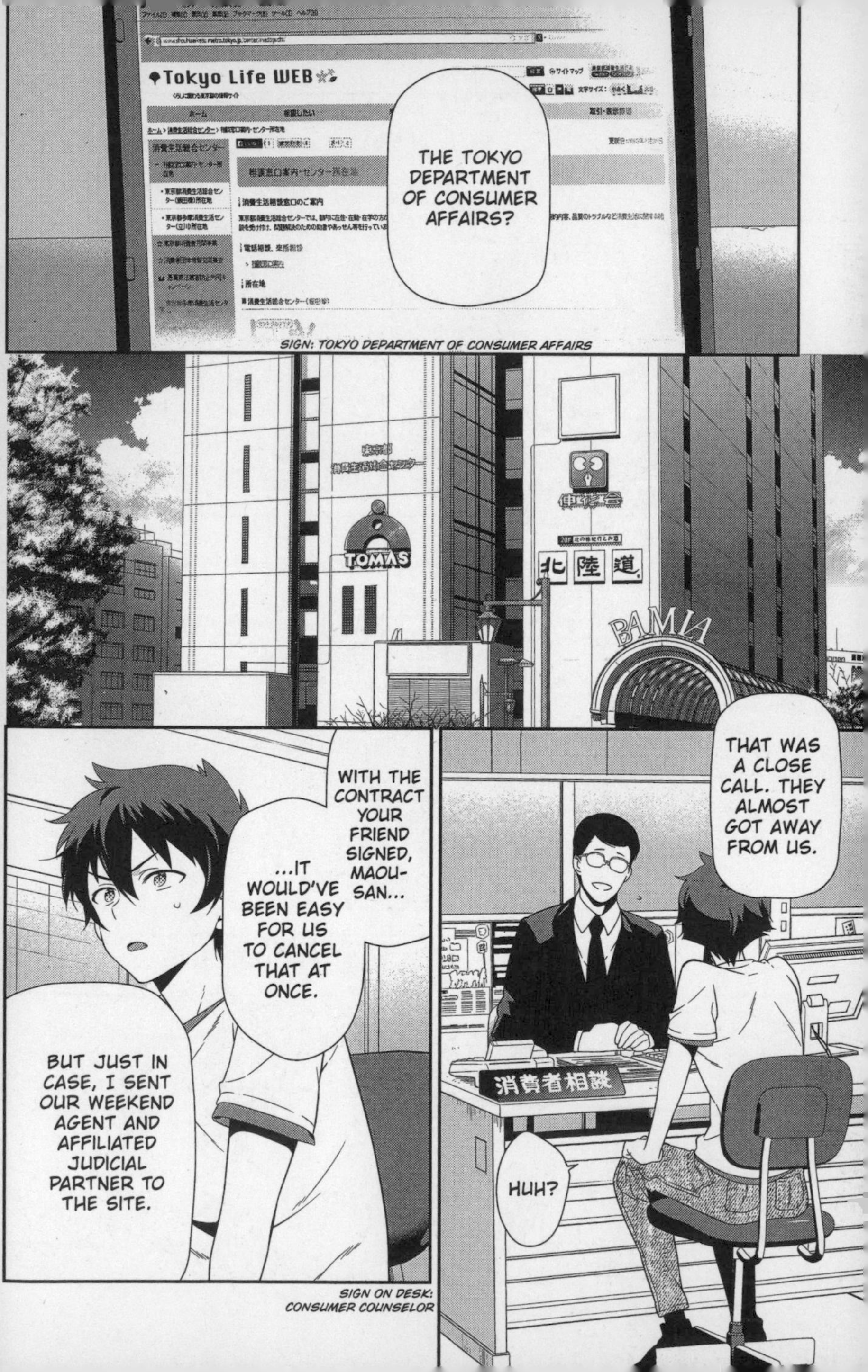
Tokyo Life WEB
THE TOKYO DEPARTMENT OF CONSUMER AFFAIRS?
SIGN: TOKYO DEPARTMENT OF CONSUMER AFFAIRS
TOMAS
北陸道
BAMIA
THAT WAS A CLOSE CALL. THEY ALMOST GOT AWAY FROM US.
HUH?
消費者相談
SIGN ON DESK: CONSUMER COUNSELOR
WITH THE CONTRACT YOUR FRIEND SIGNED, MAOU-SAN...
...IT WOULD'VE BEEN EASY FOR US TO CANCEL THAT AT ONCE.
BUT JUST IN CASE, I SENT OUR WEEKEND AGENT AND AFFILIATED JUDICIAL PARTNER TO THE SITE.

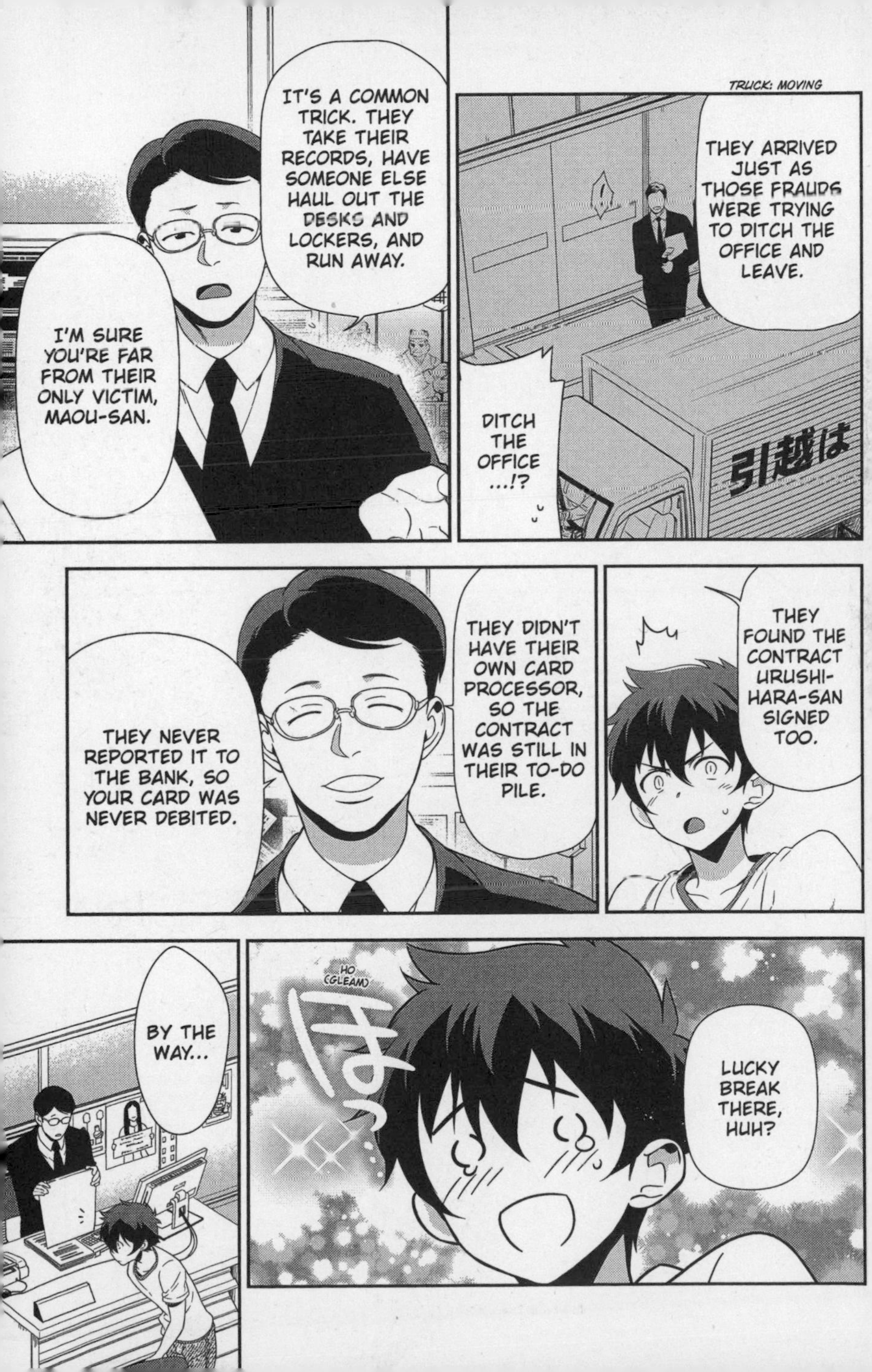
TRUCK: MOVING
THEY ARRIVED JUST AS THOSE FRAUDS WERE TRYING TO DITCH THE OFFICE AND LEAVE.
引越は
DITCH THE OFFICE ...!?
IT'S A COMMON TRICK. THEY TAKE THEIR RECORDS, HAVE SOMEONE ELSE HAUL OUT THE DESKS AND LOCKERS, AND RUN AWAY.
I'M SURE YOU'RE FAR FROM THEIR ONLY VICTIM, MAOU-SAN.
THEY FOUND THE CONTRACT URUSHI-HARA-SAN SIGNED TOO.
THEY DIDN'T HAVE THEIR OWN CARD PROCESSOR, SO THE CONTRACT WAS STILL IN THEIR TO-DO PILE.
THEY NEVER REPORTED IT TO THE BANK, SO YOUR CARD WAS NEVER DEBITED.
LUCKY BREAK THERE, HUH?
HO (GLEAM)
ほっ
BY THE WAY...

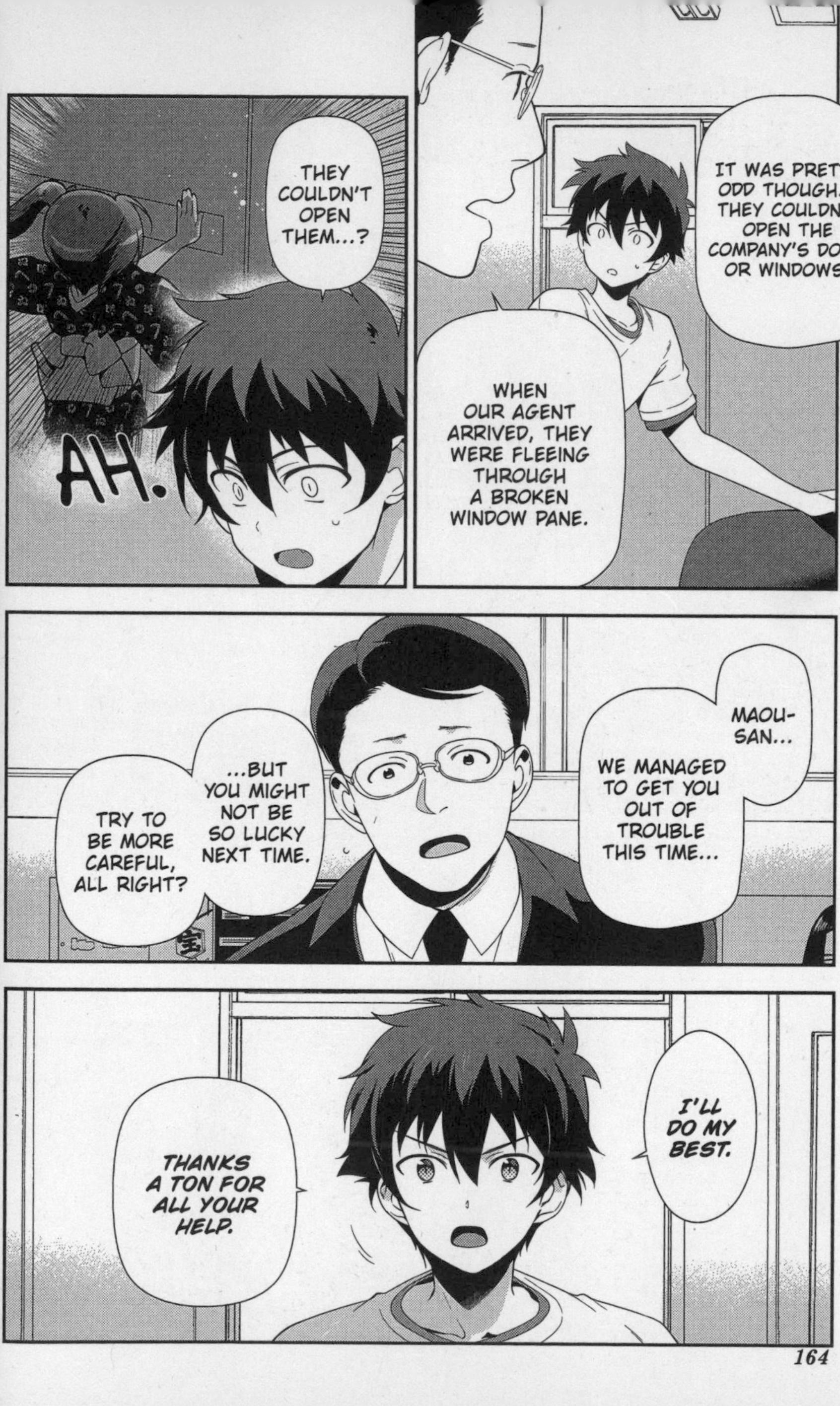

IT WAS PRETTY ODD THOUGH... THEY COULDN'T OPEN THE COMPANY'S DOOR OR WINDOWS.
WHEN OUR AGENT ARRIVED, THEY WERE FLEEING THROUGH A BROKEN WINDOW PANE.
THEY COULDN'T OPEN THEM...?
AH.
MAOU-SAN...
WE MANAGED TO GET YOU OUT OF TROUBLE THIS TIME...
...BUT YOU MIGHT NOT BE SO LUCKY NEXT TIME.
TRY TO BE MORE CAREFUL, ALL RIGHT?
I'LL DO MY BEST.
THANKS A TON FOR ALL YOUR HELP.

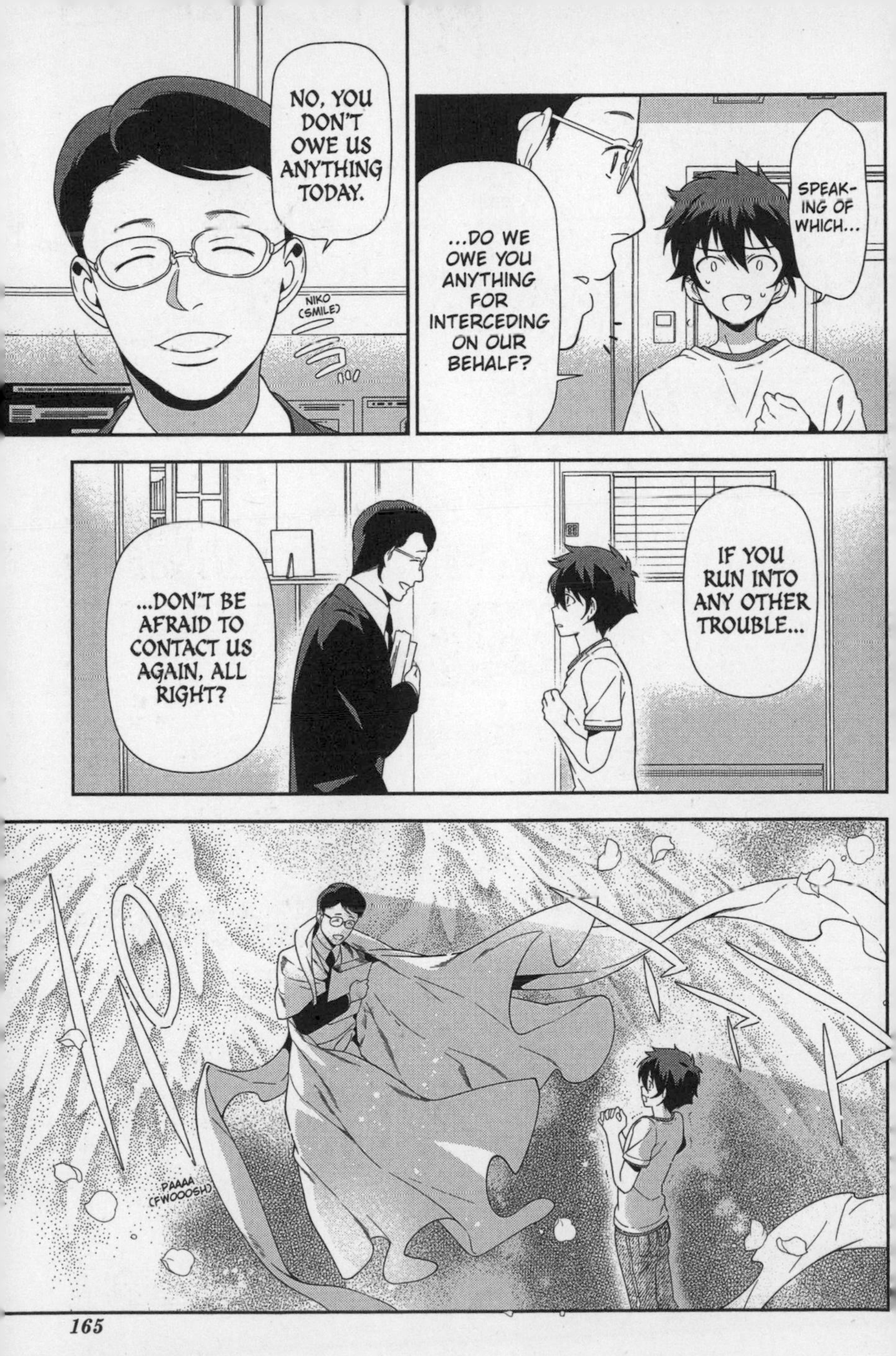
SPEAKING OF WHICH...
...DO WE OWE YOU ANYTHING FOR INTERCEDING ON OUR BEHALF?
NO, YOU DON'T OWE US ANYTHING TODAY.
NIKO (SMILE)
IF YOU RUN INTO ANY OTHER TROUBLE...
...DON'T BE AFRAID TO CONTACT US AGAIN, ALL RIGHT?
PAAAA (FWOOOSH)

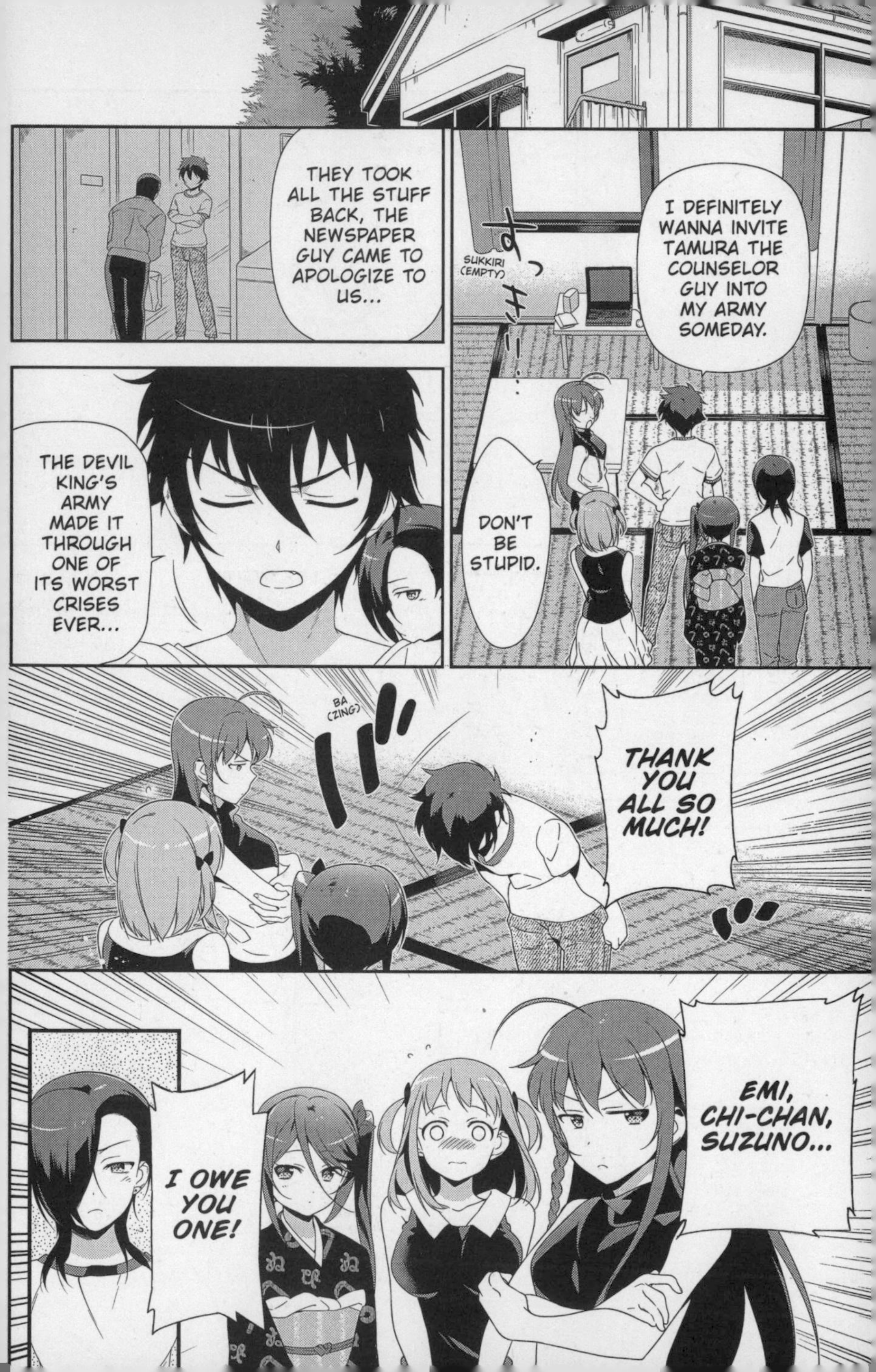
I DEFINITELY WANNA INVITE TAMURA THE COUNSELOR GUY INTO MY ARMY SOMEDAY.
SUKKIRI (EMPTY)
DON'T BE STUPID.
THEY TOOK ALL THE STUFF BACK, THE NEWSPAPER GUY CAME TO APOLOGIZE TO US...
THE DEVIL KING'S ARMY MADE IT THROUGH ONE OF ITS WORST CRISES EVER...
THANK YOU ALL SO MUCH!
BA (ZING)
EMI, CHI-CHAN, SUZUNO...
I OWE YOU ONE!

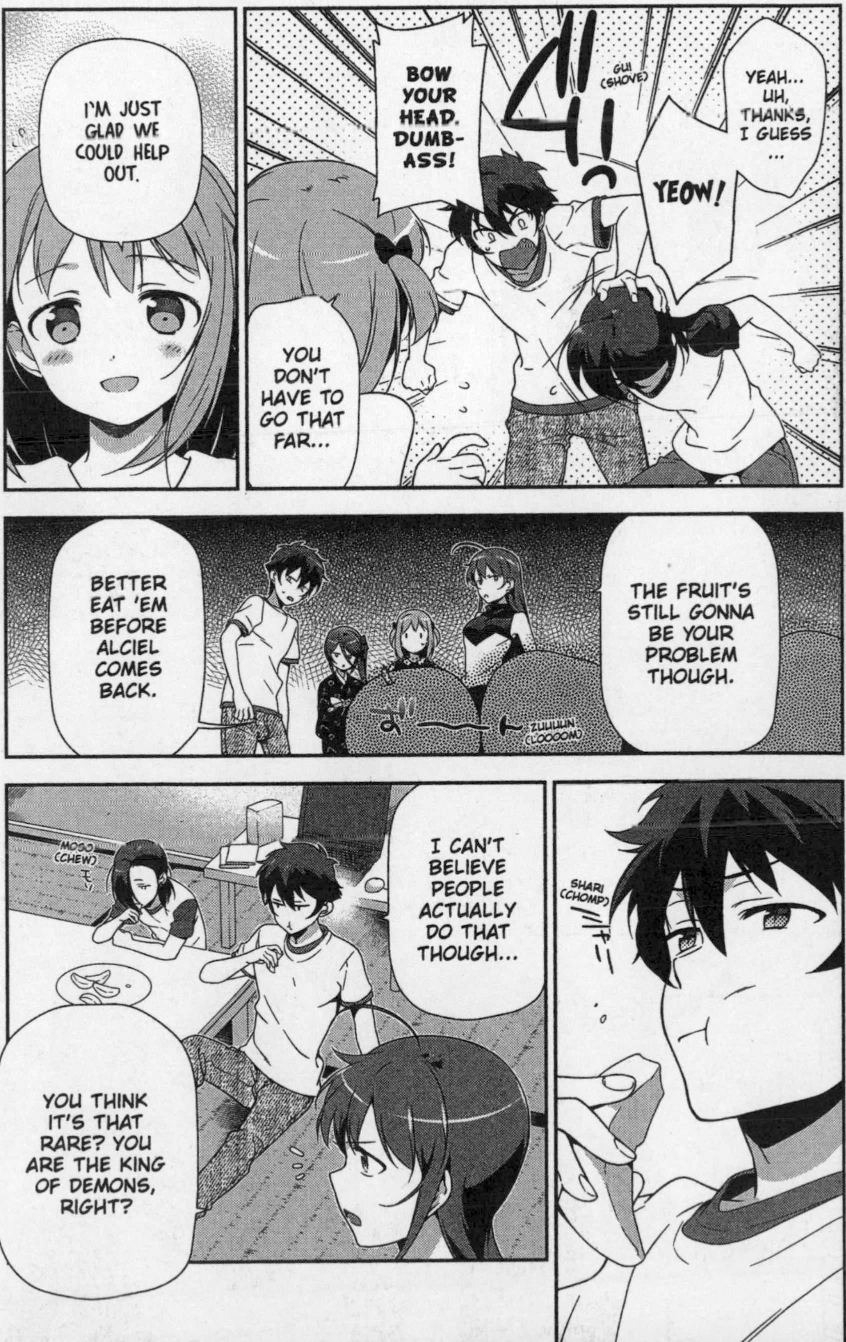
YEAH... UH, THANKS, I GUESS ...
GUI (SHOVE)
YEOW!
BOW YOUR HEAD. DUMB-ASS!
YOU DON'T HAVE TO GO THAT FAR...
I'M JUST GLAD WE COULD HELP OUT.
THE FRUIT'S STILL GONNA BE YOUR PROBLEM THOUGH.
ZUUUUN (LOOOOM)
BETTER EAT 'EM BEFORE ALCIEL COMES BACK.
SHARI (CHOMP)
I CAN'T BELIEVE PEOPLE ACTUALLY DO THAT THOUGH...
MOGO (CHEW)
YOU THINK IT'S THAT RARE? YOU ARE THE KING OF DEMONS, RIGHT?

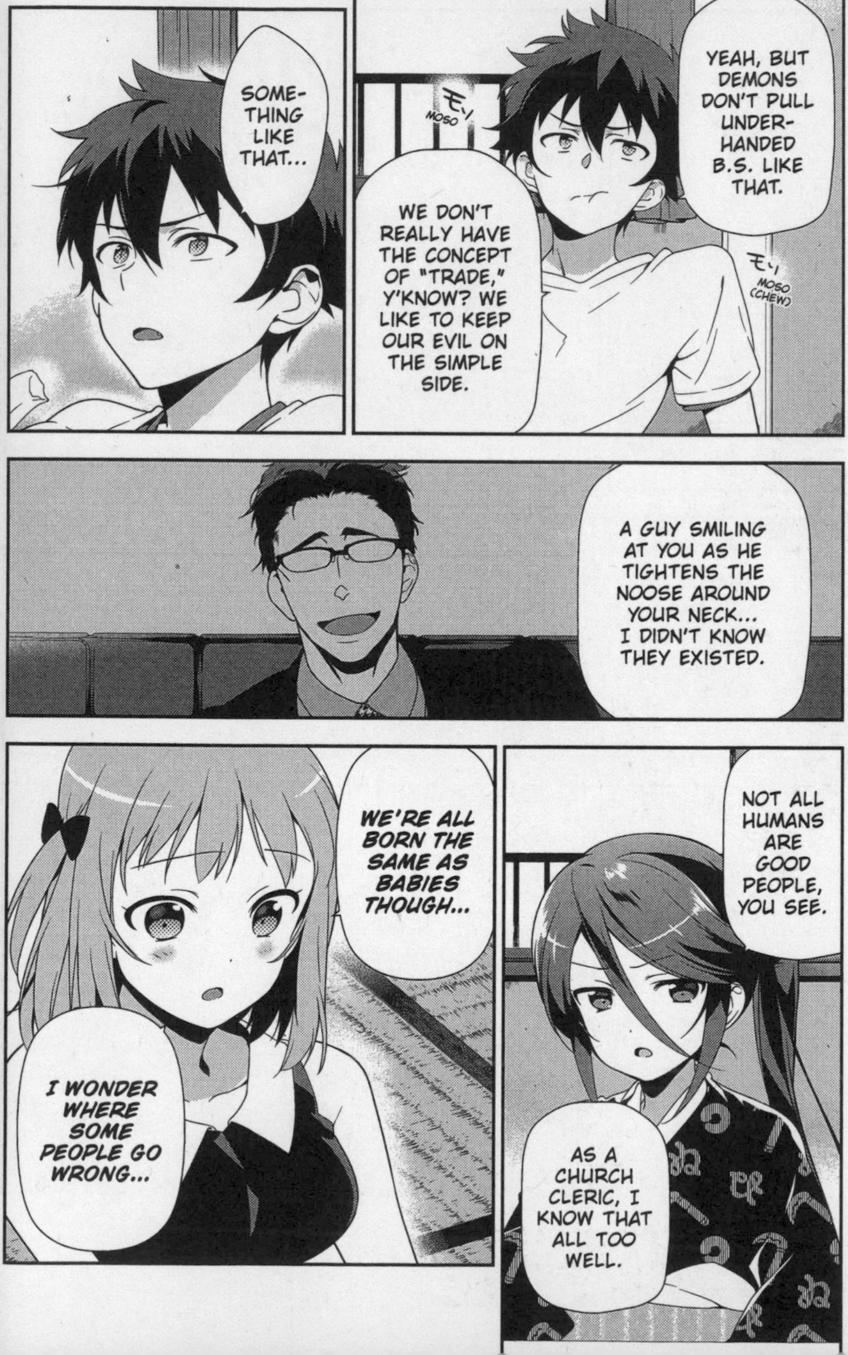
YEAH, BUT DEMONS DON'T PULL UNDER-HANDED B.S. LIKE THAT.
MOSO
WE DON'T REALLY HAVE THE CONCEPT OF "TRADE," Y'KNOW? WE LIKE TO KEEP OUR EVIL ON THE SIMPLE SIDE.
MOSO (CHEW)
SOME-THING LIKE THAT...
A GUY SMILING AT YOU AS HE TIGHTENS THE NOOSE AROUND YOUR NECK... I DIDN'T KNOW THEY EXISTED.
NOT ALL HUMANS ARE GOOD PEOPLE, YOU SEE.
AS A CHURCH CLERIC, I KNOW THAT ALL TOO WELL.
WE'RE ALL BORN THE SAME AS BABIES THOUGH...
I WONDER WHERE SOME PEOPLE GO WRONG...

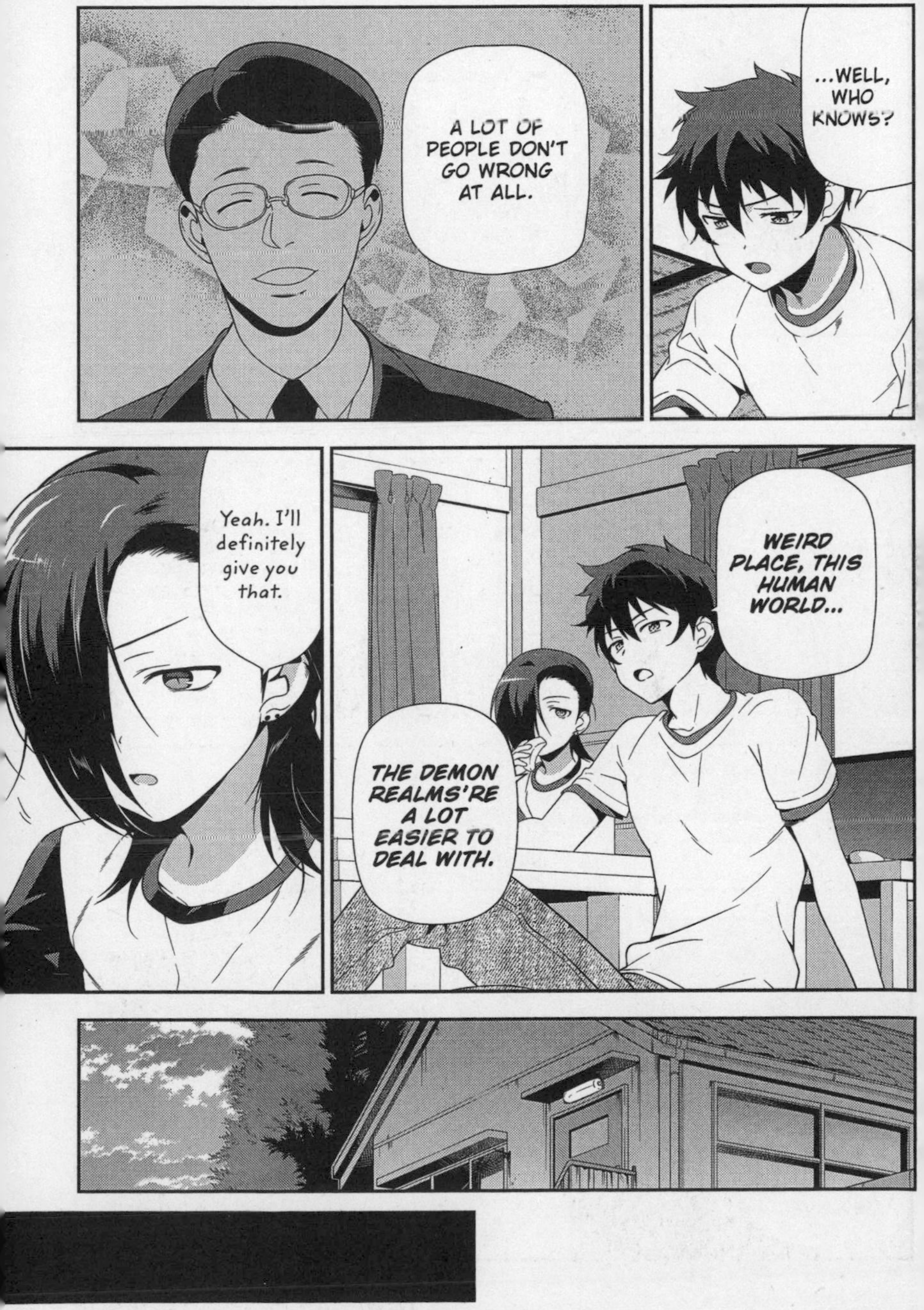
...WELL, WHO KNOWS?
A LOT OF PEOPLE DON'T GO WRONG AT ALL.
WEIRD PLACE, THIS HUMAN WORLD...
THE DEMON REALMS'RE A LOT EASIER TO DEAL WITH.
Yeah. I'll definitely give you that.

[redacted]

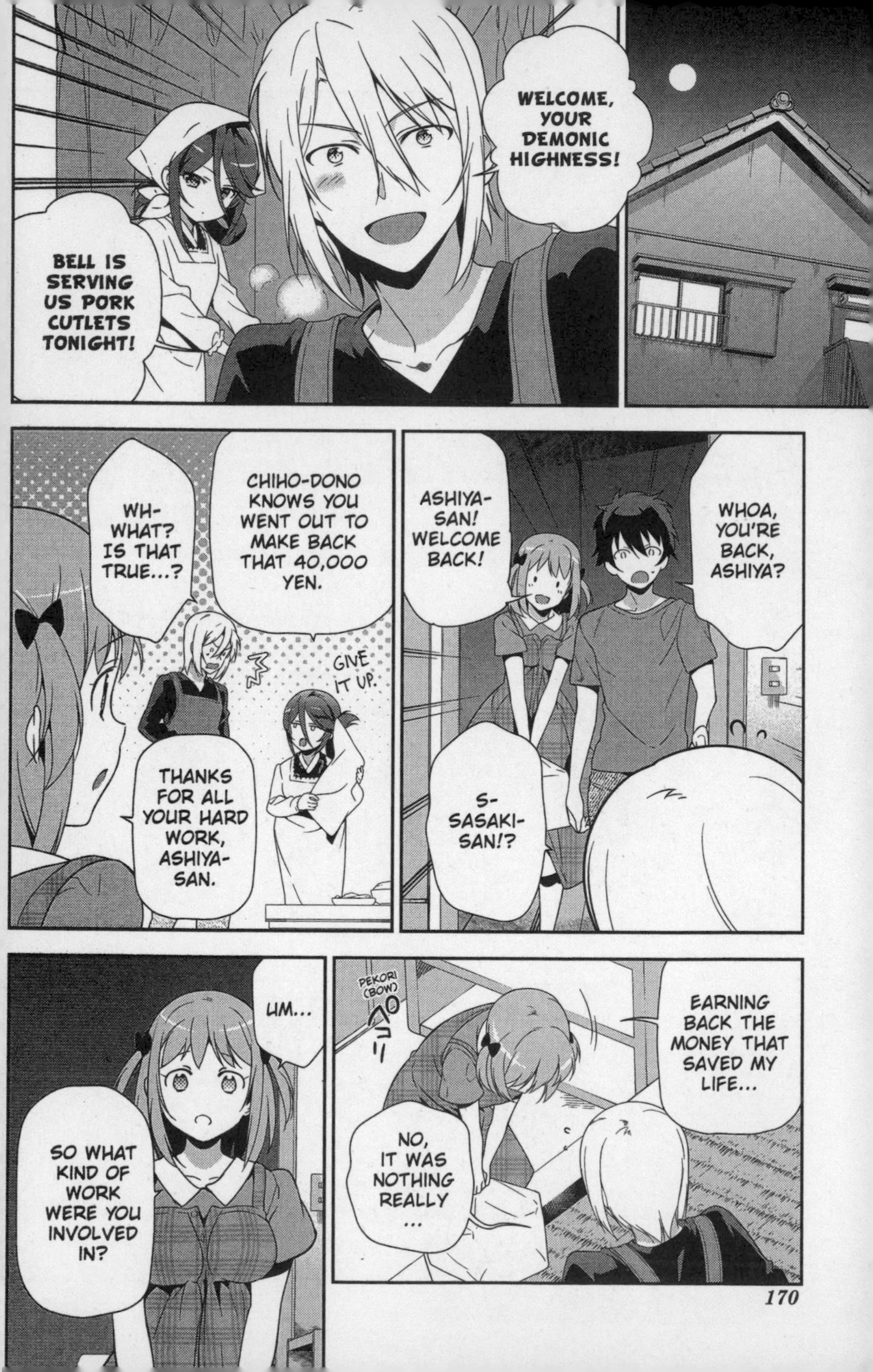
WELCOME, YOUR DEMONIC HIGHNESS!
BELL IS SERVING US PORK CUTLETS TONIGHT!
WHOA, YOU'RE BACK, ASHIYA?
ASHIYA-SAN! WELCOME BACK!
S-SASAKI-SAN!?
CHIHO-DONO KNOWS YOU WENT OUT TO MAKE BACK THAT 40,000 YEN.
WH-WHAT? IS THAT TRUE...?
GIVE IT UP.
THANKS FOR ALL YOUR HARD WORK, ASHIYA-SAN.
EARNING BACK THE MONEY THAT SAVED MY LIFE...
PEKORI (BOW)
NO, IT WAS NOTHING REALLY ...
UM...
SO WHAT KIND OF WORK WERE YOU INVOLVED IN?

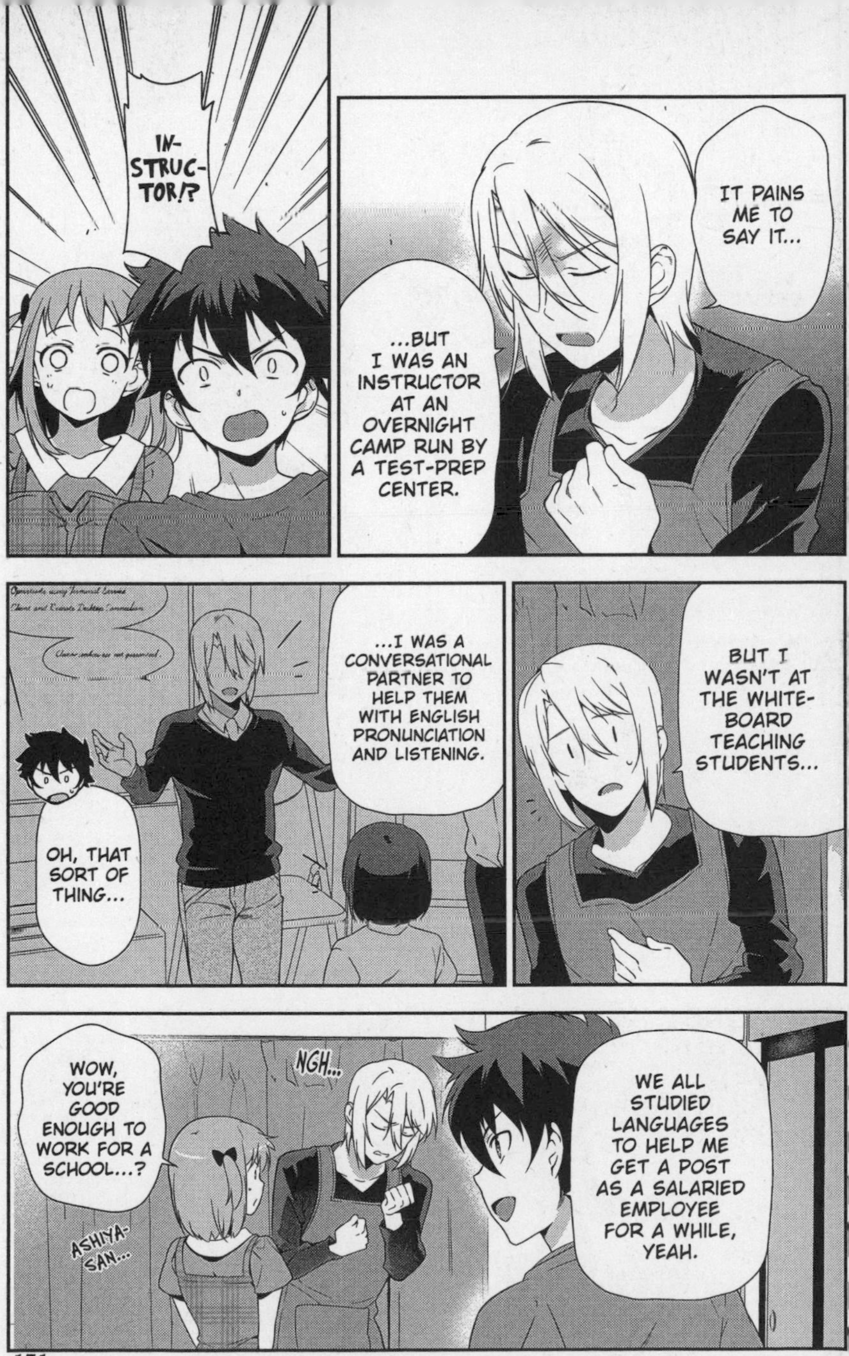
IT PAINS ME TO SAY IT...
...BUT I WAS AN INSTRUCTOR AT AN OVERNIGHT CAMP RUN BY A TEST-PREP CENTER.
IN-STRUC-TOR!?
BUT I WASN'T AT THE WHITE-BOARD TEACHING STUDENTS...
...I WAS A CONVERSATIONAL PARTNER TO HELP THEM WITH ENGLISH PRONUNCIATION AND LISTENING.
OH, THAT SORT OF THING...
WE ALL STUDIED LANGUAGES TO HELP ME GET A POST AS A SALARIED EMPLOYEE FOR A WHILE, YEAH.
NGH...
WOW, YOU'RE GOOD ENOUGH TO WORK FOR A SCHOOL...?
ASHIYA-SAN...

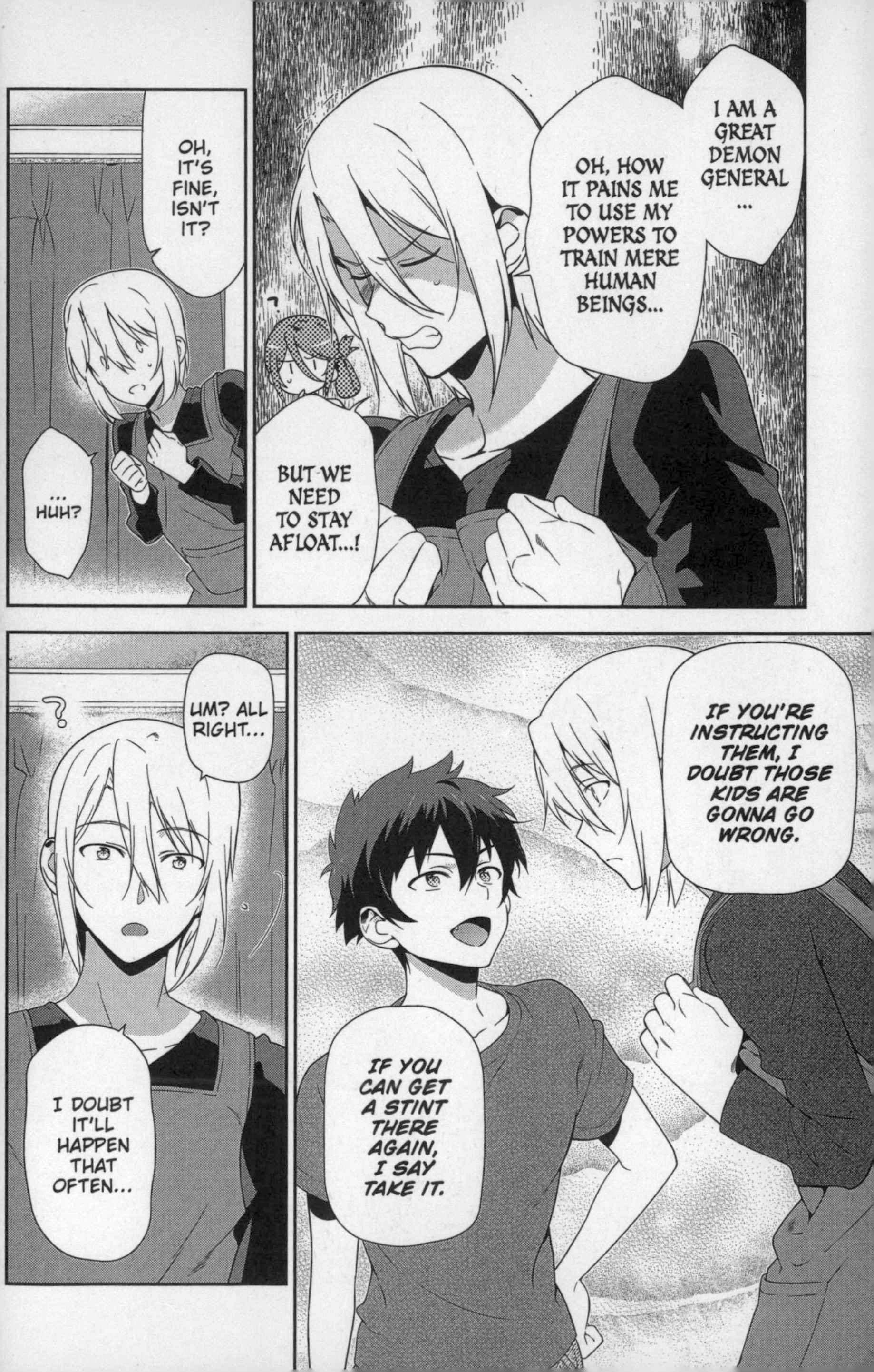
I AM A GREAT DEMON GENERAL...
OH, HOW IT PAINS ME TO USE MY POWERS TO TRAIN MERE HUMAN BEINGS...
BUT WE NEED TO STAY AFLOAT...!
OH, IT'S FINE, ISN'T IT?
... HUH?
IF YOU'RE INSTRUCTING THEM, I DOUBT THOSE KIDS ARE GONNA GO WRONG.
IF YOU CAN GET A STINT THERE AGAIN, I SAY TAKE IT.
UM? ALL RIGHT...
I DOUBT IT'LL HAPPEN THAT OFTEN...

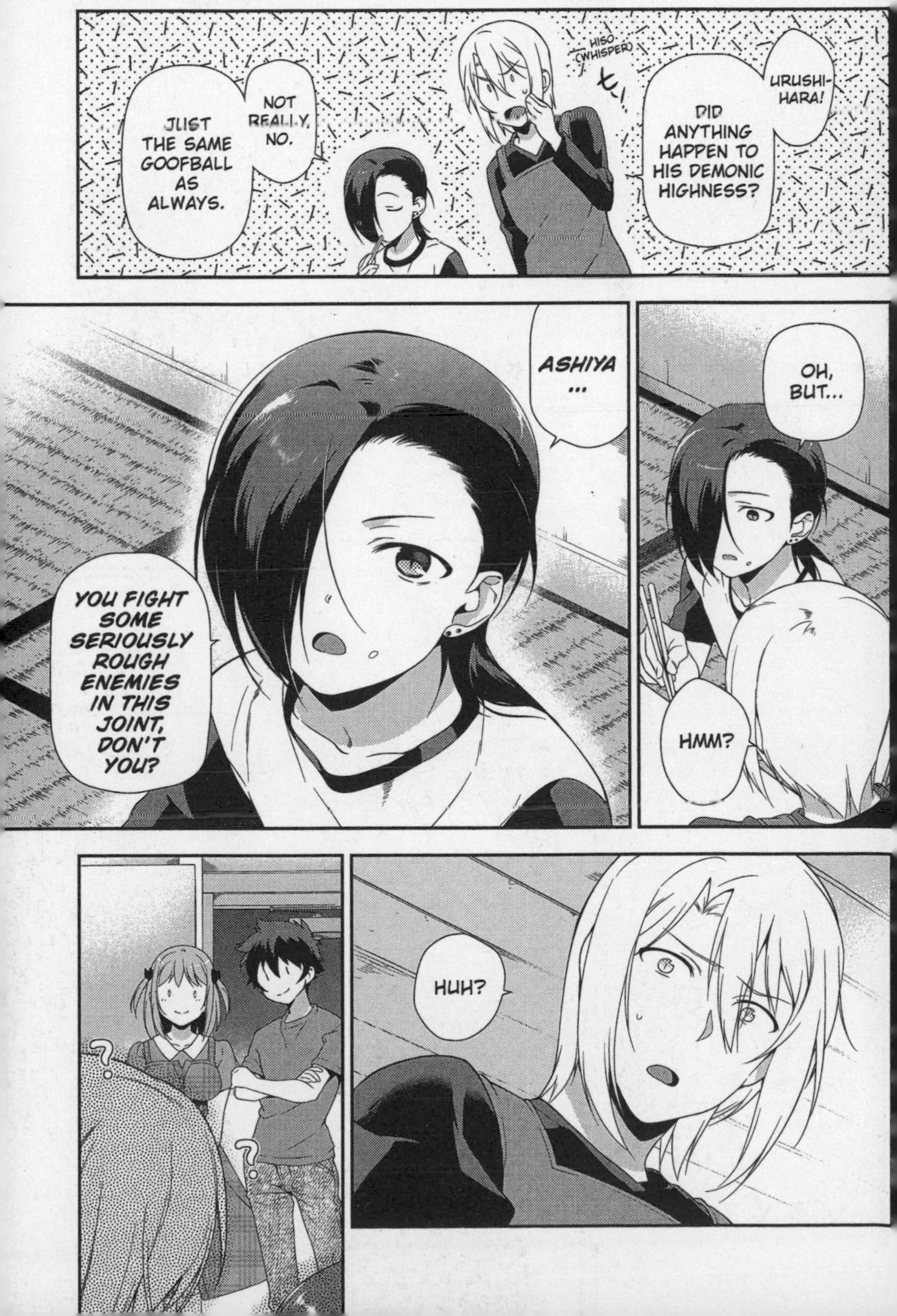
URUSHI-HARA!
DID ANYTHING HAPPEN TO HIS DEMONIC HIGHNESS?
HISO (WHISPER)
NOT REALLY, NO.
JUST THE SAME GOOFBALL AS ALWAYS.
OH, BUT...
HMM?
ASHIYA...
YOU FIGHT SOME SERIOUSLY ROUGH ENEMIES IN THIS JOINT, DON'T YOU?
HUH?
?
?

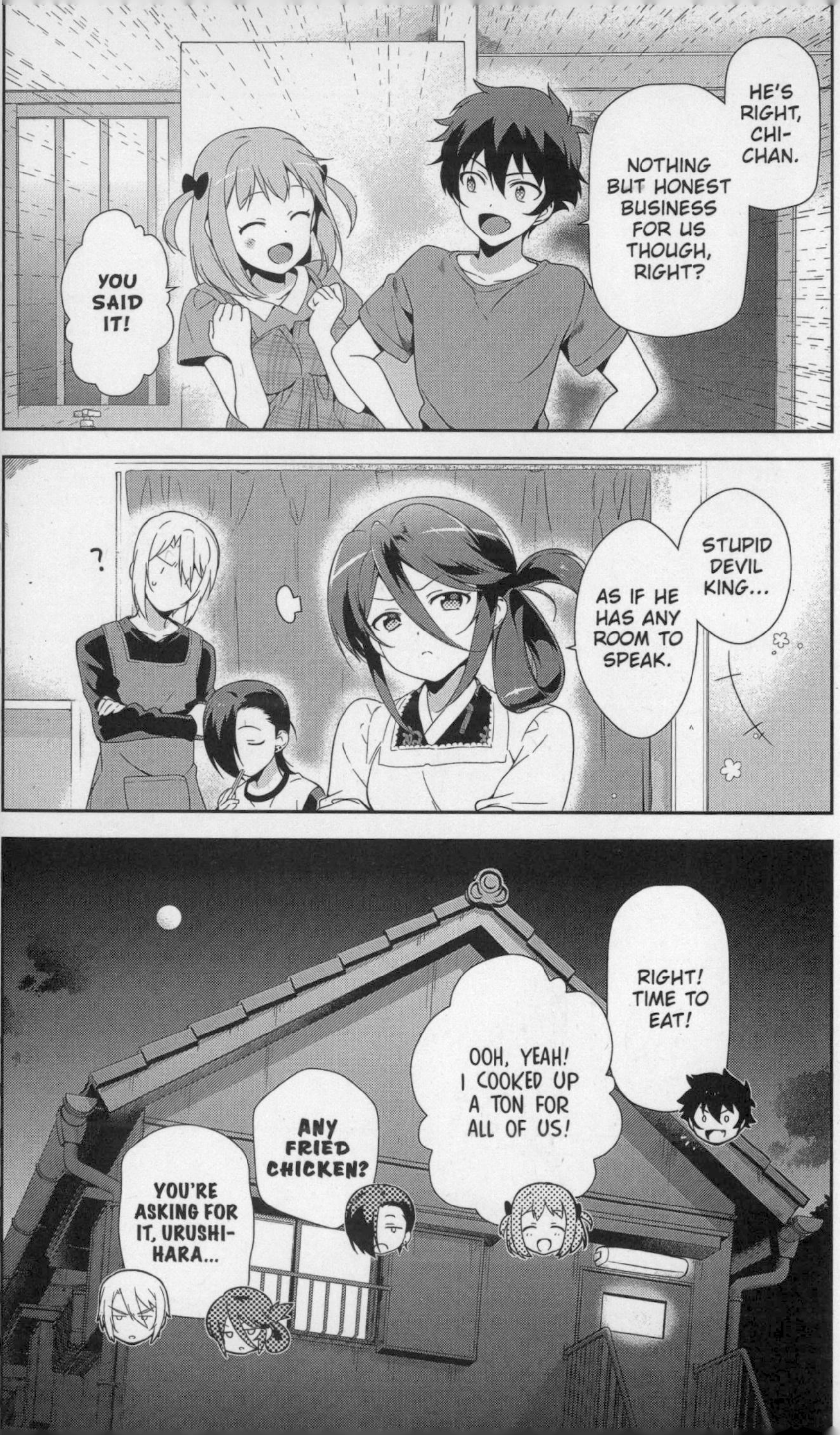
HE'S RIGHT, CHI-CHAN.
NOTHING BUT HONEST BUSINESS FOR US THOUGH, RIGHT?
YOU SAID IT!
STUPID DEVIL KING...
AS IF HE HAS ANY ROOM TO SPEAK.
?
RIGHT! TIME TO EAT!
OOH, YEAH! I COOKED UP A TON FOR ALL OF US!
ANY FRIED CHICKEN?
YOU'RE ASKING FOR IT, URUSHI-HARA...

Shirou
Ashiya

BEFORE I EVEN KNEW IT, I'M ALREADY AT VOLUME FIVE.

WITH THIS VOLUME, I'VE FINALLY WRAPPED UP EVERYTHING COVERED BY THE ANIME SERIES.

MY DEEPEST THANKS GO OUT TO WAGAHARA-SENSEI, 029-SENSEI, AND EVERYONE ELSE INVOLVED WITH THE DEVIL IS A PART-TIMER!

RIGHT NOW (MARCH 2014), I'M PREPPING TO START TACKLING VOLUME THREE OF THE NOVELS.

ALL THOSE SCENES (AND A CERTAIN NEW CHARACTER TOO!) I'VE BEEN ACHING TO DRAW OUT...I CAN'T WAIT!

I'M GONNA PUT MORE EFFORT THAN EVER INTO MY WORK, SO I HOPE YOU'LL ALL KEEP PROVIDING ME WITH YOUR SUPPORT!

I COULDN'T FIT EMI INTO THE LAST SCENE OF THIS VOLUME, SO I DREW HER BIG FOR THIS AFTERWORD.

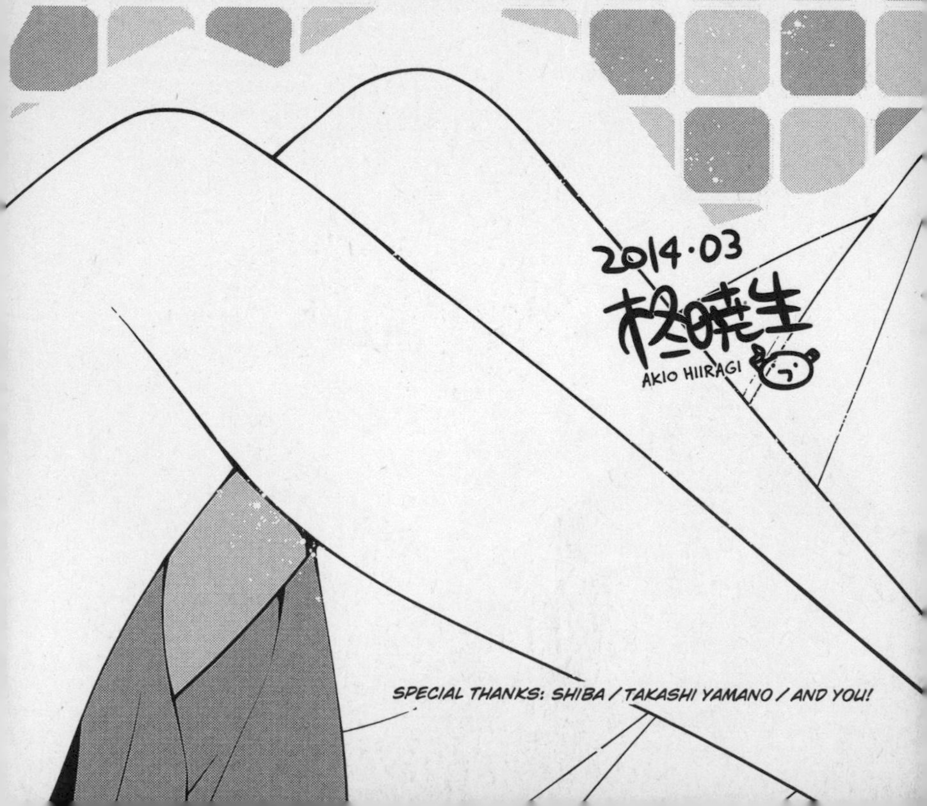

2014·03

柊暁生

AKIO HIIRAGI

SPECIAL THANKS: SHIBA / TAKASHI YAMANO / AND YOU!

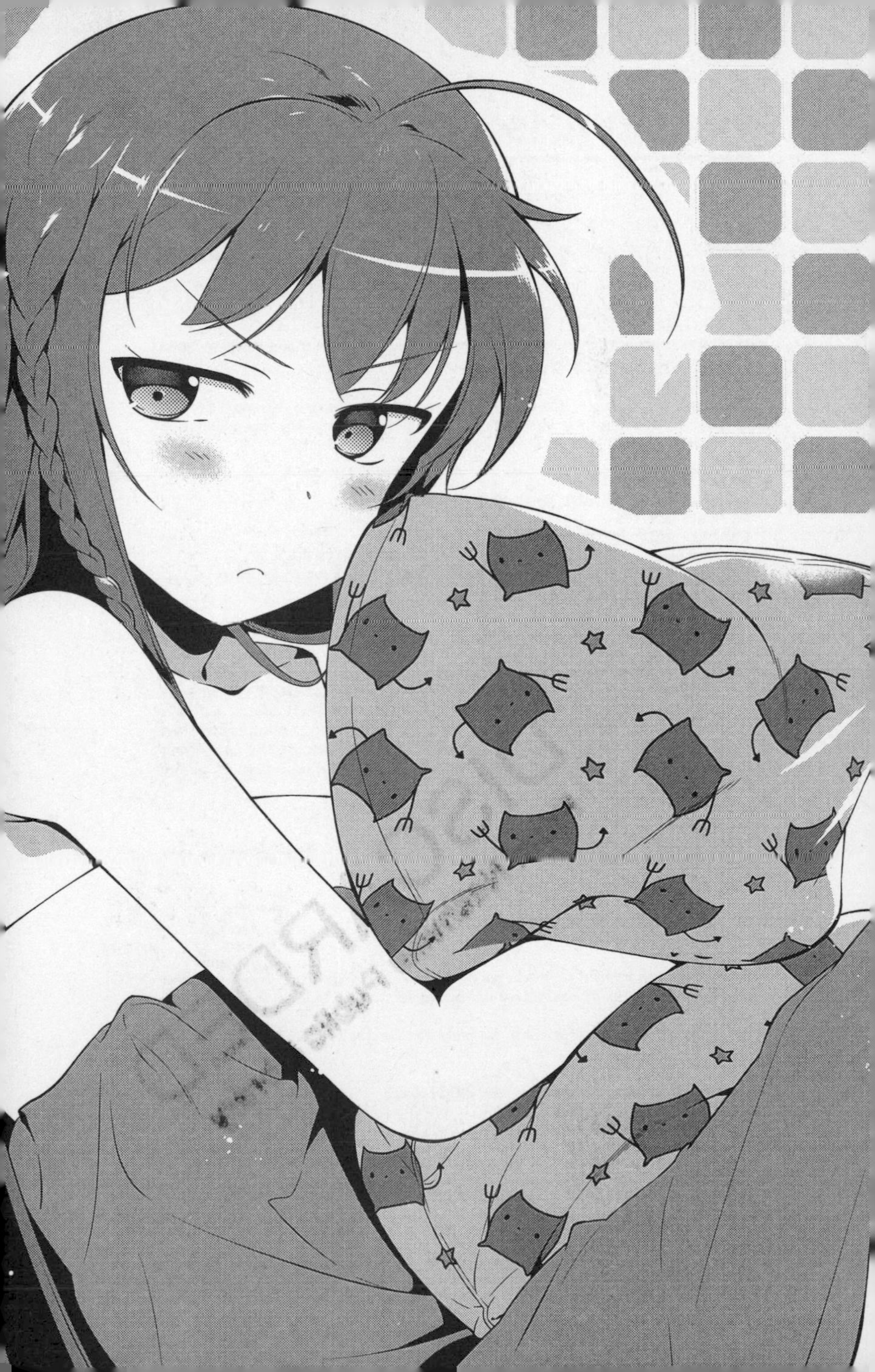

THE DEVIL IS A PART-TIMER! ⑤

ART: AKIO HIIRAGI
ORIGINAL STORY: SATOSHI WAGAHARA
CHARACTER DESIGN: 029 (ONIKU)

Translation: Kevin Gifford

Lettering: Brndn Blakeslee

HATARAKU MAOUSAMA! Vol. 5
© SATOSHI WAGAHARA / AKIO HIIRAGI 2014
All rights reserved.
Edited by ASCII MEDIA WORKS
First published in Japan in 2014 by KADOKAWA CORPORATION, Tokyo.
English translation rights arranged with KADOKAWA CORPORATION, Tokyo, through Tuttle-Mori Agency, Inc., Tokyo.

Translation © 2016 by Hachette Book Group, Inc.

Yen Press
Hachette Book Group
1290 Avenue of the Americas
New York, NY 10104

www.HachetteBookGroup.com
www.YenPress.com

Yen Press is an imprint of Hachette Book Group, Inc. The Yen Press name and logo are trademarks of Hachette Book Group, Inc.

The publisher is not responsible for websites (or their content) that are not owned by the publisher.

Library of Congress Control Number: 2015960123

First Yen Press Edition: April 2016

ISBN: 978-0-316-31489-3

10 9 8 7 6 5 4 3 2 1

BVG

Printed in the United States of America